LAYING THE FOUNDATION

LAYING THE FOUNDATION
A Handbook of Catholic Apologetics and Fundamental Theology

Fr. Joseph Clifford Fenton

Steubenville, Ohio

Emmaus Road Publishing
1468 Parkview Circle
Steubenville, Ohio 43952

© Emmaus Road Publishing
All rights reserved. Published 2016
Printed in the United States of America

Library of Congress Control Number: 2015960048
ISBN: 978-1-941447-49-9

Cover design and layout by Mairead Cameron

Nihil obstat: ANDREW A. MARTIN, Censor Deputatus
Imprimatur: † THOMAS M. O'LEARY, D.D.,
Episcopus Campifontis
December 9, 1942

CONTENTS

Foreword   vii

Introduction   xi

CHAPTER

 1 The Work of Apologetics 1
 2 The Concept of Revelation 11
 3 The Characteristics of Revelation 25
 4 The Possibility of Revelation... 37
 5 The Necessity of Revelation.. 53
 6 The Discernibility of Divine Revelation 69
 7 The Process of Proof.. 99
 8 The Historical Evidence About Jesus of Nazareth 107
 9 The Claims of Jesus 137
10 The Doctrinal Content in the Message of Jesus 171
    Part I: The New Dispensation and the Old Law
11 The Doctrinal Content in the Message of Jesus 199
    Part II: The Trinity and the Incarnation
12 The Doctrinal Content in the Message of Jesus 229
    Part III: The Redemption and the Church
13 The Apostolic Witnesses.. 257
14 The Holiness and Wisdom of Jesus................................... 271
15 The Testimony of Miracles 313
16 The Resurrection 343

CONTENTS

17 The Witness of Prophecy 385
18 The Church As a Motive of Credibility 435
19 The Conclusion of Apologetics 463
20 The Story of Apologetics 475
Index 492

FOREWORD

We like to say we believe in progress. Especially in matters related to religion, we want to believe that things are getting better all the time. Catholics are, by and large, a hopeful lot.

But in private—late into a long night's conversation, after a glass of wine or maybe two—many Catholics of my generation and younger will confess to a secret envy. We strongly suspect that we didn't get the same quality or quantity of intellectual and spiritual formation that Catholics generally received in the middle of the last century.

It's not a peculiar problem of "conservatives" or "liberals." It's not reducible to illusions about any purported Golden Age in the Church. It's an almost epidemic sense of insecurity—and, as I said, envy.

The great social scientist Msgr. George Kelly was asked about this situation shortly before his death in 2004; and in his response he described the mid-twentieth century in America as a period of religious teaching and discipline unprecedented in the history of the Catholic Church. Msgr. Kelly could be critical of the formation given during that period, and he was grateful for subsequent developments, especially in the Second Vatican Council and the pontificate of St. John Paul II. Yet he recognized the uniqueness of that singular historical moment in a particular place: the United States of America.

The man who wrote the book you're holding was one of the giants of that time and place. Born in 1906 in Springfield, Massachusetts, Joseph Clifford Fenton was ordained to the priesthood for his home diocese in 1930. After early theological studies in Montreal, he completed his doctorate at the Pontifical Angelicum in Rome. The director of his dissertation was Fr. Reginald Garrigou-Lagrange, O.P., perhaps the most brilliant theologian alive at that time.

When he returned home, Fr. Fenton showed himself to be a prodigy of holy ambition. He served for a time in parishes before finding a lasting home in academia. For twenty-five years he was professor of fundamental dogmatic theology at the Catholic University of America. For twenty years he edited the *American Ecclesiastical Review*, the most influential theological journal in the country and the standard-bearer of Catholic orthodoxy. He wrote six books.

An imposing figure, a dynamic lecturer, a tireless and prolific writer, he engaged the major controversies of his day. When Fr. Leonard Feeney advanced the argument that non-Catholics could not be saved, he found the most forceful opposition in Fr. Fenton. When Fr. John Courtney Murray, S.J., began to articulate a Catholic approach to religious liberty, it was Fr. Fenton who challenged him, debated him publicly, and required him to sharpen his thinking. He played a similar role in the career of Fr. John J. Hugo, Dorothy Day's spiritual director and a leading light of Catholic pacifism.

If the mid-century was a time of widespread Catholic intellectual engagement, as Msgr. Kelly insisted it was, Joseph Clifford Fenton deserves a good portion of the credit. His classroom lectures clarified basic doctrine for a generation of leaders, who then went out to all the States to tell the Good News. His journal delivered the same lessons to a waiting readership that ranged from bishops to motivated laypeople. Fenton's mind was the iron that sharpened iron.

The book at hand appeared in 1942 under the rather unimposing title *We Stand with Christ: an Essay in Catholic Apologetics*. It should have become a classic. It is, I believe, the greatest work of apologetics produced in a time of superstar apologists such as F. J. Sheed, Ronald Knox, and Fulton Sheen.

Apologetics was in demand because every seminarian had to study it and it was the basic freshman course for every student in Catholic colleges (some required two semesters). When it was taught well, apologetics endowed students with a vision of faith and reason, a sense of the credibility of divine revelation, and a battery of ways to demonstrate the existence of God.

The problem was (and always will be) that it wasn't always taught well. Too often, apologetics came across as something small, crabbed, contentious, reductionist, reflexively defensive, and appallingly rationalistic. It was the incipient rationalism that most concerned Fr. Fenton—the overweening confidence that the mysteries of the faith could somehow be reduced to self-evident syllogisms.

The truth is that the mysteries of faith cannot be proven. If they could, they would not require faith. But that does not obviate the need for reason, study, or apologetics. As Fr. Fenton knew, there is no way to provide a rational "proof" of the mysteries of faith. But one could provide a rational *justification* for accepting and believing the mysteries of faith.

What emerged from such efforts was the field of fundamental theology.

This book is pivotal in that history. It represents the high point of apologetics as well as a gold standard for subsequent works of fundamental theology.

Though it never saw the sales it merited, it got noticed. Fr. Fenton was increasingly called upon for consultation by the upper echelons of the hierarchy. He belonged to the Pontifical Roman Theological Academy and served as counselor to the Sacred Congregation of Seminaries and Universities. In the years leading up to the Second Vatican Council, he was summoned by Cardinal Alfredo Ottaviani, secretary of the Holy Office in the Vatican, to serve as his personal *peritus* (expert). At the Council, he served as a member of the preparatory Theological Commission, the Doctrinal Commission, and the Commission on Faith and Morals.

Once back home, he was alarmed and disillusioned by the way the Council was reported and implemented. He felt increasingly isolated in the academic establishment. Soon he retired from editorship of the review and from teaching, and he returned to parish life as a pastor. He died, in his sleep, in 1969.

His legacy, though, is formidable. It is what we, in our best moments, perhaps, admit that we envy about a particular generation of our ancestors.

It is enshrined in this book.

—Scott Hahn

INTRODUCTION

When Origen wrote his introduction to the book *Against Celsus*, he drew a picture no apologist can afford to forget. He described our Lord standing alone and silent before His accusers in the judgment hall. Shrill voices bore discordant charges against Him, and He would not speak in His own defense. The great Alexandrian made it very clear that the silence of Jesus was freighted with meaning. The important thing there in that courtroom was Jesus Himself. The men who surged about Him knew well what He had said and what He had done. The Saviour wished them to consider only that.

Now Origen knew very well that Jesus of Nazareth never would and never could stand in need of any earthly advocate. His is not a cause to which men are to be won over by skilled pleading or any merely rhetorical tactic. He wills only that men should understand what He has spoken and what He has accomplished. Hence it is that when a man is privileged to stand with Christ, it becomes his duty to conduct himself in a manner that through his speech or writing the men of his age and of his little circle may perhaps gather some more accurate appreciation of the Lord.

It was with this spirit that Origen took up the contest against Celsus. It is in this same spirit that every successful apologist since the dawn of Christianity has faced his task. The men who stand with Christ come and go. The Master remains. Each man who is privileged to plead for Him takes cognizance of the objections and calumnies that the world casts at Him. Then he bends every effort to enable men clearly to see the life and the words of Jesus. All the time he is aware that our Lord seeks for more than some mere refutation of the idle calumnies that are issued against Him, for He stands clothed in that blood which was shed for many.

The efforts of each man or group of men are sharply limited. The effective work of one defender of Christ may reach a few listeners for a short time. Others will come and these in turn will go. But while men live upon this earth there is no more precious and sacred privilege than that of standing forth and speaking for Christ.

At the moment this privilege is ours. The American Catholics of our generation are empowered, as perhaps no similar group in the world is now, to point effectively at Christ. Through our efforts the men of this warring world can come to know Him better, and knowing Him achieve that eternal life He died to procure for them. This at least is certain. If we do not show Christ to men, we shall have failed.

Each man must speak in the language of his people and according to the mentality of his time. Our people are capable of and habituated to a language of scientific accuracy. The time in which we live is by far too difficult to admit of much concern over fanciful systems and theories. We must present the claims of Jesus clearly. It is our business to show the proofs He offered in support of His claims, and to point out how they demonstrate.

In far-off lands theorizers who had no pressing business might sit around in salons and indulge their fancy about some never-never country in which perfectly impartial men set out on a search for the true religion. Now we must take cognizance of facts and act in accordance with them. The Church of God does not wait for men to come to her seeking the divine message. Urged on by the insistent command of her divine Founder, she carries that message to men who suffer and work. With that message she carries credentials, showing it to be a communication from the real and living God, which men ought to accept with the unwavering assent of divine faith and through which alone they can achieve an unending and ineffable happiness. We who are privileged to stand with Christ must be able to show that message and those credentials.

In this book I have ventured to cite the texts of pertinent documents a bit more extensively than is usual in a work of this

Introduction

type. I believe this to be an effective and satisfactory procedure since American readers are notoriously interested in direct evidence. In this way they can see what Jesus has said and what others have said about Him much more effectively than through a mere recapitulation with the inevitable references to other books. For scriptural citations, the Challoner revision of the Douay version has been used in practically every case.

Chapter 1

THE WORK OF APOLOGETICS

1. In general, the term "apologetics" designates a defense of Catholic teaching. Although the word apologetics[1] did not come into general use until the nineteenth century, the activity which it connotes is as old as Christianity itself. Since the days of Jesus of Nazareth, men have written and spoken to refute the charges advanced against His followers and His doctrine and to show decisive reason why their fellows should accept His teachings with the assent of divine faith. Thus St. Justin the Martyr and Athenagoras pointed out the injustice of that persecution which the Roman Empire raised against the followers of Christ. Origen triumphantly overthrew the accusations of evil and inconsistency which the philosopher Celsus had leveled against Christian teaching. Eusebius of Caesarea and St. Athanasius were able to disprove claims which had been set forth in favor of a cultural superiority of paganism over Catholicism. The great Augustine demonstrated that the Roman Empire's acceptance of Christianity had in no way been responsible for the calamities which befell the state during the barbarian incursions.

When men attacked the intellectual claims of Christianity in the name of the old paganism, or of Judaism, or later of Mohammedanism, there were always erudite followers of Christ able to examine these writings and to reply victoriously to them. Again from the time of St. Irenaeus until our own, the scholars of the Catholic Church have had to keep up a running battle against those men who have attacked the Church in the name of one or another of those sects which have

---

[1] The term is a derivative of the Greek, *"apologein,"* to defend or to speak in favor of. The cognate word, "apology," is much older. It was applied to several second-century Christian works which attempted to dissuade pagan rulers from persecuting the Christians.

disputed with it the title and the prerogatives of the true Christian society. Finally there have been Catholic writers who in more recent times have taken up the replies against rationalism and naturalism, and who have developed what we may term a theory for the defense of the Christian Church.

All of the writings which these men have produced can be collected under the heading of "apologetics." Thus a history of apologetics, properly written, should take cognizance of all the controversial literature designed to defend the claims of Catholicism. However, the apologetics which is taught in our seminaries and universities, which has been brought into scientific order within the past century and a half, is far more than a mere compilation of controversial information. It considers the contributions of traditional controversial literature in positive and scientific form.

2. The science of apologetics is meant to demonstrate that Catholic dogma is rationally acceptable. Catholic dogma consists in those truths which are found in sacred Scripture and in tradition, and which are presented by the Church, either by way of solemn judgment or in her ordinary and universal magisterium, as having been revealed by God to be accepted by all men with the assent of divine faith.[2] It is a body of teaching which claims at once to be living and immutable. It is living in the sense that it has been and is proposed to people of all ages and of every variety of intellectual endowment. The Church expounds this dogma in terms of every language and every cultural environment and in face of the difficulties which have arisen through every crisis of world history. Catholic dogma is immutable in that, through all this complexity of cultural approach and expression, the same identical truths are always presented to the people as having been revealed by God. Their meaning never changes.[3]

The science of apologetics, then, takes up the defense of a doctrine which is not merely set down in a book and then left to the varying

---

[2] The Vatican Council, Constitution, *Dei Filius*, Ch. 3 (Denzinger, 1792). See also Garrigou-Lagrange, O.P., *De Revelatione per Ecclesiam Catholicam Proposita* (Rome, 1929), 3rd edition of the complete work, Vol. 1, pp. 183–185; Léonce de Grandmaison, S.J., *Le Dogme Chrétien, Sa Nature, Ses Formules, Son Development* (Paris, 1927), pp.275–329.

[3] "For the doctrine of faith, which God has revealed, was not proposed as a philosophical discovery, to be perfected by human genius, but rather as a divine deposit, entrusted to the" spouse of Christ to be guarded faithfully and to be expressed

interpretations of different ages and cultural conditions. It defends this dogma by demonstrating clearly and with certitude that it gives evidence of having been revealed by God. A doctrine which offers naturally ascertainable evidence of having been communicated by God is obviously one which men can accept prudently and rationally with the assent of divine faith. The defense of Catholic dogma, then, consists in an examination of the claims advanced in favor of this teaching and then in the demonstration of the way in which these claims are justified by manifest signs of divine origin.[4]

The term defense, as it is used in connection with the function of scientific apologetics, must be properly understood. The science of apologetics is in no way construed as an answer to some definite attack which has been made against the integrity of Christian doctrine. Such a reply must be classified as a work of individual controversy or polemics. Neither is this science merely to be thought of as repertory out of which answers may be found to any charge which might be leveled against the Church or its teaching. All of the ecclesiastical sciences hold information which may be utilized in replying to such attacks. In the same way the science of apologetics is quite distinct from what is known as the apology of dogma. In this latter discipline the student learns to defend some individual dogma against the misrepresentations which have been made against it by the enemies of the Church.

The science of apologetics differs from controversy and polemics in that it is positive and irenic rather than negative. It is distinguished from apology of dogma in that it inquiries into the acceptability of

---

infallibly. Hence also that meaning of the sacred dogmas which the Church has once proclaimed is always to be held, nor can we ever abandon that meaning under the pretense or name of higher understanding" (The Vatican Council, Constitution, *Dei Filius*, Ch. 4 (Denzinger, 1800). See also Garrigou-Lagrange, op. cit., pp. 185–190; Belgeri, *Canones Tridentini et Vaticani* (Milan and Turin, 1895), pp. 567–571; Vacant, *Etudes Theologiques sur les Constitutions du Vatican - La Constitution "Dei Filius"* (Paris and Lyon, 1895), Vol. 2, pp. 281–319.

4 This is precisely the claim the Church advances for her teaching. According to her doctrine the external proofs of revelation, which primarily are miracles and prophecies, are *"signa certissima divinitus orate christianae religionis"* (The Oath against Modernists, Denzinger, 2145).

the body of revealed doctrine as a whole rather that into that of some individual statement contained in the body of divine teaching.[5]

3. Catholic dogma is intellectually acceptable only insofar as it is rationally credible. The Catholic dogma which the science of apologetics sets out to establish as intellectually acceptable is a body of teaching which claims to have been revealed by God Himself. Included in this body of teaching are certain truths which are known as the supernatural mysteries, verities absolutely beyond the natural capacity of any creature, actual or possible, to comprehend. Such truths can be seen clearly only in the light of the divine intelligence, or in that of the beatific vision which God grants as a supernatural and eternal reward to the blessed in heaven. If these truths had not been revealed to man, that is, communicated to him in a way which is at once distinct from and superior to the manner in which man naturally obtains his knowledge, he could never know of their existence. But even after they have been supernaturally revealed and accepted with the assent of divine faith, man does not see them clearly in this world.[6]

For this reason it is idle to attempt any proof of acceptability which would claim to show that all the verities contained in the deposit of Christian revelation are evidently true. As long as man is in this world he will be incapable of effecting any such demonstration. The only recourse left to one who wishes to establish the intellectual acceptability of Catholic dogma is the demonstration that these mysteries' have actually been revealed by God.

The revelation with which we are here concerned is mediate and public rather than immediate and private. In other words, it is a body of doctrine which comes to the individual "destinary" through the preaching of some one of his fellow men. It is intended for the body of mankind as a whole, rather than merely for one individual or for a limited number of persons. Hence, it is impossible for the apologist to appeal merely to the individual experience of one of the "destinaries." A man can be certain that the dogma of the Catholic

---

[5] For a more complete understanding of the place which apologetics occupies in the discipline of theology as a whole, see Fenton, J. C, *The Concept of Sacred Theology* (Milwaukee, 1941), pp. 209–211.

[6] The Vatican Council, Constitution, *Dei Filius*, Ch. 4 (Denzinger, 1795–1796).

Church is intellectually acceptable only when the divine origin of that doctrine is attested by evident and certain guarantees.

A doctrine thus guaranteed is termed rationally credible. It is, in other words, a teaching which men may prudently and reasonably accept with the assent of divine revelation. A statement is said to be rationally credible only insofar as it is capable of being accepted with the assent of divine faith by a man who does not do violence to his own human nature in believing it.

In proposing Catholic dogma as something which is evidently credible as divine revelation, the science of apologetics is quite cognizant of the fact that accepting a statement on the authority of God revealing it is indeed a serious business. Rather than honoring God, a man would commit an offense against Him were he to believe without reason that some statement had been communicated by the Creator. Christian teaching censures the man who believes without having cause to know that the statement which he accepts is actually one which should be accepted. "He that is hasty to give credit, is light of heart, and shall be lessened."[7] Furthermore, in the Scripture itself there is the direct assertion that the revealed message is actually credible. "Thy testimonies are become exceedingly credible."[8]

In general a judgment of credibility involves three elements. First of all, the man who receives a message on the authority of the one who has communicated it to him, rather than by reason of any evidence of truth manifest in the communication itself should know whether the statement is genuine, that is, whether it has actually come from the person who was supposed to have sent it. Then, he should know whether the person who has sent the message actually has knowledge of the object about which he wishes to instruct. Finally, the "destinary" should be able to judge whether the sender of the message actually intends to tell the truth.

In dealing with a message which claims to come from God, obviously only the first element need be considered. Our natural knowledge about God shows us clearly enough that He is at once all-knowing and all-truthful. Consequently, one may not reject a message which purports to come from God on the ground that He might

---

7 Eccles. 19:4.
8 Ps. 92:5.

deceive us. However, it is not only possible but even necessary to inquire as to whether this particular message actually has come from God.

The standard by which we determine the divine origin of a particular or any communication is analogous to that which we utilize in ascertaining the origin of any other message which we might receive. We recognize a message from another human being principally by means of his signature. This signature is so intensely personal that it can be considered as perfectly proper only to the individual human being involved. Others may counterfeit his signature, but they can never duplicate it. A message which bears the signature or the seal of a man is rightly considered as emanating from his person and as worthy of credence as he himself is.

Although God Himself is invisible to bodily eyes, there are certain visible effects which He alone can produce, and which are manifestly distinct from and superior to any and all counterfeits of these same effects. Such works, evident in themselves and manifestly attached to the body of a doctrine which claims to be revealed, show this doctrine to be of authentic divine teaching. The all-wise and all-just God could never permit Himself to deceive His creatures by attaching His signature to a doctrine which He knew to be false. He could never allow Himself to be called in as a witness and to attest a claim that was unsubstantiated.

A message which claims to come from God and which is authenticated by these visible and manifestly divine effects is properly termed credible. It is the business of the apologist to show that such is the case with Catholic dogma. The man who accepts with the assent of divine faith a doctrine that gives evident indications of coming from God obviously acts in accordance with the dictates of his own reason. In believing a message which gives manifest indications of its own divine origin, the Catholic acts prudently and wisely.

4. The conclusion of Catholic apologetics is meant to be acceptable in the light of pure human reason. A demonstration of rational credibility would be to no purpose, unless it were visible in the light of natural reason as such. In other words, a man need not possess the gift of divine faith in order to see that the content of that faith is something which he can accept prudently with the assent of divine faith. A man must have the gift of divine faith in order connaturally and perfectly to accept with certainty the teachings contained in the body of divine revelation. But he does not stand in need of any gift of faith in order to be able to demonstrate and to realize that the acceptance of this doctrine is perfectly in harmony with the tendencies and the demands of his own human nature.

Since it contains supernatural mysteries as a definite and specifying element, the body of divine revelation remains something above and beyond the natural intellectual capacity, not only of the individual man but of any creature actual or possible. In order that the human mind may possess these truths according to the perfection of intellectual certitude it must be strengthened and confirmed supernaturally by God. However, since the indications of divine authorship are visible to all men and comprehensible to any person who is aware of that by which the Creator is distinguished from His creatures, the evidence of credibility is attainable by any individual who will examine the realities in which the divine testimony is made manifest.

Moreover, the historical and critical doctrine which necessarily enters into the demonstration of credibility offered in support of the claims of Catholic dogma must be available to the natural understanding of man. The apologist is concerned with offering naturally ascertainable evidence that Jesus Christ really lived, that He actually taught the doctrine which is ascribed to Him, that He claimed that His doctrine was a divine message which was to be accepted as such, and finally that He adduced, in support of His claims, unmistakable evidence that His teaching actually had been revealed by God. Catholic dogma could never be accepted prudently as divine revelation unless all of this evidence can be offered to the natural mind of man.

Since the conclusion of apologetics is meant to be something naturally evident, the process of proof from which this conclusion is derived must itself be ascertainable according to the demands and the conditions of natural reason. Obviously, for the examination of the claims of Christianity, a man must look into the content of the Christian message itself. However, such an examination in no way compels an acceptance of this dogma according to the certain assent of divine faith. A man may see that the Christian dogma claims to be a doctrine actually revealed by God, a message communicated by God to man in a supernatural way, without ever accepting this message on divine faith. Likewise, he can recognize through the exercise of his natural faculty of understanding alone that this message is set forth as public and mediate revelation and as a necessary and beneficial teaching.

In the same way, a man can judge the historical competence of those books which the Christian accepts as the written Word of God. In forming his judgment he may use the same standards of recognition which he would utilize in attempting to ascertain the historical value of any other documents. Moreover, by the use of his natural reason alone, man can decide as to the possibility and the probative value of miracles, and can recognize the testimony of miracles with reference to the essential claims of Christianity. It is the business of the apologist to utilize all of the equipment of natural reason in bringing out that conclusion to which his own science is primarily directed.

Obviously the demonstration of credibility cannot depend in any way upon the assent of divine faith. Catholic dogma is rationally acceptable as divine revelation only through actual evidence that it has been communicated by God to man, and not merely through any claim to credibility contained in the body of doctrine itself. It is perfectly true that within the body of Christian dogma there is the assertion that this doctrine is designated as divine revelation through certain unmistakable indications of divine authorship. The proof of credibility, however, consists essentially in showing that such indications actually exist and are manifestly attached to the teaching of Jesus Christ.

5. The judgment of credibility to which the science of apologetics is essentially orientated must be objectively certain. A certain judgment is made without fear or danger of the contradictory proposition being true. It is essentially firm. As such it differs from those acts of the intellect which are designated as doubt, conjecture, and opinion. In doubt the mind is faced with two contradictory propositions, and is unable, either because of a paucity of motive, or because the claims of each appear to be equally balanced, to adhere firmly to either of them. By conjecture the mind assents to one of two contradictory propositions, but without an indication or motive

The Work of Apologetics

which would be objectively sufficient for such an adherence. By an opinion the mind assents to one of two contradictory propositions, but not firmly, since there is valid and objective reason for supposing that the other contradictory may be true.[9]

The judgment of credibility which would be sufficient for a doctrine which claims to be divine revelation would obviously have to be certain. The matter under consideration is far too important to lie within the field of mere opinion.[10] A message which God sends to man, and which man cannot reject without a serious moral fault would necessarily be one which carried objective and certain indications in favor of its own claims.

This is the case with the Christian message. It is on this ground, and in function of these claims that it must be judged. The history of the Church and the life of the Church in the world around us are indications that certain evidence has always been presented in favor of the fact that Catholic dogma is rationally credible as divine revelation. A course in apologetics, or a book on the science of apologetics, must be evaluated according to the clarity and the perfection in which they bring out this certainty.[11]

---

9 *Summa Theologica*, IIa, IIae, q. 2, a. I; *Disputed Questions on Truth*, q. 16, a. I.

10 The Church has rejected as false the modernist assertion that "The assent of faith is ultimately based on a combination of probabilities." *The Decree "Lamentabili,"* July 3, 1907, prop. 25 (Denzinger, 2025).

11 Some books and courses in apologetics broaden the scope of this science so as to prove that Christ is God or that the Catholic Church is truly the organization instituted by Christ. However, the first of these statements belongs to the domain of faith since it is the mystery of the Incarnation. The second should properly be treated in Ecclesiology. Confusion as to the central function of apologetics is hardly excusable since the appearance of Father Gardeil's *La Credibilite et l'Apologetique* (Paris, 1928), 3 ed.; and his article "Credibilite" in the *Dictionnaire de Theologie Catholique* (Vol. 3, Cols. 2201–2310).

Chapter 2

THE CONCEPT OF REVELATION

1. The declaration of the Vatican Council. Since apologetics sets out to explain and to demonstrate that "Catholic dogma is rationally credible as divine revelation," it is absolutely necessary that we know at the very outset in what sense Catholic teaching claims to have been revealed. Naturally, Catholic dogma is intellectually acceptable only if it can be demonstrated that the same has come from God in the very manner claimed. When we can adduce certain evidence that God has revealed this doctrine in the way that Jesus Christ and the Church say that it has been revealed, then the task of apologetics will have been accomplished. In examining the concept of revelation, we shall consider the manner in which Catholic dogma insists that it has come to man.

The Catholic Church has effectively summarized her teaching on the origin of her dogma in one paragraph in the Constitution, *Dei Filius* of the Vatican Council: "The same holy mother Church believes and teaches that God, the Principle and the End of all things, can be known with certainty in the natural light of human reason from created things, 'for His invisible things, from the creation of the world are seen, being understood by those things that are made.'[1] Nevertheless it has pleased His wisdom and goodness to reveal Himself and the eternal decrees of His will to the human race in another, and this a supernatural way. 'Diversely and in many ways in times past, God speaking to the fathers in the prophets, last of all in these days hath spoken to us in His Son.'"[2]

---

1 Rom. 1:20.
2 Heb. 1:1, 2; cf. Denzinger, 1785.

In the light of this statement it is evident that the Church considers revelation *actively* as a process of speech by which God communicates truths about Himself and His works to men in a manner at once distinct from and superior to the natural way in which man obtains knowledge. *Objectively* it is the body of truth thus communicated. The ultimate and essential purpose of apologetics is to demonstrate that the teaching which the Catholic Church proposes as a divine message and which the members of that Church accept on divine faith is actually such a revelation.

2. The word "revelation." The very term "revelation" gives us some insight into the claims made by the Catholic Church in favor of her doctrine. The word is an adaptation of the Latin *revelare*. As such it implies the removal of a veil, the taking away of some factor which has hitherto rendered an object unintelligible or invisible. A person is said to reveal something when he exhibits or makes known that which was previously concealed.

The Church claims that this is verified in her own dogma. Asserting that God has chosen "to reveal Himself and the eternal decrees of His will to the human race," she places the body of this dogmatic teaching in the class of truths which the children of men would otherwise not have known. Now it is essential that we understand that the message as a whole expresses truth which has hitherto been concealed from man. There is obviously nothing to prevent God from including in this communication some individual truths which man knew independently of the revelation.

3. The supernatural way of knowing about God. Furthermore, when the Catholic Church insists that the truth we possess in her dogmatic utterances has come to man "in another, and this a supernatural way," she makes obvious reference to a means of knowing about God which is within the natural competence of man and at the same time is quite distinct from revelation. We cannot hope to appreciate what the Church means by "a supernatural way" unless we are aware of her teaching about the purely natural manner by which man can learn about God. She has made this teaching most explicit, not only in the decrees of the Vatican Council to which we have already alluded, but in the section of the "Oath Against Modernism" which is meant to guard against misinterpretation of the Vatican doctrine. "First of all I profess that God, the Principle and End of all things, can be known with certitude and even demonstrated in the natural light of reason through those things which are made, that is through the visible works of creation as a cause (is known and demonstrated) through its effects."[3] The Church has condemned as heretical any denial that "the one true God, our Creator and Lord can be known with certitude in the natural light of human reason through those things which are made."[4] Moreover, she has taken pains to eradicate incompatible doctrines, like those of fideism and traditionalism, even when these have been set forth by her own children and, ostensibly at least, intended for her benefit.[5]

4. The natural way of knowing about God. Clearly then, the Church considers that way by which we know God as the First and absolutely Necessary Cause of the universe to be the mode of knowledge within the sphere of man's natural intellectual competence. The man who attains to this knowledge gains first a clear understanding of the visible and palpable realities which go to make up the material universe. Once he begins to realize what these things are and what they are doing, he notices that they give evidence of real and immediate dependence upon some Cause which Itself is absolutely and ineffably independent. In much the same way, a man who looking out of his window sees a wire swinging to and fro in front of it is perfectly well aware that this wire is held by something above his window. The fact that he is unable actually to see the fastening in no way militates against his certitude that it exists.

The existence, the extent, and the scientific reliability characterizing this natural manner of knowing about God are obviously matters of supreme moment in the science of apologetics. In the first place we must understand this process thoroughly in order to appreciate the way in which it differs from the supernatural means of revelation. More important still, it is the process by which we gain our basic natural notion about God, upon which, in the last analysis, every explanation and demonstration in all the science of, apologetics must depend. For when we say that God has revealed, we understand by

---

[3] Denzinger, 2145.
[4] The Vatican Council, Canon I, "De Revelatione" (Denzinger, 1806).
[5] Cf. Denzinger, 1622-27; 1649-52.

God no mere figment of imagination, but the one, infinitely perfect, First Cause whose existence we know naturally with the utmost certitude. Finally, when we assert that Catholic dogma is rationally credible as divine revelation, we must be able to demonstrate apodictically that this doctrine carries with itself manifest indication that such a God has communicated it to men and wills that all men should accept it.

5. The five ways and the existence of God. We can obtain no adequate idea of the natural process by which we know God without considering the product of that process. As we have seen, man begins with an awareness of the visible things in the universe. He sees these bodies as moved, caused, contingent, admitting of various degrees of excellence, and, finally, as ordered to some purpose. It is, of course, not at all necessary that he should acquaint himself with every object in the universe, or for that matter, with every aspect of dependence manifest in these beings. It is enough that he should see that some thing is moved by a being distinct from itself, that some thing is cause, that some reality is contingent upon another, that one being is better than another, that a design or purpose is manifest in some reality.

When man reflects upon the matter, he cannot fail to realize that the being which moves another must either receive movement from a third object, or must act independently of any other. Likewise, the being which exercises efficient causality upon a reality distinct from itself must be one which acts either as acted upon by another or as utterly independent. Hence, even at this stage of the proof, man can see that there must be some Prime Mover or some First Cause (God), if there is to be any movement or causality whatsoever. For, if the agency which moves or causes the visible object with which we are concerned is dependent upon a being beyond itself, we know that there cannot be an unending series of such beings. Just as we know that ultimately something must support the final link of a suspended chain, so we realize that finally some adequate and absolutely independent factor must be responsible for the movement and causality evident in the universe. By multiplying a series of dependent superior agencies, one succeeds only in finding added reasons for the existence of one absolutely necessary and independent agent by whom these lesser objects are influenced.

Much the same procedure is followed in observing the implications of the contingency which we find in the world. We observe that some things are contingent upon others. These others either depend upon an absolutely necessary being or are such themselves. Since contingency implies a dependence, there must be some utterly independent reality upon which the contingent being is founded.

Where there are degrees of perfection and nobility, quite evidently there must be a distinction between perfection itself and the thing which possesses it or shares in it. If one thing is better than another, there must be some goodness which has made the various mundane realities good.

Finally, since purpose is manifest among the beings of the world, there necessarily is some intelligent being who has wrought the design. Now this intelligent person is either designed by another or he is an understanding who is at once his own act and his own purpose. Thus naturally we form the basis for our notion of God.

There are two facts which we must realize carefully in evaluating and using these proofs of the existence of God. In the first place, such proofs are entirely outside of and superior to the order of time. We do not look for a cause which once, long ago, set the various substances in the material universe in motion, much as a billiards player starts the movement of the balls upon the table. On the contrary, we look for and find the necessary and primary Agent from whom *this* observable movement proceeds *here and now;* and we seek and require the necessary First Efficient Cause in this observable process of causality, the absolutely necessary being, upon which the contingent reality depends at this moment. The reality we find is the subsistent goodness which actually communicates nobility and worth to the varying objects about us. It is the subsistent intelligence which gives order and design to the things we encounter.

In the second place, we must not expect too much from these demonstrations. Directly and in themselves they give us only the information we have seen. There is nothing within the beginning of this natural process to enable us immediately to recognize the full number of those divine attributes which we are naturally capable of knowing. We must not allow ourselves to forget that the natural process through which we learn about God involves the ways of causality, removal, and excellence. Merely to avail ourselves of the data gained by way of causality is certainly not to exhaust the resources of this natural method for the other two ways are most helpful.

6. Removal of imperfections. In order to find out more about God we must perfect our natural investigation by the ways of removal and excellence. The process of removal comes first. The first statements we can make about the First Cause or subsistent Intelligence whose existence we recognize through the way of causality must be denials. At first we can know at least what this Being is not. Although the resultant propositions are negative, they are most valuable insofar as they enable us effectively and accurately to distinguish God from creatures.

Now it is evident that God cannot be denominated by any quality or characteristic proper to a being that is moved or caused or is contingent, one which merely receives perfection and order. God is immovable. It so happens that movable or caused beings are as such composite. Consequently this subsistent Understanding is not and cannot be composed in any way whatsoever. He can have no composition of integral or substantial parts. Therefore He is not a body and cannot, in any way, be subject to the extension or limitations of a body. He differs from any being distinct from Himself in that there can be no distinction between His essence and His existence, between His nature and His operation. Limitation is a characteristic of beings that are subject to causality and motion. Hence God is obviously and certainly infinite in the order of being or perfection. Time is the measure of bodily movement. Since the First Cause is supremely above all the conditions and vicissitudes of bodies, He is eternal. Because place is a bodily modification, God is not contained by any location but, on the contrary, all things existent depend upon Him. He is in all created things insofar as He can bring about change in them, inasmuch as He holds them in existence and gives them their operation, and because He understands every fiber and aspect of their being. Finally, we are aware that there could not be a multiplicity of beings infinite in perfection, and therefore we assert the sure and evident conclusion that God is One.

7. The entirely perfect attributions. The way of excellence governs the terms which we use in designating God. We find upon examination that certain terms, although commonly used to designate the finite and corporeal beings from which we draw our natural knowledge about God do not *in themselves* express any significance of limitation or imperfection. When we say, for example, that some man is good, we fully realize that his goodness is definitely of the finite order. Yet the word *good* itself carries no implication of limit or imperfection. Hence there is nothing to prevent our properly using this term to denominate the subsistent Understanding Himself. We use such terms when we say, as the natural means for knowing about God show us, that He is good, perfect, understanding, wise, and provident, endowed with the fullness of will, and loving, just, merciful, powerful, and blessed.

8. Analogy in apologetics. We use all these terms *analogously*. In other words, we are quite cognizant that, applied to God, they express a meaning and a reality infinitely distinct from that which they signify when they are utilized to designate His creatures. Yet these terms can properly be used of God because of a similarity of reference. The understanding of man is an act, limited, imperfect, and quite distinct from his existence and nature; the understanding of God, on the other hand, is manifestly identical in reality with Himself and thus with His own existence. Yet there is a certain similarity in the reference of the objects known by God to Him and that of the objects perceived in human understanding to that faculty and to the person possessing it. We know that God perceives all things in function of being and not merely according to some accidental modification. Thus the word *understanding* applies to God in its proper meaning and not merely by metaphor. We say that there is metaphorical denomination when the word applied does not fit the object according to its formal and proper signification. Thus we have metaphorical analogy when we describe God as a lion, remarking the effect which He produces upon His enemies. We use proper analogy when we designate Him as intelligent or as merciful, since neither of these two terms carries within itself any implication of finiteness which would be incompatible with the divine nature.

It is important that we realize the extent and the competence of this natural way of knowing about God, particularly with reference to those attributes which have the most influence in drawing out the conclusions of scientific apologetics. The process of causality brings us to understand the existence of a subsistent Understanding, one which is not designed or planned by any intelligence distinct from and superior to itself. The way of denial shows us that this subsistent Understanding is not a part of anything else but is Its own nature and operation, embracing in Itself all the perfections proper to the order of intelligence. We can see at once that the subsistent Intelligence possesses and *is* the fullness of perfection in the order of will and power.

It would be utterly and evidently impossible to have a subsistent, Intelligence or an absolutely necessary First Cause which would not be endowed with every perfection in the order of understanding, will, and power. Hence God is manifestly omniscient. He causes the creatures which He conserves in being by planning what they shall do and how they shall achieve the purpose He has set for them. He is provident. He loves His own goodness and wills that His creatures should possess or share in that goodness. He is eminently disposed to give to His creatures all that they should have as well as the benefits which they may possess only because of His supreme benignity. Thus He is ineffably just and merciful, all powerful and infinitely blessed.

In fine, the natural means available to man for knowing about God are effective in showing that there is an infinite, eternal, and personal Creator and Lord of the created universe. Since He alone is absolutely necessary, and since all other things possess existence only insofar as He is willing to give it to them, He makes them ultimately, utilizing no pre-existent subject whatsoever. The intelligent beings whom He has created certainly owe Him a real and serious debt of acknowledgment and service. In this way the natural means for showing us about the existence and nature of God bring us to the knowledge of an omnipotent Supreme Being who is perfectly capable of communicating with men, and quite prepared to manifest the authenticity of any message which is offered as His own. Infinitely just and veracious, He will not be party to deception. Omniscient, He cannot be deceived. Omnipotent, no other agency can prevent His communication with man or successfully imitate the means by which He verifies His message.

9. Catholic Dogma claims to have come to man through a process quite distinct from that by which man gains his natural knowledge. When the Vatican Council states that the message of the Catholic Church has been *revealed* to men in another, and this a supernatural way, the Council tacitly admits that there is reason for calling the natural mode by which man learns about God a "revelation." Obviously God is the supreme Source of all knowledge which comes to man even in the natural manner. In the first place God has fashioned the human mind itself. He is the Principle at once of understanding and of intelligibility. He has been the First Cause in all of that activity by which the ideas existent in the human mind have been formed. The understanding is able to grasp objects insofar as they possess being, and whatever being, reality, or intelligibility they have they owe to God. The archetypes of those essences which belong to created things are ideas existent from all eternity in the mind of God. Finally, as Supreme in the order of understanding, God is the Prime Mover and the First Cause of that act in which the mind understands. His influence is all pervading and intimate. The act of knowledge is one which the creature elicits as moved by God.

Yet the Catholic Church teaches, as did Jesus of Nazareth, her Founder, that the message she delivers to the world has come to man through channels quite distinct from those used in the natural process of learning about God. She tells us that her doctrine has come to man in a supernatural way and that God has given it to man by way of speech.

Man acquires knowledge in a supernatural way when he attains some truth in a manner distinct from and superior to that in which he is naturally competent to gain it. In other words, the way is supernatural when it is something which human nature as such is neither able to produce by its own unaided powers nor which it needs for its own essential operation. The knowledge which we are able naturally to obtain about the living God is quite sufficient to assure us that He is infinitely just, and that He will give to every creature whatever is requisite for its own proper activity. Now man is equipped with a faculty of understanding by which he is able to perceive the objects in the world around him. When he has examined these things closely enough, he will find, as we have already seen, that they can be as they are and act as they do only because they depend upon and are supported by an infinitely perfect God. As a result, if God chooses to *speak* to man, and thus further to inform him about the divine life and about his eternal destiny, He is thereby conferring a favor upon man; He is giving him something quite over and above that which is due to human nature as such. This is precisely the claim which Jesus Christ made for the doctrine He advanced while on earth. It is the claim made today in His name by the Catholic Church.

The Church has been most insistent upon this point. She has asserted, time and time again, that man is naturally capable of learning about God. Furthermore, she has taken the trouble to correct those of her loyal but misguided children who, wishing to further her interests, have stated that man could gain no certain knowledge about God other than by means of a message, spoken by God to men and conserved among them by means of tradition. Her rejections of fideism and traditionalism mark the high claim she sets forth in favor of her own teaching. For if her message is something which God has deigned to give man by way of utterance or speech, if it is something which man receives in a supernatural way, then manifestly it is a message which will never be certified by the simple demonstration that it is conformable to or demanded by human nature itself. Some higher criterion must be adduced in order that men may see this teaching as acceptable.

10. God speaks to man. The doctrine which the Church presents as divinely revealed contains numerous indications that it is something which God has spoken to man. We have already seen that the Vatican Council used the words of St. Paul to the Hebrews in describing the way in which man has acquired the message with which the Catholic Church has been entrusted. "God, who, at sundry times and in divers manners, spoke in times past to the fathers, by the prophets, last of all in these days hath spoken to us by His Son."[6] Holy Scripture, which Jesus of Nazareth and the Catholic Church acknowledge as a source containing the revelation explained and defended in the science of apologetics, is filled with similar expressions pertaining to this doctrine. The Pentateuch expressly claims that the statements proposed to the Israelites to be accepted on divine faith were actually

---

6 Heb. 1:1–2; Denzinger, 1785.

The Concept of Revelation

spoken by God to men and meant to be transmitted to others and to be believed with all firmness and certitude. "And the Lord spoke to Moses, saying: I am the Lord: speak thou to Pharao king of Egypt all that I say to thee."[7] The Israelites were given assurance about their future deliverance because God spoke to them. "And the Lord spoke to Moses, saying: I am the Lord that appeared to Abraham, to Isaac, and to Jacob, by the name of God Almighty, and My name Adonai I did not shew them. And I made a covenant with them, to give them the land of Canaan, the land of their pilgrimage wherein they were strangers. I have heard the groaning of the children of Israel wherewith the Egyptians have oppressed them: and I have remembered My covenant. Therefore say to the children of Israel: I am the Lord who will bring you out from the work prison of the Egyptians, and will deliver you from bondage: and redeem you with a high arm and great judgments. And I will take you to myself for my people, I will be your God."[8]

Jesus of Nazareth, likewise, was insistent that His teaching was something God had spoken or taught. "Many things I have to speak and to judge of you. But He that sent me is true: and the things I have heard of Him, these same I speak in the world."[9] "Jesus therefore said to them: When you shall have lifted up the Son of man, then shall you know that I am He, and that I do nothing of myself, but as the Father hath taught me, these things I speak."[10] When our Lord refers to His teaching as containing truths which He had *seen* with the Father, He voices His claim to divine origin and dignity. He, as God, speaks to the world. "I speak that which I have seen with My Father."[11] The burning words of St. John the Apostle explain the import of this last passage. "No man hath seen God at any time. The only-begotten Son, who is in the bosom of the Father, He hath declared Him."[12]

Isaiah the prophet vividly describes this process of divine revelation in terms of speech or teaching. "The Lord hath given me a learned tongue, that I should know how to uphold by word him that is weary.

---

7 Exod. 6:29.
8 Exod. 6:2–7.
9 John 8:26.
10 John 8:28.
11 John 8:38.
12 John 1:18.

He wakeneth in the morning, in the morning He wakeneth my ear, that I may hear Him as a Master."[13] With such emphasis upon the fact that this revelation is something which God has *spoken* to man, it is imperative that we know the meaning of "speech" as used here.

It is evident that, when God is said to speak to man, there is no implication of any limitation which characterizes the speech of one man to another. Normally man speaks to his fellows making use of articulated sound. The propositions which he forms in his mind and which he wishes to bring to the attention of another man, he expresses or signifies by means of an oral statement. This statement, in its turn, is composed of the various words, each manifesting some one of the ideas which go to make up the proposition communicated. By his very nature man is prevented from achieving truth other than by means of these propositions or sentences. Moreover, because he can understand only what has first come to his attention by way of some sense impression or other, man can only communicate and receive truth by means of these external and sensible manifestations in oral, written, or gesticulated words or signs. Materially and as applied to man, speech is necessarily clothed with these connotations. Formally, however, speech involves the conception of some truth in the mind of the speaker, and the ordering of this truth to a distinct person in such a way that the one to whom the speech is addressed will know and recognize it precisely as something which has been communicated. In this sense we can predicate speech, analogously but properly, of God Himself.

Catholic dogma claims to have been given by God to man exactly in this way. It presents itself as a message sent by God. What man has received is not the understanding of some corporeal objects; this is the type of knowledge he can attain through the merely natural use of his own faculties. He actually receives truths set forth in the form of propositions or statements of which God Himself is the Author.

In presenting these statements to man, God makes use of the ideas which man has acquired through the natural exercise of his intellectual powers. But the statements themselves are composed by God, and communicated to man in such a way that man is able to understand

---

13 Isa. 50:4.

them in some way at least and to recognize and acknowledge their divine origin.

Thus, when the Catholic Church presents its dogma as something revealed, she does not claim that it comes to man by way of infused ideas. These latter are concepts which God Himself can form in the mind of man altogether independently of that natural intellectual process through which man is capable of forming ideas. The revelation with which we deal in the science of apologetics involves the presentation of truth, and for men in this world truth is expressed in a proposition or judgment rather than through the medium of a simple idea. God wills that we should know a series of truths. He acts in such a way that we receive these truths precisely as His message. He tells us that we are meant to be His adopted children. We understand the meaning of each term which enters into this proposition, and we gain that knowledge in a natural way. But the statement, the truth itself, comes to us as a communication from God.

11. The Catholic definition of revelation and the process of apologetics. The Church insists upon this concept of revelation as supernatural in the way it has come to man. In the famous decree, *Lamentabili*, of July 3, 1907, Pope Pius X of saintly memory explicitly condemned the modernist assertion that "revelation can be nothing other than the consciousness acquired by man of his own relation to God." If revelation were what the modernists asserted it to be, then the message of the Catholic Church could be judged just as any other product of human genius is evaluated. Since the message itself claims a higher dignity and a supernatural origin, it must stand or fall in the light of that claim. If it can produce credentials adequate for its own sphere, then it is a favor and benefit of incomparable goodness. If it fails to produce guarantees that it is something which God has spoken to men in order to teach them, then no reasonable man should do other than refuse it. Catholic dogma by its definition of revelation appeals but to God. In His court alone can it be justified.

We add that the message of God to man is a kind of *teaching* in order to distinguish this form of speech from every other. Not every speech among men is, or is meant to be, instructional. Very frequently a man speaks in order to influence the attitude or the emotions of his fellow men. According to the content of Catholic dogma itself, this constitutes a message which is meant to instruct. The result of this speech is not merely a changed attitude on the part of the person who receives it; it gives, and it is meant to give, informative knowledge about God. A realistic apologetics will necessarily examine it in the light of these claims.

Chapter 3

THE CHARACTERISTICS OF REVELATION

In attempting to treat the matter of apologetics from the realistic or theological point of view, we have already seen the meaning of the term revelation as this is applied to the truth which we accept on divine faith and which we are meant to defend in this science. It now becomes necessary to see what type of such revelation this doctrine professes to be, that we may thereby realize how its credibility can be established and explained. This doctrine is presented to us as intrinsically supernatural, mediate, and public revelation, and, if it is to be shown as credible at all, it must be considered under these various characteristics.

1. The Vatican Council teaches that Catholic dogma is an intrinsically supernatural revelation. First of all, the doctrine which God has spoken to us and which we are expected to receive with the assent of divine faith contains truths which are intrinsically supernatural. The words of the Vatican Council in the Constitution *Dei Filius* express the meaning of "intrinsically or essentially supernatural truth." "This also the perpetual consent of the Catholic Church has held and now holds, that there are two orders of knowledge distinct not only by principle but by object; distinct by principle because in the one we know by natural reason, and in the other by divine faith; distinct by object because, besides those things to which the natural reason can attain, there are proposed to us to be believed mysteries hidden in God which could not be known if they had not been revealed. Therefore the Apostle who testifies that God is known to the gentiles 'by the things that are made'[1] still, telling about the

---
[1] Rom .1:20.

grace and the truth which 'came by Jesus Christ'[2] states, 'But we speak the wisdom of God in a mystery, a wisdom which is hidden, which God ordained before the world, unto our glory, which none of the princes of this world knew.... But to us God hath revealed them by His Spirit. For the Spirit searcheth all things, yea, the deep things of God.'"[3]

2. That which is intrinsically supernatural is distinguished from that which is supernatural merely in the mode of its production. The meaning attached to the term supernatural is the most important doctrine contained in the body of apologetics. As we have already seen, a thing can be spoken of as supernatural in two distinct ways. First, it can be said to be supernatural by reason of the way in which it is brought about. Second, it can be termed such by reason of its very essence. The Vatican Council, as a matter of fact, speaks of God revealing truths to men by a way which is distinct from that process through which man is naturally capable of acquiring his knowledge. It speaks of this revelation as "another and this *a supernatural way*."[4] We may note here that in order to avoid confusion on this point, certain authors like Dieckmann[5] and Dorsch use the term "preternatural" to designate what we call supernatural by reason of the way in which a thing is brought about. The intention of these writers is quite laudable, but their terminology is not in accord with the traditional wording of the Church as made manifest in the decrees of the Vatican. Furthermore, there is another meaning attached to the word preternatural, one quite incompatible with the definition of divine revelation.[6]

The thing that is supernatural by reason of the way in which it is brought about is something which is thus designated because of

---

[2] John 1:17.
[3] 1 Cor. 2:7, 8, 10; Denzinger, 1795.
[4] Denzinger, 1785.
[5] Dieckmann, Hermannus, S.J., *De Revelatione Christiana* (Freiburg im Breisgau: 1930), pp. 144–146.
[6] Dorsch, Aemilius, S.J., in *Institutiones Theologiae Fundamentalis* (Innsbruck, Austria, 1930), Vol. I, 2 and 3 ed., calls preternatural those truths which could not be known other than through the process of revelation but which, once revealed, can be comprehended as well as any other proposition in the natural order. These are mysteries insofar as this existence is not attainable by man. More commonly, a thing

its efficient cause. In other words it is an effect which could not be produced by any created agency. Thus divine revelation, which is a speaking of God to man by way of teaching him, is obviously something which could not be produced by any created agency whatsoever. It involves the activity of One who is evidently the Master of the created universe, One who is not dependent upon the laws of the world, but upon whom rather these laws themselves depend for their very existence and operation.

The reality which is supernatural intrinsically or essentially is one, the very being of which is above the order of created nature. In contradistinction, the reality which is supernatural merely by reason of its efficient causality would be something allocated within the realms of created reality, even though, as an effect, this particular reality could not be produced by the natural operation of any created power.[7]

3. God in His intimate life is the center of the intrinsically supernatural order. Now there is one, and only one substantial reality which is essentially remote from the realm of the natural competence of any creature whatsoever. This reality is the nature or the being of God Himself, as He is seen by and in Himself. The highest of creatures which could possibly be brought into existence could never have within its own natural competence the face to face vision of the living God. The most perfect of creatures could know God naturally only insofar as it recognized Him as the First Cause upon whom the being and the operation of other things depend necessarily and evidently.

Thus to the order of the intrinsically supernatural pertain all those things which are specified by God, as He is seen directly in Himself, and not merely insofar as He is recognized as the necessary and evident First Cause of created being and activity. The uncreated supernatural Reality is God Himself, as He is to be seen in and through Himself, that is insofar as He is known in the divine science which belongs to Him and in the beatific vision which the saints in heaven enjoy by

---

is designated as preternatural when it is beyond the natural competence of man but within that of higher creatures, who are pure spirits. Cf. Fenton, J. C, *The Concept of Sacred Theology*, p. 12.

7 Garrigou-Lagrange, *De Revelatione*, Vol. I, pp. 211–212.

reason of His mercy. Next, of course, the beatific vision itself is in the order of the intrinsically supernatural. It is an act of awareness or understanding, and as such it is specified by its object. The object of this act is, of course, the uncreated Supernatural itself.

With the beatific vision we must classify as intrinsically supernatural the "Light of glory" which renders the intellect of the saint in heaven connaturally able to elicit this act. In the same class also is habitual or sanctifying grace, the ultimate intrinsic principle of that life to which the beatific vision pertains and of which it is the perfect culmination. Also specified by the same ultimate supernatural object and likewise intrinsically supernatural are the infused virtues, both theological and moral, the gifts of the Holy Ghost, and all of those acts of which these virtues and gifts are the immediate principles.[8]

Obviously the supernatural mysteries also must be allocated in this class. These are the truths which refer to God insofar as He is known in Himself and through Himself. They are "hidden in God" in the very literal sense that they are truths about God which are utterly beyond the natural competence of any created intellect, actual or possible. Then if they were not revealed, that is shown by God to man through the process of speech, these truths could not be known by man.

4. The beatific vision and divine faith which is ordained to it are in the intrinsically supernatural order. When God shows Himself to the blessed in heaven in the ineffable intimacy of the beatific vision, He concedes to them a supernatural clarity of knowledge which goes beyond anything to be found in the natural, order. But this vision is precisely the end toward which we are working, the end toward which the Christian life in this world is orientated. As a result, the efforts and tendencies of this life, which is essentially a period of preparation and purification for the happiness of the next, are incompatible with the clarity of this vision. The only way, then, in which the truths seen clearly in the beatific vision, the mysteries of which the Church speaks in the passage of the Vatican

---

8 T. J. Walshe, M.A., *The Principles of Catholic Apologetics* (London, 1926), pp. 116–135; by the same author, *The Principles of Christian Apologetics* (London, 1919), p. 167; Garrigou Lagrange, *a.c.*, pp. 191–219; Fenton, J. C, *The Theology of Prayer* (Milwaukee, 1939), pp. 25–26.

Council, just cited, can be possessed with certainty by a man in this world is through the essentially obscure assent of divine faith. Faith is precisely the certain acceptance of a proposition based, not upon evidence which shows the objective identity of its subject and predicate, but upon the authority of the person who has submitted the statement under consideration. A proposition about God in His intimate life which is not evident, and which cannot be shown as evident, such as the mysteries are in respect to the men of this world, can be possessed with certainty only in the assent of divine and intrinsically supernatural faith.

5. The intrinsically supernatural order and the process of revelation. To put the matter in another way, the Object about which the mysteries inform us is God, known in and through Himself rather than merely as the First Cause of the being and the activity of creatures. This Object is not to be seen in this world. There can be no similar object open to the gaze of men for the very good reason that there is nothing in all the world of creatures which is like to God.[9] The only way, then, in which man can gain an accurate and certain knowledge of this Object is through a communication addressed to him by God Himself. God can express the truth about Himself to man through propositions intelligible to him.

We must realize, of course, that the terms in which these mysteries are expressed and spoken to man are terms known to him according to the natural process of his reasoning. In the field of human intellectual activity, truth is contained and expressed in judgment rather than in simple apprehension. It is the *truth* which is the mystery. The words in which this mystery is conveyed are quite intelligible to man, and well within the natural competence of his mind. Thus, for instance, the truth that there are, within the ineffable unity of the divine essence, three persons really distinct one from the other constitutes a mystery. It is a fact which man could never begin to know if God Himself had not presented this proposition to him as a divine teaching. But each of the terms which compose the proposition are words which enter into the expression of man's natural knowledge. Speaking involves the expression and the reception of propositions, and these propositions could not be intelligible were it not for the fact that the

---

9 St. Thomas Aquinas, *The Summa Theologica*, I, q. 12, art. 2.

terms which enter into them are understandable by the persons to whom they are addressed.

6. The supernatural mysteries and human reason. In the light of the definition of revelation as a speaking of God to man, and through the realization of divine mysteries as truths about an Object which will not be evident to men in this world, we can understand the following statement of the Vatican Council relative to the study of divine mysteries. "And reason, enlightened by faith, when carefully, piously, and soberly, it seeks some God-given understanding of the mysteries, it attains this most fruitful understanding, both from analogy with those things which it knows naturally and from the connection of the mysteries among themselves. Still, however, reason is never fitted to perceive these mysteries in the same way that it perceives those truths which constitute its own proper object. For the divine mysteries by their very nature so exceed the created intellect that even after they have been presented in revelation and received by faith, they yet remain covered with the veil of faith itself and enveloped, as it were, in a mist, as long as, in this life 'we are absent from the Lord, for we walk by faith and not by sight.' "[10]

The doctrine which the apologist presents as credible contains truths which are mysteries in the strict sense of the term. Not only would man be utterly unable to know these mysteries if God had not seen fit to reveal them to him, but even after this revelation has been made, and after the truths have been accepted with the supernatural assent of divine faith, the Object which these revealed propositions describe remains obscure. Even after the revelation has been made and the truths have been accepted with an act of divine faith, there is no way of demonstrating the objective identity of the subject and the predicate which enter into the statement of these revealed mysteries.

Man can obtain an understanding of these mysteries in the two ways which have been described in *Dei Filius* of the Vatican Council. He can make use of the process of analogy, and thus he can formulate terms which can be utilized to express and teach the revealed truths themselves. Or he can compare the mysteries among themselves and with the last end of man, and in this way he will begin to appreciate further the significance of those truths which God has

---

10 2 Cor. 5:6, 7; Denzinger, 1796.

given to us in His revelation of the mysteries. Through the process of analogy the Nicene Fathers learned to evaluate the aptitude of the word *consubstantial* to express the fact that the divine Father and Son subsisted in one and the same ineffably simple divine essence. Through the process of comparison the theologian learns more perfectly to understand the truth of the Incarnation, when he realizes that the Person who assumed a human nature in order to suffer and to die for us is that same Person who proceeds from all eternity from the Father.

The import of this truth in the science of apologetics is tremendous. Because the mysteries remain obscure even after they have been revealed and accepted with the assent of divine faith, there can be no hope of defending them by the simple process of demonstrating that the subject and the predicate in the propositions of faith are objectively identical. In other words, the mysteries cannot be defended or shown to be credible by any manner of proof which is directed to point out their evident truth. At the same time, however, the statements which express these mysteries are intelligible propositions. Man can come to understand them with ever increasing profundity. Hence the apologist will be able to seek in the consistency, sublimity, and holiness of these revealed mysteries some indication of the validity of their claim to have been spoken by God to many.

Finally, some evidence pertinent to the proof of credibility will be forthcoming from an examination of the relation between these revealed mysteries and those truths which man possesses through the natural exercise of his own cognitive faculties. This intrinsically supernatural doctrine, this revelation which is supernatural in its content as well as in the manner in which it has been received by man, is presented to us as a teaching in conformity with natural truth. The propositions which express these mysteries, propositions which are intelligible to men, are put forward as not being contradictory to the naturally evident doctrines which mankind possesses. The Vatican Council continues its Constitution, *Dei Filius*, with the words, "Although faith is truly above reason, there can never be any true dissension between faith and reason, since the same God who reveals the mysteries and infuses faith has placed the light of reason in the human soul. But God can never deny Himself nor contradict the truth.

The false appearance of such contradiction arises especially when the dogmas of the faith are not understood and exposed according to the mind of the Church or when the teachings of opinions are held for the statements of reason. Therefore we define every assertion contrary to the truth of enlightened faith as entirely false."[11]

These claims of the Vatican Council have been put forward by the Catholic Church since her very founding by Christ. That doctrine which we accept with the assent of divine faith has always been asserted as a teaching which does not and cannot contradict the facts ascertained by man through the natural use of his reason.

If the doctrine which we receive on divine faith can be shown to contradict the facts which we obtain through our natural powers of intellect, then this doctrine cannot be credible as divine revelation. It will not have lived up to the definition which is put forward in the magisterium of the revealed doctrine itself.

7. Various meanings conveyed by the word "mystery." In order that there might be no confusion whatsoever about the meaning of the term mystery, as this term is predicated of those truths which we accept as divinely revealed, we should realize clearly the significance of this word in itself. A thing is spoken of as a mystery insofar as it is unknown to man.[12] Now a thing may be unknown in two different ways. Its very existence may be unknown or, even though its existence may be known, its essence may remain unknown. Thus the stones on the bottom of the ocean are mysteries to man insofar as he has no present means of learning about their existence. In the same way the contour of that side of the moon which is turned away from the earth remains a mystery to the men of this world. Likewise those secrets which are in the heart of man and which are withheld from the knowledge of his fellows can properly be spoken of as mysteries.

Realities which are unknowable in their very essence to man may escape his understanding for either one of two distinct reasons. The essence under consideration may be so high in the scale of intelligible reality that the very perfection of its clarity surpasses the natural com-

---

11 The closing words of this citation were taken from the acts of the fifth ecumenical council of the Lateran (Denzinger, 738); Denzinger, 1797.
12 Cf. Walshe, *The Principles of Catholic Apologetics*, pp. 112–114; Garrigou-Lagrange, *De Revelatione*, Vol. 1, pp. 174–183.

petence of man. Thus those truths which pertain to the life of God as He is in Himself, rather than as He is known to His creatures by the process of causality, are mysteries precisely because they lie beyond the limits of the natural competence of the human intelligence. God is too bright in the intellectual order to be seen or understood naturally by any created intelligence. Thus its mysterious character is based upon the excess of intelligibility in the object itself. The object is invisible for much the same reason that the unaided human eye cannot look into the sun. The object is too bright, too perfect, to be the proper object of human cognition in the natural order.

On the contrary, however, an object may be mysterious because it lacks that intrinsic intelligibility which follows upon being itself. The matter pertinent to the details of the physic mathematical sciences is difficult to learn, because in treating of the make-up of bodies as such, these sciences deal with a potential and imperfect object.[13] Now that which is intelligible is in act rather than in potency, and that which is in potency can be known only in and through the act in function of which it is defined. Thus in these disciplines we hear of the activity of light rays as having something in common with the progress of a wave and certain other similarities to the movement of a projectile. The details of such studies will always have this mysterious quality precisely by reason of the low degree of intelligibility inherent in the object under consideration.

8. The spiritual and the supernatural. Finally, there can be no real knowledge of the meaning of the term supernatural without a definite knowledge of the way in which it differs in significance from the term spiritual. A spirit is a substance, the essence of which is not composed of matter and form as primary and distinct principles. Thus the human soul, although it is an incomplete substance, is a spirit, fashioned to act as the substantial form of a corporeal substance. An angel is a created spirit, and God Himself can be properly termed a Spirit, always remembering that He is not limited by any of the various categories under which the realities of the created universe are classified, and that any term which is applied to Him is used strictly in an analogical sense.

---

13 Garrigou-Lagrange, *Le Sens du Mystère et le Clair-Obscur Intellectuel* (Paris, 1934), pp. 135–140.

A thing is called spiritual insofar as it is listed as one of the characteristics of a spirit. The characteristic and basic act of a spirit is that of understanding or intelligence, and as a result all the activity involved in the process of intelligence and the volition subsequent to it is known as spiritual activity. Thus much of the natural activity of man is itself spiritual in nature. Man's supernatural activity is also spiritual in nature, since its ultimate object is God, known through revelation. Throughout the course of Holy Scripture those who live the life of habitual grace are frequently designated as spiritual, especially in the letters of St. Paul. "And I, brethren, could not speak to you as unto spiritual, but as unto carnal."[14] "Brethren, if a man be overtaken in any fault, you, who are spiritual, instruct such a one in the spirit of meekness."[15] As a result the tendency still exists to speak of the life of grace as the spiritual life. However, this use of the term spiritual should not cause us to forget that the same term has a perfectly natural connotation, and that not everything which is truly spiritual is properly supernatural.

9. Not every action connected with God can be called supernatural. Again not every movement which creatures receive from God is supernatural. No creature can act and exist except insofar as he is moved and conserved in being by the power of God. Yet movement, if it is directed toward the accomplishment of those acts which belong to the province of created nature, is perfectly natural. Thus there is a *natural* action of God upon the universe, quite distinct from the *supernatural* operation of grace. Likewise there is a natural knowledge about God distinct from the supernatural realm of faith.

10. Catholic dogma as mediate revelation. Not only is the dogma of the Catholic Church proposed to us as a revelation which is intrinsically supernatural, namely in the way it is received by man and in its very essence, but it is also offered to us as a mediate and public revelation. A mediate revelation, as opposed to an immediate, comes to the recipient through the agency of his fellow human beings. A public revelation, as opposed to a private, is addressed to all men, rather than to one man or to a limited group.[16] Catholic dogma claims

---

14 1 Cor. 3:1.
15 Gal. 6:1.
16 Cf. J. J. Baierl, S.T.D., *The Theory of Revelation* (Rochester, 1927), Vol. 1, pp. 34–36;

The Characteristics of Revelation

to have been communicated to mankind through Jesus Christ and to have been addressed to all men. Thus it presents itself as mediate and public revelation.

11. The modes of immediate revelation. An immediate revelation is made by God directly to the man to whom it is addressed, apart from any other human agency.[17] Thus the message which God gave to Moses was strictly an immediate or direct revelation. Naturally any mediate revelation is founded ultimately upon a communication made by God directly to some individual, since those who present the revealed doctrine to their fellow men could not have received this message ultimately other than from one to whom God had spoken immediately. God moves in two distinct ways in making this immediate revelation.[18] *Objectively* He presents the truth which He wishes to communicate to the mind of the recipient. *Subjectively* He enlightens the mind of the one to whom the revelation is made in such a way as to enable this man to judge accurately about the significance of the message.

Objectively He has acted and can act in various ways. By His infinite power, He is enabled to propose truth to the mind of man by acting upon external material things, by affecting the external or internal senses, or by producing or causing species or images in the intelligence itself. In any event this action is such as to bring about an objective statement of that truth which he wishes man to know as revealed by Him.

During the course of God's dealing with man by way of revelation, He has sometimes given the objective element of His teaching to one man and the subjective element to another. Thus, for example, the actual presentation of signs, or the expression of revealed truth was given to the king of Egypt, while the subjective portion, the power to understand and interpret these signs correctly, was given to the prophet Joseph.[19] Likewise, Baltasar saw the handwriting upon the

---

John Brunsmann, S.V.D., *A Handbook of Fundamental Theology*, ed. Arthur Preuss (St. Louis, 1929), Vol. 2, p. 16.

17 Mediate revelation comes to men through the agency of their fellows. Cf. John T. Langan, S.J., *Apologetica* (Chicago, 1921), pp. 6–12; Albertus Knoll a Bulsano, O.M.Cap., *Institutiones Theologiae Dogmaticae Generalis seu Fundamentalis* (Turin, 1868), p. 54.

18 St. Thomas Aquinas, *The Summa Theologica*, II^a, II^{ae} q. 173, art. 2.

19 Gen. 41:1–36.

wall, but the meaning of the message was unknown until Daniel the Prophet interpreted it.[20] In such cases the revelation in the strict sense of the term is made to the man who is endowed with the power to understand the signs which have been seen by another.

12. Catholic dogma as public revelation. It is quite obvious that the doctrine which we accept on divine faith claims to be a public revelation, as this has just been described. Our Lord Himself pointed out the public character of His message to men when He commissioned the Apostles to bring it to all men. "And Jesus coming spoke to them, saying: All power is given to me in heaven and on earth. Going therefore, teach ye all nations: baptizing them in the name of the Father, and of the Son, and of the Holy Ghost: Teaching them to observe all things whatsoever I have commanded you: and behold I am with you all days, even to the consummation of the world."[21] Again it is recounted in the Gospel according to St. Mark that our Lord's final command to the apostolic college was "Go ye into the whole world, and preach the gospel to every creature."[22]

The message which the Apostles were ordered to preach, the Gospel that they were to bring to all men, is the doctrine which had been proposed by our Lord as divinely revealed. This fact has tremendous repercussions in the field of apologetics. If the message of Jesus Christ is to be established as credible at all, it must be in function of evidence which is available to all men, rather than merely to some limited group. As we have seen, the doctrine in question sets itself forth as evidently and rationally credible to all of those to whom it is addressed. It is the province of Christian apologetics to point out its universally acceptable evidence of credibility.

---

20 Dan. 5:5.
21 Matt. 28:18–20.
22 Mark 16:15.

Chapter 4

THE POSSIBILITY OF REVELATION

1. The meaning of possibility as predicated of divine revelation in apologetics. A thing is said to be possible in so far as it is capable of existence. This capability is absolute in every case in which the notes or characteristics of the thing are not mutually exclusive. Thus a building of solid gold is possible because the elements which enter into this notion in no way destroy one another. On the other hand, the capability or possibility is relative when the thing described is something which can be brought about by the agent to which it is attributed. Thus the passing of laws for the United States is something possible for Congress but not for any other group of men. Both absolutely and relatively it can be demonstrated that divine revelation, as this is defined and described by the Catholic Church, is possible.

Naturally the first step on the way to that proof of credibility, which is the essential function of apologetics, must be a demonstration of this inherent possibility. For obviously if it could be shown that there could be no such thing as that revelation which Christian doctrine claims to be, it would be worse than idle to pursue further the inquiry into its rational credibility. Impossibility would be an attribution far more devastating than mere incredibility.

When we consider the possibility of revelation, as this has been described in the authentic pronouncements of the Catholic faith, it is clear that we must divide our study into two distinct sections. In the first place we must treat of this revelation as something supernatural in the way in which it is accomplished, as God's speaking to man in order to teach him. In the second portion of the chapter we must consider the possibility of truths which are inherently or essentially supernatural. We must study the possibility of revelation as applied to the supernatural mysteries. We can prove positively that revelation as such is possible by showing that there is neither incompatibility nor contradiction involved in the description of it given in Christian literature.

2. The basic proof for the possibility of revelation. Essentially this revelation is a speaking by God to man in order to teach him. Such a thing is obviously possible since that God whose existence can be clearly demonstrated according to the natural process of human reason is an intelligent Being, who can express His knowledge, direct that expression to those creatures which are dependent upon Himself, and can actually see to it that the intelligent creature understands both the truth which God has expressed to him and the fact that this statement has been made by God. Moreover, it is possible also from the viewpoint of man, to whom the communication is made, since man is capable of learning and of knowing about God and in no way loses perfection through receiving this instruction from his Creator.

3. Supernatural revelation is evidently possible from the point of view of an intelligent God who communicates it. In the first place it is evident that God is intelligent. One of the proofs advanced for the demonstration of the existence of God is that the existence of order in the created universe shows that there is some intelligence which is not ordered toward its own act. For, although order can be produced by any intelligence, created or uncreated, an intelligence which is distinct from its own act would have to be ordered to that act. Thus the very proof of the existence of God by way of observable order in the universe shows the existence of God as an intelligent being.

Again, even the proofs from motion and efficient causality point directly to the same result. The One who is the First Cause of the created universe must be One who acts as a cause by way of intelligence rather than by way of nature.[1] The thing which acts as a cause by way of nature, as the seal which naturally produces always the same image in the wax, is necessarily something which is ordered

---

1 Either nature or intelligence is the principle of efficient causality. The nature of a thing has to produce an effect to which it is ordered essentially and necessarily, e.g., the seal produces an impression in wax. An intelligent cause, acting as such can plan freely the type of result it wishes to produce, e.g., the artist paints a picture. Cf. St. Thomas Aquinas, *The Summa Theologica*, I^a, q. 15, art. 1.

toward the accomplishment of this effect. But this condition is quite incompatible with the nature of the First Cause, that One who causes and who is Himself utterly beyond any need of being acted upon.

When we point out the evident possibility of revelation as it is described by the Catholic Church, and as it is predicated of the doctrine whose credibility we are establishing, we must not fail to point out the naturally observable evidence that the knowledge of God is infinite in character. In this way we can show that God could actually communicate to man information which man himself does not possess, since the most obvious characteristic of human understanding is its limited and progressive quality. The First Cause is not merely intelligent; He is Intelligence, a subsisting Act which apprehends the full measure of knowable reality. This we know by the natural process of human reason. A reality which lacks something in the intellectual order could not be that First Cause which we see must exist in order to account for the existence and the activity of the finite universe.

When we speak of God as intelligent, and not as some sort of blind and uncomprehending force, we refer to Him as a personal God. The existence of a personal God, then, is something evident in the light of natural reason. If there are those who refuse to acknowledge the existence of this personal God, their refusal is based merely upon their unwillingness to examine the naturally ascertainable evidence.

4. Pantheism, which would militate against the possibility of supernatural revelation, is manifestly untrue. In showing that God can evidently express some definite truth which He knows, and then direct that truth toward the mind of some being quite distinct from Himself, we remember the naturally ascertainable and tremendously important fact that God is quite distinct from the created universe as a whole, from any of those creatures which He has brought into existence. The denial of this naturally evident truth constitutes one of the erroneous systems which are called *pantheistic doctrines*.[2]

For the purposes of apologetics it is not at all necessary to inquire into every form in which the errors of pantheism have been presented

---

[2] An excellent discussion of pantheism from the point of view of apologetics can be found in Garrigou-Lagrange, *De Revelatione*, Vol. I, pp. 233–275; and Walshe, *The Principles of Catholic Apologetics*, pp. 58–69.

to the world. It is only proper to point out that neither the material universe in which we live nor the thought of rational creatures could in any way be identified with the First Cause. In the first place, both the material universe, as a whole and in each of its individual component parts, and likewise any activity of created beings must necessarily exhibit characteristics which are utterly incompatible with the nature of that One who is the Source of all movement, being Himself unmoved. The material universe is divided, and the First Cause is obviously entirely without composition of any kind, since composition involves potency or imperfections, the very qualities which could not be possessed by a First Cause. The parts of the universe are, as such, limited, and the First Cause is obviously infinite. The activity of creatures, either intellectual or otherwise, is obviously a characteristic or quality quite distinct both from the essence and from the existence of those beings to whom the activity belongs. On the other hand, it is naturally evident that the First Cause, whose existence is shown by the fact that beings and activities which are obviously dependent upon Him exist, is actually the *Ipsum Esse Subsistens,* "One who is His own existence."

5. God can communicate with His creatures. Furthermore we know in the light of purely natural evidence that God can enter into communication with His creatures. One of the facts brought out in the purely natural science of metaphysics is the absolute dependence of the created intelligence upon the mind of God. This dependence is twofold: objective and subjective.[3] In the objective order we find that all of the created reality which the finite mind can know directly through the natural exercise of its powers has been created freely by God. Since it has been created freely, it has been produced by way of intelligence. In other words, God brought this particular being into existence using as an exemplar an idea, a concept of a way in which His essence could be participated really though inadequately. Only God Himself is eternal and absolutely necessary, and as a result the only possible ultimate exemplar of created reality is the divine essence itself.

Subjectively God remains the First Mover, and as such the ultimate source of every act which is performed in the created universe. The

---

3 St. Thomas Aquinas, *The Summa Theologica*, I\u1d43, q. 105, a. 3.

act of understanding exercised by a creature is a created reality, and as such it depends upon the movement by God Himself. The man who reasons or understands performs this particular act as his own, but by the very nature of things observable in the purely natural light of intelligence, he could not act if he were not being moved and acted upon by the First Cause Himself. Thus objectively and in the act itself any creature's understanding is obviously and absolutely dependent upon God.

Then there is no question about the possibility of God's entering into contact with the created intellect. As a matter of fact such contact is demonstrably evident in every movement of the created mind and for that matter in the very continuance of the creature's existence. Furthermore there is nothing to prevent One who is in immediate and necessary contact with the created mind from presenting to that mind, not an *object*, ultimately derived from an act of the divine science, but a *truth* conceived in the divine mind and meant to be known by the created intelligence precisely as something communicated by God.

This possibility becomes manifest when we take into consideration the divine omnipotence itself. Every creature is entirely subject to the influence of God's causality. There is no effect in all the realms of being which God cannot produce if He wills to do so. Thus since there is obviously no contradiction involved in sending man a message which is to be received, on the divine authority this is an effect which can be brought about by the infinite power of God. By reason of His omnipotence and by reason of the absolute dependence of the creature upon Him, God can bring it about that this intellectual creature receives a message which has been communicated to him by God, and understands that message in the way in which God wills that it be understood.

6. Man can know God naturally. Again, revelation, as it is described by the Catholic Church and predicated of that doctrine which we defend as credible in the science of apologetics, is possible because the one to whom this divine communication is said to be addressed can know God, and can receive instruction from other intelligent beings. Both of these truths are naturally demonstrable and as such evident. Thus the possibility of revelation from this point of view is naturally manifest.

In general that teaching which denies that man can know anything about God is termed *agnosticism*.[4] Any agnosticism is based upon a demonstrably false notion either of human knowledge or of the idea of God. It is true that the primary objects of human knowledge in this world are the essences of corporeal and created things. It is true at the same time that the One we call God is absolutely remote from the conditions and the imperfections incident to corporeal and limited reality. There would very definitely be a contradiction involved if we were to say that we know this God in the same way in which we are aware of those things which enter into the proper object of our natural knowledge. Such a knowledge would be actually impossible. The point of the matter is however that our natural knowledge about God is arrived at in a very different way from that in which we are aware of earthly things. We know bodies through the awareness of the senses. Utilizing the power of the active intellect, we prescind from the individuating conditions inherent in the sense knowledge and we apprehend intellectually the essence or the nature of the thing observed. Considering this thing in its being and in its operation, we know that it could never exist and function as it actually does, were it not dependent upon the influence of One who is the First Cause. Thus causality is the natural basis for our idea of God.

7. God and the proper formal object of the human mind. Hence our natural knowledge of God is consequent upon the realization of those things which constitute the proper formal object of our own understanding. God is not known as one of the beings which enter into the field of this proper natural object. He is seen and recognized as the Cause upon whom the things we know immediately are manifestly dependent. And, while knowing a being merely as a First Cause of others is relatively an imperfect grade of awareness, nevertheless it is real knowledge, and the object so understood can never, in any sense of the term, be spoken of as absolutely unknowable. For, while we do not see this First Cause directly and immediately in the force of this natural knowledge, it is nonetheless true that we can tell that certain things are in compatible with His

---

4 Cf. Garrigou-Lagrange, *De Revelatione*, Vol. I, pp. 276–318; Walshe, *The Principles of Catholic Apologetics*, pp. 70–78.

status as a First Cause, while certain attributes must be predicated of Him precisely for the same reason.

The Word God has a definite and objective significance for the human mind. There is demonstrably no reason why man should not be able to know the meaning of a message about God, since He can know by the force of his natural reason that which is characteristic of the Creator. Man has a workable and correct idea of God. Even while he himself naturally knows that this concept is inadequate, he recognizes that it is such that it can be used in gaining a correct appreciation of that One whom he knows as the First Cause.

8. Man is capable of acquiring knowledge through instruction. At the same time man is so constituted that he can receive instruction. As a social being, man is dependent upon the society into which he is incorporated in the attainment of his intellectual perfection. Thus as far as the knowledge which constitutes an individual man's intellectual attainment is concerned, man does not by any means gain all of it through the independent working of his own intelligence. We know very well, as a matter of fact, that the individual who is unfortunate enough to be deprived of any instruction whatsoever would live in a state more like that of an irrational animal than like the condition which befits a human being. This need of being taught is not any weakness accidental to human nature; it is the effect of the social nature inherent in man. Man would not be so constituted that he has to live as a member of society were it not for the fact that the community of his fellow men can offer him advantages without which he would not be able fully to attain the purpose toward which his own nature is directed.

Now to instruct another is to speak to that person in such a way that through the arrangement of the statements included in the matter spoken, the person who is being instructed will be able to possess that knowledge which the instructor originally possessed and which he wishes to transmit to the person under instruction. It is requisite, of course, that the instructor should originally possess some knowledge which had not as yet been attained by the person under instruction. In the imparting of that knowledge the instructor must make use of expressions which are known both to himself and to the man he is teaching. The end of instruction has been attained when that knowledge which was originally possessed by the instructor and which he wished to communicate to the person under instruction is actually possessed by that man.

We must understand that the reception of instruction, from God or from another man, in no way militates against the vitality and the spontaneity of human intellectual activity. Real teaching or instruction in no way implies any pouring in of intellectual knowledge into the passive mind of a recipient. The act by which the person who has been taught knows the doctrine in which he has been instructed is just as much his own act as was the knowledge of the teacher himself. The concepts in which that act is expressed are the concepts of the pupil. What the instructor has been doing has been an arrangement of the propositions and expressions requisite for teaching in such a way that the person under instruction is able himself to see the meaning of the statements in which the doctrine is manifest. But the instruction has not been successful until this student himself knows the doctrine which is being taught.

Furthermore, man is able to receive instruction from God because of the naturally evident fact that the knowledge of human beings is itself limited. The very fact that men can advance in knowledge is immediate evidence that there is some knowledge which here and now they do not possess. Then it follows that there could be no contradiction involved in the statement that man has received instruction from God, whose knowledge is infinite in character.

Only God Himself is such that He could not possibly receive any revelation. That One who is His own understanding, whose knowledge is absolutely without limitation of any kind, could be so situated that no other person could ever possibly cause Him to receive any information or knowledge. There have been theories to the effect that man is placed in something of the same position. According to these theories, the intellectual life of man is such that he should be considered as absolutely autonomous and thus not in a position to receive instruction from any outside source. Actually this statement is a postulate which is in no way consonant with the naturally observable facts about the scientific life of man. The fact of intellectual progress, a fact strikingly evident, makes it obvious that the knowledge of man is imperfect, and that there would be neither a contradiction nor a derogation of human dignity involved when man is taught by God. For if one man can be taught by another, then there is no possible reason why he should not be in a position to receive instruction from One who is all knowledge and who is sovereignly able to transmit this instruction to him.

9. Public revelation is possible. Obviously again there is no reason why an instruction coming from God should not be directed toward all men, rather than merely to one man or to a limited group of human beings. The same person cannot be the source and the object of instruction in one and the same act. Thus no man could possibly send out an instruction which would be destined for all men, absolutely speaking. At least this instruction would not be destined for himself. But God, who is eminently and perfectly distinct from His creatures can certainly issue an instruction which is destined for every created person. Thus there is no contradiction involved in the notion of public revelation as such.

10. Mediate revelation is possible. Neither could there be any contradiction involved in the notion of mediate as opposed to immediate revelation. Obviously a communication from my friend is just as much his message whether he gives it to me directly or sends it by messenger. There is no reason why, since God can speak to man in order to teach him, this teaching should not be conveyed to some men through the instrumentality of others.

11. The possibility of supernatural mysteries. On the other hand, we cannot positively show the possibility of revelation of mysteries which are intrinsically supernatural in this way because human reason alone is not competent to know even of the existence of these mysteries.[5]

Thus we must concentrate our demonstration on what may be termed the negative aspect of the case. We cannot, in the light of natural reason, positively show the possibility of the existence of the supernatural order. However, we can point out that the field of

---

[5] For a brilliant treatment of the possibility of revelation of supernatural mysteries, see Baierl, *The Theory of Revelation*, Vol. I, pp. 83–109; Walshe, *The Principles of Catholic Apologetics*, pp. 136–143; Garrigou-Lagrange, *De Revelatione*, Vol. I, pp. 337–403; A. C. Cotter, S.J., *Theologia Fundamentalis* (Weston, 1940), pp. 45–52; Langan, *Apologetica*, pp. 12–15; Tepe, Bernardus, S.J., *Institutiones Theologicae* (Paris, 1894), Vol. I, pp. 24–27.

our natural intellectual competence is evidently limited and that, for this reason, there would evidently be no contradiction involved in speaking of some truth as that which the human mind could never know in any way whatsoever independently of divine revelation, and which it can know only in the obscurity of divine faith as long as man remains within this life.

As we have seen, the proper field of man's natural knowledge about God embraces that which can be known about God by reason of the fact that He is evidently the First Cause of the created universe. We cannot demonstrate positively, in the light of natural reason alone, that there could be a distinct domain of truth about God, a field of reality which could only be realized through the vision of God in Himself. However, there is certainly no observable reason which would militate against this possibility.

We know from a consideration of the natural order itself that the kind of knowledge which we can derive about a cause from the study of its effects is objectively inferior to a knowledge derived from a consideration of the cause by and in itself. For example, the man who would know about the habits and the culture of Raphael merely from a study of the paintings which he produced would obviously not know as much about him as would the men who worked under his direction in painting the stanze of the Vatican. Likewise, in the light of natural reason alone, we can see that God would know more about Himself through that consideration of Himself which is the act of the divine intelligence than any creature could realize through the study of created reality as evidently dependent upon God.

It is certain and evident, in the light of this same natural reasoning, that God would have a more profound and perfect appreciation of his own essence than that which could naturally be gained by any creature. At the same time it is obviously possible that the knowledge of God in Himself might discover an entire realm of created reality. As a matter of fact we could never know of the existence of the supernatural mysteries, which lie within this naturally hidden realm of truth apart from divine revelation. Furthermore, apart from this same revelation, we could never discover even the possibility of these mysteries. But, once they have been revealed, we can point out that there is nothing in all the realm of naturally attainable truth about

God which could in any way imply that no higher order of truth existed. What we know about God from the consideration of the things which He has brought into existence will most certainly never deny that there could be a definite order of truth concerning Him not attainable in this way.

12. The divine glory as the end of revelation. We would fail in a great measure to appreciate the possibility of divine revelation were we not to consider it in the light of the known goodness of God and the naturally ascertainable orientation of human nature. That God whose existence we know as the First Cause of created reality is seen in the natural light of human reason as infinitely good. Moreover, we can realize through a purely natural process of investigation that He is infinitely wise and omniscient. The only purpose which could ultimately determine the productions of this infinitely good God is His own glory. Now glory is defined as clear knowledge with praise. This glory is a divine good, but in acting for His own glory, God confers a favor upon His creatures. We must realize that no benefit whatsoever accrues to God out of the production of His creatures. His beatitude is infinite in itself. It cannot be increased or perfected through the activity of all the creatures in the universe. The good which He intends is something which is to benefit His creatures.

As a matter of fact the good as such is that which all things desire. All things tend toward that which is perfective of themselves, and shrink from that which is seen as destructive of their own being and activity. That which is the ultimate good of any creature is not to be found in itself by reason of the fact that the creature is essentially limited and potential. That good must in the last analysis be God Himself. Now the intellectual creature alone is capable of obtaining and possessing God. Naturally, He cannot be possessed through any corporeal act. His eminently, spiritual nature makes this sort of possession utterly impossible.

A spiritual or noncorporeal possession of God is obtained by the person who knows God, and obviously that possession is more perfect in direct proportion with the perfection of the knowledge itself. As a result, any procedure which tends to increase the fullness of man's knowledge about God contributes in this way to a more perfect realization of God's glory, is strikingly beneficial to man, and thus is consonant with the goodness of God.

13. The revelation of mysteries is beneficial to man. Now it is evident, again in the natural light of human reason, that divine revelation, as this is predicated of Catholic dogma, tends to increase the fullness of man's knowledge about God. By its very essence, teaching is an act which tends to develop and perfect the knowledge of the person who is taught. This person received the propositions set forth by one who possesses the knowledge which the pupil wishes to acquire and presents them to the pupil in such a way that, as the result of this activity, the pupil possesses the knowledge which the teacher wishes him to acquire. Obviously the value of teaching in any individual case is dependent upon the competence of the teacher. In the instance of divine revelation, the teacher possesses perfect and infinite knowledge, and is the only One who could possess an exhaustive understanding of that very reality in the perception of which man is to find his only final perfection and happiness.

Thus in deigning to teach man in the activity of divine revelation God is actually doing something which is fully in accord with His own goodness. Man in receiving the direction of God through the process of revelation acquires a dignity and intellectual perfection which could not otherwise be obtained. From this point of view the revelation described in the dogmatic formulae of the Catholic Church is evidently possible.

14. Catholic teaching on the possibility of revelation. It is obvious that a person who denies the possibility and the fitness of revelation, as this is described within the authentic declarations of the Catholic Church, contradicts the message which we accept on divine faith. Thus the Vatican Council, in the canons on divine revelation which are appended to the *Dei Filius,* condemns such denials as heretical. The first three out of the four canons in this section follow.

1. "If anyone should say that the one and true God, our Creator and Lord, cannot be known with certainty in the natural light of human reason through those things which are made, let him be anathema."

2. "If anyone should say that it is not possible or that it is not fitting that man should be taught by divine revelation about God and about

the worship which must be shown Him, let him be anathema."

3. "If anyone should say that men cannot be divinely raised up to a knowledge and perfection which surpass the natural, but that, of himself he can and ought to attain the possession of everything true and good by a continuous progress, let him be anathema."[6]

The first of these three canons condemns agnosticism and fideism, both recognized as incompatible with an exact notion of supernatural revelation. The second, through its condemnation, affirms the possibility and the beneficent character of revelation as supernatural in the manner in which it is acquired by man. The third defines the possibility and the fitness of the revelation of mysteries as well as the limited nature of man's intellectual competence.

15. Catholic condemnation of atheism, agnosticism, and pantheism. The canons on God the Creator of all things, which immediately precede those on revelation are of value in so far as they contain condemnations of teachings which are incompatible with and contradictory to the possibility of divine revelation. These canons are:

1. "If anyone should deny the one true God, Creator and Lord of all things visible and invisible, let him be anathema."

2. "If anyone should not be ashamed to affirm that apart from matter nothing exists, let him be anathema."

3. "If anyone should say that the substance or essence of God and of all things is one and the same, let him be anathema."

4. "If anyone should say that finite things, both corporeal and spiritual, or at least the spiritual, have emanated from the divine substance, or that the divine essence becomes all things by a manifestation or evolution of itself, or finally that God is the universal or indefinite being which, by determining itself constitutes the universe of things distinct generically, specifically, and individually, let him be anathema."

5. "If anyone should not confess that the world and all the things which are contained in it, both spiritual and material, have been produced by God out of nothing according to their entire substance, or should say that God has not created with a will which is free from all necessity, but rather has created out of necessity, with that

---

6 Denzinger, 1806–1808.

necessity with which He loves Himself, or should deny that the world has been established for the glory of God, let him be anathema."[7]

The first canon condemns the fundamental error of atheism. The second stigmatizes that crass materialism which is totally incompatible with the divine teaching, and which at the same time is manifestly false. The third condemns the general doctrine of pantheism and the fourth some of the forms which this error had assumed in the writings of pre-Vatican Council philosophers. The fifth defines the doctrine of creation as a free act, the effect of which is ordered to the glory of God.

16. The freedom of God and revelation. Naturally it is important that the student of divine revelation should realize that the creation of the world was a free act on the part of God. For if the world, and all which is in it had been produced as a result of necessity, then it would be idle to speak of anything as supernatural in one way or in another in God's dealings with this world. And again the value of the motives of credibility with which the science of apologetics is ordered to deal is dependent absolutely upon the fact that God is always sovereignly free in dealing with the universe which He has created.[8]

The term freedom, of course, applies formally to acts of the will. An act is said to be free in so far as it is produced by a determination which comes from the act of the person who wills, rather than from the object, from the force of nature, or from the activity of some person who necessitates the act of another. Freedom of the will is the active indetermination of this faculty with reference to something which is seen as a means not necessarily connected with the attainment of a necessary end. Thus the will is not free with regard to its adequate object. The human will is not free with reference to the good as such in this world, nor is it free with reference to the divine good, seen in the perfect clarity of the beatific vision in the happiness of heaven. However it is free with reference to something which viewed as a good does not exhaust all the extent of desirability.

---

7 Denzinger, 1801–1805.

8 Cf. the explanation of this teaching in Vacant, *Études Theologiques sur les Constitutions du Concile du Vatican, La Constitution "Dei Filius"* (Paris and Lyon, 1895), 2 vols.

Thus the will is free to accept or to reject something which has as its alternative at least an apparent good.

Naturally, with reference to the divine will, there is no such thing as a merely apparent good. The will of God which follows according to our way of thinking, upon the act of the divine intelligence, can tend toward nothing but that which is really good because the divine mind itself is absolutely infallible. However, in spite of the fact that we are well aware that there are not two distinct kinds of acts elicited by God, we can distinguish actually and properly those things which God wills freely and those things which He wills out of necessity. There is one and only one object which is the adequate good toward which the divine will necessarily tends. That, of course, is Himself. The love of God for Himself is absolutely necessary. It is utterly impossible that God should not have loved Himself or that He should ever cease to tend toward this ineffable perfection which is His own essence.

There is, of course, a certain kind of hypothetical necessity to be found in the divine effects, in so far as they are related to the divine causative power. God owes it to Himself to see to it that the things which He produces, in so far as they are caused by Him, are good. Thus, in freely creating the human race, God necessarily made man good. But the point of the matter is that while the justice and the goodness of God would bring Him to give man everything which is requisite for the attainment of his natural perfection, the divine revelation described by the Catholic Church is not one of those things which belong to the natural equipment of man. It is perfectly and demonstrably possible for God to reveal truth to man in a supernatural way. However, He does this freely. The necessity which belongs to divine revelation is not any necessity which determines the act of God Himself.

Chapter 5

THE NECESSITY OF REVELATION

1. The meaning of necessity. That teaching which we hold to be divinely revealed, and which we establish as credible through the proofs of apologetics, is proposed to us as something necessary for man. A thing is said to be necessary insofar as it is incapable of nonexistence. It is necessary, in other words, insofar as it has to be.

This necessity can be of two distinct kinds. A thing may be termed necessary by reason of its own essence. Thus man is necessarily a rational animal and God exists necessarily. On the other hand, however, a thing may be said to be necessary by reason of external causes, either efficient or final. Such a necessity is called hypothetical. The necessary thing, in this case, cannot but exist *if* some agent operates or if some end is to be obtained.

Now the necessity of divine revelation is that which is defined in function of final causality. Divine revelation is necessary for the attainment of a definite end. If that end is to be obtained, there must be that reality which we know as divine revelation.

Again, a thing may be necessary for the attainment of a final cause in two different ways. It is physically necessary when that end simply is not to be obtained at all apart from the thing which is necessary. It is morally necessary when, absolutely speaking, the end could be obtained apart from it, but when this end will not be obtained properly and in a fitting manner independently of this necessary means.

2. Divine revelation is presented as something necessary for the attainment of an end. Divine revelation is thus necessary for the attainment of two distinct kinds of good which man seeks. It is physically requisite for the attainment of that supernatural happiness which is, as a matter of fact, the only ultimate end which is available to man. It is morally necessary in order that man should possess a natural knowledge of God, which is attainable by all men, easily, with certitude and free from a damaging admixture of error. In the present order of divine providence, then, man will not obtain his only ultimate good independently of this divine revelation. And, although he is competent to know about God through the very force of his reason, man will not obtain a proper natural appreciation of God and has not procured it other than with the aid of the supernatural teaching which God has communicated to the world.[1]

3. The doctrine of the Vatican Council. This necessity of revelation has been described by the Vatican Council in the following passage. It is the one which follows immediately upon the paragraph which points out the distinction between divine revelation and that knowledge of God which man obtains through the natural exercise of his own intellectual powers. Speaking of the function and of the necessity of this revelation, the council continues. "It is to be attributed to this divine revelation that those matters about the things of God which of themselves are not impervious to human reason can, in the present condition of the human race, be known readily by all, with firm certitude and with no admixture of error. However, revelation is not said to be absolutely necessary for this reason, but rather because God, out of His infinite goodness, has ordered man to a supernatural end, that is to a sharing of the divine goods which entirely surpass the intelligence of the human mind. For 'eye hath not seen, nor ear heard, neither hath it entered into the heart of man, what things God hath prepared for them that love Him.'"[2]

4. The beneficial character of divine revelation. The revealed doctrine which we show as credible in the science of apologetics is

---

[1] Good explanations of the necessity which characterizes divine public revelation are to be found in Baierl, *The Theory of Revelation*, Vol. I, pp. 123–245; Felder, Hilarinus, O.M.Cap., *Apologetica* (Paderborn, 1923), Vol. I, pp. 45–54; Nicolas Marin Negueruela, *Lecciones de Apologetica*, 5 ed. (San Sebastian, 1939), Vol. I, p. 261; Knoll, *Institutiones Theologiae Dogmaticae Generalis seu Fundamentalis*, pp. 61–71; Cotter, *Theologia Fundamentalis*, pp. 53–61; Walshe, *The Principles of Catholic Apologetics*, pp. 144–147; Garrigou-Lagrange, *De Revelatione*, Vol. 1, pp. 404–425; Vacant, *La Constitution "Dei Filius,"* Vol. I, pp. 343–360; Dieckmann, *De Revelatione Christiane*, pp. 212–241; Dorsch, *Institutiones Theologiae Fundamentalis*, Vol. 1, pp. 350-365.

[2] The Council cites 1 Cor. 2:9; Denzinger, 1786. The same teaching is to be found in St. Thomas Aquinas' *Summa Contra Gentiles*, Book I, Ch. 4.

thus an outstanding benefit to mankind. In proposing this doctrine to the world the Catholic Church is exercising the most valuable and philanthropic function which is performed among the children of men. This work is philanthropic in that very definite sense that it is a work which is carried on for the love of men. There is a love of benevolence, after all, where forces are actually placed in motion to bring about that which is objectively good for the persons loved. In proposing the divine message the Catholic Church is bringing forward a force which can aid man in attaining the only ultimate and supreme happiness which he will ever obtain and in gaining a kind of knowledge without which man will not be able to live successfully in this world, particularly with the social forces which govern the world today.

5. The necessity of revelation is a reality. We would seriously misunderstand the truth about the necessity of divine revelation were we to see in it a doctrine which must be considered as offensive to those who are not of the faith. We are, of course, perfectly aware that a person who does not wish to possess the faith will not be able to accept as certain the doctrine on the physical necessity of divine revelation for the attainment of man's eternal and supernatural beatitude. But whether this particular person cares to admit it or not, the fact is that divine revelation is thus necessary. We live in an age which prides itself upon its realism, and we cannot fail to take into serious account the transcendently important fact that man needs revelation.

6. The elevation to the supernatural order. According to the words of the Vatican Council, and according to the perpetual tradition of the Catholic Church, divine revelation is physically necessary for men because of man's elevation to the supernatural order. In order that we may be able to understand the nature and the implications of this necessity, we must first see what is meant by this sort of elevation.

First of all, as the Council teaches us, man has been assigned a supernatural end. This end of man is supernatural intrinsically, in the way in which the divine mysteries themselves are supernatural. It is not merely supernatural in the way in which a miracle is designated as such. This supernatural end is none other than God Himself, to be seen and possessed in the ineffable clarity of a face to face vision for all eternity. As such it is an end which is beyond the merely natural capacity of man, or for that matter of any creature, actual or possible.[3]

7. The natural order of human activity. It is, of course, absolutely impossible that there should be a thing without a purpose. In the case of a creature this purpose must be something distinct from its own essence. In terms of metaphysics the purpose of a thing is the good, and the good is that which is in act opposed to that which is merely in potency. Now that which is most actual in a creature is its own existence and its own operation. By the very nature of things, these are really distinct from the essence of that thing to which they belong.

Formally the purpose of man must consist in his own operation. A thing exists only in order that it may act. That which is the highest, the most perfect, the most actual in all of the operations which belong to the human being is that of understanding. As a result the purpose of man consists *formally* in an act of understanding and *objectively* in that thing which is seen as the ultimate and perfect object of such an act, God Himself.

The nature of man then demands that his purpose in life should be an intellectual knowledge of God. But man is so equipped that, by the use of his own natural faculties, he is enabled to know God as the First Cause of the created universe. Then the purely natural purpose or end of man would be this knowledge which we bring to scientific perfection in metaphysics. Since happiness is to be found in the possession of a good, and is proportionate to the importance of the good possessed, the ultimate natural happiness of man would be obtained in the complete accomplishment of that activity of which the human intellect is naturally capable. St. Thomas Aquinas has beautifully described this natural perfection. In the third book of *On the Soul* it is said that the soul is in some way all things because it is competent to know all things. Thus, according to this manner, it is possible that the perfection of the entire universe should be in one thing. Hence this is the ultimate perfection to which according to the philosophers the soul can attain, namely, that in it the entire order of the universe and of its causes should be described. In this they placed the ultimate end of man. But according to us this ultimate end of

---

[3] Man is given a destiny which is intrinsically supernatural. Cf. Chapter 3.

man will be in the vision of God, because, as Gregory says, "what is it that they should not see who behold the One who, sees all things."[4]

This natural perfection of the human soul would include, of course, far more than the content of metaphysics. It would comprise an extensive and ordered culture which would be crowned with the metaphysical truth about God as the First Cause of the created universe. As such it would be the proper end of man's activity, and it would afford him a happiness proportionate to the forces of his own nature.

8. The supernatural end of man. As a matter of fact, however, God in His infinite goodness has assigned to man an end utterly beyond that which is proportionate to the unaided forces of his own nature. This end is the Godhead, to be seen directly or intuitively in the eternal and ineffable clarity of the beatific vision. As the immutable decrees of God's providence have decided it, this supernatural end is the only ultimate purpose which is available to man. If man attains this end, then his life will always have been a success. But, should he fail to attain this, then his life will always have been a bitter and utter failure. There is no secondary end in the attainment of which man could derive a sort of consolation prize which would merely grant him an inferior sort of happiness for all eternity. As far as the life of man is concerned, it must be perfected in the attainment of the supernatural end, or not at all. The alternative open to man, as far as his final lot is concerned, is God or nothing.

Now again, the decrees of the divine providence have arranged that this ultimate and supernatural end of man is to be obtained by those who have the use of reason only as something earned or merited. And, in order that a person should properly earn a reward, it is necessary that he should know about the thing for which he is working. The supernatural end, which is God, to be seen in the light of the beatific vision, is by its very nature a reality which men could never come to know through the exercise of their merely natural intellectual activity. As a result, if they are to know this end at all, they must learn of it through some medium other than that which is natural to them. They must derive their knowledge from some source

---

4 *The Disputed Questions On Truth;* q. 2, a. 2.

to which this clear knowledge of God belongs by right. In other words, they must learn of it from God Himself.

Thus, if God had not mercifully given to the world in a supernatural manner the doctrine about the final end which man must attain in order to have eternal happiness, this happiness could not be had by men. In this way the action of divine revelation, as it is described by the Catholic Church, is physically or absolutely necessary for man. And so it is the business of the apologist to insist upon the fact that the doctrine which he defends is given to men in order that they may have through it an eternity of happiness which human words are absolutely inadequate to describe and which the human mind cannot properly conceive in this world. This happiness is a reality. It is a fact that man could not possibly attain it without a communication from God in which God informs him of truths utterly beyond the competence of man's own nature. It is then a fact that the divine revelation is to be presented to men as a transcendent benefit, as a great and precious good which men cannot afford to neglect. Because of this fact, it is only reasonable to expect that the evidences of credibility which attach to this doctrine will be clear and unmistakable, acceptable to mankind as a whole.

9. As divine revelation, Catholic dogma claims to protect men against serious evil. Or, to put the thing in another light, the evil which the divine revelation is ordered to overcome is an evil which is beyond comparison with the worst which can befall a man in this world. This doctrine is presented to men as something which will enable them to escape an eternity of suffering, an eternity of misery, which otherwise they would endure in the knowledge that they had failed to achieve their one ultimate end. By the aid of this teaching they will be able to avoid an endless frustration and misery, the fruit of absolute failure. Without this revelation they would never have been able to escape this failure.

10. A realization that divine revelation is necessary is requisite for the proper presentation of Catholic dogma. The only effective and realistic presentation of the divine message is that which is based upon a realization that men stand in absolute need of it. The attitude of the proponent of Catholic truth is admirably expressed in a passage of the ancient "Recognitiones Clementis." "Let it be in your power to accept or to reject that which we announce. But we cannot be silent about that which we know is profitable for you. For if we are silent, it is our loss and if you do not receive what we tell you, it is your ruin."[5] The tremendous urgency of the divine message was always in the mind of St. Paul. He worked unremittingly for the spreading of the Gospel because he was firmly aware that men must have this benefit if they are to attain to the only ultimate happiness which is open to them. For this reason he could command St. Timothy, his disciple, thus, "Preach the word, be instant in season, out of season, reprove, entreat, rebuke in all patience and doctrine."[6]

11. The moral necessity of divine revelation. There is, however, another way in which divine revelation is actually necessary for man. In spite of the fact that man is competent to know the existence of God and at least some of His attributes through the natural exercise of his own reason, he needs divine revelation in order that there may be available to all men a clear and easily ascertainable knowledge of this natural doctrine about God which is free from an admixture of error that would otherwise vitiate it to a great extent. It is a fact, all too easily demonstrable from the datum of history, that independently of divine revelation there has not been a clear, correct, and readily available natural knowledge of God which was actually possessed by all members of society.

We must be very careful in describing the nature and the implications of this necessity. In the first place it must be understood that no revelation is necessary in order that man may be able to know about the existence of the one true God. The need of a first cause is far too obvious to permit an inculpable, ignorance of God's existence even among those who have not received the benefit of supernatural revelation. Furthermore, man has sufficient natural intellectual equipment to enable him to know correctly the various attributes of God and to recognize God as at once the Source and the End of the moral order. Thus the revelation which God concedes to the

---

[5] Book I, Ch. 8; cf. the assertion of St. Justin Martyr with reference to the Christians' profession of faith. "It is for your sakes that we have been saying these things" (*The First Apology*, Ch. 8).

[6] 2 Tim. 4:2.

world and which is morally necessary for man is actually something supernatural. It is not demanded by the nature of man himself.

But "that about God which is not itself impervious to human reason," to use the terminology of the Vatican Council, happens to be the most important factor in all natural human knowledge. It is the basis of any objective cultural, moral, and social doctrine which may enter into man's civilization. All that is best in the operation of human nature in this world demands a clear and certain realization about the nature of the First Cause, a realization shared by all the members of society. It is the business of the apologist first to demonstrate this truth and then to point out how the requisite knowledge of God has not been possessed and will not be independently of Christian revelation.

12. The cultural implications of supernatural teaching. First of all, any satisfactory cultural order must be based upon a recognition of the fact that there is one true God, the First Cause of all beings distinct from Himself, the Creator and Lord of all things, who is endowed with the infinite perfections of being and operation which we know as the divine attributes. By its very definition, culture is the terminus of the human mind's development. It is the natural perfection of the human mind as such. It differs from those perfections with which the mind may be endowed with reference to certain restricted fields. Thus a man may train himself to be a successful accountant or a successful politician while at the same time he does not possess the intellectual perfection which is characteristically human. In the last analysis this human and natural intellectual perfection is that very reality which St. Thomas Aquinas has so well described in his *Disputed Questions on Truth*.[7]

Obviously a man cannot have described in his own mind the order of the universe and of its causes unless he knows the existence and the nature of the First Cause, upon which all things created depend. The created things of the universe themselves cannot be properly known until they are seen precisely as effects which are brought into being and maintained in existence through the divine power. The laws of created reality cannot be appreciated for what they really are unless they themselves are recognized as effects of that God who, by

---

7 Q. 2, a. 2.

His providential power, governs the universe and brings the things contained in it to the attainment of their proper end. The man who is not cognizant of the perfections of the living God then must always live in a state of dire intellectual poverty.

This culture, which is based upon a correct and substantially complete natural knowledge of God, is not merely a speculative perfection. Manifesting itself through the temperaments of the various nations and races, it is responsible for the laws, the literature, and the arts which in their turn contribute to the natural excellence of human life in this world. Thus a civilization which is vitiated through fundamental errors about the natural notion of God is doomed to express itself in ugliness and to conduct its affairs without regard for the sacredness of human life. History has shown us very clearly how such civilizations have failed in their essential function of procuring for man a fullness of natural happiness in this life.

13. Benefits of divine revelation in the moral order. Moral doctrine is absolutely dependent upon a correct and substantially complete natural idea of God also. For after all the doctrine on moral describes the activity of a good man. It makes all the difference in the world if the man who is to achieve goodness is a creature ordered for eternal beatitude by a provident and infinitely just God, or if he is to achieve merely the happiness and pleasure which he can gather in this life. A code of moral which is not based upon the recognition of God's attributes is one which will inevitably tend toward selfishness and other qualities which are incompatible with proper social existence.

The ancient civilizations of China, Greece, and Rome managed to evolve a code of moral which permitted an effective corporate life. However, these very cultures acted and legislated in such a way as to show no appreciation of the dignity of human life as such. They stained their records with the most repulsive forms of slavery and immorality. The modern states like Russia, Nazi Germany, and bolshevist Spain establishing a field of conduct absolutely apart from a correct notion of God, produced the most hideous moral codes in all the history of the human race. As a matter of fact the dignity of the individual human person, the preservation of family ties and the conduct of the state in such a way as to bring about the desired temporal well-being which belongs to human life are all rendered impossible or at least impeded greatly through a failure to observe the complete natural doctrine about God.

Apart from those peoples who have been in possession of divine revelation, there has never been a generally accepted reasonably complete knowledge of God. Certainly one of the best among the pagan cultures was that of ancient Rome. Yet, in his *De Civitate Dei*, St. Augustine was able to cite Varro, the outstanding theorist of Roman religious matters to the effect that his civilization knew three distinct kinds of "theologies" or doctrines about matters divine. One of these was the mythical theology, the second was physical and the third civil.[8] According to the teaching of Varro himself, the first of these belonged to the theater, the second to the world, the third and last to the city or the state.

The mythical theology was that exposed by the poets and the playwrights. It had to do with those fables which were intended to amuse the people and to excite their baser instincts with the suggestion that the worst crimes which could be conceived by the mind of man had already been perpetrated by the gods themselves. The so-called physical theology was nothing but the doctrine of the various philosophers about God, and was supposed to answer the questions about the identity of the various divinities, their location and classification and the characteristics, their temporal or eternal nature and their components. Thus Varro distinguished carefully the opinions of Heraclitus who believed that the gods were of the nature of fire from those of Pythagoras who believed that they were "from numbers," and Epicurus who thought that the divinities were composed of atoms.

The civil theology was that which the citizens and especially the priests were supposed to know and administer within the state. It consisted in the performance of those religious rites and in the offering of those sacrifices which were proper to the place and to the time. As far as doctrinal accuracy was concerned, this civil theology was inferior to the natural as was the purely mythical. These two, the doctrine of the theater and the civil teaching on the duties which were due to the gods comprised the popular knowledge of the divinity.

---

8 *De Civitate Dei*, Book 6, Ch. 5.

That which was available to the mass of people in the old Roman state compared at least favorably with the teachings readily available to the populace of other states.

The popular ideas respecting the divinity in the Hindu culture are grossly polytheistic. They differ sharply from those notions which are contained in a literature far too abstruse and esoteric to influence the thought of most men. The same lamentable crassness of popular appreciation of God is to be found in the story of religious life and activity among the ancient peoples of Mesopotamia and Syria. The same evidence always appears. Apart from the influence of divine revelation, the general run of mankind has never had the complete and accurate natural knowledge of God which is necessary for the perfect enjoyment of cultured social life.

But even among the philosophers who enjoyed a more perfect natural knowledge of God than that which their fellow citizens possessed, we find a lamentable lack of accuracy and coherence. The finest doctrine about God in all the run of pagan philosophical thought is to be found in the writings of Plato and of Aristotle. On the pages of his *Symposium* Plato elaborated a proof of the existence of God which was so perfect that centuries afterward St. Thomas Aquinas was able to incorporate it into the fabric of Christian teaching.[9] Yet in the same dialogue and throughout his writings Plato manifested a concept of moral which made it quite evident that this idea of God never influenced his understanding of the conduct of man. Aristotle, both in the *Metaphysics*[10] and in the *Physics*,[11] offered a real and satisfactory demonstration of the existence of the First Mover. Yet in these same volumes he gives evidence of a failure to realize the implications of his own proof. Neither of these great teachers could be said to have proposed a clear and certain complete teaching about the natural idea of God. Neither gave any evidence of understanding the truth of the divine providence. Neither understood even the natural evidence to the effect that God governs the lives and the activities of men.

---

9 This is the argument from the degrees of being, the fourth among the five ways in which St. Thomas proved the existence of God. Plato reasoned from the existence of beautiful things to that of pure beauty.

10 The twelfth book of the *Metaphysics*.

11 The eighth book of the *Physics*.

Poor as it was, their teaching was such that few men could ever avail themselves of it. The teaching of Aristotle of God is left, in its greater portion, in the books of the *Metaphysics*. These books were to be considered only by those men who had acquired all of the training in logic and in natural philosophy which were available in the culture of the day according to the intention of Aristotle himself. The ordinary man, who had neither the leisure nor the aptitude for philosophical discipline, could derive little profit from such teaching.

The force of divine revelation in offering to all men a clear and readily available natural knowledge of God becomes strikingly apparent if we look into the actual accomplishments of Christian teaching. The tiniest child who learns his prayers to God and who is trained in the teaching of the little catechism has a clear and accurate knowledge of God which surpasses the highest accomplishments of Plato and of Aristotle.[12] In the mind of that child there is certainty about the facts of creation, the divine providence and the divine government. There is no questioning about the material of the gods, as there was among the most brilliant of the thinkers cited by Varro. The simplest person who has been the beneficiary of the divine revelation knows full well that God is a spirit, infinitely perfect. He knows, too, that God is utterly immutable, that He is infinitely good, and omniscient. He knows that this same God loves man, and that He is a holy God, who will not have uncleanness in His sight.

14. The benefits of Catholic dogma for a democracy. Although divine revelation is morally necessary for all men, it is strikingly requisite for, and beneficial to, those who are fortunate enough to live as members of a democratic state. For, as the observers of political philosophy have pointed out very clearly, the ruler in a state must be endowed with virtue in order that the state may function successfully, and actually be of service in procuring for its citizens the material well-being and temporal advantages which will enable those citizens to realize their human capabilities. In a democratic state the people as a whole control the destinies of the government. The rulers act in the name and by the authority of the people themselves. As a necessary consequence, the people in a democracy must be a virtuous people if their state is to work out its own destiny.

---

12 Cf. Vincent McNabb, O.P. (New York, 1927), pp. 107–111.

Thus in any event, or under any form of government, the people must possess the moral virtues in order that they may live together successfully. There could be no social action in the proper sense of the term which is not based upon the right actions of those individuals who compose the society. However, in the case of other forms of rule, the first direction toward right activity can come from the ruler, who directs the activities of the state in a way which is at least theoretically independent of the choice of the populace. In the democracy the first impulse must be from the people themselves, for the choice of rulers lies within their hands. Naturally with the choice of rulers there comes a choice of policy or direction of government for which the people as a whole are responsible. Thus, within the framework of a democracy, the people must possess those virtues which are characteristic of rulers as well as those which are simply requisite for proper living in a social order.[13]

Our own state is, and with the help of God will continue to be, democratic. As a result it is the sort of society which stands specially in need of that ineffable benefit which is the divine revelation.

Through the agency of this revelation, and only in this way, there will be available to the citizenry at large a correct and complete natural knowledge of God. This knowledge alone can sustain the culture and the morality, both individual and civic, which are requisite for the proper functioning of our nation.

In the light of that culture, which will not be generally and successfully attained apart from the force of the divine teaching, the people of our nation will be able to discern the true import of the problems which they must resolve, in their capacity as directors of national policy. Through this cultural knowledge the true hierarchy of values is evident. The people can and will be able to see the worth of alternative courses which are proposed to them, and the effectiveness of the media which are supposed to be used in the attainment of the purposes of the state. In short that intellectual perfection which, in a monarchy, must characterize the prince who rules his country successfully can and will belong to the people of our own nation through the beneficent activity of divine revelation.

---

13 Cf. the Encyclical Letter of Pope Leo XIII, *Longinque Oceani*, Jan. 6, 1895, in the *Great Encyclical Letters of Pope Leo XIII* (New York, 1903), pp. 320–335.

15. Divine revelation and civic honesty. In the light of recent history, it is quite apparent that public immorality is definitely destructive of the life and the functioning of a democracy. A nation that winks at civic dishonesty, which tolerates or encourages activity destructive of the family and of individual morality, is a nation which tends away from the blessings and the benefits of democratic processes. However, it is quite as obvious that there will be no such thing as corporate justice and corporate morality apart from the justice and the honor of those men who actually compose the commonwealth. A nation composed of individuals who are devoid of private ideals of justice will never react successfully against the raids of larcenous politicians. A state whose members have individually no regard for veracity will never be able to escape the fatal pitfall of corporate hypocrisy, which has vitiated the activity of so many nations. Finally, only in that state whose members have a love of purity and honor will there be the same family life without which the life of any country is inevitably doomed.

Now all of these qualities are aspects of an objective moral which rests only upon a complete and accurate natural knowledge of God, or upon the knowledge derived from divine revelation through which this natural awareness is developed and perfected. They are qualities which must be implanted in the members of the state through a process of education. Actually that education, to be effective and successful, must center about this dominant idea of God. The education which is objectively requisite for the proper functioning of our own democracy must be a religious education. It must point out God as One to whom service and reverence are due precisely because of His supreme excellence. Democracy is not only an excellent form of government, but it is also by far the most exacting. Precisely because of its excellence, it is worth all of the labor and all of the accomplishments which must contribute to its perfect functioning.

16. The teaching of divine revelation is a patriotic function. Since divine revelation is requisite for the successful functioning of our own democracy, it is evident that the work of presenting this teaching to the citizens of this country constitutes a work of patriotism in the strictest sense of the term. Patriotism is, after all, that virtue by which a man tends to give to his own country the service and the respect which are its due. To give service to the country is nothing more or less than to render to the state that which is good for it, and, of course, that which is requisite for it, according to the capacity of the individual who is called upon to do so. Divine revelation is good for our nation. It is a benefit of incomparable importance. Thus the Christian who possesses the gift of divine revelation would not be doing good to his country were he to withhold this benefit from his fellow citizens.

Primarily, then, it is the work of the apologist to manifest the credentials of this doctrine which is presented to men as a great and ineffable benefit. If he can bring forward evidence that this doctrine is what it claims to be, actually a teaching which has been communicated by God to men, then he will have demonstrated the reliability of his contribution to the life of his own nation. The apologist does not ask anyone to take his word to the effect that his teaching can be of service to his fellow men. It is his function to bring forward the clear and irrefutable evidence which is at his disposal. He claims that his doctrine is sovereignly important. It is within his power to adduce evidence proportionate to the magnitude of his claims.

That evidence must be both striking and extensive. After all, the apologist presents a doctrine which he claims to have been taught to men by the living God. He says that this doctrine is addressed to all men, that it comes to them through the instrumentality of their fellows. It is his contention that his doctrine contains truths which are absolutely beyond the natural competence of any created intellect, actual or possible. He can show that there is nothing contradictory in the claims which he has made, and, furthermore, he asserts that this doctrine is necessary for the men who live upon this earth. He says that through this doctrine, and through this alone, men can achieve the eternity of perfect happiness for which they are intended. He claims that by the use of this teaching men can derive that natural knowledge of God which will direct and guide the successful operation of their individual and corporate lives. Only the most conclusive evidence could render the acceptance of such claims rational and prudent. Yet such evidence can be adduced in the science of apologetics.

Chapter 6

THE DISCERNIBILITY OF DIVINE REVELATION

1. The general conditions of credibility. In order to show that the testimony of some man is reliable we must point out three distinct facts. In the first place, we must demonstrate that the man himself is truthful, that he has no intention of doing other than tell the truth about the matter under consideration, and secondly that he actually knows what he is talking about in this given case. Finally, we must be at pains to show that the testimony in question was really and actually given by the person who was supposed to have given it.

When we are dealing with the matter of divine revelation, we obviously need offer only one of these proofs. There is no special need of insisting upon the fact that God is truthful. We know of the divine veracity and of the divine omniscience through the proofs of metaphysics. These qualities are known naturally as divine attributes. We demonstrate the existence of these attributes from the fact that God is that First Cause whose existence we know through the consideration of those beings which could neither be or act apart from His causality. The study of the divine attributes from the purely natural point of view belongs rather to metaphysics than to apologetics.

On the other hand, it is the central and essential purpose of apologetics to point out the evident indications that Catholic dogma, offered as a message from God to man, has actually been revealed by God Himself. Because this teaching is put forward as mediate rather than immediate revelation, we cannot rely merely upon the experience of that one who has directly received the divine communication. We can establish the proper divine authorship of this message in the light of natural reason, only in that same way in which we can discern the authorship of any other communication which comes to us through indirect channels. We must look for something which is analogous to a divine signature, really attached to the message which comes to us in His name.[1]

If we can show that the message is thus as it were signed by God, we shall evidently have sufficient reason for giving a prudent assent of divine faith to the truths contained in it. The message will be evidently and rationally credible, since obviously the all-just and veracious God could not knowingly signify His assent to a claim of divine authorship for a doctrine which He knew to be merely human in character. The point which we must consider then is the nature of this divine signature and its application to the doctrine which we propose as divinely revealed.

A signature, even that of a human being, is established as some mark which can be made by this person alone. A signature may be counterfeited, but it cannot be duplicated. In the case of men, theoretically at least, any counterfeit can be discovered and demonstrated as such. Only, this individual man can competently affix his own signature.

2. The various signs of revelation. But there is one sort of visible effect which can be produced by God alone and which can be recognized as such by those men to whom His message is addressed. Such an effect will be an act obviously beyond the competence of any creature, actual or possible. It will be an act performed independently of the laws of created reality, and as such evidently the production of One who is not dependent upon those laws but rather upon whom the created laws themselves depend. It can be shown clearly that such actions are possible, that they can be discerned as such, and thus seen evidently as divine works, and finally that they are attached to this teaching which we call Catholic dogma, and that they thus unerringly designate this dogma as a divine teaching. These divinely produced effects, visible as means by which we may judge the authenticity of a doctrine which is proposed as divinely revealed, are called criteria of revelation or motives of credibility. They are criteria of revelation insofar as they are the positive signs by which we may establish with certitude the divine origin of some message which is proposed to us as God's teaching. They are motives of credibility insofar as the

---

1 Negueruela, *Lecciones de Apologetica*, Vol. I, pp. 162–164; Dieckmann, *De Revelatione Christiane*, pp. 242–259.

doctrine which is evidently endowed with these signs is evidently and rationally credible as divine revelation.

Apart from these positive signs of the divine authorship, there are certain negative criteria which can be utilized to recognize the falsity of claims that certain doctrines have been taught by God. Thus a series of pronouncements which express palpable untruths can evidently not have come from the God of truth. And teaching which incites men to acts of immorality can obviously never have come from the God of holiness. But obviously a doctrine is not evidently credible merely by reason of the fact that it does not contain inconsistency and immorality. The point of these proofs is only that a doctrine which is obviously incorrect and morally unclean can have no serious claim to divine origin, and thus could never be accepted prudently and rationally with the assent of divine faith.

Furthermore, there are what are called internal criteria of revelation which can give solid, yet secondary, assurance of credibility. These internal criteria are to be found in the satisfaction of man's aspirations in the acceptance of the doctrine itself. It is obvious that the God who created and preserves His creatures is the same One who is the Author of a divinely revealed doctrine. When He chooses to speak to His people, it is evident that He could do so in such a way that these people could as it were experience the fitness and the perfection of His message. That message would be something perfectly adapted to the needs and to the best aspirations of those to whom it was addressed. When a doctrine which actually corresponds to these needs and aspirations is found, and when that doctrine is proposed as a message from God Himself, there is certainly objective reason to suppose that the teaching is actually what it claims to be. A counterfeit revelation could hardly manifest the same aptitude for the exigencies and the tendencies of human nature as one which had really come from the God who founded and designed that nature and who unfailingly guides its operation.

3. The Church appeals to motives of credibility in support of her claims. The Church herself makes a definite appeal to all of these motives of credibility. Unhesitatingly she states that her teaching is rationally acceptable as divine revelation because it is guaranteed by unmistakable signs of God's testimony to this effect. She realizes, of course, that the assent of divine faith, as the acceptance of a doctrine which is intrinsically supernatural, must be made with the aid of an intrinsically supernatural grace coming from God Himself. This essentially supernatural aid, which enables man to assent firmly to the truth of a revealed doctrine which is absolutely beyond the natural competence of any creature, actual or possible, is what the Church terms the internal help of the Holy Ghost. According to the teaching of the Vatican Council, the motives of credibility are quite distinct from these internal helps of the Holy Ghost. It is their function to render the service of our faith something reasonable and prudent.

"Nevertheless, in order that the service of our faith may be conformed to reason, God has willed that there should be joined with the internal aids of the Holy Ghost external proofs of His own revelation, namely *divine works*, and *first of all miracles and prophecies*, which, since they clearly manifest the omnipotence and the infinite knowledge of God, are most certain signs of divine revelation and adapted to the understanding of all men. Wherefore both Moses and the prophets, and especially the Lord Christ Himself exhibited many and most manifest miracles and prophecies, and we read about the Apostles, 'But they going forth preached everywhere, the Lord working withal, and confirming, the word with signs that followed' (Mark 16:20). And again it is written, 'We have the more firm prophetical word: whereunto you do well to attend, as to a light that shineth in a dark place.'"[2]

The Church reasserts this claim in the text of her oath against the modernists. "I admit and acknowledge the external proofs of revelation, that is the divine worlds and first of all miracles and prophecies as most certain signs of the divine origin of the Christian religion and I hold them to be perfectly adapted to the understanding of men of all ages, and even the understanding of the men of this time."[3] Thus she clearly claims that divine effects, or works which evidently could be performed only by the divine power itself, demonstrate the credibility of the doctrine which she advances as divinely revealed.

---

2 2 Pet. 1:19; The Vatican Council, The Constitution *"Dei Filius,"* Ch. 3 (Denzinger, 1790).

3 Denzinger, 2145.

The Discernibility of Divine Revelation

In the same way, she boldly claims the fullness of what we have seen as the negative criteria to establish the credibility of her teaching. In the same constitution of the Vatican Council she declares, "Although faith is above reason, yet there can never be any true conflict between faith and reason: since the same God who reveals the mysteries and infuses faith has granted the light of reason to the human soul. But God cannot deny Himself, nor can the true ever contradict the true. However, the empty appearance of such contradiction arises especially when either the dogmas of faith have not been understood and expounded according to the mind of the Church or when the voice of opinion is mistaken for the statement of reason."[4] Concluding this same statement the Church utilizes the terms of the Fifth Council of the Lateran in defining as false every assertion which is contrary to the truth of enlightened faith.

However, the Church goes still farther in her claims for the credibility of her own teaching. She asserts that the doctrine which she proposes as divinely revealed is actually of service to human science and not merely something entirely out of its field and compatible with it. "Not only can faith and reason never contradict each other but they actually do one another a mutual service. For right reason proves the foundations of faith and illumined with the light of this same faith cultivates the science of divine things while faith frees and guards reason from errors and endows it with a multiple knowledge."[5] These are obviously claims which are easy to verify. It is not too difficult to see whether or not the doctrine which is proposed by the Catholic Church as divinely revealed is actually in contradiction to those propositions which we see to be true in the light of our own natural knowledge. In the case where there is such contradiction, then, evidently the doctrine which is presented as divine teaching is not what it claims to be.

These claims have obvious reference to what we have seen as the internal motives of credibility. A doctrine which is in conformity with the truths which are seen as such in the natural light of human reason and which actually is of assistance in the mastery of natural knowledge will manifestly be a sort of doctrine which is eminently satisfac-

---

4 Denzinger, 1797.
5 Denzinger, 1799.

tory to human beings and in conformity with the highest aspirations and tendencies of human nature. An individual can experience this satisfaction himself in the possession of Christian truth, and as such it constitutes an individual internal motive of credibility. More important from a scientific point of view is the demonstration that a doctrine proposed as divinely revealed has been found eminently satisfactory and consoling by men who obviously expressed in their own lives the highest accomplishments of which human nature is capable. The fact that a doctrine has been a source of joy and consolation to those who have been sincere seekers after truth is manifest confirmation of a claim which has been advanced that this doctrine is divinely revealed to man.

However, the Church advances one more indication of the divine origin of the doctrine which she proposes. She claims that she herself is manifestly a divine work, a miraculous phenomenon which could not have been produced and maintained by the natural power of any creature or creatures whatsoever. "Moreover the Church by herself, because of her admirable propagation, her eminent sanctity, and her inexhaustible fruitfulness in all good things, because of her Catholic unity and her unconquered stability, is a certain great and perpetual motive of credibility and an irrefutable witness of her own divine messengership."[6] This claim, like the others advanced for the credibility of Catholic dogma, is reasonable and very easy to verify. In the event that she is not manifestly a divine work, she cannot reasonably propose her own doctrine as divine revelation. On the other hand, if she does manifest in her own constitution and in her activity elements which could not possibly be the effects of any merely created power, then she has established herself as a true indication of the divine origin of that doctrine which is proposed as divine revelation.

---

6 Denzinger, 1794.

Those signs which are manifestly indications of divine origin in a doctrine, which is proposed as divinely revealed may thus be classified:

A) Negative criteria.
B) Positive criteria.
  a) External signs (external with reference to the person to whom the message in question is addressed).
    a* Extrinsic criteria (extrinsic this time with reference to the doctrine under consideration). Under this heading we find miracles and prophecies.
    b* Intrinsic criteria. These are manifest qualities found in the doctrine itself, in the one who delivered the teaching, or in that social agency by which this teaching is guarded and preserved.
  b) Internal signs or criteria, and these may be either:
    a* Individual, or
    b* Universal.[7]

In the process of establishing, in the light of natural reason, the credibility of Catholic dogma as divine revelation, it will be necessary to apply all of these criteria to the doctrine in question. In the event that this doctrine, and only this doctrine, is manifestly signed by these

---

[7] The division of positive motives of credibility is that of Garrigou-Lagrange, De Revelatione, Vol. 1, p. 556. Dieckmann, De Revelatione Christiane, p. 255, following the same pattern uses a different terminology.

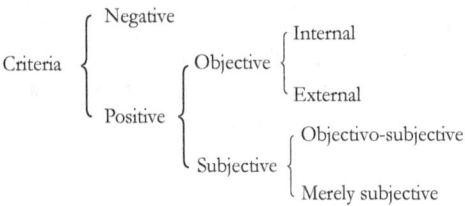

The "internal" motives of Dieckmann are those which Garrigou-Lagrange, and Walshe, The Principles of Catholic Apologetics, p. 180, call intrinsic to the message under consideration. The external motives of Dieckmann are those which we denominate as extrinsic. The objective of Dieckmann are the external motives to which we refer while his subjective criteria are our internal motives.

evident indications of divine authorship, then we can conclude that an acceptance of this doctrine with the assent of divine faith is a reasonable and prudent act. For only a teaching which gives evidence of having been revealed by God can possibly be accepted as divine revelation according to the exigencies of human reason itself.

4. The order among the motives of credibility. However, before we can proceed to the work of examining Catholic dogma in the light of these manifest criteria, we must first realize the order which exists among the motives of credibility themselves. The Catholic Church herself has qualified miracles and prophecies as motives of credibility which occupy the most important position among those criteria which can manifest the divine origin of her own message. Both in the Vatican Council and in the oath against the modernists she has taken pains to condemn those who rejected the demonstrative value of these miracles and prophecies in the work of apologetics. Furthermore, she insisted that these signs were fitted to give certain evidence of the divine origin of the Christian message to the men of all ages, and even to those of modern times.

There is a real and valid reason for this insistence. The Church takes cognizance of the fact that a doctrine which is revealed in the sense in which she speaks of revelation could not be fully demonstrated as credible apart from these external motives or criteria. Since the message which we are asked to accept on the authority of God revealing contains truths which are set forth as intrinsically supernatural mysteries, the only way in which this message can offer valid evidence of credibility is by making it unmistakably clear that God actually has given this message to man as a special communication.

If the message were merely natural in its import, then it would be perhaps sufficient to show that this teaching was in accord with the best tendencies of human nature in order to establish it as rationally acceptable. If revelation were what the modernists said it was, merely the consciousness which man acquires of his own relation to God, then obviously it would be demonstrated as acceptable in the same way any other merely natural truth is presented for the acceptance of men. But since it is proposed as an actual message communicated by God to man, there must be some incontestable evidence that God is really its Author. That incontestable evidence can be nothing but

The Discernibility of Divine Revelation

some sign which is proper to God, an effect which could not possibly be brought about by any created agency whatsoever.

5. The miracle is a manifest divine work. Now an effect which is obviously proper to God is one evidently performed by the Master of the universe. The Master of the universe is the One upon whom the laws of created nature depend. He is not in the least restricted by these laws. The laws of created nature are those observable and unchanging tendencies which are manifest in the activity of created things. When we say that a thing acts in accordance with the physical laws, we mean that it performs that type of activity to which its nature is directed. Basically, then, the law is the expression of the nature itself. The activity which is in accordance with this law is necessarily something quite distinct from the nature of a created thing. For in every created thing the nature is quite distinct from the operation of which it is the principle or the source.

Only the Master of the universe, the One who has created the universe and who holds all the things contained in it in their existence, can act in such a way as to impede the activity which is the immediate consequence of the created nature. Creatures must act upon other creatures in utilizing the forces which follow from the nature of these beings. When there is an effect which is obviously independent of the physical laws which govern the activity of created things, it is obvious that this is something which God has done in the world independently of the natural activity of His creatures.

A creature could very well act upon another by utilizing the forces which are consequent upon the nature of that other creature. Thus a physician can heal his patient, but in doing this he must employ those very forces of the human body which tend toward physical well-being. But he could never bring back to life a man who has died for the simple reason that the forces native to man's body will carry him from the status of childhood through maturity to old age. He can arrange to have these forces work for the health of the person which is his patient. He can certainly never reverse the direction of the forces themselves.

6. Three types of miracles. These divine works in the physical order are miracles in the proper sense of the term when they are apparent as such.[8] They may be divided into three classes. First of all there are certain effects which could not be brought about at all by any created agency. These are the miracles substantially such. The second class includes effects which could be brought about by purely natural forces, but which could never be accomplished in this definite subject. These are the miracles which are thus named by reason of the subject in which they are brought about. In the final class are those effects which could have been brought about in this particular subject by the natural forces themselves, but evidently could not be produced in the way in which actually it has been brought about other than by the divine power itself. These are the miracles which are such by reason of the manner in which they are brought about.[9]

Within the first category we find such manifestations as the multiplication of the loaves and the fishes and the compenetration of matter incident to the passage of a body through the walls of a room. These are effects which lie altogether outside of the competence of any created power.

In the case of the multiplication of the loaves and the fishes, we have evidently an effect which lies outside of the natural capacity of these things. Only that Being from whom these created realities obtain their natural effects and their real though secondary causality can bring them to produce effects to which their nature is evidently not ordered at all. As something which is itself included in the order of the universe, a created cause would have to avail itself of the actual and natural tendencies of such things in order to produce an effect through them. Thus when we know that this effect has actually taken place, we are certainly aware that it has been brought about by no natural created power. It is an effect which is brought about in the visible and created universe by a power which is outside of and thus independent of the laws of this universe. It is visibly something which has been produced by that One upon whom the laws and the activities of the created universe themselves depend.

---

[8] Thus the act of transubstantiation is manifestly beyond the natural competence of any creature, actual or possible. However, it is not a *miracle*, in the sense of a criterion of revelation because it is not sensibly manifest. It is an object of faith rather than a motive of credibility.

[9] This classification of miracles is found in St. Thomas Aquinas, *The Summa Theologica*, I[a], q. 105, a. 8.

Within the second category, that of the miracles which are such by reason of the subject in which the effects are produced, we find such things as the raising of a man from the dead, or the granting of sight to a man who is born blind. This class of miracles is just as truly a category of obviously divine works as the division which includes miracles such by their very substance. Yet they are miracles because they constitute the production of an effect of which this particular subject is obviously incapable, but which could naturally be produced in some other body. Thus when a man is raised from the dead, the kind of life which he lives is exactly that which is enjoyed by the other persons who constitute the human race. His body and its functions are no different from those which he possessed before his own death. His activities are those which are quite natural to man, and which can be produced by purely natural forces in a living human body. But what constitutes this effect as a miracle is the evident fact that such activities could never be produced naturally in a body which is dead and which has been corrupted.

Obviously such a miracle is ascertainable in the same manner as any purely natural phenomenon. The fact of death is something which can be known with perfect certainty. Men can be as sure that this particular individual is dead as they are about the death, the burial, and the corruption of the body of any other. They can know that this man who has been really dead now lives as well as they can be aware that any other individual is alive. They can see the deformed eyes of a man who was born without the gift of sight, and then they can certainly know that this man sees. Furthermore, they can be quite well aware that these effects are beyond the power of any merely natural agency.

To the third class of miracles belong particularly healings of diseases which of themselves are curable, but which are certainly not curable merely at the word or the command of some person or through the instantaneous application of some substance like common mud. Again such miracles are evidently divine works, although they are not as easily ascertained as such as are the miracles of the first two orders. It is possible for nervous disorders which are generally classed under the somewhat inadequate heading of hysteria to simulate or counterfeit some of the symptoms of recognized organic ailments. Such nervous disorders may well cease to have their effects through the application of mental hygiene. However, such cases are ascertainable not only by men of the medical profession, but also by those who come into close contact with the ailments simulated or imitated. Or, to put the matter positively, an ordinary man of the world can tell a case, of genuine organic ailment, and can see that such a case has been cured suddenly and without the application of such specific remedies which are ordinarily utilized for the relief of this condition. And when there is unmistakably a condition which could not be cured suddenly or without specific remedies in the natural course of events, and this ailment is cured instantly at the command of some person or as the result of some petition made to God, men can easily see in this an effect which is beyond the natural competence of any creature.

7. The miracle and the divine causality. There have been, and unfortunately there still are, men who refuse *a priori* to admit the possibility of a miracle. It is absolutely certain that such a refusal is based either upon a false judgment about the causality of God Himself or upon an unwarranted and inaccurate notion of created reality. There would, of course, be no possibility whatsoever of a miracle if God had been limited by, and determined to, the actually existing order of the universe. But in this case the material things in the world would have had some existence and reality apart from the causative power of God, and this is evidently not true. The creative action of God was not exercised upon a previously existing mass of objects. Every fiber and aspect of created reality, insofar as it is real and good, is the product of the divine causality. Consequently there is and there could be nothing in all of the created universe which would limit or confine the power of God.

Furthermore, the power of God is in no way limited by any necessity on the part of His own activity. He created the world with absolute freedom. He stands in no need of it. He created it freely, knowing well that through it He was obtaining the one object or end which could ultimately motivate His effects, but He saw that this end could be obtained other than through this particular universe which was actually established. If He had caused as One determined by His very nature to produce this effect, rather than freely and intelligently, He could not have been the First Cause, since every cause which is determined to its effect is by that very reason something which is potential and which is acted upon by something superior to itself.

Making the world freely, He obviously established it in such a way that not only the substances within it but also the very operation and tendencies of those substances were subject absolutely to His power. Since the created thing only exists insofar as it has been brought into being and there sustained by the power of God, and since it operates and exercises causality only insofar as it is moved by the divine power, God has it within His choice to direct that activity either according to the direction of the created nature itself, or otherwise.[10] Now it is quite obvious that the usual course of the activity of created things will be in accordance with the tendencies expressed in their own natures. Thus a fire is something which is naturally capable of burning human flesh which comes in contact with it, and it is natural that it should thus consume the matter with which it actually comes in contact. If at some time it is observable that fire does not consume the combustible material it touches, it is acting in a way which could only be brought about by God Himself, and for a definite and laudable purpose.

8. The miracle and order in the universe. Thus when we assert the certain and obvious truth that miracles are possible, we in no way deny that there is such a thing as a fixed order in the material universe. As a matter of fact exactly the opposite is the case. For there could be no such thing as an ascertainable work of God as such in the world if there were not an evident and fixed order within the universe of bodies. Furthermore, we know that this order is fixed, not as some merely artificial disposition of corporeal reality but as something which flows from the very natures of things which are in this world. To utilize an example to which we have already appealed and which has particular importance in this field of miracles, the dead body of a human being tends to corrupt by reason of the very chemical and physical forces at work within it. That tendency is in it by the very fact that it is what it is. When, by reason of His infinite wisdom, God chooses to bring about the Resurrection of that body, he causes an effect quite distinct from that to which the thing itself is orientated. The miracle is obvious and is in the technical sense a sign, precisely because that tendency and its otherwise inevitable effect are so easily observed.

---

10 The effect of God's omnipotence in creatures, their capacity to be used in any way by Him, is called their *obediential potency*.

All bodies or all things in the material universe except man himself act in a definite and determined way. Each substance has its own activity which it will not and from a purely natural point of view cannot change. Fire will consume unprotected human flesh which comes in contact with it. The water of the sea or of a lake will submerge rather than sustain the human being who attempts to walk upon it. We can know not merely that these reactions occur, but also we can understand why these effects take place rather than any others. The nature and the composition of material things are obviously purposive, and a nature achieves its immediate end precisely in the performance of that activity.

9. The miracle and possibility. Again, when the assertion is made that a miraculous effect is impossible, we must be careful to note the meaning which is attached to the term impossible. A thing may be impossible in two different ways. There is such a thing as absolute impossibility. Thus it is impossible that the sum of two plus three should be other than five. To make two plus three equal six or four would not be a miracle. It would be nothing at all. It is something which is beyond the possibility of existence since its terms or components are mutually exclusive. A two plus three which would equal six would be something which did not have a nature of any sort, and as such there could be no possibility or its existence.

On the other hand, however, a thing may be impossible from a relative point of view. Thus the thing which would be possible for a strong man would be relatively impossible for one who is weak. It would be an effect to which his physical condition is not proportioned. Likewise, what would be possible for a created pure spirit would be relatively impossible for any human being. Finally, what is possible to the unlimited power of God would be impossible to any of His creatures whatsoever. It is in this way that the true miracle, of any of the three classes to which allusion has been made, is impossible to the creature but certainly not to the power of the living God. A miracle is obviously something beyond the power of any creature as such, but it is not something fantastic or absolutely impossible.

If a man refuses absolutely to admit the possibility of miracles, we can only show him that his refusal is devoid of objective foundation. If he admits the existence of a First Cause, who obviously is possessed of all perfection and who freely produces and preserves the universe, then he can have no trouble in seeing that such a being can produce effects which are obviously beyond the natural competence of any creature. But without that accurate notion of God which can be acquired naturally by man, he is in danger of failing to see the possibility of that which is the outstanding sign of divine revelation.

10. True and false miracles. We come now to consider precisely how a man, in a given order of circumstances, can distinguish between a real miracle and that which is merely a counterfeit. The doctrine which we defend as credible in our science of apologetics takes cognizance of the fact that counterfeit miracles are not only possible but unfortunately real. Our Lord Himself incorporated a foretelling of such false signs into His preaching. "For there shall arise false Christs and false prophets, and shall show great signs and wonders, insomuch as to deceive (if possible) even the elect."[11] Like any other counterfeits, these false miracles are intended to deceive men, and they can well do so. Consequently we have the right to ask whether there is, at our disposal, some means of discerning with unfailing accuracy the false miracle from the true one.

Actually we possess such criteria. The portent or wonder which is set forth as a counterfeit miracle will inevitably prove, upon examination, to be other than the work of the true God: Obviously it is possible for a clever magician to produce effects which the untrained onlooker will not be able to explain. Again it is possible for a created spirit to perform works which could not be duplicated by the natural power of any man whatsoever. But any one of these tricks is put forward as a trick. It is something prepared and at the same time something which can never attain the manifest perfection of the real miracle. Any one of these tricks will be based upon a clever or powerful use of the natural forces themselves. There is not and there cannot be in them any indication of independence of the physical laws.

There are, of course, certain types of miracles which can never be efficiently counterfeited at all. There is not and there will not be in all the claims of counterfeit miracles any reasonably credible account of raising a dead person to life. Where such a counterfeit is attempted, it is an obviously shoddy substitute. The person who is "raised" was not one who was known to be dead at all, or if the fact of his death

---

11 Matt. 24:24.

was unquestioned, there was no valid evidence of any vital activity on his part whatsoever. Such tricks as the movement of tables or other objects without any apparent corporeal force being exercised in this task are hardly convincing as substitutes for miracles. It is clear in the first place that the raising of a table without any apparent corporeal cause is not something beyond the natural competence of any created thing.

Even apart from the possibility of trickery, through the use of magnets or some similar device, there is the possibility of some action on the part of created spirits. There is certainly nothing beyond the competence of created nature in the raising of the table in itself. The part which would demand an explanation is the fact that this table has been raised without the use of any visible cause. But we know that there are invisible realities which are actually capable of such causality. The miracles which have been cited, and those which have been scientifically accepted as such throughout the course of Christian history, have never been anything like these vulgar manifestations.[12]

But there is still another way in which the true miracle may easily be discerned from the counterfeit. The true miracle is an act of the living God, produced visibly in the created universe for some reason which is consonant with the holiness and the wisdom of God. Thus it is evident from the very outset that a sign which is intended to induce men to the practice of immorality or to the rejection of that which is naturally evident could not in any sense of the term be con-

---

12 The Fathers were quite cognizant of the fact that proponents of error had cited miracles in support of their own doctrine. St. Irenaeus offers a relatively complete norm for distinguishing true motives of credibility from counterfeits. These latter are not real cures of people manifestly sick or injured. The heretics do not even believe that it is possible to raise the dead to life. They are "magical illusions impiously wrought in the sight of men," apart from any exercise of virtue (Book 2, *Against the Heresies*, Chs. 31 and 32.) Origen shows that the manifest moral excellence of Jesus and His opposition to sorcery precluded any possibility of considering Him as a deceiver (*Contra Celsum*, Book 1, Ch. 68). Arnobius glories in the fact that the real miracles of Jesus are far more numerous than even the fictional wonders ascribed to pagan deities or personages (Book 1, Ch. 43). Both St. Irenaeus and Quadratus stress the fact that persons known to have been dead, and then raised again to life, existed for a long time in the sight of all (Irenaeus, *loc. cit.* Quadratus cited in the *Ecclesiastical History* of Eusebius, Book 4, Ch. 3).

sidered as a miracle. Furthermore, a sign which is orientated merely toward flattering the vanity of some individual could certainly never be considered as a work which God Himself freely performs in the created universe.

11. The purpose of the miracle. It is essential to our concept of a miracle that we recognize it as something which is freely brought about in the visible world by that God who is infinitely wise, and who is perfectly cognizant with all of the circumstances which accompany its production. The miracle, by its very nature, is an unusual thing; it is something which excites wonder. At the same time it is something which God performs for a definite reason. Every action which is produced in all the extension of the universe is and must be something which has a reason sufficient to explain its appearance. The miracle as such is obviously not intended to make up for some deficiency in the universal order. It is not necessary because of some congenital inefficiency of the created causes themselves. It is necessary in order that it may serve as a sign to teach men some lesson which they would not be able to grasp through the inspection of the natural workings of created causes.

Now through the inspection of created being and activity men may learn with perfect certainty that there is a God who is all powerful and omniscient. But only through a manifestation of this infinite power or boundless knowledge could they know that God approves the claim that this or that individual doctrine actually has been revealed by Him. Only through such signs can man know the divine approval of this or that individual claim which is made to them. This value of testimony is the primary purpose which dominates the production of the true miracle. It is true that the miracle need not necessarily be performed directly to show the truth of a claim that a certain doctrine has been divinely revealed. It has happened more than once in the course of history that miracles have been performed in order to show the innocence of certain men who have been under suspicion. Furthermore, we know quite well that miracles have been and are being performed in order to testify to the sanctity of certain persons whose cause of canonization is being advanced. But always there is some evidence of the divine testimony, an evidence which is unshakable because the miracle is an indication that God who knows the claim which is being advanced, and who is certainly under no compulsion to act, freely produces this effect which no creature could possibly produce when it is asked of Him as a sign of the validity of the claim.

Since a miracle necessarily has this power of testimony, and since it is something freely performed by an omniscient and all-holy God, it is obviously a motive of credibility. It is the most valuable criterion of revelation actually at our disposal. We have no means of seeing the object of supernatural revelation clearly as long as we live in this world. Then it is obvious that the only means we can have for obtaining evidence of the acceptability of this doctrine will be the indication that it really has been taught by God to man. This evidence is not direct, at least for those persons who receive this message by way of mediate or indirect revelation. Then the only way in which there can be evidence of the divine origin of this intrinsically supernatural doctrine will be through clear and unmistakable indications of God's testimony to that effect. This indication is best obtained through the medium of miracles.

12. The miracle and the judgment of credibility. For if God were to give His signature of approbation to a doctrine which claims to be divinely revealed but which actually is not, He would be either ignorant of the claim or actually a partner in a work of deception. The divine work is something as characteristic of God as the signature of any human being could possibly be to him. Only God can produce it. But obviously, even in the light of natural reason alone, it can be seen that God is all holy, and thus incapable of any prevarication. Likewise, it is evident in the same way that He is omniscient, and so unable to be deceived. Thus when the infinite power of God is evidently exercised in support of a claim that some doctrine is divinely revealed, there is every reason to admit that this claim is justified.[13]

---

13 Alfred E. Garvie, author of the article on Miracles in the *Dictionary of the Bible*, edited by James Hastings (New York, 1939, pp. 621–624), manifests the opinion that miracles are possible but that they lack force as motives of credibility. The old apologetic view of miracles as the credentials of the doctrines of Christianity is altogether discredited. It is the truth of the doctrines that makes the fact of the miracles credible (pp. 623–624). The reader may compare this view with the accurate and scientific investigation by Baierl, *The Theory of Revelation*, Vol. 2, pp. 207–425; Garrigou-Lagrange, *De Revelatione*, Vol. 2, pp. 35–106; Walshe, *The Principles of Catholic Apologetics*, pp. 190–205; Dieckmann, *De Revelatione Christiana*, pp. 291–328; the article "Miracle" in the *Dictionnaire de Theologie Catholique*, Vol. 10, columns 1798–1859 by A. Michel; the article *"Wunder"* in the *Lexicon fuer Theologie und Kirche*, Vol. 10, columns

13. The conditions of prophecy. The second among these outstanding divine works which can stand as evidences of credibility is the prophecy.[14] By a prophecy we mean here a clear and certain foretelling of some event which could not possibly be known through the light of any created intelligence. A future event which could not be known naturally by any created mind is that which depends upon some indeterminate secondary cause, namely the free will of some intelligent being. A cause is necessary as such when it is ordered to produce this particular effect rather than another. Thus a falling body will travel at a rate of speed which increases, all other things being equal, in proportion with the square of the distance through which it is falling. Thus if a man knows the distance a thing will fall, and if he can find the check which will inevitably be made in the speed of the fall by the air pressure, he can foretell exactly how long it will take this object to reach the ground. But the will of man, or that of any other intelligent being, is free with reference to any good which is not seen as its proper and adequate object. Thus there is no way of foretelling with certainty, through an examination of the intellectual being himself, exactly how this being is going to act. Furthermore, the impossibility is even clearer when it is seen with reference to an effect which will follow out of the free acts of various and distinct rational beings.[15]

Now the only one to whom a certain and clear knowledge of effects which depend upon free activity is natural is God Himself. God's knowledge of His creatures and of their activity is practical. He sees these things for what they actually are, realities which derive every portion of their being from His causality. They have no being apart from Him, and hence they cannot be considered by Him in a

---

980–984 by H. Straubinger; the article "Miracles" in the *Catholic Encyclopedia*, Vol. 10, pp. 338-348 by John T. Driscoll.

14 There is another use of the word prophecy. In the scholastic terminology the prophet is the man who receives revelation immediately from God and is charged with the duty of communicating this doctrine to his fellows. Cf. St. Thomas Aquinas, *The Summa Theologica*, II^a, II^{ae}, q. 171–174.

15 That prophecy which is a criterion of revelation is thus the certain prediction of future contingent events which in no way depend upon the man who foretells them, and which he could not possibly know apart from a communication made to him by God. The accomplishment of the prophecy shows that the prediction, which had claimed divine origin, actually was what it purported to be.

merely speculative way. Thus He knows from all eternity, in one perfect and ineffable act of intelligence, all the events which are to occur in the course of history. No other being can have this knowledge as natural to itself because no other being is the First Cause of the created universe. Thus when there is a certain foretelling of some future event which depends upon the activity of free secondary causes, this is evidently an article of knowledge which could only have come from God Himself.

The man who cites this prediction as an indication of the divine origin of some doctrine offers what is obviously a proper divine signature. However, this signature is verified only in the actual realization of the prophecy. If a prediction about some future event which could not possibly be known by a creature is made in support of a claim that a certain doctrine has been divinely revealed, and then this prediction is realized, it is a certain indication that God has approved this claim by delivering to the man who has made the prediction a knowledge which could only come from Himself.

14. True and counterfeit prophecy. There are and there always will be counterfeits of true prophecy. Such foretellings are fairly common in the course of history.[16] At sometimes they have occurred in such a way as to be cited for the authentication of no particular claim. In such cases it is obviously impossible to consider them under the headings of motives of credibility. At other times there have been foretellings which have been realized, but which have shown no evidence of any divine origin. We must remember that in spite of the fact that only God has certain knowledge of what is going to follow from free activity, there are still certain tendencies manifest in the conduct of human affairs which can give rise to definite and sometimes well-founded opinions upon future results. Thus a man who predicted twenty years ago that in this year of 1942 there would be airplanes capable of attaining the speed of four hundred miles an hour would have been able to base his prediction rationally upon the tendencies even then manifest in the manufacture of these objects. Those persons who long ago predicted the manufacture and use of instruments of transportation which would be independent of any

---

16 An interesting account of many of these predictions will be found in *The Story of Prophecy*, by Henry James Forman (New York, 1936).

animal power had basic and correct reasons which would authorize this opinion.

However a prophecy like that given by our Lord relative to the siege and the destruction of Jerusalem could not possibly have been the result of any mere investigation of naturally observable political or military trends. At the time that our Lord made His prophecy the relations between the Roman empire and the Jewish commonwealth were relatively satisfactory. As a matter of fact the treatment accorded the Jews by the Romans had been at least as good as that given to any other subject race. Furthermore, it was not the custom of the Romans to destroy utterly a city which was within their own empire and thereby to cut down the revenue which they could expect to gain out of that city. When He made that prediction, and made it with such certainty that His followers within it actually left the doomed capital when the signs which He foretold began to be manifest, He was evidently offering to men an article of knowledge which could have come from God alone.

That knowledge then constituted a real and ascertainable divine signature. To have given it in support of a claim which was unjustified, God would have had either to lie to His creatures or to have been ignorant of the matter under consideration. Both of these alternatives are obviously impossible. As a result the assent of faith which is given to doctrine whose divine origin has been attested by means of verified prophecy is a reasonable act. The prophecy is a valid and important motive of credibility.[17]

The oracles with which the ancient world abounded were for the most part couched in terms so ambiguous that there could be some reason for thinking that the prediction had been accomplished in any event. Thus there was nothing certain about them. The true prophecy is, of course, one which is understood by the persons to whom it is addressed. It must be understood by them in such a way that, after it has been fulfilled, these people will be able to remember the prophecy itself and to know that this fulfillment brings evidence that the claim in favor of which the prophecy was cited is thereby shown to

---

17 Cf. Baierl, *The Theory of Revelation*, Vol. 2, pp. 424–532. This is the most complete treatise on the nature, the discernibility, and the evidential value of prophecy available in English.

be rational and credible. It will be the business of apologetics to show that such has been the case with regard to the Christian message.

15. Miracles in the moral and social order. But the physical miracle and the prophecy, which is itself a miracle of the intellectual order, are by no means the only divine works which can and should be cited as motives of credibility. There are such things as effects produced evidently and visibly in human society, effects which obviously never could have been brought about through the power of a merely natural cause. These are the so-called moral and social miracles. The Church puts herself forward as a social miracle, as something which could not have been produced and maintained in the world through merely natural agencies. The history of the human race and the experience which we have with men and societies in the world around us are able to show us very clearly how human beings and the societies which they constitute react to the operation of created agencies. The Church claims that she herself exhibits characteristics which never could have been brought about other than through the action of God Himself, carried on independently and outside of the laws which govern the ordinary and natural procedure of human societies. "Moreover the Church by herself, by reason of her wonderful propagation, her eminent holiness and her unexhausted fruitfulness in all good things, by reason of Catholic unity and unconquered stability, is a certain great and perpetual motive of credibility and an unshakable testimony of her own divine messengership."[18]

Under this heading we can consider the naturally inexplicable patience of the martyrs, the perseverance of the Church through the centuries as a holy society and all of the other aspects of her life which the traditional apologists have described. Associated with this are such obviously divine works as the ineffable holiness and wisdom of Christ who is the vehicle through whom the doctrine of the Church has been presented to the world, the admirable consistency of the teaching itself and its outstanding holiness. All of these are effects which could not have been produced by any merely created power. They thus constitute motives of credibility external to us but intrinsic to the teaching which is shown to be credible. They are motives less striking than the miracles and prophecies, but they demon-

---

18 The Vatican Council, The Constitution, *Dei Filius*, Ch. 3 (Denzinger, 1794).

strate the credibility of any doctrine in conjunction with the primary motives themselves.

16. The internal motives of credibility. The internal motives are valuable as adjuncts to the external. By themselves alone they are not competent to engender that certitude which is requisite for a real and effective judgment of credibility. But they can offer real evidence to show that the doctrine which claims to be revealed by God really has come from Him. The individual internal motives may in the lives of those concerned offer evidence far more consoling, and for that matter far more compelling than that afforded by the objective criteria of revelation. They have their own place and function in the field of apologetics. They are only abused when an attempt is made to substitute them for the external motives of credibility. They must not be expected to offer evidence which they were never intended to give.

A divine work as such can be a motive of credibility. It is, however, a criterion by which we can judge that this particular body of doctrine is divinely revealed only when it is cited in support of the claims of this teaching before the work has actually been performed. Thus a miracle shows the credibility of that teaching to which it is attached, and no other. It is attached to a body of doctrine when the man who offers this doctrine promises to perform a miracle in order to show that it has come from God, or when he states that what he is going to do will be an unmistakable indication of his own office as a divine messenger. The appeal can obviously be made to an individual miracle or to a group of these acts. In any case it is obvious that the omniscient and all-holy God could not perform works which would mislead His people. He could not be party to a lie. His performance of a work which is cited in support of a claim of revelation makes the doctrine He signs something which can be believed reasonably. The miracle constitutes a signature of God, and the placing of the miracle is as much the effect of His power and wisdom as is the performance of the act itself.

17. Certitude and the judgment of credibility. It is obvious that, in a matter as far reaching as an acceptance of a doctrine which claims to be divinely revealed, there must be a real certitude in the judgment of credibility. A man would certainly not act with prudence if he were to accept on the authority of God some doctrine which offered merely probable evidence of divine authorship. If there were any fear or danger that the doctrine had not been revealed by God, then a man would have no sufficient reason to alter the course of his whole life in accepting it firmly on the divine authority. The Catholic Church, in proposing this doctrine which she knows to be divinely revealed, and which she realizes is absolutely necessary for the men to whom it is addressed, insists that these men should receive certain and clear indication of its divine origin. She is quite well aware that a prudent act of faith could not follow upon a mere grouping of probabilities.[19]

However, we can well ask what sort of certitude we may expect in the judgment of credibility which would precede a prudent and reasonable act of faith. First of all, of course, there is perfect and metaphysical certitude about the possibility of miracles, prophecies, and the other divine works which are cited as criteria of revelation and about their demonstrative function in the proof of credibility. The certitude is that which we obtain through the analysis of an object, seeing exactly what is contained in that object. We have metaphysical certitude about the possibility of "divine works" and about their effectiveness as motives of credibility. The divine work is possible and is seen as such because we know that God is the First Cause of the universe, creating and maintaining the things of this world in existence with absolute freedom from any restriction by the laws which govern the activity of creatures. They are valid criteria of revelation because they are obviously effects which could be produced only by the power of God Himself. They can be motives of credibility for this particular doctrine, when they are performed obviously and clearly in support of a claim that this teaching has come from God.

However, the evidence that these divine works have actually been accomplished in favor of a particular teaching does not come to all men in the same way. There is one kind of evidence which the onlookers at the working of a miracle could have which would not come

---

19 She has condemned as a modernistic error the statement that "the assent of faith is ultimately based on an assembly of probabilities" *(The Decree Lamentabili,* July 3, 1907, Denzinger, 2025), and has stated clearly in the antimodernist oath that external proofs of revelation, that is, divine works and first of all miracles and prophecies are *most certain* signs of the divine origin of the Christian religion, most perfectly adapted to the intelligence of men of all ages and also to the intelligence of men of this time (Denzinger, 2145).

to someone who heard of this miracle through the testimony of others. The first kind of evidence is visual and immediate. It goes with the type of certitude which is spoken of as physical. The man who could see the actual performance of a miracle could be as sure of this as he ever could be of the production of any other effect in the world around him. The second kind of evidence is historical. It is of the same type as that which is offered to man for the existence and the nature of things which he has never seen, but about which he is quite as certain as he is about the realities with which he has come into physical contact. It belongs to that sort of certitude which is called moral. This moral certitude, a real and objective firmness of assent to a proposition, an assent which is faced neither with the fear nor the danger of error, is the certitude which comes to the men of our time in their grasp of the judgment of credibility.

We must understand fully the perfection of this certitude. The judgment which is based upon the testimony of the human race or the testimony of reliable witnesses is just as strong as that which proceeds from physical evidence. The fact of the matter is, of course, that by his very nature man is meant to accept knowledge from others. He would not be a social being were it not for the fact that through communication with his fellow men he receives the information and the knowledge which are requisite to him. Some of the most important items in all his store of knowledge are facts of which he could not possibly be aware except through the testimony of other men.

Now there are certain definite criteria by which we are able to judge the acceptability of testimony which is offered by men in order that we may form this morally certain judgment. In the first place, we can only accept that testimony which is in harmony with evidence offered by those who have had a chance actually to observe the events about which the testimony is given. We must be sure that the person who offers the testimony actually knows what he is telling us about, and at the same time certain that he has no intention of deceiving us. That evidence is not difficult to obtain. We can easily discern the historical reliability of those sources which tell us about the motives of credibility offered in favor of Jesus and His Apostles. At the same time we must not forget that we have always with us that manifest social miracle which is the Catholic Church.

18. The distinction between the certitude of credibility and that of faith. However, the certitude of the judgment of credibility is something quite distinct from the certitude of faith itself. The reason why we assent to a proposition which is received on divine faith cannot be other than the authority of God revealing. As such it is the most perfect and powerful certitude of which man is capable in this life. On the other hand, the certitude which is attached to the judgment of credibility is based upon the evidence of these divine works, which are the criteria of revelation. Such certitude is necessarily less than that of divine faith itself.

19. The freedom of faith. It must be understood that the assent of divine faith is in no way necessitated by the acceptance of the judgment of credibility. The Vatican Council insisted upon this fact. "If anyone should say that the assent of Christian faith is not free, but is necessarily produced by arguments of human reason; or that the grace of God is necessary only for the living faith which operates through charity, let him be anathema."[20] The judgment of credibility is presented to man as a conclusion which follows properly from certain premises, themselves manifestly correct. It is something which can be made in the light of human reason alone, although as a matter of fact when it is made by a man who is tending toward the acceptance of divine faith, it is something in which the man is actually aided by the grace of God. The fifth canon of the Second Council of Orange makes the Church's teaching on this point quite clear. "If anyone says that, as the increase, so also the beginning of faith and the very tendency toward belief (*ipsumque credulitatis affectum*), by which we believe in Him who justifies the man who is averted from God and by which we attain to the regeneration of holy baptism, is within us not through the gift of grace, that is through the inspiration of the Holy Ghost correcting our will from infidelity to faith, but (says) that it is in us naturally, he is shown to be an adversary of the apostolic dogmas, since the blessed Paul says, 'We are confident of this very thing, that He, who hath begun a good work in you, will perfect it unto the day of Christ Jesus.'[21] And again, 'For unto you it is given for Christ, not only to believe in Him, but also to suffer for

---

20 Canon 5, *De Fide* (Denzinger, 1814).
21 Phil. 1:6.

Him.'[22] And 'by grace you are saved through faith, and that not of yourselves: for it is the gift of God.'"[23]

The same truth is brought out even more clearly in a subsequent canon of the same council. "If anyone affirms that a person can think as is fitting or choose any good which pertains to the salvation of eternal life or consent to the salutary, that is, to the evangelical preaching through the power of nature and without the illumination and the inspiration of the Holy Ghost, who gives to all the savor *(suavitatem)* in consenting to and believing the truth, he is deceived by the heretical spirit, not understanding the voice of God in the gospel, saying, 'Without Me you can do nothing'[24] and that of the Apostle, 'Not that we are sufficient to think anything of ourselves, as of ourselves: but our sufficiency is from God.'"[25]

20. The motive of faith and the judgment of credibility. But even though the certitude of the judgment of credibility in the man who tends toward the essentially supernatural assent of divine faith is something which is brought about with the aid of divine grace, the evidence on which that certain judgment is based is natural. Thus it is more probable that the certitude about the fact of divine revelation which we gain through the examination of the motives of credibility is essentially distinct from that which we possess in the act of faith itself. According to the doctrine of St. Thomas Aquinas and of his school, in the act of faith the fact of divine revelation is at once the thing which we believe and the motive reason which specifies the act. It is that in the light of which all the other truths which have been communicated by God to man are accepted. However, it is at the same time something which we accept as having been revealed by God. In the same way, in the act of sight, the light is something which is seen and is at the same time that by which all other objects are perceived.

There are definite reasons for making this assertion. In the first place the act of faith itself is something essentially supernatural. It belongs to a realm of being which is absolutely beyond the natural

---

22 Phil. 1:29.
23 Eph. 2:8; Cf. Denzinger, 178.
24 John 15:5.
25 2 Cor. 3:5 Canon 7, Denzinger, 180.

competence of any creature, actual or possible, because it consists in the perception of the divine mysteries themselves. It is, as St. Paul has put it, "the substance of things to be hoped for, the evidence of things that appear not."[26] The intellectual possession of these truths constitutes an act which is distinctively and intrinsically supernatural.

But after all, an act is specified ultimately by its formal motive. And, if the act of faith were motivated by the fact of divine revelation, as this is known naturally through the inspection of the motives of credibility, the same intellectual operation would be at once intrinsically supernatural insofar as it consisted in the possession of the divine mysteries, and formally natural insofar as it was motivated and specified by a reality as true in the light of natural reason alone.

Furthermore, the expressions of Holy Scripture imply the thesis that revelation, as it is the motive of divine faith, is something which is seen in the light of faith itself rather than merely something which is accepted on naturally attainable evidence. As Garrigou-Lagrange remarks,[27] in the Scriptures the motive of faith, or the reason why we believe is spoken of as the voice of the Father or of the Son, and as the testimony of the Holy Ghost. It is said that even the Pharisees and the scribes who had seen the miracles performed by our Lord "had never heard the voice of the Father."[28] These men had most certainly seen the evidences of credibility, and had seen them more clearly than most of those to whom the message of Jesus Christ is addressed. But they had not seen that which was the motive of faith. They had not perceived that reality through which alone men can accept the teaching of God on His authority. They had not become aware of the fact of divine revelation in the only way in which that fact enters into the act of faith itself.

It is perfectly true that their failure to hear the voice of the Father was to be ascribed to their own hardness of heart. They did not wish to believe. But at the same time they were perfectly cognizant of the effectiveness of our Lord's miracles. "Many therefore of the Jews who were come to Mary and Martha, and had seen the things that Jesus did, believed in Him. But some of them went to the Phari-

---

26 Heb. 11:1.
27 *De Revelatione*, Vol. 1, p. 463.
28 John 5:36.

sees, and told them the things that Jesus had done. The chief priests therefore and the Pharisees gathered a council, and said: 'What do we, for this man doth many miracles? If we let Him alone so, all will believe in Him: and the Romans will come, and take away our place and nation.'"[29] The action of these men makes it clear that the act of divine faith is free, and that it is not forced through the evidences of credibility. But at the same time it indicates that the knowledge of divine revelation which enters into the act of faith is something of a different order from that knowledge of revelation which proceeds from the inspection of naturally observable criteria.

This question of the ultimate resolution of faith, as it is known in the technical literature of sacred theology, has more than a merely academic interest in the field of apologetics. On the solution of this problem depends the attitude of the Christian toward the content of apologetics, and in some measure at least, his appreciation of the faith as a gift of God. If the fact of divine revelation, as known with certainty through the inspection of the motives of credibility were as such the formal motive of faith, the apologetics would be properly the approach to the faith itself. The act of faith would be more properly spoken of as something supernaturalized, rather than as something distinctively and essentially supernatural because the very motive or reason which governs it would be something ascertainable in the natural light of human reason.

Actually, of course, there is nothing to confirm the teaching that the fact of revelation, seen through the motives of credibility, is the motive of divine faith in all the observable activity of Christians.

The faith of the unlettered, of those who have at best an imperfect cognizance of the motives of credibility, is frequently more intense than the faith of the men who are most perfectly cognizant with the criteria of revelation. It is true that this perfection of faith can be explained in some way by the transcendent truth of the freedom which characterizes our belief in God. But, unless we accept the common and Thomistic teaching, we shall have the embarrassing difficulty of trying to explain how this faith of the unlettered could be more perfect *as faith*. For, if the motive of faith were the fact of divine revelation or the authority of God revealing, as this is seen through the

---

29 John 11:45–48.

natural processes of human reason, then obviously the faith of that man who does not know how to discern this naturally obtainable evidence should be less perfect than the belief of the man who is able to formulate and appreciate the naturally obtainable proofs. We could see how the unlearned man's charity might be stronger than his fellow's. But there would be at least grave difficulty in trying to demonstrate how this faith could be superior to that of the trained apologist. And the fact of the matter is that the strength of faith is of itself independent of training in the sciences requisite for the proper presentation of the motives of than his fellow's credibility.

Accepting this traditional and Thomistic conclusion, we may confidently expect of the science of apologetics only that which it is qualified to give a demonstration of the rational credibility of Catholic dogma. We do not expect to obtain out of the proofs of apologetics a grasp of the motive of the faith itself. Obviously the demonstration of credibility is cogent, even though the truth which we ascertain through this process is not formally the motive of divine faith. The divine works which are motives of credibility can show us that the naturally knowable Creator of the universe has attested the validity of a claim put forward that this message is divinely revealed. The man who is cognizant of that proof and of its force can reasonably accept the revelation which is presented to him as the teaching of God. He can reasonably assent to the evident credibility of Catholic dogma as divine revelation.

Chapter 7

THE PROCESS OF PROOF

1. All apologetics should be organized in such a way as most effectively to demonstrate the credibility of Catholic dogma. Once we have ascertained what is meant when we say that a doctrine has been revealed by God, and once we have learned the objective and satisfactory criteria, in the light of which we can know whether a doctrine has been revealed or not, it is our work to examine the teaching in question in the light of these criteria. The doctrine which we, as Catholic apologists, put forward as revealed is obviously that which we accept on divine faith. According to the testimony of the Vatican Council expressing the official and solemn teaching of the Church, "All of those things must be believed with divine and Catholic faith which are contained in the written Word of God or in tradition and which are proposed by the Church, either in her solemn judgment or in her ordinary and universal magisterium to be believed as divinely revealed."[1] The truths thus proposed by the Church and accepted by her children, the truths which we mean to demonstrate as rationally credible in the process of apologetics, constitute what is known as Catholic dogma.

This Catholic dogma is presented to men as the teaching of Jesus Christ, the Son of God. In describing the divine revelation entrusted to her as something quite distinct from a merely natural knowledge about God, the Church uses the words of St. Paul which assert that this divine teaching came to man through the prophets and then finally through the Son of God Himself. "God, who at sundry times and in divers manners spoke in times past to the fathers by the prophets: last of all, in these days hath spoken to us by His Son."[2]

---
1 The Constitution *Dei Filius*, Ch. 3 (Denzinger, 1792).
2 Heb. 1:1, 2. The pertinent passage from the council may be found in Denzinger 1785.

As a result, the central function of apologetics is to ascertain whether or not we have any naturally attainable evidence to the effect that this Person whom we know as Jesus of Nazareth really claimed to have a divine message and actually demonstrated the credibility of this teaching. It is the business of apologetics to examine this doctrine in the light of all those motives of credibility which are manifestly objective and satisfactory criteria and to which the Catholic Church actually appeals. Furthermore, the apologist must be able to show that here and now, in the twentieth century and in the United States of America, it is reasonable to accept with the assent of divine faith some teaching which claims to be the same divine revelation which was made through Jesus Christ.

2. Divisions in traditional apologetics. For the attainment of this purpose, many of the books of apologetics which appeared during the early years of this century, and even some of the more recent ones have divided their matter into two distinct sets of proofs. One of these is the Christian demonstration, the process of manifesting evidence to show that the message preached by Jesus Christ actually was rationally credible as divine revelation. The second portion is the Catholic demonstration, the proof that only within the Catholic Church is the teaching of Christ to be found in all its completeness and perfection. The conclusion of this Catholic demonstration, according to the texts which distinguish it as a separate portion of apologetics, is that the Catholic Church is actually essential for man's salvation, and that membership in the Catholic Church and the acceptance of its creed is thereby a rational and prudent thing. In such manuals these two proofs, the Christian and the Catholic demonstration, were added to the general part of apologetics, the investigation of the meaning of revelation as this term is applied to the Catholic message, so as to form with it the complete science of apologetics.[3]

---

[3] Antonius Michelitsch in his *Elementa Apologeticae sine Theologiae Fundamentalis* (Graz and Vienna, 1925) 3 ed., p. 5, divides this science into four parts: (1) Philosophy of Religion, (2) The treatise on Revelation, (3) The Christian demonstration, (4) The Catholic demonstration. Archbishop Valentine Zubizarreta, O.C.D., in his *Theologia Fundamentalis*, 3 ed. (Bilbao, 1937), p. 67, considers apologetics as composed of two treatises: (1) on the true religion and (2) on the institution of the Church. Canon J. M. Hervé adopts the same division in his *Manuale Theologiae Dogmaticae* (Paris, 1929), Vol. 1, p. 19; as does Ad. Tanquerey, *Synopsis Theologiae Dogmaticae Fundamentalis*, 21 ed.

3. The procedure most consistent with the scientific unity manifest in apologetics. However, since the masterly methodological study of Gardeil[4] and the classical treatise *De Revelatione* of Garrigou-Lagrange, there has been a manifest tendency to adopt another mode of procedure. The eminent theologian of the Angelico called attention to the inefficacy of any demonstration which showed the credibility of a Christian message merely as something which had been given in the past. The thing to be proven in the process of apologetics is obviously the credibility of this doctrine as it is accepted here and now by those who profess the Catholic faith.

4. This doctrine which asserts the prerogative of divine revelation to living and present. As a matter of fact a man would form an inadequate notion of the workings of apologetics if he were to think of it as ordered, even in one integral part, to establish the rational credibility of a body of teaching which had been brought forward centuries ago but which, as far as the proofs of credibility themselves are concerned, has no direct bearing on the conditions and the men of our own time. For, according to this division of special apologetics into a Christian and a Catholic demonstration, the latter would merely indicate that the teaching of Christ is now entrusted to an infallible agency which Christ Himself founded and which He wished all men to join. It happens that this conclusion belongs to a treatise on the Church rather than directly to the process of apologetics itself. Apologetics is meant to lead to a demonstration of credibility, and the proof that the Catholic Church is the true

---

(Paris, 1925), p. 544; and Felder, in his *Apologetica*. Among the more popular works thus divided is *Christian Apologetics*, by W. Devivier, S.J., edited by Bishop Messmer (New York, 1903). Archbishop Sheehan, *Apologetics and Catholic Doctrine*, 4 ed. (Dublin, 1940), Canon Boulenger, *Manuel d'Apologetique*, 3 volumes (Paris, 1924, and Canon Eugene Duplessy, *Apologetique*, 8 ed. (Lyon and Paris, 1937), all divide apologetics into three parts, prefacing the Christian and Catholic demonstrations with a treatise on the necessity of religion.

4 *La Credibilite et L'Apologetique*, New Edition (Paris, 1928). This book and the masterly article "Credibilite" in the *Dictionnaire de Theologie Catholique*, Vol. 3, columns 2201–2310, were written to clear up the existing confusion about the extent and the exact function of apologetics. The excellent article "Apologetique" by Maisonneuve in the *Dictionnaire de Theologie Catholique*, Vol. I, columns 1511–1580, had shown the need for advance in the methodology of this science.

Church is by no means identical with the process of showing that the doctrine which it presents is actually credible as divine revelation.

5. The procedure in apologetics must be governed by the fact that the Church herself claims to be a motive of credibility. However, there is still another factor to be taken into consideration in deciding how to proceed with the proofs of credibility in apologetics. The fact of the matter is that the Catholic Church resolutely claims that the motives of credibility as such belong to her, and that furthermore she is herself a motive of credibility, clear and perpetual. "To the Catholic Church alone belong all those things, so many and so wonderful, which are divinely disposed to the evident credibility of the Christian faith. Moreover, the Church by herself, through her admirable propagation, her eminent holiness her unexhausted fruitfulness in all good things, through her unconquered ability is a certain great and perpetual motive of credibility and an irrefutable witness of her own divine mission."[5]

Now the only meaning which can be drawn from the claim that the motives of credibility belong to the Catholic Church alone is that we are not to regard Christianity or the message of Jesus Christ as something which is in any way really distinct from the teaching of this same Catholic Church. In other words, in demonstrating the rational credibility of that message which Jesus of Nazareth preached to men, we are actually proving the credibility of the Catholic doctrine. The Christian message cannot be regarded as a sort of general good which is somewhat restricted when it is presented by the Catholic Church exclusively. Christianity and Catholicism are one in such a way that there could be no valid proof of the credibility of the Christian message which would not be by that very fact a proof of the acceptability of Catholic dogma. Thus there is, according to the dogmatic claim of the Church herself, only one process of demonstrating the credibility of her doctrine.

The thing which we set out to demonstrate as credible in the science of apologetics is that teaching which here and now we receive on the authority of God revealing. The assertion that the motives of credibility belong to the Catholic Church alone is a part of this Catholic dogma. Furthermore, the very fact that the Church is willing

---

5 The Constitution *Dei Filius*, Ch. 3 (Denzinger, 1794).

to present herself as a motive of credibility, and entrust the results of an investigation into the acceptability of her own doctrine to an examination of her supernatural character, is an indication that logically the demonstration of apologetics should not be divided arbitrarily into a Christian proof as opposed to a Catholic proof. If the Church really is a motive of credibility by reason of the characteristics manifest in her constitution and in her activity, she is obviously a kind of divine work which shows the credibility of the Christian message exactly as it is being proposed by herself. And if the motives of credibility are to be grouped together, then the demonstration of credibility which comes from the consideration of these motives will apply to the teaching of Jesus Christ exactly as it is expounded by and in the Catholic Church.

On the other hand, if she herself turns out to be an organization which is obviously explicable in function of merely natural causes, then the validity of her claim as a whole is destroyed. If such a result could be shown, then there would be no question of the credibility of Catholic dogma, here and now proposed to all men. The only thing which could be demonstrated as credible would be a teaching which was brought to the world over nineteen hundred years ago. If Catholic dogma as it is expressed here and now is not shown to be evidently credible, then the faith of the men of our day is not defended in the science of apologetics.

6. The implications consequent upon immutability of dogma. Thus the realism which must govern the processes of apologetics demands or at least suggests that we should conduct our proof directly toward the credibility of Catholic dogma. This is, according to the claim of the Church herself, something which is absolutely unchanging in substance. There is no mutation in the meaning of those formulae which have once been submitted by the Catholic Church as articles to be accepted by all men on the authority of God revealing. "Nor is the doctrine of faith which God has revealed proposed as a philosophical finding, to be perfected by human genius. It is rather entrusted as a divine deposit to the Spouse of Christ, to be cared for faithfully and to be declared infallibly. Hence that meaning, of the sacred dogmas is to be retained which holy mother the Church has once declared, nor must we ever abandon that meaning under the pretext and the name of a higher understanding. 'Let the understanding, the knowledge, the wisdom of individuals as well as of all, of one man as well as of the entire Church grow and advance much and powerfully by the degrees of the ages and of the eras: but always within its own class alone, that is in the same dogma, with the same sense and the same meaning.'"[6] The unchanging character of her teaching would be manifested as a credible doctrine if the Church herself can be alleged as a motive of credibility. But, as we have seen, this motive of credibility is not meant to be separated from those other signs of the divine origin of the Catholic teaching.

7. The progressive method. We have, however, two distinct alternatives in proceeding to show the rational credibility of that teaching which was preached by Jesus Christ and which is proposed as such by the Catholic Church. In the first place we can proceed historically or by what is known as the progressive method. Thus we consider the teaching which was brought forward by our Lord in the way in which it was presented to the people of His time. We know that He claimed His teaching to be the fulfillment of a revelation which had begun with the very origins of the human race, and which had developed during the ages until the period in which He lived and preached. Thus there was, according to His own teaching, a primitive, a patriarchal, and a Mosaic revelation, all of which were continued and finally perfected in the message which He presented to the people of God. Obviously, then, it is possible to consider the indications of credibility as these attach themselves to each of these parts into which the divine message is divided. We could consider the divine works which testified to the authenticity of that message which was proposed as God's own teaching by the patriarchs and the prophets of the Old Testament. As a matter of fact several prominent and well-written books of apologetics proceed in exactly this manner.[7]

8. The regressive method and its advantages. Or, on the other hand, we can proceed by what is termed the regressive method. We

---

6 Denzinger, 1800. The Council cited the words of Vincent of Lerins in his *Commonitorium* at the end of this passage credibility.

7 Among such traditional works we find the treatise *de Religione* which is the second volume of the *Theologia Wirceburgensis*, 3 ed. (Paris, 1880); Dorsch, *Institutiones Theologiae Fundamentalis*, Vol. 1; Knoll a Bulsano, *Institutiones Theologiae Dogmaticae Generalis seu Fundamentalis*.

can consider the signs of credibility exactly as these are attached to the message which is proposed by Jesus Christ and presented as such by the Catholic Church.[8] This regressive or concrete method has several obvious advantages. In the first place it is considerably more effective. The teaching of Jesus Christ came as the terminus and the perfection of that message which had been in the possession of men since the time of Adam himself. As a consequence the criteria of revelation which manifested the credibility of this message are much more readily available to us than those which were used to show the divine origin of that teaching that was presented by the patriarchs and the prophets of the Old Testament. The natural light of human reason, which alone can be used in drawing the conclusion of credibility, will shine with much greater clarity on events which are placed within the limits of definite historical and literary criticism. Furthermore, the divine attestation to the effect that the teaching presented by Jesus Christ and proposed by the Catholic Church is actually credible would not have been given by an all-wise and all-just God if the claim inherent in this message, to the effect that it constitutes the completion and the perfection of a previously existing body of divine teaching, had not been substantiated.

Through the use of this regressive and direct method, we come to the understanding of the credibility of Catholic dogma, exactly as it stands and as it is brought to the men of our own time. Through the use of this method the purpose of apologetics as a science is properly attained. It is best adapted to the study of apologetics according to the method which has been elaborated and demonstrated by Gardeil.

In utilizing this method, it is first incumbent upon us to show that we have naturally acceptable historical evidence about the life and the teachings of Jesus of Nazareth. Once we have shown the existence of this evidence, we must utilize it in order to see if this Man actually claimed to be the Bearer of a divine message. Obviously there would be no possibility of treating His teaching as something credible and acceptable for divine revelation, if He Himself never made the claim that His teaching was of divine origin. The third step must consist in examining this same evidence to see if actually He set forth a distinct

---

8 This is the procedure followed by Garrigou-Lagrange, *De Revelatione*; by Felder, *Apologetica*; by Dieckmann, *De Revelatione Christiana*; and by most modern authors.

body of doctrine, rather than merely certain principles of morality. Finally, once we have seen that He did teach a body of doctrine, we must examine this teaching in the light of the wonders which were accomplished to convince men that this teaching really was from God, and had to be received with the assent of divine faith. After this second and essential portion of apologetics has been completed, there will only remain the task of seeing what sort of obligation binds man to accept a teaching which is shown to be credible as divine revelation.

Chapter 8

THE HISTORICAL EVIDENCE ABOUT JESUS OF NAZARETH

1. The need for historical evidence in apologetics. There can be no such thing as a rational demonstration of credibility for the teaching of Jesus of Nazareth unless we have at our disposal historical sources which are obviously reliable. Since He lived and died over nineteen hundred years ago, the only naturally and historically acceptable testimony about Him and about His activity is ultimately to be sought in genuine and incorrupt volumes, written during the lifetime of His contemporaries by men who intended to tell the truth and who actually had at their disposal means for ascertaining the matters about which they wrote. Actually we do possess such historically reliable testimony. It is the business of apologetics to point out the existence of these writings and their evidence of reliability.

The writings pertinent to the life and the teaching of our Lord are both Christian and non-Christian. Among these latter books are some of pagan origin and others of Jewish origin. The extant pagan sources tell us very little about the activity of our Lord, although even in themselves they show that He existed and exercised an incomparably powerful religious influence during the first century of our era. In spite of their many imperfections, they constitute valuable sources for the science of apologetics, testifying as they do to the knowledge about Christ and His work of contemporary pagan writers.

2. The pagan sources. Gaius Suetonius Tranquillus, the Roman historian who flourished around the end of the first century of our era, wrote in his life of the emperor Claudius, "Since the Jews constantly made disturbances at the instigation of Chrestus, he (Claudius) expelled them from Rome."[1] The event he describes is one

---

1 Suetonius, *De Vita Caesarum. Vita Claudii*, Ch. 25. Cf. *Documents Illustrative of the History*

which took place in either the year 51 or 52 of our era. It is interesting to note that this same event is mentioned by St. Luke. "After these things departing from Athens, he came to Corinth. And finding a certain Jew named Aquila, born in Pontus, lately come from Italy, with Priscilla his wife (because that Claudius had commanded all Jews to depart from Rome), he came to them."[2] The arrival of St. Paul in Corinth, after his Athenian preaching, was in the year 52.

The fact that Suetonius referred to Jesus of Nazareth as Chrestus is patent from another excerpt from his own work. In his life of Nero he lists among the accomplishments of this emperor his punishment of the Christians. "Punishment was inflicted upon the Christians, a class of men given to a novel and pernicious superstition."[3] Writing at the time he did, Suetonius (*Vita Neronis*, No. 16) was fully aware that the Chrestus to whom he referred was the founder of the hated society of the Christians. Christians were still under the ban of the empire, and it was known by all that they had been founded by One who was a Jew and had been condemned by the Roman authorities at the instigation of His own people. Furthermore, at the end of the year 197, when the matchless Tertullian wrote his *Apologeticus*, the pagans still mispronounced the name of Christiani as Chrestian. "There is no good great enough to overcome the hatred of the Christians. Now, therefore, if this be the hatred of a name, what is the fault of a name? What accusation can be raised against words save that the very sound of a certain name is barbarous or unlucky or accursed or shameful? But 'Christian' as far as its interpretation goes, is derived from 'anointing.' But even when you mispronounce it 'Chrestian' (for you have not even a sure knowledge of the name), it is composed of sweetness and benignity."[4]

Tacitus, an older contemporary of Suetonius, gives much clearer and more correct teaching about our Lord, even though his prejudice against the Christian name was no less apparent. This is his account of the persecution of the Christians which took place under Nero,

---

of the Church, edited by B. J. Kidd, D.D. (New York and London, 1938), Vol. 1, No. 37.
2 Acts 18:1, 2.
3 Suetonius, *Vita Neronis*, Ch. 16. Cf. Kidd, *Documents*, Vol. 1, No. 38.
4 Tertullian, *Apologeticus*, Ch. 3. There is a similar play on the term "Chrestian" in the *First Apology* of St. Justin Martyr, Chapter 4.

the first emperor to proscribe the followers of our Lord. "Neither human aid, nor imperial munificence, nor all the modes of placating heaven, could stifle scandal or dispel the belief that the fire had been started by order. Therefore, to scotch the rumor, Nero substituted as culprits, and punished with the utmost refinements of cruelty, a class of men, loathed for their vices, whom the crowd called Christians. Christus, the founder of the name, had undergone the death penalty during the reign of Tiberius, by sentence of the procurator, Pontius Pilatus, and the pernicious superstition was checked for a moment only to break out once more, not merely in Judea, the home of the disease, but also in the capital itself, where all things horrible or disgraceful in the world collect and find a vogue. First, then, the confessed members of the sect were arrested; next, on their disclosures, vast numbers were, convicted, not so much on account of arson as for hatred of the human race. And derision accompanied their end: they were covered with the skins of wild beasts and torn to pieces by dogs; or they were fastened on crosses, and, when daylight failed, were burned to serve as torches by night. Nero had offered his gardens for the spectacle, and gave an exhibition in his circus, mixing with the crowd in the attire of a charioteer, or mounted on his car. Hence in spite of a guilt which had earned the most exemplary punishment, there arose a sentiment of pity, due to the impression that they were being sacrificed not for the welfare of the state but to the ferocity of a single man."[5]

The correspondence between Gaius Plinius Caecilius Secundus, and his superior the emperor Trajan while the former was prefect of Bithynia gives valuable information about the followers of Christ and shows that even a pagan knew that Christians considered Him as divine. This correspondence was carried on in the years around 113. The younger Pliny reported on his treatment of the Christians. "I have conducted myself in this manner with regard to those who were brought before me as Christians. I have asked them if they were Christians. When they confessed I interrogated them a second and a third time, threatening punishment. I have ordered those who persevered to be put to death. Nor did I doubt (whatever it was that

---

[5] Publius Cornelius Tacitus, *The Annals*, Book 15, Ch. 44. Cf. Kidd, *Documents*, Vol. 1, No. 22.

they might have admitted), that this stubborn and certainly inflexible obstinacy ought to be punished. But they affirmed that this was the extent of their fault or error: that it was their custom on a stated day to gather together before dawn to sing in concert a hymn to Christ as to a God; and to bind themselves by oath, not to any crime but rather not to commit robbery, thievery, or adultery, not to break faith nor to refuse to return goods deposited with them when they were called upon to do so. Having done these things, it was their habit to disperse and then again to gather to take food, which, however, is common and harmless. They have, however, ceased to do this after my edict in which I forbade secret meetings as you ordered. For so much greater reason, I believed it necessary to seek what is true by torture from two servant women who were called deaconesses, but I found nothing other than an evil and extravagant superstition. And so, having adjourned the inquiry, I have had recourse to your advice. It seemed to me a matter worth consulting about, especially because of the number of those endangered. For many persons of every age, of every order, and of both sexes are called and will be called into peril. For the contagion of this superstition has spread, not only through the cities but also through the villages and the country, yet still it seems possible to check and correct it."[6]

The emperor Trajan replied to this letter of Pliny's with another epistle which is still extant. "You have followed the proper procedure, my dear Secundus, in dealing with the cases of those who had been brought to you as Christians. Nothing, however, can be decided as a universal rule which would have any definite form. They are not to be sought out. If they are brought to court and convicted, they are to be punished, but in such a way that he who denies that he is a Christian, and who makes this most evident by the deed itself, that is by supplicating our gods, may obtain acquittal through his recantation, even though he was suspect in the past. Anonymous accusations must not be used in any process, for this procedure is of the very worst example, and does not belong to our age."[7]

---

6 The Letters of Pliny, Book 10 No. 96; cf. Kidd, *Documents*, Vol. 1, No, 14.
7 Trajan to Pliny. This document is found among the letters of Pliny, Book 10, No. 97; cf. Kidd, *Documents*, Vol. 1, No. 15.

A few years later, around 125, the emperor Hadrian sent a similar letter to the proconsul of Asia, Minucius Fundanus. This letter is cited by St. Justin Martyr at the end of his *First Apology*.[8]

These pagan sources about the life of Christ tell us very little. They give evidence of the confusion existing in the comfortable and self-sufficient fashionable pagan world with reference to those men who had been condemned by the law of the empire. But there is no confusion whatsoever on certain fundamental points. The pagans knew very well that Jesus of Nazareth was by no means a mythical person. They knew very well that He had lived, and that He had suffered the death of a condemned malefactor in Judea during the reign of their own prefect, Pontius Pilate. They were very well aware that the empire was quickly filling up with men who worshiped this Jesus of Nazareth as God, and who were sincere and firm enough in their belief to prefer death itself to a denial of Jesus.

3. The Jewish sources. We have also certain Jewish teachings about the life of Christ, although even the Jewish Encyclopedia is honest enough to classify some of these writings as myths and legends about our Lord, rather than as truly historical data about His life and teaching.[9] The stories thus castigated are developments of those insults the Pharisees directed against Jesus during His own lifetime.

The first Jewish source is the paragraph from the Antiquities of Flavius Josephus, a writer who was born in AD 37 and died in the year 94. This has obviously no connection with the fabulous stories to which we have just referred. "At that time there existed Jesus, a wise man, if indeed it is proper to call Him a man at all. For He was a worker of wonderful deeds, the Master of those men who receive the true with pleasure: and He attracted many Jews and also many gentiles to Himself. He was the Christ. Those who had first loved Him did not cease to love Him when Pilate condemned Him to the punishment of the cross after He had been accused by the leaders of our men. He appeared to them again on the third day, revivified, the

---

8 The Rescript of Hadrian to Caius Minucius Fundanus, Proconsul of Asia. The complete text was given by Tyrannius Rufinus in his translation of Eusebius' *Ecclesiastical History*, Book 4, Ch. 9; see Kidd, *Documents*, Vol. I, No. 25.
9 The Jewish Encyclopedia, article "Jesus."

divine prophets having told these and a thousand other wonderful things about Him. And the nation of the Christians, named for Him, endures even until this day."[10]

Although the preponderance of evidence is in favor of the genuineness of this passage, there are still serious reasons for doubting that it was in the work as Josephus actually wrote it. The first Christian apologists who disputed against the Jews never cited this work, and it would seem likely that they would have cited it had they known of its existence. Eusebius of Caesarea mentions it in his *Ecclesiastical History*,[11] and although he was an eminent scholar, far beyond most of his contemporaries in critical powers, he has admitted as genuine certain documents which later writers came to recognize as spurious. Origen, however, expressly states that Flavius Josephus denied that Christ is the Messiah, a statement obviously contained in the passage under discussion.[12] The statement of Origen is by far the most serious objection which can be brought to bear against the authenticity of this passage.

On the other hand, all of the early codices of the Antiquities which exist in the world carry this passage. It would be at least surprising if all of the manuscripts of this Jewish author had fallen into the hands of the Christians, who had taken the trouble to insert into the text an approbation of Christ, attributing this to an author for whom they obviously cared very little. Furthermore, the paragraph occurs in Latin translations as well as in manuscript versions of the Greek original. Thus, from a point of view of documentary evidence, the passage is at least as well attested as any other portion of the works of Josephus.

---

10 *The Antiquities of the Jews*, Book 18, Ch. 3, No. 3. A good evaluation of this testimony, interesting although of no great moment in the apologetical process, will be found in *Jésus Christ, Sa Personne, Son Message, Ses Preuves*, by Father Leonce de Grandmaison, S.J., 17 ed. (Paris, 1931), Vol. 1, pp. 7–8.

11 Eusebius, *The Ecclesiastical History*, Book 1, Ch. 11.

12 Origen, *Contra Celsum*, Book 1, Ch. 47. The great Alexandrian blames Flavius Josephus for having described the destruction of Jerusalem as a punishment for the Jews' sin in slaying James, the brother of Jesus rather than as a retribution for the murder of Jesus Himself. The passage in Josephus to which Origen refers is to be found in *The Antiquities of the Jews*, Book 20, Ch. 9. Josephus mentions the stoning of "James, the brother of Jesus who was called the Christ."

The Historical Evidence About Jesus

As far as merely internal evidence is concerned, there can be no question of any serious decision against the authenticity of these words. Josephus was a Jew, but one who wrote for and among the Romans, the bitter enemies of his own people. The man who favored the cause and the arms of Rome could hardly have been expected to contradict the written proclamation of the Roman procurator who had condemned Jesus of Nazareth to the death of the cross. This procurator had written in the three languages that Jesus of Nazareth was the King of the Jews, the true Messiah. That inscription was visible above the head of the dying Christ. It is hardly to be wondered that the pro-Roman Jewish writer should insert into his text a notice which after all did nothing more or less than sum up the judgment of a Roman governor. Pilate who first wrote that message did not accept the faith of Jesus Christ. Then there is no reason for surprise in the fact that Josephus who set down the same statement should have remained outside of the society of those who followed the Master.

However, by reason of the objections which are raised against its authenticity, the passage of Flavius Josephus has very little moment in the proofs of Catholic apologetics. It is, however, something far more worthy and credible than the other notices about Jesus contained in Jewish writings. For there are remarks about Jesus of Nazareth contained in the Talmud, stories evidently colored by the hatred with which the leaders of the Jewish people never ceased to follow the most illustrious member of their nation. These stories were gathered together in a certain "Toledot Ieschu" (the Generations or the Life of Jesus), which appeared during the early middle ages. These stories which attribute every sort of infamy and wickedness to our Lord are rejected now even by Jewish scholars as sources for real historical knowledge about Jesus of Nazareth. They constitute one of the most grotesque and abominable exhibits in all of the line of literary perversity.

However, these same stories are of ancient origin. The writings of the Talmud were not brought together until long after the death of our Lord, but the teaching expressed in these writings was something handed down from rabbi to rabbi over a period of many generations.[13]

---

13 Strictly speaking the Talmuds contain interpretations of the Old Testament law. They are grouped around the Mischna, a sort of commentary which was taking form

Basically the stories about Christ contained in Talmudic literature are those which the Pharisees, the enemies of Jesus, circulated in order to interfere with the success of His mission. However, in spite of their blasphemous and scandalous character, they stand as indications of the reality and of the importance of Christ and His teaching. It is another example of that "unfortunate astuteness"[14] mentioned by St. Augustine, that the very stories which were spread abroad to defame Jesus, actually show forth the strength and the importance of His claims. It would be more than miraculous if the sort of person described in the Jewish legends could win adherents and found a society which actually covers the world. They picture a Man who is said to be weak, vacillating, uncertain, vicious, and stupid. Yet they testify that this Man was strong enough to win away thousands of adherents of the Mosaic Law, and to be adored as God by countless throngs of men.

Furthermore, these stories ape the actual facts in the life of Christ, as these are described in authentic and reliable historical documents.[15] In so doing they show very clearly the basic outlines of His work. They show Him as One who was born in a village of their own country and to a woman of royal blood. Their very charge of illegitimacy constitutes a recognition of the fact that their original teachers were aware of the story that He had been conceived apart from the activity of any human father. They describe a long sojourn in Egypt, and thus testify that the men who originated the stories were quite cognizant of the flight into Egypt. They speak of Jesus as a magician who went about performing wonders, and thereby they indicate the reality of His miracles. The gross and fantastic legends of His death mirror and

---

in the time of Jesus and which was set in definitive order by the Rabbi Juda who died in the year 220. The Talmud of Jerusalem was completed in the fourth century while the more authoritative and complete Babylonian Talmud was not finished until the beginning of the sixth.

14 Enarratio in Psalmum LXIII, cap. 15.

15 Celsus, writing against the Christians at the beginning of the third century knew these stories. The first portion of his "True Discourse" comprises a recital of these fables, put into the mouth of a fictitious Jewish adversary of Christianity. Origen, *Contra Celsum*, Book 1, Ch. 38 and 40, shrewdly remarks that both the myths and Celsus who cites them use and thereby acknowledge the historical value of the gospel narratives.

ape, with unspeakable malevolence, the true recountal of the Passion and the crucifixion.

The men who composed the stories about Jesus in the Talmud and in the Toledot Ieschu[16] saw Him with all the clarity of hatred, which, after all, is only a little less vivid than love itself. They hated Him and His works far too fiercely to be content with the obviously ridiculous charge that He was only a myth. It remained for the clouded minds and the flaccid wills of men in later times to attempt the historically absurd hypothesis that there had never been a man named Jesus of Nazareth.

4. The Christian sources and their reliability. The most important sources of historical knowledge about Jesus of Nazareth and His teaching are, of course, the books which were written by His own followers. Some of these books are actually received by the Church as divinely inspired, that is, as books which have been written by God Himself through the agency or the instrumentality of certain human authors. These constitute the canonical books of the New Testament. Naturally, in the science of apologetics we are not concerned with these books precisely insofar as they are inspired by God. To believe that they are so inspired and this statement that they have been written by God Himself constitutes one of the propositions to which we assent on the authority of God revealing, one of the truths which enter into that body of doctrine which we explain and demonstrate as rationally credible in the science of apologetics.

Thus it would be wildly illogical to utilize these documents as divinely revealed in attempting to show that the very belief is reasonable. It so happens, however, that these books were written by definite and ascertainable human authors, at times and in places which have been recorded. Thus it is possible for us to examine these books as we would examine other writings, for evidence of their historical reliability. There are certain definite criteria in the light of which we can ascertain with perfect certainty that this or that document is trustworthy in an historical sense. We can certainly apply these criteria to the canonical writings of the New Testament. If they conform to the standards of historical reliability, there is absolutely no reason

---

16 A medieval Jewish "life" of Christ.

why we should not accept what is contained in them as historically accurate, in the same way as we receive the doctrine contained in the Commentaries of Julius Caesar.

However, not all of the teaching about the life and the works of Jesus Christ which has come to us from Christian sources of one sort or another is contained in the books of the New Testament. There are certain writings which are called apocryphal gospels. These are far more numerous than the canonical books themselves, and certainly they claim to give information about the conduct and the teaching of Jesus Christ. Furthermore, there are certain sayings attributed to Him and set down in the compositions of early ecclesiastical writers. These statements, not contained in the canonical books of the New Testament, are known as the Agrapha, or as the Logia or the Antilegomena of Jesus.[17]

5. The Agrapha. In the first place, as far as these Agrapha are concerned, we must admit that they throw no light whatsoever upon the problem of the credibility of that teaching which is proposed by Jesus Christ. They are interesting because of the tremendous importance of our Lord and of His message. But they contain no doctrine nor manifest any evidence of credibility not already expressed in the existing monuments of sacred Scripture and of apostolic tradition

---

17 The term *Logia* is occasionally applied to a collection of the sayings of Jesus which some nineteenth-century critics supposed that the synoptic evangelists used as a common source. There is, of course, no historical basis for such an assertion. The Agrapha or unwritten sayings of Jesus are those statements attributed to Him in documents other than the canonical books of the New Testament but not mentioned in the text of the New Testament itself. Some of these are contained in the apocryphal gospels. Others are found in the works of patristic writers, e.g., Clement of Alexandria, Origen, and Tertullian. Still others are found written on recently discovered papyri.

Among these last documents the most important are those contained in two collections of Oxyrhynchus papyri, the first series of which were published by their discoverers, Grenfell and Hunt in 1897 (cf. the article "Unwritten Sayings" in the *Dictionary of the Bible*, edited by James Hastings, 1939) by J. C. Lambert, and Sir Frederick Kenyon, *The Bible and Archeology* (New York and London, 1940), pp. 208–217, and another group of papyri acquired by the British Museum in 1935 (Kenyon, *a.c.*, pp. 216–217). The first group of agrapha found at Oxyrhynchus can only be classified as early. The second Oxyrhynchus writings date from the third century. The British Museum pieces are written in a hand not later than the middle of the second century (Kenyon, *a.c*, p. 216).

6. The Apocrypha. The Apocrypha, on the other hand, are documents written as counterfeits to existing and recognized canonical books. Most of them imitate the four authentic gospels.[18] The most important New Testament apocryphal writings which have been mentioned in the course of history or which are still extant include the gospel according to the Hebrews, that according to the Egyptians, the gospel of Peter, and that of Thomas as well as the Protoevangelium of James as spurious gospel accounts. There were also spurious acts published under the names of Peter, of John, and of Paul, as well as a tiresome number of false epistles which claimed to have apostolic origin.

These books were termed apocryphal or hidden because they were considered first as belonging to certain esoteric sects which claimed to be in possession of a teaching which Christ had never deigned to reveal to the common run of men. Some of them, however, are works written in a spirit of misguided pietism by men who were trying to edify the Christian public. Most of them, however, had a distinctively heretical orientation.

These documents have absolutely no historical authority. They cast no light whatsoever upon the life and the teachings of Jesus Christ. As they appeared, they were rejected by the universal Church, even though some individual churches were inclined for a short time to regard them as authentic. Even a cursory examination of these documents will manifest their extravagant character and their obvious unreliability.

However, the apocryphal writings of the New Testament contribute to the work of Catholic apologetics only insofar as they show the existence and the authority of the existing gospels. These

---

18 A generally acceptable summary of this literature may be found in *The Apocryphal New Testament*, translated by Montague Rhodes James, Oxford, 1926. Kenyon, *a.c*, gives useful information about four more apocryphal gospels, fragments of which have recently been discovered, *(a)* A third-century manuscript of a gospel showing dependence upon Synoptic sources—Oxyrhynchus; *(b)* a life of Christ in the hand of the first half of the second century, and manifesting dependence upon the fourth gospel. This is among the British Museum pieces to which we have referred in note 17; (c) a vellum leaf of the fourth or fifth century containing conversation between our Lord and a pharisee—Oxyrhynchus; *(d)* a small fragment of a large codex, fourth century—Oxyrhynchus. Cf. *The Bible and Archeology*, 215–218.

apocrypha are obviously counterfeits, and just as the existence and nature of counterfeit money is an indication of the existence and the form of an authorized currency, these false books may be utilized to show the reliability of the accepted gospels. Men would not have taken the trouble to set forth even such obvious substitutes as the apocryphal books unless they had been perfectly aware that the people recognized the real gospels as authentic and reliable accounts of Christ and His teaching.

7. The canonical sources. The only complete and authentic books which can offer historically reliable information about the life and the activity of Jesus of Nazareth are the books of the New Testament, recognized as authentic and canonical by the Church. Naturally the books which give the most direct teaching on these points are the four Gospels, written by SS. Matthew, Mark, Luke, and John.[19]

The first of these gospels was written by St. Matthew in Palestine itself, and probably in the city of Capharnaum, between the years 40 and 45 of our era. It was originally written in Aramaic, the mother tongue of Jesus Himself.[20] However, in apostolic times it was translated into Greek, the common language of the entire Mediterranean basin. There were originally many of these translations, but at a very early date one Greek text took precedence over the rest. This gospel was written for Christians of Hebrew origin.

The gospel according to St. Mark[21] was written by this evangelist at Rome about the year 53. St. Mark had first been the companion

---

19 For scientific discussion about the historical reliability of the New Testament books and of the four gospels in particular, see Felder, *Christ and the Critics,* Vol. 1, pp. 26–117; De Grandmaison, *Jesus Christ,* Vol. 1, pp. 19–194; the article "Le Christ et l'Evangile de Jésus-Christ," by C. Lavecgne, O.P., the section included in pp. 317–352, in *Apologetique,* published under the direction of M. Maurice Brillant and M. l'Abbe M. Nédoncelle (Paris, 1939); J. P. Arendzen, *The Gospels, Fact, Myth or Legend?* 2 ed. (London, 1929), pp. 1–94.

20 See the article, pp. 124–126, by J. Huby in *Initiation Biblique, Introduction à l'Etude des Saintes* Écrittures, published under the direction of A. Robert and A. Tricot, Paris, Tournai, and Rome, 1939, and the book, *The Church and the Gospels,* by Joseph Huby, translated by Fenton Moran (New York, 1931), pp. 45–76, as also the writers cited under note 19.

21 I. H. Ianssens, *Hermeneutica Sacra, Editio Quarta, Reformata et Aucta a C. E. Morandi* (Turin, 1922), pp. 223–228; Huby, in *Initiation Biblique,* pp. 127–128; idem, *The Church and the Gospels,* pp. 77–107.

The Historical Evidence About Jesus

of St. Paul. Afterward he attached himself to the service of St. Peter. His gospel, written like all the other books of the New Testament with the exception of St. Matthew's gospel, in Greek was actually his rendition of the message of St. Peter, as this had been preached to the Romans.

St. Luke wrote his gospel during the captivity of St. Paul,[22] either at Caesarea or at Rome. This first captivity is described in the closing chapters of the Acts of the Apostles, the book which St. Luke wrote as a sequel to his gospel. Thus the gospel was written during the year 61 or 62. St. Luke was the inseparable companion of St. Paul, and it was his intention to set down the events of our Lord's life, as these had been recorded in the other gospels, according to a more complete chronological plan.

These first three gospels are frequently called the synoptics[23] (from the Greek *sunoptikos*, agreeing), because they narrate practically the same series of facts and of sayings of our Lord. Each one of these three gospels recounts at least some incidents not mentioned by the other two, and each has its own peculiar style of narration. Nevertheless, the striking resemblance among these justifies the common name of synoptic.

St. John the Apostle, the beloved disciple of Jesus, wrote the fourth gospel most probably at Ephesus, about the year 100.[24] He set down incidents and sayings which had not been recorded by the other three evangelists, and brought out that portion of the teaching of our Lord which was most effectively contrary to the doctrine advanced by the heretics at the end of the first century.

Besides the four gospels there is one other historical book in the canon of the New Testament. This is the Acts of the Apostles, written at Rome during the year 63 by St. Luke himself.[25] The first

---

[22] Ianssens-Morandi, *Hermeneutica Sacra*, pp. 228–243; Huby, in *Initiation Biblique*, pp. 129–130; *idem, The Church and the Gospels*, pp. 108–151.

[23] The word was first employed by Scripture scholars after the publication of J. J. Griesbach's *Synopsis* in 1776.

[24] Ianssens-Morandi, *Hermeneutica Sacra*, pp. 244–254; Huby in *Introduction Biblique*, pp. 130–132; *idem, The Church and the Gospels*, pp. 152–223; see also *The Authorship of St. John's Gospel*, by John Donovan, S.J., edited by Edmund F. Sutcliffe, S.J. (London, 1935).

[25] Ianssens-Morandi, *Hermeneutica Sacra*, pp. 254–257; Huby in *Introduction Biblique*, pp, 132–134.

nine chapters deal with the first propagation of the Church among the Jews and the Samaritans in Palestine. The remaining nineteen chapters deal with the spreading of the Church and its teaching among the gentiles, especially through the efforts of St. Paul.

There are also in the authentic canon of the New Testament twenty-one didactic books, written in the form of letters either to individual Christians or individual churches, or to the body of believers as a whole. Fourteen of these letters were written by St. Paul, three by St. John, two by St. Peter, while St. James the Lesser and St. Jude produced one each. The one prophetical book was written by St. John.

The letters of St. Paul asserted the universality of that salvation which had been procured through the Passion and the death of Jesus and thus fought the Judaizing tendencies of the early heretics.[26] The first letters written were the two epistles to the Thessalonians, in 51 and 52. From 55 to 57 there appeared the two letters to the Corinthians, the epistle to the Galatians, and that to the Romans. The epistle to the Colossians and that addressed to the Ephesians, the little note to Philemon and the epistle to the Philippians were all written from 61 to 63. During the last four years of his life St. Paul wrote the epistle to the Hebrews and the three pastoral epistles. These last included one letter to Titus and two to Timothy. The Catholic epistle of St. James was written sometime between the years 50 and 60. The two epistles of St. Peter and that of St. Jude were composed between the years 60 and 65, while the three letters of St. John the Apostle were composed around the end of the first century. The first of these epistles stands as an epilogue to the fourth gospel.[27] The Apocalypse, the last of the canonical books of the New Testament, dates from the same period.[28]

Now it is the business of the apologist to utilize these books, and in particular the four gospels, which deal directly with the life and

---

[26] For the letters of St. Paul, see L. Pirot in *Initiation Biblique*, pp. 135–151. Ianssens-Morandi, *Hermeneutica Sacra*, pp. 257–275; F. Prat, S.J., *La Theologie de St. Paul*, 18 ed. (Paris, 1930).

[27] For the Catholic epistles, see Ianssens-Morandi, *Hermeneutica Sacra*, pp. 275–287; Pirot in *Initiation Biblique*, pp. 151–154.

[28] See E. B. Allo, O.P., *St. Jean, L'Apocalypse*, 3 ed. (Paris, 1933); also Pirot in *Initiation Biblique*, pp. 154–158; Ianssens-Morandi, *Hermeneutica Sacra*, pp. 287–292.

the accomplishments of Jesus of Nazareth, in demonstrating the rational credibility of Catholic dogma. For this dogma is set forth as the teaching of Jesus of Nazareth, as a doctrine which He showed very convincingly to be credible through the testimony of those divine works which are obviously valid criteria of divine revelation. Obviously, then, we could never hope to show that Catholic dogma as such is rationally credible, unless we are able to advance some definite and naturally acceptable evidence that Jesus Christ really existed, that He, claimed to be a divine messenger, and that He really advanced, as divinely revealed, a system of truth which is actually that now presented by the Catholic Church. Once we have ascertained these facts, we can logically inquire into the evidences of credibility which have appeared to authenticate the claims set forth in favor of the Christian message.

Obviously, then, the apologist must consider the reliability of the books of the New Testament, and in particular that of the four gospels, as historical documents. In the event that they are such as to offer historical evidence equal to that given by other authentic and recognized works, we can know through them what our Lord did and what He said and claimed to be. But, should they prove to be other than scientifically acceptable, then we shall have no means of knowing with anything like historical exactness the very truth which we must understand in order to prove the credibility of Catholic dogma.

8. The canonical books are used in apologetics merely as reliable historical documents and not in their capacity as inspired writings. As Catholics, of course, we know that these books are divinely inspired.[29] They are books which have been written by God in the same sense that any book has been written by the man who is its author. What is contained in them is precisely the message which God intended to communicate to the human race. However, not all of that message which constitutes public revelation is actually contained in these inspired works. Moreover, these works had human

---

29 For an excellent modern treatise on inspiration, see John E. Steinmueller, *A Companion to Scripture Studies*, Vol. 1 (New York, 1941), pp. 6–43; also Fenton, *The Concept of Sacred Theology*, pp. 84–97; Pirot, *Initiation Biblique*, pp. 7–27; G. Van Noort, *Tractatus de Fontibus Revelationis necnon de Fide Divina* (Bussum, Holland, 1920), pp. 17–67.

authors, who were the writers of these books just as fully and perfectly as any other men have ever been the authors of works which have been ascribed to them. The human authors of these inspired works have been the instruments used by God in the production of books of which He is the Author. With a power beyond that of any creature, actual or possible, God has utilized the entire power and spontaneity of a human being in order to have that human being cooperate toward the accomplishment of an end which obviously surpasses the capabilities of merely created nature, a book which is the expression of the teaching of the living God.

However, it would be worse than idle to attempt to utilize these books as inspired in accomplishing the task of apologetics. The inspiration of Holy Scripture is one of these truths which we accept as divinely revealed, and consequently it belongs to that body of teaching which, as a whole, we show to be rationally credible as divine revelation through the process of apologetics. Thus we cannot and do not know the inspiration of the canonical books in a merely natural way. If it cannot be known in the light of natural reason, then it can obviously never enter into a demonstration which is meant to be cogent precisely in this same light. And the demonstration of credibility is meant to be something which can be grasped and seen by any person who is willing to recognize naturally observable truth.

It is quite evident, from a critical point of view, that the four gospels and the other canonical books of the New Testament can be used in the demonstration of apologetics as documents naturally acceptable from the historical point of view. We speak of a document as historically reliable when it gives us definite and accurate information concerning the deeds and the sayings of ancient times. We can distinguish such a document when we ascertain that it has been written by those who were competent to describe the scenes and the discourses about which they wrote and when it is evident that the writers intended to tell the truth rather than merely to attempt to arouse emotions. When such a book has manifestly come down to our own times substantially as it was written by its author, we know that this book now before us is historically reliable as an historical source. Such is demonstrably the case with the four gospels.

The Historical Evidence About Jesus 123

9. The genuineness of the four gospels. In order to prove this point, we must first point out the evidence that these books were actually written by the authors to whom they are ascribed. The evidence which can be adduced in support of this conclusion is either extrinsic or intrinsic. The extrinsic evidence is formed from the testimony of reliable early writers, to the effect that these four books were actually written by SS. Matthew, Mark, Luke, and John. The intrinsic evidence consists in the manifest indication in the text itself that it was produced during the first century by men who were cognizant of conditions in Palestine before the destruction of Jerusalem and were anxious to tell the truth about the life and the sayings of Jesus.

Obviously the extrinsic evidence is of prime importance. The four gospels were not written secretly, to be distributed among the initiates of some esoteric sect. They were the public books of the Christians, and as such they have been recognized in the earliest Christian writings as authentic and truthful documents, actually produced by the men to whom they are commonly ascribed. We have written and recognizably reliable testimony about the human authorship of the four gospels from apostolic times themselves.

10. The testimony of Papias. The first of the writers who testify to the human authors of the gospels is Papias, bishop of Hierapolis in Phrygia during the first half of the second century. He left as a literary legacy five books *The Interpretations of the Lord's Sayings*, which have long since been lost. In fragments of these which have been preserved in the five books *Against the Heresies*, by St. Irenaeus, bishop of Lyons in France (202), and in the *Ecclesiastical History* of Eusebius of Caesarea in Palestine (circa 340), he testified about the writing of two of the four gospels. "Mark, having become the interpreter of Peter, wrote whatever he remembered accurately, but still not in that order in which the things had been said and done by the Lord. For he had not heard the Lord, nor had he followed Him, but afterward, as it has been said, he was the companion of Peter, who did not teach the sermons and the precepts of the Lord, in that order which the Lord Himself had followed in teaching them, but followed that arrangement in preaching which he judged opportune and best fitted to aid the minds of his hearers. Hence Mark has not erred in anything when he wrote things as he remembered them. For he had this one intention seriously in his mind and in his thought, not to leave out any of those things which he had heard nor to interpose anything false."[30] Papias has this to say about the writing of the gospel according to St. Matthew, in a passage which follows immediately after that which refers to St. Mark in the text of Eusebius. "Matthew wrote a gospel in the Hebrew tongue about the sayings and the deeds of Christ, which every man interpreted according as he was able."

This Papias was known both to St. Irenaeus and to Eusebius as the hearer of John and the companion of Polycarp. The John he had heard would seem to have been a disciple of the Lord, distinct from St. John the Apostle and Evangelist, since Papias expressly declared that he had neither heard nor seen the holy Apostles themselves. However, it had been his pleasure and his custom to travel about and to seek out the elders who had actually been in company of the Apostles.[31] From these men he asked about the sayings or the explanations of the Apostles themselves, and of the most illustrious among the disciples who lived in the churches of Asia. Hence his testimony has unique value. Tenacious of tradition, as was every orthodox Christian teacher, he testified that the first two gospels had been written by Matthew and Mark. Furthermore, on the authority of his friend and master, John the presbyter, he cites the circumstances attendant upon the writing of the second gospel and the plan of composition which governed its production.

11. Pantaenus. The tradition of the Church in Alexandria, with which Eusebius was very well acquainted, was explicit about the missionary career of its first notable catechist, Pantaenus. This president of the famous Didiscalion, predecessor of Clement and Origen, flourished as a teacher in that city from around the year 180 until after 190. Before settling in Alexandria he had performed missionary service in foreign lands, and had gone as far as India where "he found his own arrival anticipated by some who there were acquainted with the gospel of Matthew, to whom Bartholomew, one of the Apostles, had preached, and to whom he had left the gospel of

---

30 Cited in Eusebius, *The Ecclesiastical History*, Book 3, Ch. 39. St. Irenaeus states that Papias was "a hearer of John" and that he had written five books. *Adversus Haereses*, Book 5, Ch. 33, No. 4.

31 Cf. Eusebius, *The Ecclesiastical History*, Book 3, Ch. 39.

Matthew in Hebrew, which was also preserved until this time."[32] Like Papias, from whose tradition incidentally he is quite independent, Pantaenus had visited many of the churches of Christendom. He labored "to increase and to build up the word of God" which he knew very well was the doctrine that was believed on the authority of God by the Church scattered throughout the world. When he testified about the first gospel as the work of St. Matthew, and as a document which had been written in Hebrew, he was simply taking cognizance of an unquestionable and universal conviction that this gospel was genuine.

12. The Muratorian fragment. The Muratorian fragment, a manuscript statement of the canon of sacred Scripture which was most probably written during the second half of the second century, attributes the "fourth gospel" to the disciple John.[33] Since the first three, according to the ordering which was universal in the Church, were most certainly those of Matthew, Mark, and Luke, this manuscript stands as a clear indication from an officially recognized source of the genuineness of all the four gospels.

13. St. Justin Martyr. St. Justin Martyr (circa 165) cites all of the four gospels in the three authentic works of his which have come down to our own time. In his *First Apology*[34] when he comes to describe the Eucharistic sacrifice, he states, "For the apostles, in the memoirs composed by them, which are called gospels, have thus delivered to us what was enjoined upon them."

In the *Dialogue with the Jew Trypho*, he cites a statement taken from St. Matthew as being "written in the gospel,"[35] and again in the same work,[36] he speaks of "the memoirs which I say were composed by the apostles and by those who followed them." Although he does not ascribe any passage to an individual evangelist, he uses many of the passages which are obviously taken out of the texts of the four gospels, particularly those of SS. Matthew and Luke. It is clear then that the memoirs or gospels to which he refers are actually the four gospels which we know today.

---

32 Eusebius, *a.c.*, Book 5, Ch. 10.
33 There is an excellent translation of this fragment in Steinmueller, *a.c.*, pp. 390–392.
34 Ch. 66.
35 Ch. 100.
36 Ch. 103.

14. Tatian. However, the most valuable indication of St. Justin Martyr's teaching on the genuineness of the four canonical gospels is to be found in the procedure of his disciple, the unfortunate Tatian. This brilliant but violent scholar was converted to Christianity and became a disciple of St. Justin at Rome. Some time after his great teacher's death, he left the Church and, according to Eusebius[37] and to St. Irenaeus,[38] founded the heresy of the Encratites. Tatian, about the time of his separation from the Church, composed a certain Diatesseron, written originally in Syriac. It was a sort of harmony of the four gospels, or rather one account which utilized the statements of all the evangelists in bringing out the life and the teachings of our Lord. Eusebius speaks of it[39] as "the gospel of the four or a gospel formed of the four, which is in the possession of some even now." As a matter of fact the Diatesseron remained the received gospel text among the Syrians, both Catholic and dissident, until the fourth century. The exegetical works on the gospels by St. Ephraem, who died about the year 373, as well as his discourses on the mysteries of our Lord, are all based on the text of this work of Tatian.[40] And the four writings out of which Tatian had drawn the material for his works were the gospels of SS. Matthew, Mark, Luke, and John.

15. St. Irenaeus. Another outstanding witness to the genuineness of the four gospels is St. Irenaeus. Like Papias, he was a disciple of St. Polycarp. He had visited the various churches situated within the Roman empire both as a missionary and as a delegate of his predecessor in the see of Lyons, St. Pothinus. Like St. Justin, he composed books against the heretics who attempted to change the belief of the Christians in the second century. However, while the controversial works of Justin have been lost to history, those of Irenaeus, the famous *Adversus Haereses*, have remained. The dominating motive of his life, expressed in his writings, was an enthusiasm for the purity of the Christian faith. It was insufferable to him that anyone, on any pretext whatsoever, should presume to alter one word or statement

---

37 *The Ecclesiastical History*, Book 4, Chs. 28–29.
38 *Adversus Haereses*, Book 1, Ch, 28.
39 *The Ecclesiastical History*, Book 4, Ch. 29.
40 Cf. F. Cayré, A. A., *Precis de Patrologie et d'Histoire de la Theologie*, 2 ed. (Paris, Tournai, and Rome), Vol. 1, p. 370 and page 125; also Sir Frederick Kenyon, *Our Bible and the Ancient Manuscripts* (New York, 1940) (reimpression, 1941), pp. 156–159.

in that doctrine which the Church received as the divine teaching from the hands of the apostles themselves. He valued his friendship with St. Polycarp as one of the truly consoling memories of his life. By reason of his travel, and his extraordinary erudition, he was in a position to know with unique accuracy what was taught as Christian truth, and attested by the words of the Apostles, throughout the Christian world. His words about the human authorship of the four gospels deserve to be cited at some length.

"From none others have we learned the plan of our salvation than from those through whom there came down to us the gospel, which they at one time manifested in public and then later, by the will of God, gave to us in the Scriptures, to be the pillar and the ground of our faith. For it is wicked to say that they taught before they had perfect knowledge, as some are arrogant enough to claim, while they boast that they have improved upon the Apostles. For, after our Lord rose from, the dead, they (the Apostles), were filled with power from above and possessed perfect knowledge. They went to the ends of the earth, preaching the gospel of God's benefits to us and announcing the peace of heaven to men who possess God's gospel equally and individually. Matthew also composed a written gospel among the Hebrews, in their own tongue, while at Rome Peter and Paul preached and laid the foundations of the Church. After they had gone away, Mark the disciple and the interpreter of Peter also gave to us in writing that which had been preached by Peter. Also Luke, the companion of Paul, set down in a book the gospel he had preached. Afterward John, the disciple of the Lord, who had also leaned upon His breast, himself published a gospel during his sojourn at Ephesus in Asia."[41]

16. Origen. The tradition of the Alexandrian Didiscalion reached its epitome in the writings of the peerless Origen (*circa* 254). His account of the writing of the four gospels is found in his commentary on the gospel according to St. Matthew. It is cited in the *Ecclesiastical History* of Eusebius. "I have learned from tradition about the four gospels, which alone are undisputed in the whole Church of God throughout the world. The first is written according to Matthew, the same who was once a publican, but later an apostle of Jesus Christ,

---

41 *Adversus Haereses*, book 3, Ch. 1.

who, having written it for Jewish converts, set it down in the Hebrew. The second is according to Mark, who composed it as Peter explained it to him. Peter acknowledges him as his son in his general epistle, saying, 'the elect Church in Babylon salutes you, as also Mark, my son,' And the third is according to Luke, the gospel commended by Paul, which was written for the converts from the Gentiles: and last of all the gospel according to John."[42]

17. Tertullian. Finally, Tertullian (240), the most forceful of the Latin Apologists, declared expressly that John and Matthew from among the Apostles themselves have manifested the faith to us while Mark and Luke from among the apostolic men have repeated their teaching.[43] His testimony, manifesting the traditions of the Latin church of Africa, completes the evidence offered by the Christian writers to the effect that the four gospels were actually composed by Matthew, Mark, Luke, and John.

18. The value of patristic testimony about the authorship and historical nature of the gospels. The value of this testimony becomes apparent when we begin to consider the mentality of those men among whom this teaching existed. So impressed were these early Christians with the value of their teaching that they were absolutely unwilling that there should be even the slightest modification introduced into their doctrine. If anyone had attempted to retail the four gospels which we know as canonical as the works of these four men, Matthew, Mark, Luke, and John while they had actually been written by other men, the Church which prides itself on its unwavering and absolute fidelity to the apostolic teaching would never have accepted them. We know very well that during apostolic times apocryphal gospels were in circulation, documents falsely ascribed to some of the most important personalities within the infant Church. Such was the intelligent critical appraisal of the contemporary Christians that these documents were universally rejected as spurious. The same fate would have undoubtedly befallen the four canonical gospels, were it not for the fact that these Christians of the apostolic age had ample evidence that they really had been produced by the human authors to whom they are assigned.

---

42 Books 6, Ch. 25, *The Ecclesiastical History*.
43 *Against Marcion*, Book 4, Ch. 2.

These Christians of the apostolic age were men who took seriously that command which came to them from St. Jude. "But you, my dearly beloved, be mindful of the words which have been spoken before by the Apostles of our Lord Jesus Christ."[44] St. Paul had warned them to "stand fast and hold the traditions which you have learned, whether by word or by our epistle."[45] The unwavering tradition of the Christians was that these four gospels, and these alone, were genuine apostolic documents.

Naturally this tradition and constant testimony of the Christians is enhanced in the consent of those men who opposed the true teaching of Jesus Christ. The men who were enemies of the Christian Church and its teaching, the heretics, pagans, and Jews never denied the authorship of these documents. Their task of denying the Christian position would, of course, have been rendered much easier, if they could have asserted that the books which the Catholics utilized in expressing their knowledge of Jesus and His teaching were not genuine. The fact that the authorship of these books was never questioned, even by the most painstaking adversary like Celsus, against whom Origen wrote so brilliantly, is ample indication that even the most serious opponents of the Catholic position could find no possible ground for denying that the four gospels had actually been written by SS. Matthew, Mark, Luke, and John.

We must not forget that contemporaries of Jesus and of the Apostles were living throughout the world during the early years of the second century. Many of these men had known the Lord and His chosen witnesses. It would have been impossible for all of these men throughout the world to have been deceived into accepting as authentic apostolic documents, writings which were merely forgeries.

19. The question of veracity. The next point which we must consider in determining the actual historical reliability of the gospels, and of the New Testament writings in general, is the question of their veracity. Granting that the four gospels were actually written by the authors to whom they have been traditionally ascribed, we must further inquire if these books were actually written as historical narratives, or merely as religious romances, intended only to set down

---

44 Jude 1:27.
45 2 Thess. 2:14.

legends which had gathered around the name of Jesus of Nazareth. At the present time even the enemies of the faith are impelled to admit the historical character of the three synoptic gospels. However, it can easily be shown that not only these, but also the fourth gospel, are real historical documents, which contain a record of the actual teaching and the accomplishments of our Lord.

We possess both internal and external evidence to this effect. As far as the internal evidence is concerned, the four gospels evidently set forth the brief public career of a Man who lived and taught in Palestine over nineteen hundred years ago. Written as they were during the first century, and in the lifetime of many people who remembered the conditions and the events in Jerusalem prior to the wars of Vespasian and Titus, these documents describe places and conditions in a matter of fact and entirely historical way. There is neither inconsistency nor incoherence in the presentation of facts. There is no straining for effect, no attempt to increase the prestige of the writers by ascribing any outstanding goodness to themselves. On the contrary, the faults and the imperfections within the apostolic college are noted, and even the betrayal of the Master by one of the twelve is set down. A comparison of the texts of the four gospels with those of the apocryphal imitations can best bring out the sober and scientifically accurate character of the former.

As far as the fourth gospel itself is concerned, it bears within itself evident marks of historical accuracy no less obvious than those manifested by the three synoptics. The events in the gospel according to St. John are even better localized than those described in the other documents. The fact that the style of the discourses of our Lord, as recounted by St. John, differs somewhat from the style set forth in the synoptics is obviously accounted for by the fact that John was the privileged disciple, the Apostle privileged above all the others to hear the intimate statements of Jesus of Nazareth. As a matter of fact the so-called antilogies of the four gospels constitute one of the best guarantees of their historical veracity. They do not contradict the statements found in reliable contemporary historians, and, moreover, the statements of the various evangelists are not opposed one to the other. However, the evangelists frequently, as in the recountal of the

Resurrection, describe the same event in the capacity of obviously independent witnesses, as falsifiers would certainly never have done.

However, the most important evidence for the veracity of the four gospels is to be found in the acceptance of these books as reliable documents both by the Christians of early times and by their adversaries. The evangelists described events which had taken place, not in some unknown corner of the world, but in the province of Judea, regularly administered by the forces of the Roman empire. A tremendous number of people had witnessed these events. The followers of Christ, who knew of these happenings, and who were scattered throughout the entire Roman world toward the end of the first century, received these books as expressions of the truth about Jesus, and unanimously rejected other writings which pretended to offer the same information. Moreover, even enemies of Christ, like Celsus and the heretics, attempted to base their reasonings on facts which had been recorded in the writings of the four evangelists. Thus the historicity of the four gospels is at least as well attested as that of any other documents which have ever been presented to mankind.

20. The authenticity of available texts. Finally, the apologist has absolutely convincing evidence that these documents which accurately described the life and the teaching of Jesus have been preserved for mankind in a substantially incorrupt condition. The text of the gospels and of the other inspired books which convey information about our Lord is manifestly that which was originally set down by the human authors of these documents, according to incontestable evidence. There exist in the world today upward of 2,700 Greek manuscripts of the New Testament. There are, moreover, about 1,600 lesson books in which the greater portion of the gospel text is contained in the form of readings arranged for the various seasons of the year. There are three important series of translations of the gospels made in ancient times into languages other than Greek, all of them testifying to the wording of the manuscripts utilized by the churchmen who made these translations.[46]

---

46 Sir Frederick Kenyon, in his *Our Bible and the Ancient Manuscripts*, pp. 105–108, speaks of about 170 fragments on ostraka, papyrus, or vellum found with them, slightly more than two hundred uncial manuscripts (including fragments), on vellum, 2,429 listed cursive manuscripts, 1,678 lectionaries. There are four versions of the New Testament

With this overwhelming mass of evidence, we can be perfectly certain that the text reproduced in the critical editions of today is practically identical down to the least detail, with that order of words set down by the apostolic authors themselves. The variants in the wording of the important manuscripts reduce themselves almost entirely to questions of arrangements of words. There is no substantial change manifest in the versions.[47]

21. The historical value of New Testament literature. In the light of this evidence we can be sure that here and now we possess a series of documents which will inform us correctly about the life and the accomplishments of Jesus of Nazareth. We can examine the content of these documents and from this examination we shall be able to see if this Man really claimed to be a divine messenger, the

---

in Syrian, five in Egyptian, and two in Latin. Scholars recognize three families of old Latin versions. Manuscripts of the Vulgate are counted by thousands and about 700 of these are anterior to the eleventh century (cf. Tricot, in *Initiation Biblique*, p. 278). One of the papyrus fragments is the famous Rylands manuscript containing a short portion of St. John's gospel written during the first half of the second century (cf. Kenyon, *Our Bible and the Ancient Manuscripts*, 128; *idem, The Bible and Archeology*, p. 226). The fragment has received the designation P^{52} and is known as the Rylands Papyrus 457.

47 The reliability of the Scripture text now available is beautifully explained by Kenyon, *Our Bible and the Ancient Manuscripts*, p. 23. "It cannot be too strongly asserted that in substance the text of the Bible is certain. Especially is this the case with the New Testament. The number of manuscripts of the New Testament, of early translations from it, and of quotations from it in the oldest writers of the Church, is so large that it is practically certain that the true reading of every doubtful passage is preserved in some one or other of these ancient authorities. This can be said of no other ancient hook in the world. Scholars are satisfied that they possess substantially the true text of the principal Greek and Roman writers whose works have come down to us, of Sophocles, of Thucydides, of Cicero, of Virgil; yet our knowledge of their writings depends on a mere handful of manuscripts, whereas the manuscripts of the New Testament are counted by hundreds and even thousands." Kenyon makes his own the now classical statement of Hort, contained on page 2 of the introduction to Westcott and Holt's edition of *The New Testament in the Original Greek*, that the proportion of words about which there is some doubt can be placed at about one eighth of the entire text, and that by far the greater number of these are merely differences in order or other unimportant variations. Thus "the amount of what can in any sense be called substantial variation...can hardly form more than a thousandth part of the entire text." The most complete listing of New Testament manuscripts in English is, in spite of its antiquity, *A Plain Introduction to the New Testament, for the Use of Biblical Students*, by Frederick Henry Ambrose Scrivener, 3 ed. (Cambridge, England, 1883).

bearer of a doctrine which was communicated by God to men and which men are expected to receive on the divine authority itself. We can ascertain His presentation of a definite doctrine and not merely an exhortation to spiritual improvement among the men of Judea and of Galilee. Finally, we can find, through the reading of these sources, the motives of credibility or signs of revelation which confirmed the claim of Jesus that His teaching was actually of divine origin, and as such destined to be accepted by all men.

22. Some opponents. Those men who have rejected and who still reject the historical authority of the gospels may be grouped, for the sake of convenience, under the headings of certain schools or hypotheses in scriptural criticism. The proponents of these hypotheses are by no means in complete agreement among themselves, but there are definite claims, which, though utterly false, should be known by the student of Catholic apologetics.

First of all the German professor, Hermann Reimarus, who died in 1768, claimed that the four gospels were written by the Christian leaders of the first century with the simple object of deceiving their followers. It was his contention that our Lord had attempted to foment a political revolution. After the failure of this move, according to Reimarus, the Apostles simply presented their crucified leader as a Savior of humanity. This claim had absolutely no scientific standing, and it has only served to give Reimarus the unfortunate distinction of being the first among western Europeans to have alleged the deliberate untruthfulness of the gospel narratives.

Another professor, Gottlieb Paulus, who died in 1851, is known as the father of the "naturalistic" interpretation of the gospel narratives. According to his teachings, the authors of the four gospels simply gave an erroneous interpretation to the reporting of purely natural facts. In the light of the "superstition" common in apostolic times, a story like that of the feeding of the four thousand was developed from a recountal of a prosaic event in which Jesus of Nazareth, by the example of his own generosity, induced a tremendous number of His followers to share their repasts with those who were in need to an account of a miracle. The "naturalism" of Paulus was the dominating influence in the famous "Life of Christ" by Renan. It has long since been abandoned by the great mass of critics who are aware that the accomplishments of One whom even His enemies regarded as a wonderworker could never have been as banal as those proposed by the naturalists.

David Strauss (d. 1874) attempted to explain the gospel accounts of our Lord's activities and teachings as the results of mythological predication. According to his teaching, the early Christians, living as they did in a world which abounded in pagan myths, simply took some of the stories which had been circulated about the heathen gods and attributed them to their hero. He was logical enough to see that such a proceeding would take a considerable time, and consequently he denied that the gospels were written until late in the second century. His teaching constituted a gross and obvious misinterpretation of facts, easily ascertainable to students of literary history.

Another nineteenth-century rationalistic professor, Christian Baur, distinguished himself by sponsoring the claim that the four gospels were in reality a sort of irenic literature, intended to terminate, by compromise, a strife which had grown up in the ranks of the Christians between the followers of Peter and those of Paul. The fact that there was no evidence whatsoever to support this assertion did not in any way lessen its popularity among the nineteenth-century anti-Christian critics.

Still more bizarre was the doctrine of Bruno Bauer (d. 1882). This man carried the principles of destructive and unscientific criticism to their logical term, and denied the actual existence of Jesus. This weird teaching was never, of course, taken seriously in enlightened circles. It has, however, had a certain vogue among the followers of various sorts of free thought.

Finally, there is the liberal or evolutionary hypothesis, which is generally attributed to Albrecht Ritschl (d. 1889). He and his followers, chief among whom we must number Adolph Harnack, consider that the evangelists actually set down the doctrine which appealed to the mentality of the men of their own time, without, of course, intending to deceive their readers. According to their doctrine the men of apostolic ages were prone to explain every occurrence in terms of the miraculous, and thus the Apostles themselves seriously related miraculous effects which had never been brought about by our Lord. It is the contention of these men that our Lord had preached and had Himself expected the physical destruction of the world as an event which was to take place within a very short time from the period in which He began to teach. He and His disciples were supposed to have expected that He was to rule in glory over the survivors of this universal catastrophe. This eschatological concept of the gospel narrative is shown to be false by the very fact that the earliest Christians rejected this same doctrine as manifestly an error and contradictory to the teaching which had been given by our Lord.

All of these hypotheses fail in that they fail to take into account the manifest and clear assertions of the very documents which they attempt to explain. These gospels were not written in obscurity. The teaching conveyed in them had been proposed by a living and active society for some years before these documents were put in writing. The very men who had known Jesus of Nazareth most intimately were the ones who received these gospels as statements of the truth about Him. They were in a position to know. We who wish truth have authentic and historically reliable documents out of which we can learn of the claims and the accomplishments of Jesus can most certainly find such documents in the four gospels. They are authenticated from a purely natural and scientific point of view more perfectly than other historical narratives which have come down to us from ancient times.

Chapter 9

THE CLAIMS OF JESUS

1. The fact of Christian revelation. According to the testimony of those reliable and authentic historical documents which we know as the four gospels, Jesus of Nazareth openly professed that He was the bearer of a message from God to men. He asserted that the doctrine He preached was actually what we call divine revelation, public rather than private, mediate rather than immediate as far as the body of mankind is concerned. He described His teaching as a doctrine which is supernatural, not merely by reason of the way in which it comes to man, but also by reason of its content.

It is of course absolutely requisite to establish and demonstrate this fact in a course of scientific apologetics. In this science we are concerned with proving the rational credibility, not of some vague and unknown system of religious teaching, but of this definite doctrine which was propounded by Jesus of Nazareth and which is proposed as such in the magisterium of the Catholic Church. If there were no naturally ascertainable evidence that Jesus of Nazareth had actually claimed that this teaching was divinely revealed, then obviously this teaching could never be acceptable from a rational point of view as Christian revelation. However, we have at our disposal abundant reliable historical evidence to show that Jesus Christ taught a definite religious doctrine, which He proposed to man as a communication from God.

The historical evidence of the four gospels makes it quite clear that Jesus of Nazareth claimed that His doctrine was actually a teaching from God. Furthermore, He continually spoke of Himself as a messenger from God, as the Messiah, and as the true and natural Son of God. Thus in every way possible He pointed to His teaching as a body of truth which men were bound to accept as divine revelation.

2. The Word of God. The doctrine which He set forth is the teaching of God rather than of man. "My doctrine is not Mine, but His that sent Me."[1] It is the actual speech of God, insofar as the words in which it is conveyed are the words of God. "He that is of God, heareth the words of God. Therefore you hear them not, because you are not of God."[2]

The teaching of Jesus was something which He designated as "the gospel of the kingdom."[3] In explaining the parable of the sower to His disciples, He designated this "word of the kingdom" under the image of the seed which fell upon various types of soil.[4] He stated openly that this doctrine is "the word of God."[5] The people who thronged about Jesus came in order to hear the "word of God."[6] At several other times during the course of His public ministry it is recorded that He designated His teaching in exactly this fashion.[7]

3. The doctrine all men must accept. Furthermore, Jesus of Nazareth asserted that His teaching was a divine revelation which all men are bound to accept under penalty of losing their eternal salvation. "I am come a light into the world: that whosoever believeth in Me, may not remain in darkness. And if any man hear My words, and keep them not: I do not judge him: for I came not to judge the world, but to save the world. He that despiseth Me, and receiveth not My words: hath one that judgeth him; the word that I have spoken, the same shall judge him in the last day. For I have not spoken of Myself, but the Father who sent Me, He gave Me commandment what I should say, and what I should speak. And I know that His commandment is life everlasting. The things therefore that I speak, even as the Father said unto Me, so do I speak."[8] He insisted upon

---

1 John 7:16.
2 John 8:47.
3 Matt. 24:14, also 4:23 and 9:35.
4 Matt. 13:19.
5 Luke 8:11.
6 Luke 5:1.
7 Cf. Luke 8:21, 11:28; John 3:34, 8:47 (St. John recounts that Jesus spoke of His doctrine as "the words of God").
8 John 12:46–5.

The Claims of Jesus

the mediate, public, and necessary character of the revelation which He had brought to mankind in the commission which He gave to the Apostles immediately before His Ascension. "And He said to them: Go ye into the whole world and preach the gospel to every creature. He that believeth and is baptized, shall be saved: but he that believeth not, shall be condemned."[9] "And Jesus spoke to them, saying: All power is given to Me in heaven and in earth; Going therefore, teach ye all nations: baptizing them in the name of the Father, and of the Son, and of the Holy Ghost: Teaching them to observe all things whatsoever I have commanded you: and behold I am with you all days, even to the consummation of the world."[10]

4. The Messenger from God. Very frequently during the course of His public life, Jesus of Nazareth asserted that He had been sent by God. Thus He characterized Himself as a divine messenger, the bearer of a communication which God had addressed to mankind. In speaking thus He was obviously claiming that the doctrine He presented was something to be accepted with the assent of divine faith.

He described the limits of His own immediate preaching field at the very time that He affirmed His function as a delegate sent by God, in answering the Canaanite woman whose faith He praised and whose petition He granted. "I was not sent but to the sheep that are lost of the house of Israel."[11] In sending His Apostles upon their first teaching venture He explained that they were His legates just as He was the bearer of a message from God. The teaching which they were commissioned to bring to the people was the very doctrine which He had set forth as having been divinely revealed. "He that receiveth you, receiveth Me: and he that receiveth Me, receiveth Him that sent Me."[12] In the parable of the evil husbandmen Jesus referred to Himself as the Son whom the heavenly King sent to the rebellious subjects in order to offer them a last opportunity to repent. The chief priests and the Pharisees were very well aware that in speaking in

---
9 Mark 16:15–16.
10 Matt. 28:18–20.
11 Matt. 15:24.
12 Matt. 10:40; Luke 9:48; John 13:20.

this way Jesus had reference to them and to their rejection of His teaching.[13]

Actually, according to the words of Jesus, the rejection of His teaching involved the rejection of God Himself, because He was sent by God. He told His disciples, "He that heareth you, heareth Me; and he that despiseth you, despiseth Me. And he that despiseth Me despiseth Him that sent Me."[14]

Although references to the divine legateship of Jesus of Nazareth abound in the three synoptic gospels, they are far more numerous and striking in the historical account of His life set forth in the Gospel according to St. John. In the beautiful colloquy with the pharisee Nicodemus, which took place during the early portion of His public life, Jesus stated clearly that He had been sent by God as the bearer of a message which was to be accepted on divine faith. "For God sent not His Son into the world, to judge the world, but that the world may be saved by Him. He that believeth in Him is not judged: but he that doth not believe, is already judged: because he believeth not in the name of the only begotten Son of God."[15] The evangelist appends his understanding of the statement to the account, of the same discourse. "For He whom God hath sent, speaketh the words of God."[16]

5. The teaching of the Father. The One who has sent Jesus, according to His own assertion, is so perfect and amiable that in doing His will a man will find delight and strength above that which he could obtain through earthly nourishment. "My meat is to do the will of Him that sent Me." He informed the Pharisees who opposed Him that they were setting themselves up against the living God, whose message He carried to men. "He who honoreth not the Son, honoreth not the Father who hath sent Him. Amen, amen, I say unto you, that he who heareth My word, and believeth Him that sent Me, hath life everlasting, and cometh not into judgment, but is passed from death to life."[17]

---

13 Matt. 21:33–46; Mark 12:1–12.
14 Luke 10:16.
15 John 3:17–18.
16 John 3:34.
17 John 5:23–24.

The fact that He has been sent by God the Father renders His judgment just, according to the explicit statement of Jesus. "I cannot of Myself do anything. As I hear, so I judge: and My judgment is just: because I seek not My own will, but the will of Him that sent me."[18] Likewise, according to the claims which Jesus made explicitly, the Father made manifest the fact that He was the bearer of the divine teaching. "For the works which the Father hath given Me to perfect: the works themselves, which I do, give testimony of Me, that the Father hath sent Me: and the Father Himself who hath sent Me, hath given testimony of Me: neither have you heard His voice at any time nor seen His shape; and you have not His word abiding in you: for whom He hath sent, Him you believe not."[19] In this same reproachful discourse to His enemies, Jesus of Nazareth made it clear that His doctrinal mission was such that He spoke in the name of God. "I am come to you in the name of the Father, and you receive Me not: if another shall come in his own name, him you will receive."[20]

6. The word of everlasting life. Acceptance of the teaching which is set forth by Jesus is said to be the work of God, precisely because He is declared to have been sent by God as the bearer of a divine message. "Jesus answered, and said to them: This is the work of God, that you believe in Him whom He hath sent."[21] The insistence upon His character as a divine legate runs throughout the famous sixth chapter in the gospel according to St. John. Jesus insisted that those who believed Him, and accepted on divine faith the message which He proposed as divinely revealed, were to be given eternal life, and a glorious Resurrection on the last day. "I came down from heaven, not to do My own will, but the will of Him that sent Me. Now this is the will of the Father who sent Me: that of all that He hath given Me, I should lose nothing, but should raise it up again on the last day. And this is the will of the Father that sent Me: that everyone who seeth the Son, and believeth in Him, may have life everlasting, and I will raise him up on the last day."[22] Furthermore, Jesus asserted that no

---

18 John 5:30.
19 John 5:36–38.
20 John 5:43.
21 John 6:29.
22 John 6:38–39.

man could accept his teaching with the assent of divine faith except by the power of God whose message Jesus brought to the world. "No man can come to Me, except the Father, who hath sent Me, draw him."[23] Again, in the same discourse, He connected the doctrine of the Eucharist, which He then set forth, with the fact that He had been sent by God. "As the living Father hath sent Me, and I live by the Father: so he that eateth Me, the same also shall live by Me."[24]

7. A message acceptable as divine revelation. Jesus was careful explicitly to assert that the acceptability of the teaching which He offered to men was based upon the evidence that He really had been sent by God. To the leaders of the Jews He stated, "My doctrine is not Mine, but His that sent Me. If any man will do the will of Him: he shall know of the doctrine whether it be of God, or whether I speak of Myself. He that speaketh of himself seeketh his own glory; but He that seeketh the glory of Him that sent Him, He is true, and there is no injustice in Him."[25] Jesus repeated this assertion, crying out in the Temple of Jerusalem, "You both know Me, and you know whence I am and I am not come of Myself, but He that sent Me is true, whom you know not. I know Him: because I am from Him, and He hath sent Me."[26] It was the contention of Christ that He could and would return to the God who had entrusted Him with this doctrinal mission. "Jesus therefore said to them: yet a little while I am with you: and then I go to Him that sent Me."[27]

The testimony which Jesus alleged in favor of His own teaching was such as to show that He had been sent by God. "If I do judge, My judgment is true: because I am not alone, but I and the Father that sent Me. And in your law it is written, that the testimony of two men is true. I am one that give testimony of Myself: and the Father that sent Me, giveth testimony of Me."[28] The One who had sent Jesus with the message which He preached, and for which He demanded the assent of faith was One competent to send that message. "He that

---

23 John 6:44.
24 John 6:58.
25 John 7:16–18.
26 John 7:28–29.
27 John 7:33.
28 John 8:16–18.

sent Me is true."[29] Furthermore, the One who sent Jesus, according to His explicit claim, is ever with Him. "And He that sent Me is with Me, and He hath not left Me alone."[30] The divine mission which He claimed for Himself was such as to demand an affection for Him on the part of every man who loved God. "Jesus therefore said to them: If God were your Father: you would indeed love Me: for from God I proceeded, and came: for I came not of Myself, but He sent Me."[31]

8. God commands the preaching of this doctrine. The work which He had been commissioned to perform was incumbent upon Him. "I must work the works of Him that sent Me, whilst it is day: the night cometh when no man can work."[32] The mission which He had been sent to perform was a holy work, a task which He had been sanctified to accomplish, for Jesus was One "whom the Father hath sanctified and sent into the world."[33] The fact that He was consubstantial with the Father in no way detracted from the reality of His mission. "But Jesus cried and said: He that believeth in Me, doth not believe in Me, but in Him that sent Me. And he that seeth Me, seeth Him that sent Me."[34] Furthermore, Jesus declared that His mission was such that the content of His teaching had been determined by God Himself. "For I have not spoken of Myself, but the Father who sent Me, He gave Me commandment what I should say, and what I should speak,"[35] "And the word which you have heard is not mine: but the Father's who sent Me."[36]

He explained to His followers that they would be persecuted by those men who did not know who had given Him His doctrinal mission in the world. "But all these things they will do to you for My name's sake: because they know not Him that sent Me."[37] The God at whose right hand He is to sit for all eternity and to whom He returned after His earthly life is actually the One who has sent

---

29 John 8:26.
30 John 8:29.
31 John 8:42.
32 John 9:4.
33 John 10:36.
34 John 12:44–45.
35 John 12:49.
36 John 14:24.
37 John 15:21.

Him for this work. "And now I go to Him that sent Me: and none of you asketh Me, Whither goest Thou?"[38] Finally, He likened the commission which He gave to the Apostles to preach the doctrine He had given them in His name to that mission with which He had been entrusted by the Father. "As the Father hath sent Me, I also send you."[39]

9. The fact of revelation and the prayer of Jesus. Jesus of Nazareth not only asserted that He had been sent by God in the course of the instructions and warnings He gave to men, but He integrated this claim into the sublime prayers which He offered to God. In the petition which He addressed to His Father immediately before He called Lazarus from the dead He made it strikingly clear that this miracle, like the other signs which He had given, was meant precisely to indicate the fact of His divine commission. "Jesus, lifting up His eyes said: Father, I give Thee thanks that Thou hast heard Me: And I know that Thou hearest Me always, but because of the people who stand about have I said it: that they may believe that Thou hast sent Me."[40]

In the sublime sacerdotal prayer, which is recounted in the seventeenth chapter of the gospel according to St. John, Jesus clearly indicates in His petition the fact and the nature of the mission He had received. The eternal life, which He came to merit for men, includes the contemplation of Himself as One sent by God. "Now this is eternal life: That they may know Thee, the only true God, and Jesus Christ, whom Thou has sent."[41] The work of Jesus in this world has resulted in a firm belief or conviction that He had been sent by God. "The words which Thou gavest Me, I have given to them: and they have received them, and have known in very deed that I came out from Thee, and they have believed that Thou didst send Me."[42] This same truth is reasserted at the conclusion of this prayer. "Just Father, the world hath not known Thee: but I have known Thee: and these have known that Thou hast sent Me."[43] Thus, according to the

---
38 John 16:5.
39 John 20:21.
40 John 11:41–42.
41 John 7:3.
42 John 17:8.
43 John 17:21.

explicit statement of Jesus, the truths which the disciples received from Him were actually verities which had been confided to Him by God. In accepting this teaching, the disciples had recognized the fact that He was a messenger from God.

Before God He protested that the mission of His Apostles was patterned after the mission which He had received from on high. "As Thou hast sent Me into the world, I also have sent them into the world."[44] The society which He had founded was to exist as a manifest social miracle, attesting the fact of His own divine messengership. "That they all may be one, as Thou, Father, in Me, and I in Thee, that they also may be one in Us: that the world may believe that Thou has sent Me."[45] "I in them, and Thou in Me: that they may be made perfect in one: and the world may know that Thou hast sent Me, and hast loved them, as Thou hast also loved Me."[46]

It is evident, then, in the light of these statements attributed to Jesus of Nazareth in reliable historical documents, that He claimed His doctrine to be divinely revealed. There is, then, nothing which would militate against the credibility of Catholic doctrine by reason of the great Teacher of that doctrine having failed to assert its character as a message of divine origin.

10. The messianic claim and the office of deliverer. The claims of Jesus in favor of His teaching stand out still more clearly when we examine His contention that He was the Messiah expected by the children of Israel.[47] The sacred books of the Hebrews, which they accepted as the Word of God, were filled with information about a deliverer whom God was going to send into the world, and through whose activities the children of Israel and, as a matter of fact, all men were to be benefited immensely. The Jewish people and their leaders were waiting for this deliverer at the very time that Jesus was carrying out His work in the world.

In explaining the doctrinal claims of Jesus, it is necessary to point out the characteristics which the books of the Old Testament at-

---

44 John 17:25.
45 John 17:23.
46 John 17:18.
47 For a discussion of the messianic claims of Jesus, see De Grandmaison, *Jesus Christ*, Vol. 2, pp. 3–59; Felder, *Christ and the Critics*, Vol. I, pp. 119–237.

tributed to this Messiah, and then to demonstrate clearly that Jesus claimed for Himself not only this office, but all of the prerogatives associated with it. In making this explanation, we must take special cognizance of the various interpretations of the messianic office and dignity which were current among the Jews during the time when Jesus was preaching.

The Messiah was to be a deliverer, one whose duty it would be to undo the evil wrought upon the human race through the malice of Satan who had brought about the fall of Adam and the consequent baneful effects felt by the descendants of Adam. This deliverer was to be a descendant of Eve, and thus truly a "son of man." God said to the serpent in whom the enemy of the human race is represented, "I shall place enmities between thee and the woman, between thy seed and her seed. It will lie in wait for thy head, and thou wilt lie in wait for its heel."[48]

11. The Messiah was to bring a message from God. Furthermore, this Messiah was to be a prophet in the strict and technical sense of the term. He was to speak the words which God gave to him. In other words, He was commissioned to deliver to men a message which was actually from God a communication which God had spoken to man, and which man received in a way at once distinct from and superior to the natural way in which he derives his knowledge about the things of God. In the last book of the Pentateuch, Moses, the great prophet of the Old Law, is represented as saying to the people, "The Lord thy God will raise up to thee a prophet of thy nation and of thy brethren, like unto me: him thou shalt hear. As thou desiredst of the Lord thy God in Horeb, when the assembly was gathered together, and saidst: Let me not hear any more the voice of the Lord my God, neither let me see any more this exceeding great fire, lest I die. And the Lord said to me: They have spoken all things well. I will raise them up a prophet out of the midst of their brethren like to thee: and I will put My words in his mouth, and he shall speak all that I command him. And he that will not hear his words, which he shall speak in my name, I will be the revenger."[49]

---

48 Gen. 3:15.
49 Deut. 18:15–19.

According to the sacred text of the Hebrews, the people had asked God for a revelation which was mediate rather than immediate. They had feared the direct reception of the message which God willed to give them and which they desired to possess. So, in answer to their petition, God had first sent His teaching through Moses. Then He had promised them to send another prophet who would be empowered to speak to them as Moses had done before.

12. The Messiah as king. Again, the Messiah, or as the Greek form has it, the Christ or the Anointed One, was promised as a king having universal domination. "The sceptre shall not pass from Juda, nor the rod from between his feet, until he comes to whom the sceptre belongs, his is the domination of the nations."[50] "He shall rule from sea to sea: and from the river unto the ends of the earth. Before him the Ethiopians shall fall down: and his enemies shall lick the ground. The kings of Tharsis and the islands shall offer presents; the kings of the Arabians and of Saba shall bring gifts. And all the kings of earth shall adore him: all nations shall serve him."[51]

Thus the doctrinal authority of the Messiah, for with this we are principally concerned in this section of the science of apologetics, was meant to be absolutely universal. All the peoples of the earth, regardless of their power or position, were expected to receive the teaching which God offered to mankind through the preaching of this deliverer. In claiming the dignity and the prerogatives of the Messiah, Jesus of Nazareth asserted that He was the bearer of a revelation which was public rather than private. Furthermore, it was necessary, since God Himself had threatened to punish the individual who refused to accept this teaching.

13. The sacerdotal office of the Messiah. Finally, the Messiah was promised as a priest. In this way He was meant to stand as an intermediary between God and man. He was to offer the sacrifice acceptable to God, and thus perform the act in which the favor of God would be gained for those who were united with Him. "The Lord hath sworn, and He will not repent: Thou art a priest forever according to the order of Melchisedech."[52] He was to be the servant

---

50 Gen. 49:10.
51 Ps. 71:8–10.
52 Ps. 109:4.

of God in a special way, a friend of God and in every sense a just man. "Behold My servant shall understand, he shall be exalted and extolled, and shall be exceeding high."[53] In spite of the fact that, as the servant and the chosen friend of God, the Messiah was to be exalted above all other men, He was to suffer and die the most excruciating death. The fifty-third chapter in the book of Isaiah describes the death which the Messiah is to undergo. This death was to constitute the sacrifice which should continue, a clean oblation offered throughout the world for the glory of God until the end of time. "For from the rising of the sun even to the going down, My name is great among the gentiles, and in every place there is sacrifice, and there is offered to My name a clean offering: for My name is great among the gentiles, saith the Lord of Hosts."[54]

It is perfectly clear, from an examination of these reliable historical documents which we know as the four gospels, that Jesus of Nazareth claimed the dignity and the prerogatives of the Messiah. Furthermore, He applied to Himself this messianic dignity exactly as it had been described in the divinely inspired books of the Old Testament, and not as it had been distorted in the minds of a great many of his contemporaries. However, the fact that such a misconception of the messianic office existed and was fostered by the most powerful teachers among the Jewish people at the time when Jesus of Nazareth preached had a great deal to do with the manner in which He notified the people of His messianic character. In order to meet the religious needs of the moment He had to be careful not only to insist that He was actually the deliverer promised by God from ages past, but He had to be on His guard to see that His hearers realized that His office was not the one which had been described in the sermons of the rabbinical masters or in the writings of the eschatological school.

14. The rabbinical concept of the Messiah. Those rabbis who constituted the school of the Pharisees and whose doctrine was to become the official teaching of Judaism after the fall of Jerusalem and the subsequent disappearance of the Sadducee party had constructed and proposed a definite messianic concept.[55] Colored

---

53 Isa. 52:13
54 Mal. 1:11.
55 An expression of this rabbinical and popular messianic teaching is to be found in

and motivated by an intense nationalism, this concept utilized some of the Old Testament prophecies concerning the promised deliverer, but took these promises altogether apart from their context. The stern traditionalism of the Jewish masters kept this teaching extant until the time came when it was incorporated into the Talmud, to become thenceforth the official and orthodox doctrine of Judaism.

The messianism of the pharisaical rabbis centered about the Mosaic Law itself. The deliverance of Juda was to be accomplished in the mathematically accountable fidelity of the Jewish nation to that law. It would be brought about through a condition of things in which the balance sheet of the activities of this nation would show a definite preponderance in favor of those works which were prescribed by the law. Only after this state of things had been established was the Messiah Himself to arrive. Then His function was to establish that reign in which the promises of God to His people were to be fulfilled.

As these promises of the Creator were understood by the rabbis, they included the dominance of Juda over all the other kingdoms and peoples of this world. Palestine itself was to become a land of incredible fertility and pleasure. The other peoples of the earth were to be allowed access to it merely for the purpose of paying tribute and in order to glorify the perfection and felicity of its inhabitants.

15. Jesus rejected the rabbinical concept of the Messiah. Such a racial, political, and material concept of the messianic office was evidently in direct opposition to the implications of that teaching which Jesus of Nazareth presented to the world. Actually the reliable historical teaching which we find in the four gospels assures us that He rejected that rabbinical concept several times during the course of His preaching. After His teaching had been rejected by the leaders of the people who had been given full opportunity to learn about it, He assured His enemies that their traditions which included this rabbinical concept of the Messiah were contrary to the divine doctrine itself. "But He answering, said to them (the scribes and the Pharisees): Why do you also transgress the commandment of God for your tradition?"[56] He informed the Jewish populace which had rejected

---

the apocryphal Psalms of Solomon. Cf. Hans Lietzmann, *The Beginnings of the Christian Church*, translated by Bertram Lee Woolf (New York, 1937), pp. 27–34.
56 Matt. 15:31; see also Mark 7:8.

His teaching, that although they were children of Abraham according to the flesh, they were not the offspring which was to possess the messianic kingdom.[57] He told the people explicitly that the kingdom of God, which was the messianic realm, was to be peopled by those who were not members of the Jewish race, while the Jews themselves, heirs to the kingdom by reason of their physical descent, were to be cast out as unworthy of it. "There shall be weeping and gnashing of teeth: when you shall see Abraham and Isaac and Jacob, and all the prophets in the kingdom of God, and you yourselves thrust out. And there shall come from the east and the west and the north and the south, and shall sit down in the kingdom of God. And behold they are last that shall be first, and they are first that shall be last."[58]

The pointed parable of the murderous husbandmen was understood by the leaders of the people as a statement of their own rejection.[59] Finally, He commissioned His Apostles to carry His message to all nations,[60] or to every creature.[61]

The nonpolitical and nonmaterial character of His mission is evident from His conduct as well as from His words. When, after the first miracle of the loaves and the fishes, the people wished to take Him by force and make Him king, "He fled again into the mountain, Himself alone."[62] When the Roman procurator, Pontius Pilate, asked Him openly if He were the king of the Jews, knowing full well that this title belonged to the person whom the Jewish people expected as Messiah and deliverer, Jesus replied, "My kingdom is not of this world; If My kingdom were of this world, My servants would certainly strive that I should not be delivered to the Jews; but now My kingdom is not from hence. Pilate therefore said to Him: Art Thou a king then? Jesus answered: Thou sayest that I am a king. For this was I born, and for this I came into the world, that I should give testimony to the truth: every one that is of the truth, heareth My voice."[63]

---

57 John 8:31–59.
58 Luke 13:28–30; see also Matt. 8:11.
59 Matt. 21:45; Mark 12:12; Luke 20:19.
60 Matt. 28:19; Luke 24:46.
61 Mark 16:15.
62 John 6:15.
63 John 18:36–37.

The Claims of Jesus

The activity of Jesus, as well as His explicit teaching indicates very clearly that He did not accept the common pharisaical interpretation of the messianic office. It was His unmistakable assertion that He had not come as the ruler of a people destined to enjoy some vain triumph over its political and military rivals. He even refused to act as a secular judge, alleging that His mission did not include this office.[64] He claimed to be a king, but a king in the realm of truth. His messianic claims were in line with the assertions He had made about the divine origin of the doctrine which He offered to the children of men. They were likewise in line with the portrait of the Messiah, as this had been drawn in the authentic Old Testament sources, rather than in the tradition which He found opposed to the real law of God.

16. The eschatological concept of the messianic dignity. An apocalyptic or eschatological interpretation of the messianic concept, likewise foreign to the teaching of the Old Testament and to the doctrine of Jesus of Nazareth, is to be found in certain of the apocryphal books which appeared about the time Jesus of Nazareth lived in this world.[65] According to this teaching the duties of the Messiah were to be carried out after the end of the physical universe in which we live and have our being. The splendor of the messianic kingdom, and the humiliation of the enemies of God, who were also, of course, the foemen of the Jewish nation, was to be reserved to a time after a catastrophe regarded as imminent, which was to terminate the course of nature and to result in the death of all men. Where the Pharisees had hoped for the renovation of the Davidic kingdom in this corrupted world of ours, the producers of these eschatological works preferred to think of this triumph as taking place in a world far more fitted to receive the glory of the dominant Jewish state.

Naturally this concept was not as widespread among the people as that which had been introduced and fostered by the intellectual leaders. Jesus of Nazareth, however, clearly indicated that it did not enter into His teaching on those frequent occasions when He referred to His kingdom as something which was to exist in this world.

17. Jesus and the eschatological notion. It must be understood very clearly that Jesus did not deny that a certain portion of the

---

64 Luke 12:13–14.
65 This notion appeared in the apocryphal book of Esra. Cf. Lietzmann, *a.c.*, pp. 43–46.

messianic activity was to take place only at the end of the world. Several times during the course of His instructions He affirmed that He would come again to mankind at the end of the world, this time to act in the capacity of a just Judge. When the disciples asked Him "What shall be the sign of Thy coming, and of the consummation of the world?"[66] He informed them: "And then shall appear the sign of the Son of man in heaven: and then shall all the tribes of the earth mourn: and they shall see the Son of man coming in the clouds of heaven with much power and majesty."[67] Again, when the high priest adjured Jesus to inform the Sanhedrin if He was actually the Christ, the Son of the Blessed God, He replied: "I am, and you shall see the Son of man sitting on the right hand of the power of God, and coming with the clouds of heaven."[68]

Jesus evidently claimed to exercise the messianic functions, and thus to be the Messiah at the moment He was being questioned by the tribunal of the Jewish nation. At the same time He made it clear to His enemies that the messianic work included another element, a task which was not to be accomplished until a future time. What Jesus rejected out of the eschatological and apocalyptic notion of the messianic dignity was the claim that the office of the deliverer was not to begin until after the end of this world. Naturally He did not countenance the childish concept of material prosperity which both these writers and the Pharisees incorporated into their notion of the messianic kingdom.

The messianic realm which Jesus of Nazareth set out to found and to instruct was one to which a contumacious sinner might be cited.[69] Furthermore, it was an organization which was destined to include within its membership both just and unjust, precisely during the period which was to intervene between His preaching and the end of the world. The angels of heaven were to assist at the judgment on the last day. It was to be their function to cast the evil out of the kingdom which had existed during the years of human history as the

---

66 Matt. 24:3.
67 Matt. 24:30; see also Mark 13:26 and Luke 21:27.
68 Mark 14:62; see also Luke 22:69 and Matt. 26:54.
69 Matt. 18:17.

The Claims of Jesus

cockle is separated from the wheat at the time of harvest,[70] or as the fishes that are unfit to eat are separated from the rest of the catch by the fishermen who have come to the shore.[71]

In this world, the kingdom was to endure persecution and suffering, rather than enjoy the idle material benefits which are described both in the rabbinical and the eschatological writings.[72] It was to be an organization which would have corporate cause for sorrow.[73] But in the last analysis, the evils which the kingdom of the Messiah were to endure in this world were to be made bearable here and to be turned eventually into the ineffable joy of heaven.[74] The benefit which was to be conferred upon the citizens of the kingdom was something far greater than any of the rabbis had been able to imagine. It was the vision and the possession of the living God.[75]

18. Jesus took cognizance of the prevailing erroneous doctrines in asserting His true messianic dignity. However, the prevailing false interpretations of the messianic dignity made it necessary for Jesus of Nazareth to proceed with caution in instructing the multitudes about His office. During the earlier portion of His public life, He had occasion several times to forbid the publication of His messianic mission. Naturally He refused to allow this fact of His messianic character to be brought to the attention of men through the agencies of the demons, who were able to recognize Him.[76] It was certainly anything but proper that the enemies of God should have been allowed to publicize the divine message itself, and thus bring it into discredit. Furthermore, upon occasion He charged the very beneficiaries of His miracles not to tell the people about them. He acted thus with a leper whom He cleansed miraculously during the course of His Galilean ministry.[77] He asked the crowd before whom He had cured the deaf-mute not to tell about this marvelous operation, and the evangelist records that they failed to heed His

---

70 Matt. 13:30.
71 Matt. 13:47 and the following.
72 John 15:18–24.
73 John 16:20.
74 John 17:2.
75 John 17:3.
76 Mark 3:12; Luke 4:41
77 Matt. 8:4; Mark 1:43; Luke 5:14.

injunction.[78] Again, He forbade the blind men to whom He gave sight to inform their fellows about what had taken place, and this time also they disobeyed His command.[79]

With the current interpretations about the nature of the messianic office, and in view of the opinions about Himself which were current, not only at the court of Herod but also among the individuals with whom the Apostles themselves came in contact, it is small wonder that Jesus did not wish to offer proofs of the reality of His divine messengership until He had been accorded the opportunity of informing men exactly what His function was. Herod Antipas was of the opinion that Jesus was merely John the Baptist risen from the grave to reproach him for his sins.[80] (The third gospel merely says that Herod had heard this opinion advanced about Jesus. SS. Matthew and Mark, however, point out that he adopted this opinion himself and communicated it to his servants.) Others, some of them in the court of Herod, had ventured the conjecture that Jesus was Elijah, or one of the other prophets who had risen from the dead. Finally, there were others who thought that He was a prophet like one of the ancient bearers of the divine message.[81] When Jesus asked His disciples on that day near Caesarea Philippi about what men thought of Him, they were able to report only these same conjectures.[82] When such misunderstanding existed, it was only prudent that Jesus should reserve to Himself the work of explaining the nature of that office of which the miracles were regarded as divine testimonies of approbation. As a result He explicitly forbade the Apostles who had just heard the confession of Peter, but who had yet to understand the full importance of the messianic dignity, to announce to the people that He was the Christ.[83]

19. The messianic claim and consciousness of Jesus at the beginning of His public life. However, from the very outset of His public life, Jesus of Nazareth made it perfectly evident to all those who came in contact with His teaching that He was the Messiah who

---

78 Mark 7:36.
79 Matt. 9:30.
80 Matt. 14:2; Mark 6:14; Luke 9:7.
81 *L.c.* Both SS. Mark and Luke mention the opinion that Jesus was Elijah.
82 Matt. 16:13–14; Mark 8:27–28; Luke 9:18–19.
83 Matt. 6:20; Mark 8:30; Luke 9:31.

had been promised and foretold in the Old Testament. John the Baptist announced himself as the precursor of the deliverer who was to come,[84] and then clearly indicated Jesus as the One from whom the world was to expect its salvation.[85] When Jesus was coming out of the water after having been baptized by John, phenomena occurred leading the people to believe that Jesus was actually the Messiah. Jesus allowed that impression to exist.[86] John the Baptist afterward made explicit mention of these events when he indicated Jesus as the "Lamb of God," or the Messiah who was to be sacrificed in accordance with the prophecies which had been made and recorded in the Old Testament.[87]

Jesus of Nazareth claimed the messianic dignity for Himself in many ways. Sometimes He cited messianic prophecies and pointed out that these had been fulfilled in Him. At other times He applied to Himself one or other of the titles by which the Messiah had been designated in the Old Testament, and by which He was named among the Jewish people. Clearly, then, before His own disciples, before His own people, and before those foreigners who came into contact with Him, Jesus of Nazareth affirmed that He was a divine messenger insofar as He was the Messiah awaited by the Jewish people as the bearer of a communication from God to man.

20. The citation of Messianic prophecies. At the occasion of His first public preaching in Nazareth, where He had lived with Mary and with Joseph since their return from the flight into Egypt, Jesus cited an indubitably messianic prophecy recorded in the Old Testament, and then asserted that this prophecy had been written about Himself. "And He came to Nazareth where He was brought up: and He went into the synagogue, according to His custom, on the sabbath day; and He rose up to read. And the book of Isaiah the prophet was delivered unto Him. And as He unfolded the book, He found the place where it was written: The Spirit of the Lord is upon Me: wherefore He hath anointed Me, to preach, the gospel to the poor, He hath sent Me to heal the contrite of heart, to preach

---

[84] Matt. 3:11–12; Mark 1:7–8; Luke 3:16–17; John 1:30–33.
[85] John 1:19–35.
[86] Matt. 3:16–17; Mark 1:10–11; Luke 3:22.
[87] John 1:34.

deliverance to the captives, and sight to the blind, to set at liberty them that are bruised, to preach the acceptable year of the Lord, and the day of reward. And when He had folded the book, He restored it to the minister, and sat down. And the eyes of all in the synagogue were fixed on Him. And He began to say to them: This day is fulfilled this scripture in your ears."[88] This passage was taken from the sixty-first chapter of the prophecy of Isaiah. It is of undoubtedly messianic import. In asserting that He was the One pointed to by Isaiah, Jesus of Nazareth clearly indicated that the message which He brought to men was actually a divine revelation.

Not only did Jesus point out a definite and individual messianic prophecy, as He did in Nazareth, but He also claimed that the messianic prophecies as a whole applied to Him. "Search the scriptures, for you think in them to have life everlasting: and the same are they that give testimony of Me."[89] The messianic passages in the Pentateuch applied to Jesus, according to His own assertion. "Think not that I will accuse you to the Father; there is one that accuseth you, Moses, in whom you trust. For if you did believe Moses, you would perhaps believe Me also: for he wrote of Me."[90] The only personage who is described in the Pentateuch, as well as in the other books of the Old Testament, as coming to the rescue and for the instruction of the people is the Messiah. Hence, in asserting that Moses and the other authors of the sacred books had written of Him, Jesus of Nazareth clearly asserted that His message was divine revelation and was to be accepted as such by men. It was in this same fashion that Jesus replied to the disciples of John the Baptist who were sent to ask Him directly, "Art Thou He, that art to come, or look we for another? And Jesus making answer said to them: Go and relate to John what you have heard and seen. The blind see, the lame walk, the lepers are cleansed, the deaf hear, the dead rise again, the poor have the gospel preached to them: And blessed is he that shall not be scandalized in Me."[91]

---

88 Luke 4:16–21.
89 John 5:39.
90 John 5:45–46.
91 Matt. 11:4–6.

21. The Apostles understood from the outset that Jesus claimed to be the Messiah and recognized Him as such. The Apostles themselves considered Jesus as the Messiah, and they summoned their fellows to follow Him by informing them of His messianic dignity. St. Andrew informed Simon Peter, his brother, "We have found the Messiah: which is being interpreted, the Christ."[92] St. Philip summoned his friend Nathanael to follow Jesus by telling him, "We have found Him of whom Moses in the law, and the prophets did write, Jesus the Son of Joseph of Nazareth."[93] When Nathanael was loath to believe that the deliverer of the world could come from the town of Nazareth, which seems to have had a poor reputation among the people of Galilee, Jesus supported the assertion of Philip by telling Nathanael a closely guarded secret of his own life. And when, influenced by this obviously supernatural power, Nathanael openly professed the belief that Jesus was "the Son of God the king of Israel,"[94] he was not corrected but informed that he would experience far greater demonstrations of the divine messengership of Jesus.

22. Jesus claimed and was accorded the title of Messiah or Christ. The actual term *Messiah* occurs only twice in the Scriptures, both times in the gospel according to St. John. On both occasions the evangelist is at pains to inform his readers that the term is the term of which the Greek form *Christ* is the equivalent. The second time it was used, it is to be found in a setting in which Jesus asserted directly to the woman of Samaria that He was the Messiah. "The woman saith to Him: I know that the Messiah cometh (who is called Christ); therefore when he is come, he will tell us all things. Jesus saith to her: I am He, who am speaking with thee."[95] It is interesting to note that even at this time, to a woman who was not one of the children of Israel, Jesus took occasion to claim His messianic dignity precisely with reference to its doctrinal function.

The word *Christ* is found fifty-three times in the four gospels. St. John the Baptist stoutly denied that he was to be designated in this way. On the other hand, the four evangelists continually apply the

---

92 John 1:41.
93 John 1:45.
94 John 1:49.
95 John 4:25–26.

term to Jesus. Sometimes the word Christ is employed by itself as a proper name of Jesus.[96] Again, very frequently, they designate the Saviour as Jesus Christ, conjoining the messianic title with His given name.[97] Jesus Himself promised a reward to the one who would give the disciples even a cup of water "in My name, because you belong to Christ."[98] When He forbade His followers to assume the title of rabbi, He gave as a reason "for one is your Master, Christ."[99] Explicitly He affirmed that He was the Christ in the sacerdotal prayer which He offered to the Father the night before He was crucified. "Now this is eternal life: That they may know Thee, the only true God, and Jesus Christ, whom Thou hast sent."[100] After He had asked His Apostles about the conjectures which men had been making in His regard, He interrogated them about their belief and received the glorious confession of faith from Peter. "Jesus saith to them: But who do you say that I am? Simon Peter answered and said: Thou art Christ the Son of the living God. And Jesus answering, said to him: Blessed art thou, Simon Bar-Jona: because flesh and blood hath not revealed it to thee, but My Father who is in heaven. And I say to thee: That thou art Peter, and upon this rock I will build My church, and the gates of hell shall not prevail against it."[101]

Clearly and solemnly then He affirmed that He was the Christ. He maintained that the recognition of this fact had been due to the influence of God Himself; in other words, that it was a truth which unaided human nature would be unable to grasp. He rewarded the profession of Peter precisely by constituting him the visible head of the organization which He was in the process of founding. It is interesting to note in this respect that, while Jesus claimed that the recognition of His messianic status was something which had necessarily to depend upon the free grace of God, He made no such statement about the recognition of the fact that He claimed this dignity. All men might know, as the unbelievers who were His contemporaries knew very well, that He had taught that He was the

---

96 E.g., Matt. 1:18.
97 E.g., Matt. 1:1; Mark 1:1.
98 Mark 9:41. Cf. Matt. 10:42.
99 Matt. 23:10.
100 John 17:3.
101 Matt. 16:15–18.

Messiah. However, the certain assent to that claim, and the acceptance of the teaching which He gave with the assent of divine faith was actually something which could not be brought about other than with the aid of divine grace.

Solemnly again, at His trial before the Sanhedrin, Jesus claimed for Himself the title and the prerogatives of the Christ. "And the high priest said to Him: I adjure Thee by the living God, that Thou tell us if Thou be the Christ the Son of God. Jesus saith to him: Thou hast said it."[102] The very soldiers who tortured and insulted Him while He was being detained in the palace of the high priest knew of this claim and used it to mock Him. "Prophesy onto us, O Christ, who is he that struck Thee?"[103]

23. Jesus claimed the messianic royalty. Another messianic title which Jesus of Nazareth claimed and which His contemporaries applied to Him was that of king. As a matter of fact the Christ or the Messiah is really the anointed king, the descendant of David, whom God had promised to His people. This was the title under which the Magi thought of Jesus, and asked Herod about Him. "Where is He that is born king of the Jews?"[104] The populace wished to make Jesus king after they had witnessed the multiplication of the loaves and the fishes.[105] The throngs hailed Jesus as king when He entered triumphantly into Jerusalem on the first Palm Sunday.[106] It was a title by which Jesus was greeted at the outset of His public life by Nathanael.[107] The Jews brought Him before Pilate precisely as One who claimed to be Christ the King. "And they began to accuse Him saying: We have found this man perverting our nation, and forbidding to give tribute to Caesar, and saying that He is Christ the king."[108] To the interrogation of Pilate, Jesus answered, "Thou sayest that I am a king."[109] The cross on which He died was surmounted by an inscription, set there by the command of Pilate himself, "Jesus of

---

102 Matt. 26:63–64; Mark 15:61–62; Luke 22:70.
103 Matt. 26:68.
104 Matt. 2:2.
105 John 6:15.
106 Luke 19:38; John 12:12–13.
107 John 1:49.
108 Luke 23:2.
109 John 18:37.

Nazareth the King of the Jews."[110] Finally, when the Jews realized the import of this inscription, written as it was in Hebrew, Latin, and Greek, they sought to have Pilate change the wording to read merely that He said that He was the King of the Jews. This Pilate refused to do.[111] Thus that One whom the angel had promised would be given the throne of David His father[112] died proclaimed by the Roman judge as the royal ruler of the house of Israel.

24. The title Son of Man. The messianic title which Jesus of Nazareth used most frequently to designate Himself was that of the *Son of Man*. This title was used almost exclusively by Jesus Himself. The few times that the four gospels record it as having been spoken by others are precisely on occasions when these others merely quote the terms of the Master. For instance, St. John records that the crowd who heard Jesus in Judea during the last period of His public life asked Him about the meaning of the term. "The multitude answered Him: We have heard out of the law, that Christ abideth forever: and how sayest Thou: The Son of Man must be lifted up? Who is this Son of Man?"[113] Otherwise, in the course of the seventy-nine times this term appears in the four gospels, it is used by Jesus clearly to denominate Himself, as He is endowed with the characteristics of that deliverer who had been promised to the people of God.

The expression had occurred many times in the Old Testament. Very frequently it is employed simply to designate a human being. At other times, particularly in the prophecies of Ezechiel and Daniel, it was used to denominate the person to whom God's revelation is addressed, or man, precisely insofar as he is the beneficiary of the divine teaching. However it was used in an unquestionably messianic sense in the book of Daniel. "I beheld therefore in the vision of the night, and lo one like the son of man came with the clouds of heaven, and he came even to the Ancient of days: and they presented him before him. And he gave him power, and glory, and a kingdom: and all peoples, tribes and tongues shall serve him: his power is an everlasting power, that shall not be taken away: and his kingdom, that

---

110 John 10:19; Matt. 27:37; Mark 15:26; Luke 23:38.
111 John 19:21–22.
112 Luke 1:33.
113 John 12:34.

The Claims of Jesus

shall not be destroyed."[114] The four gospels record clearly that Jesus of Nazareth utilized the term "Son of Man" in the same messianic sense in which Daniel the prophet had employed it, since explicitly He applied to Himself, as the Son of Man, various characteristics which had qualified this figure in the message of Daniel.

As the Son of Man, Jesus asserted that He would have that power and glory which Daniel had described. "And Jesus said to them: Amen I say to you, that you who have followed Me, in the regeneration, when the Son of Man shall sit on the seat of His majesty, you also shall sit on twelve seats, judging the twelve tribes of Israel."[115] He promised to come in the clouds of heaven, in exactly the same manner as Daniel had stated that the Son of Man or the Messiah would come. "And then they shall see the Son of Man coming in a cloud with great power and majesty."[116] Furthermore, according to the express declaration of Jesus, the empire of the Son of Man, which was His own kingdom, would in no way be limited by bounds of territory or earthly dominion. "And He shall send His angels with a trumpet, and a great voice: and they shall gather together His elect from the four winds, from the farthest parts of the heavens to the utmost bounds of them."[117]

The power of the Son of Man is not restricted in any way to merely material concerns. He is able to exercise, in His own right, the divine prerogative of forgiving sins. "But that, you may know that the Son of Man hath power on earth to forgive sins, then said He to the man sick of the palsy: Arise, take up thy bed, and go into thy house."[118] His dominion is divine in the strictest sense of the word, since He vindicated for Himself as the Son of Man absolute power over the very day which had been set aside by God for His service. "For the Son of Man is Lord, even of the Sabbath."[119]

Jesus asserted that His mission, as the Son of Man, was doctrinal in character. "For he that shall be ashamed of Me, and of My words in this adulterous and sinful generation, the Son of Man also will be

---

114 Dan. 7:13–14.
115 Matt. 19:28.
116 Luke 21:27; Matt. 24:30; Mark 13:26.
117 Matt 24:31; Mark 13:27.
118 Matt. 9:6; Mark 2:10; Luke 5:24.
119 Matt. 12:8; Mark 2:28; Luke 6:5.

ashamed of him, when He shall come in the glory of His Father with the holy angels,"[120] Conversely, the man who adheres to the teaching of the Son of Man, and confesses Him before his fellow men, will be acknowledged by the same Son of Man when He comes in power with the angels of heaven to judge the peoples of the world. "And I say to you: Whosoever shall confess Me before men, him shall the Son of Man also confess before the angels of God: but He that shall deny Me before men, shall be denied before the angels of God."[121]

It is extremely clear in the teaching of Jesus that the Son of Man, as such, was sent into this world for the first time to aid men in their attainment of eternal happiness, and for their sake to suffer and to die at the hands of His enemies. He announced this for the first time clearly to the Apostles immediately after they had heard the glorious confession of Peter, and after Jesus had forbidden them to tell the world that He was really the Messiah. "The Son of Man must suffer many things, and be rejected by the ancients and chief priests and scribes, and be killed, and the third day rise again."[122] As a matter of fact it was precisely because the Apostles had not as yet been instructed about this essential portion of the messianic function that He refused to allow them immediately to proceed with their task of informing the people that He was the Christ.

Shortly afterward He announced again to the disciples that the Son of Man was to be abandoned and put to death, and even then the evangelists tell us that they were unable to understand and to bear this aspect of the messianic work.[123] "And all were astonished at the mighty power of God: but while all wondered at all the things He did, He said to His disciples: Lay you up in your hearts these words: for it shall come to pass that the Son of Man shall be delivered into the hands of men. But they understood not this word, and it was hid from them so that they perceived it not: and they were afraid to ask Him concerning this word."[124] During the instructions which He gave to the throngs on the first Palm Sunday, again, He announced this task which lay before Him.[125]

---

120 Mark 8:38; Luke 9:26. See also Matt. 16:27.
121 Luke 12:8–9; Matt. 10:32–33.
122 Luke 9:22; Mark 8:31. See also Matt. 16:21.
123 This was due to the profound influence exercised by the rabbinical teaching.
124 Luke 9:44–45; Mark 9:31–32; Matt. 17:22–23.
125 John 12:20–33.

The Claims of Jesus 163

However, neither the fact of the redemptive death of Jesus, announced and later described by Him as a function of the Son of Man,[126] nor the future glorious appearance of this same Son of Man in any way detracted from the fact that He claimed, as the Son of Man, to have a divine message which men were expected to accept on divine faith. In the discourse which is recorded in the sixth chapter of the gospel according to St. John, Jesus had spoken of Himself as the Son of Man.[127] But it is exactly as such that men are to believe in Him, that they are to accept Him as the messenger sent by God. "And Jesus said to them: I am the bread of life: he that cometh to Me, shall not hunger and he that believeth in Me, shall never thirst."[128] Again He told the Pharisees, after showing them the terrible prophecy that they were to die in their sins, "When you shall have lifted up the Son of man, then shall you know that I am He, and that I do nothing of Myself, but as the Father hath taught Me, these things I speak."[129]

There could be no clearer indication of the fact that Jesus claimed, precisely in His capacity as the Son of Man, to be the bearer of a divine message.

25. Jesus claimed the messianic prophetical function. Another title of messianic import by which Jesus of Nazareth was designated during the course of His earthly life was that of prophet. Obviously not every prophet who had labored among the children of Israel could lay claim to the dignity of the Messiah. But, from that portion of the revealed message which is expressed in the book of Deuteronomy, the Jews had been led to think of the deliverer who was to come in terms of prophetic activity. "The Lord thy God will raise up to thee a prophet of thy nation and of thy brethren like unto me: him thou shalt hear. I will raise them up a prophet out of the midst of their brethren, like unto thee: and I will put My words in his mouth, and he shall speak all that I command him."[130]

The historical books of the New Testament show very clearly that the contemporaries of Jesus chose to speak of the Messiah as the prophet "per excellentiam," the messenger of God gifted above all

---

126 Luke 24:27.
127 John 6:27.
128 John 6:33.
129 John 8:28.
130 Deut. 18:15, 18.

others who had been favored with that office. The delegation from the elders in Jerusalem, inquiring from John the Baptist about his right to teach and to baptize, received from him the information that he was neither the Christ nor the prophet.[131] The Samaritan woman recognized the prophetic dignity of Jesus Himself. "The woman saith to Him: Sir, I perceive that Thou art a prophet."[132]

St. Matthew recounts how the multitude in Jerusalem itself considered Jesus to be a prophet. "And seeking to lay hands on Him, they feared the multitudes: because they held Him as a prophet."[133] The response of the multitudes who had witnessed the feeding of the five thousand men with the five barley loaves and the two fishes was expressed in an act of faith in the prophetic mission of Jesus. "Now those men, when they had seen what a miracle Jesus had done, said: This is of a truth the prophet that is to come into the world."[134] Some of the people who were privileged to hear His teaching offered that selfsame observation. "Of that multitude therefore, when they had heard these words of His, some said: This is the prophet indeed."[135] This same title was given to Jesus by the man to whom He had given sight. "They say therefore to the blind man again: What sayest thou of Him who hath opened thy eyes? And he said: He is a prophet."[136]

When the people of Nairn had witnessed the raising up of the widow's son, they attributed the dignity and the office of prophet to Jesus who had performed this miracle. "And there came a fear on them all: and they glorified God, saying: A great prophet is risen up among us: and God hath visited His people."[137] Finally, when the risen Christ appeared to the discouraged pair of disciples on the road to Emmaus, they spoke of their Master as a prophet. They spoke "concerning Jesus of Nazareth, who was a prophet, mighty in work and word before God and all the people."[138]

In spite of the fact that certain of His contemporaries chose to think of Him as the reincarnation of one of the ancient Hebrew

---

131 John 1:21, 25.
132 John 4:19.
133 Matt. 21:46.
134 John 6:14.
135 John 7:40.
136 John 9:17.
137 Luke 7:16.
138 Luke 24:19.

prophets,[139] Jesus of Nazareth applied the prophetic title to Himself on several occasions. He told His fellow townsmen of Nazareth, "A prophet is not without honor, save in his own country and in his own house."[140] He used this same designation when He taught of the reward which would be due to those who accepted and aided Himself and His emissaries. "He that receiveth a prophet in the name of a prophet, shall receive the reward of a prophet."[141] Finally, He spoke of His own Redemptive mission when He told the Pharisees who had come to Him, "It cannot be that a prophet perish out of Jerusalem."[142]

26. He who was to come. Another specifically messianic title which Jesus claimed for Himself, and through which He asserted that the doctrine He preached was in reality a message from God to be accepted by all with the assent of divine faith, was that of "the one who was to come." The only dominating personality who was awaited by the righteous among the people of Israel was the promised Messiah. Consequently when John the Baptist sent his disciples on their last mission to Jesus, they were empowered and expected to ask Him officially if He was this Messiah. Their question was, "Art Thou He that art to come, or look we for another?"[143] The response of Jesus was the most solemn and certain assurance that this title actually belonged to Himself.

27. The Son of David. Another messianic title by which Jesus of Nazareth was hailed among His people was that of the Son of David. Two of the blind men to whom Jesus gave their sight appealed to Him under this title. "And as Jesus passed from thence, there followed Him two blind men, crying out and saying: Have mercy on us, O Son of David."[144] The throngs who greeted Jesus on the first Palm Sunday acknowledged Him as the descendant of the great king of Israel and consequently as the promised possessor of the messianic kingdom. "And the multitudes that went before and that followed cried saying: Hosanna to the Son of David: Blessed is He that cometh

---

139 Cf. Luke 9:19.
140 Matt. 13:57. Cf. Mark 6:4; Luke 4:24; John 4:44.
141 Matt. 10:41.
142 Luke 13:33.
143 Luke 7:19; cf. Matt. 11:3.
144 Matt. 9:27; 20:30–31; Mark 10:47–48; Luke 18:38–39.

in the name of the Lord: Hosanna in the highest. And when He was come into Jerusalem, the whole city was moved, saying: Who is this? And the people said: This is Jesus the prophet from Nazareth of Galilee."[145] When the chief priests and the scribes protested against this demonstration to Jesus, He informed them in no uncertain terms that this was pleasing to Him. Thus He accepted the designation of Son of David in the most public and open manner possible.[146]

The contemporary misunderstandings among the Jews relative to the nature and the function of the messianic kingdom were sufficient to force a clarification of the title, Son of David. The response of the multitudes in Jerusalem and the spontaneous petitions of those persons who called upon Jesus for aid show us very clearly that this designation was a popular term for the Messiah.

As a result Jesus had to see to it that men did not consider that He claimed the messianic dignity merely in the way in which this dignity was described in the rabbinical teaching of that time. Although He approved the use of this title by others, the gospels do not record that He ever directly applied it to Himself. Furthermore, on one occasion, described in all of the three synoptic gospels, He taught explicitly that His messianic dignity as the Son of David was far superior to that which had been ascribed to the deliverer in the teaching of the Jewish masters, "And the Pharisees being gathered together, Jesus asked them, saying: What think you of Christ? Whose son is He? They say to Him: David's. He saith to them: How then doth David in spirit call Him Lord, saying: The Lord said to my Lord: sit on my right hand, until I make thy enemies thy footstool? If David then call Him Lord, how is He his son?"[147]

It is obvious from the account of Jesus' reaction to the title Son of David, described throughout the synoptics, that He did not in any way attempt to deny that He was physically the descendant of the great Israelitic king, and consequently the heir to the promised kingdom. All that He set out to do, and that He actually accomplished, was to advance a demonstration that the Messiah, the bearer of the divine

---

145 Matt. 11:9–11.
146 Cf. Mark 11:10
147 Matt. 22:41–45. Cf. also Mark 12:35–37; Luke 20:41–44.

message, was not to be merely the possessor of an earthly kingdom of the type over which David had ruled.

28. The claim of divinity and that of revelation. Most important of all, from the point of view of the doctrinal claims advanced by Jesus of Nazareth, was the fact that the historical records which we know as the four gospels clearly indicate that He asserted Himself to be a divine person in the strictest sense of the term. Since, according to His own claims, He was not only the bearer of a divine message, but actually God Himself, it follows clearly that He taught that His doctrine was something which men were expected to receive on divine faith. Thus, from this point of view at least, Catholic dogma is rationally credible as divine revelation, since it claims to be the message which was brought to men as the teaching of God by Jesus of Nazareth. It is abundantly and immediately clear, from the reliable historical documents which we have available to us, that Jesus of Nazareth really asserted that He was the bearer of such a divine teaching.

29. Jesus asserted that His doctrine was intrinsically supernatural. However, this chapter would be lamentably incomplete were we not to consider what Jesus said about the intrinsically supernatural character of His teaching. We know very well that this divine revelation with which Jesus was concerned might have been supernatural merely from the point of view of the way in which it was given to men, while it remained at the same time intrinsically natural in quality. If this had been the case, then there would have been no need for the act of divine faith, precisely as the Catholic Church claims it for her own dogmatic teaching. For an intrinsically natural teaching could be accepted on natural evidence, even though it had come to man by avenues other than those naturally available to him for the attainment of his knowledge about God. If, for example, the teaching of Jesus had been such as to contain merely truths like that of the existence of God, or of the natural norms of morality, men could treat this teaching in the same way as they deal with the teaching of any great philosopher or scientist. They could have adduced the evidence which was brought before them, and then from the examination of this evidence realized that the statements contained in the teaching were necessarily true.

However, according to the words of Jesus, such was not the case. He asserted that the doctrine which He presented to the world was something which could not possibly be gained through any merely human process of reasoning. In the interview which He granted to Nicodemus, He stated, "Amen, amen I say to thee, that we speak what we know, and we testify what we have seen, and you receive not, our testimony. If I have spoken to you earthly things, and you believe not: how will you believe if I shall speak to you heavenly things?"[148] The heavenly things to which Jesus referred were obviously matters about which men could not learn apart from the revelation which He brought to them. The evangelist appended this explanation to the words of St. John the Baptist. "He that cometh from above, is above all. He that is of the earth, of the earth he is, and of the earth he speaketh. He that cometh from heaven, is above all. And what He hath seen and heard, that He testifieth: and no man receiveth His testimony."[149] The doctrine of Christ is thus described explicitly as a teaching which results from the vision of the living God, something obviously beyond the natural competence of any creature, actual or possible.

Jesus Himself declared that faith in Him, that is to say acceptance of His teaching with the certain assent of divine belief, was something which could be possessed only by those to whom God Himself had given the grace to make this act. It is consequently an act over and above the capacity of the creature as such. "No man can come to Me, except the Father, who hath sent Me, draw him."[150] After the defection of the false disciples, consequent upon the sermon of Jesus about the Eucharistic sacrifice, Peter expressed the conviction of the other Apostles and the teaching of the Master Himself when he made his illustrious response. "Then Jesus said to the twelve: Will you also go away? And Simon Peter answered Him: Lord, to whom shall we go? Thou hast the words of eternal life."[151] The evident connotation of this statement by the prince of the Apostles is that they realized that the truths taught by Jesus Christ were such that they could be

---

148 John 3:11–12.
149 John 3:31–32.
150 John 6:44.
151 John 6:68–69.

obtained from no other source. They were thus obviously statements which were intrinsically supernatural in their meaning.

After Peter had spoken for the other Apostles and expressed the belief that Jesus was actually the Christ, the Son of the living God, Jesus pointed out the intrinsically supernatural character of this truth. "And Jesus answering, said to him: Blessed art thou Simon Bar-Jona: because flesh and blood hath not revealed it to thee, but My Father who is in heaven."[152] In other words, the truth which Peter had enunciated was beyond the range of those verities which might be perceived through the natural operation of the human faculties.

30. The beneficent revelation. In His discourse in the temple on the feast of the tabernacles, Jesus of Nazareth made it quite clear that His doctrine came from a source which was not seen by those who chose to oppose Him. "Jesus therefore cried out in the temple, teaching and saying: You both know Me, and you know whence I am: and I am not come of Myself; but He that sent Me is true, whom you know not. I know Him: because I am from Him, and He hath sent Me."[153] The doctrine which He offered then was something which depended upon the knowledge of the living God, a sort of knowledge not available to creatures as such. Likewise, the Master made it abundantly evident that the acquisition of this knowledge did not in any way depend upon the natural brilliance nor on the intellectual training of the individual man. It was communicated by God in the way of divine and supernatural revelation, and only those who had been favored with the gift of God's grace would possess it. "At the same hour He rejoiced in the Holy Ghost, and said: I confess to Thee, O Father, Lord of heaven and earth, because Thou hast hidden these things from the wise and prudent and hast revealed them to little ones. Yea Father: for so it hath seemed good in Thy sight."[154] Furthermore, this supernatural revelation was such as to be inaccessible to the merit even of the good men who had lived in former times. "And turning to His disciples, He said: Blessed are the eyes that see the things which you see. For I say to you, that many prophets and kings have desired to see the things that you see, and

---

152 Matt. 16:17.
153 John 7:28–29.
154 Luke 10:21; Matt. 11:25.

have not seen them: and to hear the things that you hear, and have not heard them."[155]

It is evident, then, from the records of Jesus' own life, that He made exactly the same claim for His teaching that the Catholic Church to this day sets forth in favor of that doctrine which she presents to the world as having been preached by Him. If it can be shown that Jesus actually taught a doctrine which is that now offered by the Catholic Church in the form of her own dogma, and if this doctrine is actually signed with unmistakable marks of authenticity, manifesting it as a doctrine which God Himself visibly approves as His revelation, then the teaching of Jesus as the dogma of the Catholic Church will have been established as rationally credible in its claim for the assent of divine faith.

---

155 Luke 10:23–24; Matt. 13:16–17.

Chapter 10

THE DOCTRINAL CONTENT IN THE MESSAGE OF JESUS

PART I:
The New Dispensation and the Old Law

1. The reason for this study. The crucial problem for the modern apologist concerns the content of that teaching which Jesus of Nazareth preached to His disciples and to His fellow countrymen. If His doctrines had been only general and vague in character, if He had occupied Himself merely with attempting to form a religious attitude in the minds of those who were privileged to hear Him, then, of course, there could be no possible question of my rational credibility on the part of the definite teaching that the Catholic Church offers in His name. If, on the other hand, He proposed a definite system of truth and claimed for this dogmatic teaching the characteristic of divine revelation, and, furthermore, if it can be shown that this is the very doctrine which is now brought before the world as Catholic dogma, then, from this point of view at least, there is nothing to stand in the way of a declaration of credibility being issued in favor of this Catholic dogma.

2. The modern liberal view. This examination of the message of Christ, as it is made known to us in the historically reliable documents, is of utmost importance to the present-day apologist precisely because it is on this point that the most serious attacks of modern opponents have centered. It is a commonplace contention among liberal writers about the Christian message that Jesus of Nazareth never intended to set forth a definite and particular system of religious teaching. In recent times Nathaniel Micklem, principal of Mansfield College, Oxford, has suggested "this contention that the work of Christ is action rather than doctrine, and that the doctrine is but the commentary on the action" as the most effective means for answering the objections of those who suppose that St. Paul the Apostle changed the message of Christ and actually founded the Christianity which we know today. He states that this contention "is increasingly recognized by modern scholarship, but it can never be demonstrated beyond cavil that such is the only possible interpretation of the facts."[1] According to this eminent writer, however, the denial of this contention would involve an admission either that "the Jesus of history" is misrepresented in the books of the New Testament or that He Himself was in error.

Professor McCown who, in spite of the preponderant evidence offered by modern critical research, still refuses to admit the historicity of St. John's Gospel and who professes to see in the synoptics a meager tradition about a Jesus who actually lived in Palestine nineteen hundred years ago spread through expressions of apostolic faith in an already idealized mystical Christ and biased apostolic propaganda in favor of the gospel, asserts that, "because they are not intellectualistic or philosophical, the basic qualities in Jesus which have always appealed to men can be fitted into the Orient and the Occident, into ancient and modern civilization with equal ease and difficulty."[2] It is his contention that the Jesus of history will never be fully known, and indeed that it is well for the world that He will not be so known. In any event he is perfectly convinced that there is no evidence to show that the system preached as Christianity was ever set forth by Jesus of Nazareth.

Naturally the greater number of non-Catholic scholars are sufficiently abreast of the times not to take seriously the brash dicta and attitudes of a long since outmoded nineteenth-century radical criticism. But even relatively conservative writers like Morrison, while conceding that Jesus taught a definite doctrine and established a definite religious organization, refuse to admit certain elements in that teaching.[3] Dodd, less conservative, tells us that "Jesus stood

---

[1] *The Primitive Church*, by Nathaniel Micklem, included in the symposium *The Christian Faith, Essays in Explanation and Defense*, edited by W. R. Matthews (New York and London, 1936). p. 179.

[2] *The Search for the Real Jesus, A Century of Historical Study*, by Chester Charlton McCown (New York, 1940), p. 301.

[3] *What Is Christianity?*, by Charles Clayton Morrison (Chicago and New York, 1940).

The New Dispensation and the Old Law

isolated among the movements of His time. He took no side in the conflict of ideals. Nor did He form a party of His own. It is true that He collected a band of followers who might be variously regarded as the disciples of a rabbi or the accomplices of a conspirator. But when He commissioned them to carry His message through the towns and villages of Palestine, He gave them, as far as our records tell, no programme and no body of teaching to propagate."[4] The teaching of Moore is just as perfectly indicative of this attitude toward the content of Christ's doctrine. "Jesus was not in his own thought nor in the apprehension of those who heard him, friend or foe, the founder of a new religion. However different the emphasis of his teaching from that of the school and the synagogue, he had no doctrine about God's nature and character, or about what he requires of men, or on his relation to his people and his purpose for them, or concerning the hereafter of the individual and the world, that would have been unfamiliar to a well-instructed Jew of his time." The distinguished Harvard Professor thus expresses his positive conviction about the nature of that teaching which was offered by Jesus. "Here, then, is the emphasis of Jesus' teaching—piety, morality, and charity."[5]

3. The duty of the modern apologist. In the face of this frankly expressed attitude, it is obviously the business of the Catholic apologist to undertake the not too difficult work of showing that, in the teaching of Jesus which is recorded in reliable historical documents, there is abundant evidence that He founded a new religion, that He did set forth dogmatic teaching which was not only not familiar to the well-instructed Jews of His own time, but which was so difficult in itself as to occasion the withdrawal from His company of the majority of those who had formerly professed to be His disciples. It was this definite, positive, and personal teaching which He set forth as divinely revealed and as a body of doctrine which, as essentially supernatural in character, men could not possess except insofar as they were strengthened by the free gift of divine grace. Furthermore, it can be shown that this doctrine is and has always been proposed

---

See Lecture X, pp. 250–275.
4 *History and the Gospel*, by C. H. Dodd (New York, 1938), p. 123.
5 *History of Religions*, by George Foot Moore, Vol. 2 (New York, 1941, original edition, 1919), p. 114.

by the Catholic Church as the divine revelation which came to men through the preaching of Jesus of Nazareth.

4. New Testament books and Catholic dogma. Naturally, one paramount fact must be kept in mind in the course of this portion of apologetics. Holy Scripture is by no means the only source of divine revelation, acknowledged and utilized by the Catholic Church. According to her own dogmatic definition, she finds those truths which she proposes as divinely revealed and to be believed with the assent of divine faith by all men in Scripture and in the divine apostolic tradition. There are truths which belong to the deposit of divine public revelation, truths which were proposed by Jesus Christ as divinely revealed, which are not clearly contained on the pages of the inspired books. Obviously then, when we utilize the books of the New Testament, and in particular the four canonical gospels, as naturally verifiable historical sources, we cannot hope to see in them a complete picture of that Catholic dogma, the rational credibility of which we are meant to demonstrate in the science of apologetics. But, conversely, we can expect to recognize, in the authentic dogmatic teaching of the Catholic Church, every doctrine which the historical sources at our disposal show that Jesus of Nazareth actually set forth as divinely revealed during the course of His earthly life.

It is perfectly true that unwritten divine apostolic tradition is, along with sacred Scripture, a genuine source of revelation. Likewise it is certain that, according to the teaching which has always been current in the Church, the actual process of public revelation did not close with the death or even with the ascension of Jesus, but only with the death of the last Apostle. Thus evidently such truths as the content of the New Testament canon could not have been allocated, and must not be sought, in the content of that teaching of Jesus Christ which is set forth on the pages of the four gospels. However, we can expect to find, in the message of Jesus, as it is set forth on the pages of these historical sources, a clear *outline* of the complete dogmatic teaching, the rational credibility of which we wish to demonstrate. And in the stage in which the science of apologetics finds itself today, the process of this discipline would in no way be complete and convincing if we were to neglect this inquiry.

5. The modern objections and apologetical science. The matter contained in this chapter was, as we have seen, incorporated into the science of apologetics by reason of the direction from which the present-day opposition to Catholic dogma proceeds. Nevertheless, we must not allow ourselves to think that it is foreign to the proper content of this science of apologetics. This discipline has been in the process of development during the course of all those centuries in which the Catholic mind has been concerned with the defense of revealed truth against the strictures of its opponents. Actually the sections which go to make up the content of this science, in its present-day stage of development, have been incorporated into it originally by reason of some definite objections raised against the credibility of the divine teaching. The modern contention that Christ did not set forth a definite and proper religious message has only served to call attention to the proofs which establish the contradictory truth. By inserting this portion of the apologetical demonstration into the science, the modern apologist not only responds to the contentions advanced against Christianity in his own day. Actually he contributes to the full perfection of that demonstration of credibility of which the science of apologetics is essentially capable.[6]

6. Jesus and the Mosaic dispensation. In proving that Jesus of Nazareth offered as divinely revealed a definite system of religious truth which had not been proposed by any teacher before Him, we must not allow ourselves to lose sight of the fact that not every truth which entered into the religious teaching of Christ was first brought to the attention of men through His preaching. According to the teaching of Jesus Himself, the doctrine which He brought to the world had been introduced to mankind in the revelation given by God through the agency of Moses and the prophets of the Old Testament. In His Sermon on the Mount, the Master made this point very clear. "Do not think that I am come to destroy the law, or the prophets: I am come not to destroy but to fulfill. For amen I say unto

---

[6] Unfortunately too many modern apologists neglect this section of their science entirely. However, a fine treatment of the definite dogmatic content in the message of Jesus is to be found in Garrigou-Lagrange, *De Revelatione*, Vol. 2, pp. 167–215; in *Critique et Catholique*, by Father Hugueny, O.P., Vol. 2, parts 1 and 2 (Paris, 1924), and by C. Lavergne, O.P., in his treatise *"Le Christ et l'Évangile de Jesus-Christ"* (pp. 366–379), in *Apologetique*.

you, till heaven and earth pass, one jot or one tittle shall not pass of the law, till all be fulfilled."[7] It was His contention that the prophecies had been fulfilled since Moses, the chief human author of the Old Testament, and the one to whom the Old Law had been directly communicated by God, had written concerning Him. "For if you did believe Moses, you would perhaps believe Me also: for he wrote of Me."[8] At the very outset of His public life, He so instructed His first disciples that they proposed Him to their fellows as the fulfillment of the prophecies contained in the Old Testament. "Philip findeth Nathanael, and saith to him: We have found Him of whom Moses in the law, and the prophets did write, Jesus the Son of Joseph of Nazareth."[9]

7. The speculative truths. The body of speculative doctrinal truths which were contained in the revelation of the Old Testament were included as a whole in the religious teaching which He proposed to men as divinely revealed. "Then Jesus spoke to the multitudes and to His disciples, saying: The scribes and the Pharisees have sitten on the chair of Moses. All things therefore whatsoever they shall say to you observe and do: but according to their works do ye not: for they say and do not."[10] The scribes and the Pharisees, among whom the most deadly of the enemies of Jesus were to be found, had their teaching approved by Him precisely insofar as that teaching was the expression of that doctrine which God had given to Israel through Moses, and with Moses the school of the prophets which had been the vehicle through which the additional revealed truths contained in the Old Testament dispensation had come to mankind. What God had given to man in the way of truth during those years remained true, and remained matter which men were meant to accept with the assent of divine faith even when these verities came to them in the instruction of unworthy teachers of the type of the scribes and the Pharisees.

8. The Mosaic Ritual. The ceremonial or ritual observances contained in the revelation of the Old Testament were, of course,

---

7 Matt. 5:17–18; Luke 16:17.
8 John 5:46.
9 John 1:45.
10 Matt. 23:1–3.

abolished through the institution of that new sacrifice, the "clean offering" of which the prophet Malachi had written. "For from the rising of the sun even to the going down, My name is great among the Gentiles, and in every place there is sacrifice, and there is offered to My name a clean offering: for My name is great among the gentiles, saith the Lord of hosts."[11] This great act of the New Testament was explicitly instituted by Jesus Himself. "And whilst they were at supper, Jesus took bread, and blessed, and broke, and gave to His disciples, and aid: Take ye, and eat: This is my body. And taking the chalice He gave thanks: and gave to them, saying: Drink ye all of this. For this is My blood of the New Testament which shall be shed for many unto remission of sins."[12]

Obviously the institution of the great sacrificial act for which the ceremonies of the Old Testament were merely a preparation involved the abolition of these preparatory rituals. The prophecy of Malachi explicitly connects the institution of the new with the cessation of the old, since these words are prefixed to the announcement of the "clean oblation." "I have no pleasure in you, saith the Lord of hosts: and I will not receive a gift of your hands."[13] The hand from which God had received the offerings of the people under the Old Testament dispensation were those of the Aaronitic priesthood. Clearly then God states in this portion of His message that, with the advent of the new sacrifice, the work of the ancient priesthood will have come to an end. In the institution of the new sacrifice by Jesus, there was the fulfillment of that ancient rite which had been essentially preparatory in character.

9. The moral doctrine of the Old Testament. Still another procedure was followed in the fulfillment of that portion of the law which had to do with morals. Those acts which of their very nature were sinful and destructive of the life of grace which Jesus Christ had come to give to men were forbidden both in the Old and in the New Testaments. To the young man who asked Him how everlasting life was to be obtained, Jesus replied, "Thou knowest the commandments: Thou shalt not kill: Thou shalt not commit adultery: Thou shalt

---

11 Mal. 1:11.
12 Matt. 26:26–28; Mark 14:23–24; Luke 22:19–20. See also 1 Cor. 11:23–26.
13 Mal. 1:10.

not steal: Thou shalt not bear false witness: Honor thy father and mother."[14] Likewise, the love of God above all things else, which was commanded in the Old Testament,[15] remained the central and focal point of all the moral teaching inculcated by Jesus of Nazareth. "And behold a certain lawyer stood up, tempting Him, and saying: Master, what must I do to possess eternal life? But He said to Him: What is written in the law? How readest thou? He answering, said: Thou shalt love the Lord thy God with thy whole heart, and with thy whole soul, and with all thy strength, and with all thy mind: and thy neighbor as thyself. And He said to him: Thou hast answered right: this do, and thou shalt live."[16] However, even in the case of these primary rules of the natural law, the teaching advanced by Jesus of Nazareth contained elements distinctly more perfect than the portion of revealed truth which had been brought to men through His predecessors.

While the basic command to love God above all things was naturally included in the Mosaic dispensation, the application of this rule in the love to be accorded to one's neighbor was somewhat restricted. In the Old Law, frankly, the obligation of loving one's neighbor did not go beyond prescribing an affection for those who were members of the Israelitic community. "Thou shalt not hate thy brother in thy heart, but reprove him openly, lest thou incur sin through him. Seek not revenge, nor be mindful of the injury of thy citizens. Thou shalt love thy friend as thyself. I am the Lord."[17]

When the lawyer who is spoken of in the gospel according to St. Luke as having tempted Jesus and having consequently been interrogated by Him about the content of the law wished to gain an advantage over the Master, it is recorded that He pushed the question by asking about the meaning attached to the term "neighbor" in the response which he himself had just given. Jesus answered him with the magnificent story of the Good Samaritan.[18] As everyone knows, there existed between the Jews and the Samaritans of that day an enmity which, as a matter of fact, the passing years have never

---

14 Luke 18:20.
15 Deut. 6:5.
16 Luke 10:24–28. See also Matt. 22:37; Mark 13:30.
17 Lev. 19:17–18.
18 Luke 10:29–37.

lessened. It was the contention of Jesus, and an integral part of the doctrine which He proposed to the world as divinely revealed, that the object of that love of man which is the expression of the love accorded to the Creator Himself could even be a member of the despised and hated race of the Samaritans. This was very definitely an aspect of Jesus' teaching which was "unfamiliar to the well-instructed Jew of His time."[19] Not only was this teaching above the content of the Jewish religion as it existed at the time of Jesus, but even in modern times the Jewish encyclopedia article relative to this matter professes to see in this story recounted in Luke an obvious mistake in recording the words of Jesus. It is the contention of this author that Jesus had spoken, not of the Good Samaritan, but of some "Good Israelite" since no Jew of the time of Christ could possibly have spoken well of this race so hated by his confreres. In this way obviously the teaching of Jesus presented a real advance over the hitherto received revealed truth and a real fulfillment of the moral code set forth in the Mosaic revelation.

This same perfectional development is manifest in His treatment of the negative precepts contained in the Mosaic moral law. "You have heard that it was said to them of old: Thou shalt not kill: and whosoever shall kill, shall be in danger of the judgment. But I say to you: that whosoever is angry with his brother, shall be in danger of the judgment. And whosoever shall say to his brother, Raca: shall be in danger of the council. And whosoever shall say, Thou fool: shall be in danger of hell fire. If therefore thou offer thy gift at the altar, and there thou remember that thy brother hath anything against thee: Leave there thy offering before the altar, and go first to be reconciled to thy brother: and then coming thou shalt offer thy gift."[20] This universality and strict consistency in the love of benevolence which is to be accorded to our fellows will obviously be found to go far beyond the requirements imposed in the moral portion of the Mosaic code. In this respect the teaching of Jesus of Nazareth was quite clearly a religious teaching advanced by Him independently of the doctrine current among the people of His time. It represents a

---

19 Cf. Moore, *History of Religions*, l.c.
20 Matt. 5:21–24.

definite set of truths for which He could reasonably claim the dignity of a definite and individual divine revelation.

10. The permissions granted in the old dispensation. There is still another aspect under which the moral doctrine put forth by Jesus of Nazareth can be recognized as His own teaching, and not merely the restatement of truths which were universally accepted as divinely revealed. Certain permissions had been accorded by God to the people of Israel in the revealed message of the Old Testament. For instance, it had been permitted to the Jews to put away their wives and then to marry another woman, and likewise it was permissible for the dismissed woman to be taken by another man. "If a man take a wife, and have her, and she find not favor in his eyes for some uncleanness: he shall write a bill of divorce, and shall give it in her hand, and send her out of his house. And when she is departed and marrieth another husband, and he also hateth her, and hath given her a bill of divorce, and hath sent her out of his house, or is dead: The former husband cannot take her again to wife, because she is defiled, and is become abominable before the Lord: lest thou cause thy land to sin, which the Lord thy God shall give thee to possess."[21] It is clear in this instance that the rejected wife cannot be taken again by a former husband, but there is nothing to prevent her marrying another man with whom she has not been married before.

Jesus of Nazareth clearly withdrew this permission which had been given to the children of Israel, and which had been integrated into the Mosaic moral code itself. "And it hath been said: Whosoever shall put away his wife, let him give her a bill of divorce. But I say to you, that whosoever shall put away his wife, excepting the cause of fornication, maketh her to commit adultery: and he that shall marry her that is put away, committeth adultery."[22] We read in the historical accounts of the life of the Master which are accessible to us that the leaders of the Jewish nation did not fail to push their inquiries into a teaching with which they at least, as well-instructed Jews of the time of Jesus, were not at all familiar. "There came to Him the Pharisees tempting Him, and saying: Is it lawful for a man to put away his wife for every cause? Who answering said to them: Have ye not read, that He who made

---

21 Deut. 24:1–4.
22 Matt. 5:31–32. See also Luke 16:18.

man from the beginning, made them male and female and He said: For this cause, shall a man leave father and mother, and shall cleave to his wife, and they two shall be, in one flesh; Therefore, now they are not two, but one flesh. What therefore God hath joined together, let no man put asunder. They say to Him: Why then did Moses command to give a bill of divorce, and to put away? He saith to them: Because Moses by reason of the hardness of your heart permitted you to put away your wives: but from the beginning it was not so. And I say to you, that whosoever shall put away his wife, except it be for fornication, and shall marry another, committeth adultery: and he that shall marry her that is put away, committeth adultery."[23]

11. The authority of Jesus. It is interesting to note that here, as in many other places where He dealt with the moral prescriptions of the Mosaic Law to which He brought fulfillment and perfection, Jesus of Nazareth utilized the formula, "But I say to you." This expression occurs sixty-five times in the course of the four gospels as a clear indication of the fact that the teaching which is offered is that of Jesus alone, a portion of that message which they are to receive on the authority of God revealing if they are to have the faith in Him which He prescribed. The expression is found, in this sense, thirty-one times in St. Matthew, twice in St. Mark, twenty-nine times in St. Luke, and thrice in St. John.

12. The counsels and the new covenant. The moral prescriptions of the Mosaic covenant were fulfilled in the teaching of Jesus of Nazareth in still another manner. The portion of the Old Testament which had dealt with morals had contented itself with commanding those acts which were actually requisite for proper human activity and forbidding those operations which were of themselves sinful and offensive to God. Jesus, however, included in His message recommendations or counsels which men were not by any means obliged to follow in order to attain eternal life, but in the following of which they would be enabled to serve God more perfectly and efficiently. The evangelical counsel of perfect chastity is illustrative of this class of recommendations. Jesus gave this advice to the Apostles who professed themselves surprised at the new teaching which Jesus had given on the indissolubility of marriage. "His disciples say unto

---

23 Matt. 19:3–9. See also Mark 10:2–12.

Him: If the case of a man with his wife be so, it is not expedient to marry. Who said to them: All men take not this word, but they to whom it is given. For there are eunuchs, who were born so from their mother's womb: and there are eunuchs, who were made so by men: and there are eunuchs, who have made themselves eunuchs for the kingdom of heaven. He that can take, let him take it."[24]

In fulfilling the Mosaic Law, Jesus of Nazareth professed also to teach those truths which had been communicated by God to man in the way of public revelation before the time of Moses himself. The God whom Jesus preached was "the God of Abraham, and the God of Isaac, and the God of Jacob."[25] Furthermore, Abraham, Isaac, and Jacob, the patriarchs, are described as pertaining to that kingdom into which the followers of Jesus were to be incorporated. "And I say to you that many shall come from the east and the west and shall sit down with Abraham and Isaac and Jacob in the kingdom of heaven."[26] The revelation which had been made by God to Adam, the first man, and to the patriarchs who had preceded Abraham was likewise fulfilled and perfected in the same way by Jesus, insofar as this doctrine was incorporated into the body of Mosaic revelation itself.

13. Jesus and the Pharisaic tradition. Although Jesus professed to fulfill the law which had been given to the Israelites through Moses, He rejected entirely the body of human tradition which the Pharisaic party had built up as a sort of fence around this law. Not only did He refuse to incorporate these traditions into His teaching, but He asserted that these traditions actually ran counter to the precepts which God Himself had given to the people. "You have made void the commandment of God for your tradition."[27] St. Mark in his gospel shows the nature of these traditions and the attitude which Jesus adopted in their regard. "And there assembled together unto Him the Pharisees and some of the scribes, coming from Jerusalem. And when they had seen some of His disciples eat bread with common, that is, with unwashed hands, they found fault. For the Pharisees, and all the Jews eat not without often washing their hands,

---

24 Matt. 19:10–12.
25 Matt. 22:32; Mark 12:26; Luke 20:37.
26 Matt. 8:11; Luke 13:28.
27 Matt. 15:6; Mark 7:8–9.

holding the tradition of the ancients: And when they come from the market, unless they be washed, they eat not: and many other things there are that have been delivered to them to observe, the washings of cups and of pots, and of brazen vessels and of beds. And the Pharisees and the Scribes asked Him: Why do not Thy disciples walk according to the tradition of the ancients, but they eat bread with common hands? But He answering said to them: Well did Isaias prophesy of you hypocrites, as it is written: This people honoreth Me with their lips, but their heart is far from Me: And in vain do they worship Me, teaching doctrines, and precepts of men. For leaving the commandment of God, you hold the tradition of men, the washing of pots and of cups: and many other things you do like to these. And He said to them: Well do you make void the commandment of God, that you may keep your own tradition. For Moses said: Honor thy father and thy mother. And He that shall curse father or mother, dying let him die. But you say: If a man shall say to his father or mother, Corban (which is gift) whatsoever is from me will profit thee: And further you suffer him not to do anything for his father or mother, making void the Word of God by your own tradition, which you have given forth: and many other such like things you do."[28]

14. God the Creator. Having seen the relation of that teaching which was set forth as divinely revealed to men by Jesus of Nazareth, it becomes our work as apologists to examine the dogmatic content of that message. Jesus taught about the nature of God, although there was no great need to insist upon certain portions of this doctrine, since it had been properly and sufficiently presented in the Mosaic revelation and accepted by the monotheistic Jewish nation. The essential unity of God is brought out in perfect clarity, not only in the background of His entire teaching, but explicitly in the instruction which He gave to the most enlightened among His fellow countrymen. "And there came one of the scribes that had heard them reasoning together, and seeing that He had answered them well, asked Him which was the first commandment of all. And Jesus answered him: The first commandment of all is: Hear O Israel, the Lord thy God is one God: And thou shalt love the Lord thy God with thy whole heart, and with thy whole soul, and with thy whole mind, and

---

28 Mark 7:1–13; Matt. 15:1–9.

with thy whole strength. This is the first commandment. And the second is like to it: Thou shalt love thy neighbor as thyself. There is no other commandment greater than these. And the scribe said to Him: Well, Master, Thou hast said in truth, and there is no other besides Him. And that He should be loved with the whole heart, and with the whole understanding, and with the whole soul, and with the whole strength: and to love one's neighbor as one's self, is a greater thing than all holocausts and sacrifices. And Jesus, seeing that he had answered wisely, said to him: Thou art not far from the kingdom of God."[29]

Jesus taught the truth that God had created the world. "For in those days shall be such tribulations as were not from the beginning of the creation, which God created, until now" (Mark 13–19). The disciples were told to be "perfect also as your heavenly Father is perfect."[30] In the same way they are meant to be "merciful as your Father also is merciful."[31] Jesus insisted upon the spirituality of God, upon the fact that any bodily imperfection would be incompatible with the nature of the Creator. "God is a Spirit: and they that adore Him must adore Him in spirit and in truth."[32] Likewise, God knows all things, even those human actions which are utterly beyond the ken of other men's understanding. "Thy Father, who seeth in secret will repay thee."[33] He knows what we stand in need of before we ask it from Him in prayer.[34] In the religious teaching of Jesus we find the explicit declaration that God is omnipotent. "He said to them: the things that are impossible with men, are possible with God."[35]

God not only knows the needs of men, but provides for them. "Behold the birds of the air, for they neither sow, nor do they reap, nor gather into barns: and your heavenly Father feedeth them. Are not you of much more value than they?"[36] His knowledge of creatures extends to the ultimate details, far too exact ever to be measured by

---

29 Mark 12:28–34.
30 Matt. 5:48.
31 Luke 6:36.
32 John 4:34.
33 Matt. 6:4, 6, 18.
34 Matt. 6:8.
35 Luke 18:27.
36 Matt. 6:26, 30, 32.

the standards of created knowledge. This knowledge goes with a power which is in no way limited to the exigencies of this earthly life. "And fear ye not them that kill the body, and are not able to kill the soul: but rather fear Him that can destroy both soul and body into hell. Are not two sparrows sold for a farthing: and not one of them shall fall on the ground without your Father. But the very hairs of your head are all numbered."[37] The divine government of the world will finally result in a judgment which belongs to God. "For the Son of man shall come in the glory of His Father with His angels: and then will He render to every man according to his works."[38]

The justice of God is apparent, in the teaching of Jesus, not only through the conduct of God with regard to angels and men, but also through the explicit designation of God as just. "Just Father, the world hath not known Thee, but I have known Thee, and these have known, that Thou hast sent Me."[39]

15. Created spirits, angels and demons. In the teaching of Jesus of Nazareth there is the recognition of the existence of created spirits, some of whom are friendly with God while others are ranged as His enemies, and as the foemen of the human race. In the passage above, and in a good many others in the gospels, Jesus spoke of the function of the angels in the general judgment.[40] In His teaching was also the declaration that certain angels at least were assigned to the care of His beloved little ones. "See that you despise not one of these little ones: for I say to you, that their angels in heaven always see the face of My Father, who is in heaven."[41] Their spirituality is such that the condition of men after the resurrection can be likened to them insofar as these men will be freed from all of those exigencies that in this world necessarily accompany the conduct of bodily life. "For in the resurrection they shall neither marry nor be married: but shall be as the angels of God in heaven."[42] They are in great numbers, powerful beyond the competence of men, and entirely at the disposition of Jesus Himself. "Thinkest thou that I cannot ask

---

37 Matt. 10:28–30.
38 Matt. 16:27.
39 John 17:25.
40 Matt. 13:39, 41, 49; 25:31; Mark 13:27; Luke 9:26.
41 Matt. 26:10.
42 Matt. 22:30; Mark 12:25.

My Father, and He will give Me presently more than twelve legions of angels?"[43]

The evil spirits or devils, on the other hand, express their hatred of God by attempting to tear men away from His friendship, and in particular by laboring to take the Word of God, preached by Jesus, out of the hearts of men. In explaining to the Apostles the parable of the wheat and the cockle, Jesus told them, "The enemy that sowed them (the children of the wicked one), is the devil."[44] Among these evil spirits there is a certain hierarchy, so that one of them has a position of command with reference to the rest. Furthermore, these devils are capable of taking possession of a man. The man so possessed by the devils could be freed by the power of Jesus, or by those who had received their commission from Him. At the same time His teaching makes it clear that the Jews themselves, through their prayers and ritual observances, had the power to cast out devils. "But the Pharisees hearing it, said: This man casteth not out devils but by Beelzebub the prince of devils. And Jesus knowing their thoughts, said to them: Every kingdom divided against itself, shall be made desolate: and every city or house divided against itself, shall not stand. And if satan cast out satan, he is divided against himself: how then shall his kingdom stand? And if I by Beelzebub cast out devils, by whom do your children cast them out? Therefore they shall be your judges. But if I by the Spirit of God cast out devils, then is the kingdom of God come upon you."[45]

The evil spirits have a definite influence among the men of this world, so that the Jews who resisted the teaching of Jesus could actually be spoken of as men whose father was the devil. "You are of your father, the devil: and the desires of your father you will do: he was a murderer from the beginning, and he stood not in the truth: because truth is not in him: when he speaketh a lie, he speaketh of his own, for he is a liar, and the father thereof."[46] As a matter of fact the influence of the devil is so strong that he is spoken of in the teaching

---

43 Matt. 26:53.
44 Matt. 13:39.
45 Matt. 12:24–28; Mark 3:23–26; Luke 11:17–20.
46 John 8:44.

of Christ as "the prince of this world."[47] The "prince of this world" is already judged, and he has no part whatsoever in Christ. "For the prince of this world cometh, and in Me he hath not anything."[48] This last statement of Jesus was an indication that the persons who had conspired to put Him to death were approaching. Thus He taught that this action, insofar as it was performed by the leaders of the Jews and by Judas who betrayed Him to them, was an activity inspired by the leader of the forces of darkness. Finally, it was the contention of Jesus that the devil had a special hatred for His disciples, and that he had attempted to gain control of Peter, the leader of the apostolic college. "And the Lord said: Simon, Simon, behold satan hath desired to have you that he may sift you as wheat: But I have prayed for thee that thy faith fail not: and thou being once converted, confirm thy brethren."[49] The efforts of the devil and of those who chose to cooperate in his work will finally be confounded, for on the last day the Judge will consign the wicked to the everlasting fire "which was prepared for the devil and his angels."[50]

16. The eschatology of Jesus. The judgment. The teaching on the last things which Jesus set forth as a part of that message which He characterized as divine revelation represented a considerable development over the previously revealed and accepted doctrines on this subject. In the first place He announced that the act of judgment was to be His special prerogative, conceded to Him by God the Father. "For neither doth the Father judge any man: but hath given all judgment to the Son."[51] Those who have followed Jesus as His disciples are to be associated with Him in the work of the judgment. "And Jesus said to them: Amen I say to you, that you who have followed Me, in the regeneration, when the Son of man shall sit on the seat of His majesty, you also shall sit on twelve seats, judging the twelve tribes of Israel."[52] The judgment which Christ is to administer has its beginnings in this life, insofar as those who refuse to accept His teaching are already under the ban. "He that believeth in Him (the

---

47 John 16:11.
48 John 14:30.
49 Luke 22:31–32.
50 Matt 25:41.
51 John 5:22.
52 Matt. 19:28.

Son of God) is not judged: but he that doth not believe, is already judged: because he believeth not in the name of the only begotten Son of God."[53] The man who refuses to accept the divine teaching is likened to "the prince of this world" who himself is already judged.[54]

The judgment of Jesus is just. "As I hear, so I judge: and My judgment is just: because I seek not My own will, but the will of Him that sent Me."[55] Likewise, that judgment is correct. "And if I do judge, My judgment is true: because I am not alone, but I and the Father that sent Me."[56] Jesus will come for this judgment in the glory of His heavenly Father and surrounded by the angels who will assist Him. "For the Son of man shall come in the glory of His Father with the angels: and then will He render to every man, according to his works."[57] Thus the judgment of Christ will be absolutely universal.

Great signs will precede this judgment, which is to take place at the end of the world.[58] However, the time of this last judgment was, according to the explicit teaching of Jesus, a secret locked in the intellect of God Himself, in such a way that not even the Son Himself, in His capacity as true man, was aware of it. "But that day or hour no man knoweth, neither the angels in heaven nor the Son, but the Father."[59]

The final and definitive judgment which awaits the evil, according to the teaching of Jesus, is consignment to an everlasting fire in company with the demons who have motivated or assisted in their detestable deeds. "Then shall He say to them also who shall be on His left hand: Depart from Me you cursed into everlasting fire which was prepared for the devil and his angels."[60] Thus the great penalty in which the essential unhappiness consequent upon unrepented sin will consist will be banishment from the face of the living God. The unjust, after this judgment, will be permanently banished from the presence of Jesus.

---

53 John 3:18.
54 John 16:11.
55 John 5:30.
56 John 8:16.
57 Matt. 16:27.
58 Matt. 24:21–31; Mark 13:19–27; Luke 21:25–27.
59 Mark 13:31; Matt. 24:36.
60 Matt. 25:41

17. The eternal reward. Naturally, one of the most important elements in the doctrinal message delivered by Jesus and proposed by Him as divinely revealed is the nature of the reward which awaits those who are faithful to Him. This reward consists in the final and definitive incorporation into that kingdom which was begun in this world and which, in the next, is to be the possession of the just alone. "Then shall the king say to them that shall be on His right hand: Come ye blessed of My Father, possess you the kingdom prepared for you from the foundation of the world."[61] To give this eternal life to men was the reason for the mission of Jesus Himself. "As Thou hast given Him power over all flesh, that He may give eternal life to all, whom Thou hast given Him."[62] This is the reward, the great good which men sought from Jesus of Nazareth, and which He designated as the guerdon that would be granted to those who obeyed the law of God. The questions which were put to Jesus very frequently were couched in terms of this eternal life. "Good Master, what good shall I do that I may have life everlasting?"[63] In the words of Jesus Himself the reward of the just is called eternal life. "And every one that hath left house, or brethren or sisters or father or mother or wife or children or lands for My name's sake, shall receive a hundredfold, and shall possess life everlasting."[64] Jesus defined the everlasting life which was the reward offered to His followers and in this way the purpose of His mission among men. "Now this is eternal life: That they may know Thee, the only true God, and Jesus Christ whom Thou hast sent."[65] This vision of the living God brings with it an ineffable union of the blessed with the divinity. "That they all may be one, as Thou, Father, in Me, and I in Thee, that they also may be one with Us: that the world may believe that Thou hast sent Me."[66] The norm by which the union of these blessed with God is measured is thus the unity of the divine nature in which both the Father and the Son subsist. At the same time the glory of the blessed brings with it an understanding and a vision of the glory of Jesus Himself. "Father, I will that where

---

61 Matt. 25:34
62 John 13:2.
63 Matt. 19:16; Mark 10:17; Luke 10:25; 18:18.
64 Matt. 19:19; Mark 10:30; Luke 18:30.
65 John 17:3.
66 John 17:21.

I am, they also whom Thou hast given Me may be with Me: that they may see My glory which Thou hast given Me, because Thou hast loved Me before the creation of the world."[67]

18. The moral foundation. In the moral order there was also a definite and individual doctrine set forth as divinely revealed in the preaching of Jesus of Nazareth. In the first place the ultimate standard of ethical perfection demanded of the followers of Jesus was not any one of the creatures, even the highest among them, but the perfection of the living God Himself. "Be you therefore perfect as also your heavenly Father is perfect."[68] The perfection and the beatitude which Christians are meant to possess can beheld only by work. There is no such thing as an idle or useless perfection seen in the preaching of Jesus. "Not every one that saith to Me, Lord, Lord, shall enter into the kingdom of heaven: but he that doth the will of My Father who is in heaven, he shall enter into the kingdom of heaven."[69]

The Christian is expected to model his conduct upon that of Jesus Himself. "Take up My yoke upon you and learn of Me, because I am meek and humble of heart: and you shall find rest to your souls."[70] Those who follow the commands of Christ are to be constituted as His brothers and sisters. "For whosoever shall do the will of God, he is My brother and My sister and mother."[71]

19. The doctrine on faith. The teaching of Jesus contained definite instructions of faith not given in previously existing religious systems. In the first place Jesus demanded faith in Himself and in His teaching as distinct entities under penalty of the loss of eternal life. "He that believeth in the Son, hath life everlasting: but he that believeth not the Son, shall not see life, but the wrath of God abideth in Him."[72] Actually and specifically He demanded acceptance, on divine faith, of the doctrine which He preached, to the effect that He was the true and natural Son of God and not merely able to speak of God as His Father in the way in which mere creatures could do. "Therefore I said

---

[67] John 17:24.
[68] Matt. 5:48. See also Luke 6:36.
[69] Matt. 7:21. See also Luke 6:46.
[70] Matt. 11:29.
[71] Mark 3:34; Luke 8:21.
[72] John 3:36.

to you, that you shall die in your sins: for if you believe not that I am He, you shall die in your sin."[73]

Jesus was specific also in declaring that the object of that faith which He demanded of His followers was actually a message that had been communicated by the living God. "I will not now call your servants: for the servant knoweth not what his lord doth. But I have called you friends: because all things whatsoever I have heard of My Father, I have made known to you."[74] This faith was intrinsically supernatural, in the sense that a man could not accept this teaching on the authority of God revealing without a special and supernatural help given by God. "And He said: Therefore did I say to you, that no man can come to Me, unless it be given Him by My Father."[75] The effect of this faith is to be the possession of the truth, which alone can make men free. "Then Jesus said to those Jews who believed in Him: If you continue in My word, you shall be My disciples indeed: And you shall know the truth and the truth shall make you free."[76] It will likewise result in the performance of miraculous works of the order which Jesus Himself accomplished in demonstrating the credibility of His teaching. "Amen, amen, I say to you, he that believeth in Me, the works that I do, he also shall do, and greater than these shall he do, because I go to the Father."[77]

According to the explicit teaching of Jesus, faith in Him will result in a glorious resurrection. "Jesus said to her (Martha of Bethany): I am the resurrection and the life: he that believeth in Me although he be dead, shall live: And every one that liveth and believeth in Me, shall not die forever."[78] Finally, the effect of this faith is eternal life itself. "Amen, amen, I say to you, that he who heareth My word, and believeth Him that sent Me, hath life everlasting, and cometh not into judgment, but is passed from death to life."[79]

20. The teaching on hope. In the direction of the virtue of hope, Jesus taught first of all that the object in which alone men would

---

73 John 8:24.
74 John 15:15. See also the first section of Chapter 9.
75 John 6:66. See the last section of Chapter 9 above.
76 John 8:31–32.
77 John 14:12.
78 John 11:25–26.
79 John 5:24.

find their everlasting happiness was the vision and possession of the living God. "Now this is eternal life: That they may know Thee, the only true God, and Jesus Christ whom Thou hast sent."[80] Confidence in God was taught in the religious system of Jesus both directly and in the incomparable clarity of the parables. "And seek not you what you shall eat or what you shall drink: and be not lifted up on high: For all these things do the nations of the world seek. But your Father knoweth that you have need of all these things. But seek ye first the kingdom of God and His justice, and all these things shall be added unto you. Fear not, little flock, for it hath pleased your Father to give you a kingdom."[81] The parable of the prodigal son[82] points out again the ineffable mercy of God in which the hope of the follower of Christ is meant to be rooted.

21. Charity in the message of Jesus. With reference to charity, which consists in a love of benevolence for God, and for our neighbor insofar as he is connected with God, the teaching of Christ is abundantly clear. In the first place, Jesus frequently during the course of His public life enunciated the double commandment of charity. "Jesus said to him: Thou shalt love the Lord thy God with thy whole heart and with thy whole soul and with thy whole mind. This is the greatest and the first commandment. And the second is like to this: Thou shalt love thy neighbor as thyself. On these two commandments dependeth the whole law and the prophets."[83] Thus He taught with perfect clarity that the act of charity is the bond which gathers together the acts of the other virtues and renders the operation of man fully pleasing to God. All the other ordinances which man has received in divine revelation depend for their perfection and efficacy upon the precept of love.

The love which the followers of Christ are expected to have for God is truly a love of friendship, a mutual love of benevolence. Furthermore, it is essentially a dynamic thing, a love which does not exist except insofar as it is actually in operation. The operation of charity involves obedience to all of the other commandments which

---

80 John 17:3.
81 Luke 13:29–32; Matt. 6:30–33.
82 Luke 15:11–32.
83 Matt. 22:37–40; Mark 12:30–31; Luke 10:25–28.

God has given to the human race. "As the Father hath loved Me, I also have loved you. Abide in My love. If you keep My commandments, you shall abide in My love, as I have kept My Father's commandments, and do abide in His love."[84] Thus, according to the explicit teaching of Jesus, the charity by which the Christian loves his God is meant to be modeled upon the love in which the Son of God Himself tends toward His divine Father.

Furthermore, according to Jesus, the love of charity brings with it an inhabitation of the Blessed Trinity in the soul in a manner obviously distinct from that in which God is in all things necessarily. "He that hath My commandments, and keepeth them: he it is that loveth Me. And he that loveth Me, shall be loved of My Father: and I will love him, and will manifest Myself to him."[85] "Jesus answered and said to him (St. Jude the Apostle): If any one love Me, he will keep My word, and My Father will love him, and we will come to him, and will make Our abode with him. He that loveth Me not, keepeth not My words."[86] Furthermore, Jesus Himself prayed to the Father that His followers might possess this love of charity in which they were to find their perfection and union with God. "And I have made known Thy name to them, and will make it known: that the love, wherewith Thou hast loved Me, may be in them, and I, in them."[87]

The operation of this charity with reference to our neighbors is meant to be intensely practical. The teaching of Jesus gives a standard in the light of which the beneficial character of our activity in our neighbor's regard can easily be evaluated. "All things therefore whatsoever you would that men should do to you, do you also to them. For this is the law and the prophets."[88] This love is to be shown not merely to those who are our friends and brethren but also to those who stand as our enemies. This was set forth as a distinctively Christian teaching, not clearly presented in the Old Testament at all, and certainly contradicted in that false tradition which the teaching of Jesus set out to overthrow. "You have heard that it hath been said:

---

84 John 15:9–10.
85 John 14:21.
86 John 14:23–24.
87 Matt. 17:12; Luke 6:31.
88 Matt. 7:12; Luke 6:31.

Thou shalt love thy neighbor and hate thy enemy. But I say to you: Love your enemies, do good to them that hate you: and pray for them that persecute and calumniate you: That you may be the children of your Father who is in heaven, who maketh His sun to rise upon the good and bad: and raineth upon the just and unjust. For if you love them that love you, what reward shall you have? Do not even the publicans this? And if you salute your brethren only, what do you more? Do not also the heathens this?"[89]

Also in the teaching of Jesus there are definite implications attached to this charity. The sin of scandal is to be avoided at all costs. "Woe to the world because of scandals. For it must needs be that scandals come: but nevertheless woe to that man by whom the scandal cometh."[90] There is also a definite command of almsgiving, the obligation to supply those who are in need with that portion of the individual's resources which is not necessary for him. "But yet that which remaineth, give alms: and behold all things are clean to you."[91] However this charity to the poor is something which Jesus recommended as well as ordered. For, if it is, according to His teaching, absolutely requisite to give alms from the superabundance of a person's possessions, it is counseled to exercise this form of charity even to the extent of giving what belongs to the upkeep of one's state in life for the relief of the indigent. "Sell what you possess and give alms."[92]

However, the giving of alms as well as the other activities which enter into the life of Christ's followers must, according to the teaching of Jesus Himself, be carried on in such a way as to avoid the hypocrisy which He so despised. "Take heed that you do not your justice before men, to be seen by them: otherwise you shall not have a reward of your Father who is in heaven. Therefore, when thou dost an alms-deed, sound not a trumpet before thee, as the hypocrites do in the synagogues and on the streets, that they may be honored by men: Amen I say to you, they have received their reward. But when thou

---

89 Matt. 5:43–47; Luke 6:27–35.
90 Matt. 18:7; Luke 17:1.
91 Luke 11:41.
92 Luke 12:43.

The New Dispensation and the Old Law

dost alms, let not thy left hand know what thy right hand doth."[93] The service of God through charity, according to the teaching of Jesus, is inseparable from sincerity. His enemies, the scribes and the Pharisees, who finally encompassed His death are condemned not only for their infidelity and rapacity but precisely insofar as they offend God through their hypocrisy.[94]

22. Prayer according to the Christian message. Again there was a definite instruction on prayer contained in that message which Jesus proposed to men as divinely revealed. In the first place He taught His disciples how they should pray. "And it came to pass: that as He was in a certain place praying, when He ceased, one of His disciples said to Him: Lord, teach us to pray, as John also taught his disciples. And He said to them: When you pray, say: Father, hallowed be Thy name. Thy kingdom come. Give us this day our daily bread. And forgive us our sins, for we also forgive every one that is indebted to us. And lead us not into temptation."[95] Thus He made it an integral part of His message that the prayer which His followers were expected to pour forth to God should consist in certain definite petitions for the things which God desired them to possess. This idea was expressed by St. John Damascene in the definition of prayer as "the petition of fitting things from God,"[96] a definition which was destined to become classical in the literature of Catholic theology.

The text of the Lord's Prayer illustrates very well the things for which the follower of Christ is expected to petition God. First of all there is the petition for the glory of God to be brought about in the sanctifying of the divine name. Then there is the accomplishment of God's glory in the soul of the person who makes the petition that the kingdom of God should arrive and be fulfilled in himself. Again there is the expression of the intention that the law of God should be obeyed, primarily, of course, by the person who is making the prayer.

Under the heading of the daily or the supersubstantial bread, the person praying asks God for all of those temporal and spiritual goods which might be requisite for, or contributory to, the gaining of his

---

93 Matt. 6:1–3.
94 Matt. 6 and 23.
95 Luke 11:1–4; Matt. 6:7–13.
96 *De Fide Orthodoxa*, Book 3, Ch. 24. Cf. Fenton, *The Theology of Prayer*, pp. 1–15.

eternal salvation. He requests the forgiveness of the sins which he has committed in the past, showing the requisite disposition for receiving this forgiveness in asserting that he has already granted pardon to those who have offended against him. He begs that, in being delivered from temptation, he may be freed from the danger of offending God now or in the future. In seeking the freedom from evil, the person who prays according to the directions given by Jesus petitions for the removal of those temporal evils which might be hindrances in his work of pleasing God and attaining his salvation.

Jesus followed His directions for prayer with definite assurances that such petitions, addressed to that God who is actually the Father of those who are adopted in Jesus, will be infallibly efficacious. This lesson is brought out in striking clarity in the parable of the importunate friend, which, in the gospel according to St. Luke, follows immediately upon the recital of the Lord's Prayer. However, it is brought out in such a way as to show that this petition must be persevering if its object is infallibly to be attained. "And He said to them: Which of you shall have a friend, and shall go to him at midnight, and shall say to him: Friend, lend me three loaves, because a friend of mine is come off his journey to me, and I have not what to set before him: And he from within should answer and say: Trouble me not, the door is now shut, and my children are with me in bed, I cannot rise and give thee. Yet if he shall continue knocking, I say to you: although he will not rise and give him because he is his friend, yet because of his importunity he will rise, and give him as many as he needeth."[97]

He assured His disciples that the response given to the prayer which is offered according to the directions which He gave would be both infallible and good. God will, according to the explicit teaching of Jesus, answer the prayer of His followers in the same way that a loving father fulfills the desires of his children. "And I say to you: Ask, and it shall be given you: seek and you shall find: knock, and it shall be opened to you! For every one that asketh, receiveth: and he that seeketh, findeth: and to him that knocketh, it shall be opened. And which of you, if he ask his father bread, will he give him a stone? of a fish: will he for a fish give him a serpent? Or if he shall ask an

---

[97] Luke 11:5–8.

egg: will he reach him a scorpion? If you then being evil, know how to give good gifts to your children: how much more will your Father from heaven give the good Spirit to them that ask Him?"[98]

Jesus insisted, however, that the prayer which men should offer according to His directions must be an exercise directed to God and not some sort of hypocritical activity meant to impress men. "And when ye shall pray, you shall not be as the hypocrites, that love to stand and pray in the synagogues and corners of the streets, that they may be seen by men: Amen I say to you, they have received their reward. But thou, when thou shalt pray, enter into thy chamber, and having shut the door, pray to thy Father in secret: and thy Father who seeth in secret will repay thee."[99] Moreover, the prayer which we offer to God is not necessary in order to inform God of our needs. It is for the benefit of the man who prays, in order that he may direct and order his intentions in the sight of God. "And when you are praying, speak not much, as the heathens; for they think that in their much-speaking they may be heard. Be not you therefore like to them; for your Father knoweth what is needful for you, before you ask Him."[100]

The prayers of the followers of Jesus are to be addressed to the Father in His name. Furthermore, the disciples are to petition Jesus Himself, and the results of the prayer will constitute the work of Jesus. "And whatsoever you shall ask the Father in My name, that will I do: that the Father may be glorified in the Son. And if you ask Me anything in My name, that I will do."[101] Prayer in the name of Jesus was undoubtedly a process which had not existed before, either in the Jewish religious practices or in the activities among the pagans. In propounding it Jesus was very definitely setting forth a religious teaching with which the well-educated Jews of His own time were not at all cognizant. "And in that day you shall not ask Me anything. Amen, amen, I say to you: if you ask the Father anything in My name, He will give it you. Hitherto you have not asked anything in My name: Ask and you shall receive, that your joy may be full."[102] Finally, he asserted

---

98 Luke 11:9–13; Matt. 7:7–11.
99 Matt. 6:5–6.
100 Matt. 6:7–8.
101 John 16:23–24.
102 3 John 14:13–14.

that the efficacy of this prayer was due to the faith manifested to God in the petition itself. "In that day you shall ask in My name: and I say not to you, that I will ask the Father for you: For the Father Himself loveth you, because you have loved Me, and have believed that I came out from God." Prayer in common, the petition of the Church itself has special efficacy according to the doctrine of Jesus.[103]

23. The beatitudes. As a distinctive note of the religious teaching which He preached, Jesus described the blessedness or the happiness of those who lived according to His doctrine. The conditions in which this happiness was to be found were quite different from those which were considered as occasions of happiness in other and less spiritual religious teachings. "Blessed are the poor in spirit: for theirs is the kingdom of heaven. Blessed are the meek: for they shall possess the land. Blessed are they that mourn: for they shall be comforted. Blessed are they that hunger and thirst after justice: for they shall have their fill. Blessed are the merciful: for they shall obtain mercy. Blessed are the clean of heart: for they shall see God. Blessed are the peacemakers: for they shall be called the children of God. Blessed are they that suffer persecution for justice sake: for theirs is the kingdom of heaven."[104] Finally there is an application of these beatitudes to the conditions in which the disciples must expect to live in this world. "Blessed are ye when they shall revile you, and persecute you, and speak all that is evil against you, untruly, for My sake: Be glad and rejoice, for your reward is very great in heaven; for so they persecuted the prophets that were before you."[105]

---

103 Matt. 18:19.
104 Matt. 6:3–10; Luke 6:20–22.
105 Matt. 5:11–12; Luke 6:22–23.

Chapter 11

THE DOCTRINAL CONTENT IN THE MESSAGE OF JESUS

PART II:
The Trinity and the Incarnation

1. The Incarnation and the Trinity in the teaching of Jesus. The central contention in all of that teaching for which Jesus of Nazareth demanded the assent of divine faith was His assertion that He was actually a divine person, distinct from the Father and yet perfectly equal to Him in all things, while still a third divine Person, designated as the Holy Ghost, proceeded both from the Father and from the Son and thus was perfectly distinct from both of them, while He was coequal to Them in the perfection of His divinity. This teaching was to form the distinctive doctrine of that kingdom of which He, Jesus of Nazareth, was the founder and the head.

Nothing could be clearer, from an examination of those reliable historical documents in which the teachings of Jesus are recorded, than the fact that He claimed to be the Son of the living God, in a sense at once distinct from and infinitely superior to the manner in which other men could possess divine sonship. While He was taught this, He obviously was and asserted Himself to be a man, possessing the full perfection of human nature. He claimed for Himself a double-series of attributes. As man He could advance in wisdom and age and grace with God and men.[1] He could be wearied.[2] Finally, He could suffer and die. But as God He was eternal, the master of the angels and of the created universe, immortal and forever glorious. The words of Jesus, recorded in the four canonical gospels and

---

1 Luke 2:52.
2 John 4:6.

mirrored in the abiding tradition current among His disciples after His death, show very clearly that He claimed this divine dignity.

2. The divinity of Jesus and the science of apologetics. In dealing with the divinity of Jesus in the science of apologetics, we must realize exactly what we seek to know about it for the purposes of this study. In the first place, it is not within the competence of apologetics to demonstrate that Jesus was really God. The truth of the Incarnation remains one of the great central Christian mysteries. It is one of those facts which men could never know independently of divine revelation, and which must remain obscure even to those who accept it with the certain assent of divine faith, "as long as, in this mortal life 'we are absent from the Lord: for we walk by faith and not by sight.'"[3]

Since it is such a truth, it certainly does not lie within the province of apologetics nor for that matter of any science attainable by man in this life to show clearly, merely from naturally ascertainable evidence, that Christ is God. There is a strict theological demonstration of the divinity of Jesus, but it is of the same sort as all of those other demonstrations which belong to the body of the science of sacred theology. This science is competent to show, from the documents of the deposit of faith itself, that the thesis, Jesus Christ is God, expresses a truth actually contained in this same deposit of faith. It can show, likewise, that the denial of this statement would imply a rejection of the other truths which enter into the content of that revelation which we accept on the authority of God Himself. Or, to put the matter in another way, the science of sacred theology in its special dogmatic treatise on the Incarnation can derive the conclusion that Jesus Christ is God by a proper syllogistic process, utilizing as a principle of scientific knowledge one or more statements contained in the complexus of Catholic dogma. Such a proof, however, does not fall within the province of apologetics. Rather, the dogma of the divinity of Jesus is one of those truths, the rational credibility of which is meant to be demonstrated in the process of apologetics.

3. Two functions of this teaching in apologetics. In the demonstration of credibility, which is the central and essential function of the science of apologetics, the treatment of the divinity

---

3 The Vatican Council, The Constitution, *Dei Filius*, Ch. 4 (Denzinger, 1796).

of Jesus can be taken up from two distinct angles. In the first place, we can show that Jesus of Nazareth declared Himself to be a divine Person in order to lend weight to our demonstration that Jesus of Nazareth obviously declared that the message He brought to men was actually revealed by God, and as such to be received by all with the assent of divine faith. In order that this demonstration may be effective, it must be such as to appeal to any man who is able to interpret and judge the dicta of history.

In the same way, it belongs to the science of apologetics, as it is at present constituted, to demonstrate that Jesus of Nazareth taught that He was God in order precisely to show that there was a definite and individual religious teaching proposed by Him as divinely revealed. This statement obviously was one which brought with it tremendous implications, both in the doctrinal and in the purely practical order. Obviously the conduct of the followers of Christ, directed by Him, would have been quite different if He had not openly and clearly asserted that He was the natural and proper Son of God. Moreover, all the teaching on the life of God and on the dependence of creatures upon Him acquires a new meaning in the light of this assertion. Thus there would be no proper demonstration of the fact that Jesus really taught a definite religious system which could be shown as credible without a proof that He declared Himself actually divine.

Again this demonstration is meant to be attainable in the light of purely natural evidence. Prescinding from the obvious fact (ascertainable in the light of sacred theology) that grace is really requisite for a successful approach to divine faith, the proof that Jesus declared Himself to be the true and natural Son of God, would not be in any way effective were it not attainable in the natural process of human reason. Consequently, in this chapter, as in those which have gone before, we shall utilize the dicta of sacred Scriptures, and in particular the citations from the four canonical gospels, not insofar as these are inspired utterances but only insofar as they are statements contained in documents of demonstrable historical reliability.

4. The claim of divinity and the gospel sources. In dealing with the historical evidence toward Jesus' assertion of His own divinity, we must remember that there is a great deal of difference between the attitude modern critics take with reference to the statement of this fact in the synoptics and the declarations in the gospel according to St. John and in the Epistles of St. Paul. No one could deny from even a cursory reading of the fourth gospel that according to its teaching Jesus of Nazareth obviously proposed Himself as God, the monotheistic Lord of the Jews. As a matter of fact, the author states explicitly that his purpose in writing this narrative had been to show the divinity of Jesus. "But these are written that you may believe that Jesus is the Christ, the Son of God: and that believing you may have life in His name."[4] The only resource of those who refuse to concede the New Testament teaching about Christ as God has been to reject *in toto* the historical value of the fourth gospel. Some evidence of the scientific worth of such procedure carried on in the face of overwhelming testimony from critical sources in our own time may be gained from the fact that one, at least, of those who flatly reject the historicity of St. John takes seriously one of the Talmudic stories about Jesus, utilizing a source which has been rejected as historical even by the Jews themselves.[5]

On the other hand, certain writers have attempted to show that the synoptic gospels contain no clear indication that Jesus ever predicated the divine dignity of Himself. Usually this result is obtained by the amazingly simple process of rejecting as later interpolations any and all passages which militate against their own views. Such procedure may have seemed serious in the mid-nineteenth century when the imagination of "higher critics" was allowed to run wild, unhampered by such prosaic realities as versions and codices. But it is of little moment in the background of comparatively mature scientific mentality of our own times. The situation in which the "Catholic connections" of a scholar would militate against recognition of his work belongs to an age which is fortunately past.[6] However, because of the claims which have been made in this direction, it is of importance for the apologist to show that the synoptic gospels themselves carry clear indications that Jesus actually claimed to be divine.

5. The gospel of the infancy. In the first place, the synoptic gospels show that others denominated Jesus as the "Son of God." The gospel of the infancy shows that He was hailed as such by the angel

---

4 John 20:31.
5 McCown, *The Search for the Real Jesus*, p. 292. Cf. the article, "Jesus Christ," in the Jewish Encyclopedia.
6 *Ibid.*, p. 236.

The Trinity and the Incarnation

of the Annunciation. "He shall be great, and shall be called the Son of the Most High, and the Lord God shall give unto Him the throne of David His father: and He shall reign in the house of Jacob forever. And the angel answering said to her: The Holy Ghost shall come upon thee, and the power of the Most High shall overshadow thee. And therefore also the Holy which shall be born of thee, shall be called the Son of God." St. Elizabeth greeted her cousin, the Blessed Virgin Mary, as "the mother of my Lord."[7] The angel who brought the news of the birth of Jesus to the shepherds outside of Bethlehem announced Him as the "Lord," a title which was reserved among the Jewish people for the divinity. "For this day is born to you a Saviour, who is Christ the Lord, in the city of David."[8]

6. The Temptation of the Son of God. In the temptation of Jesus, as recounted in the gospels of SS. Matthew and Luke, the devil twice addressed the Master "if Thou be the Son of God."[9] A man possessed by the devil cried out in the synagogue at Capernaum, "Let us alone, what have we to do with Thee, Jesus of Nazareth? Art Thou come to destroy us? I know Thee, who Thou art, the 'Holy One of God.'"[10] Many of the devils which He cast out of the men whom they had possessed went out hailing Him explicitly as "The Son of God."[11] Naturally, Jesus did not wish to be announced to the world by such testimony, either then in Capernaum or later when He was greeted as the "Son of the Most High God" by the devils whom He cast out in the country of the Gerasens.[12] Finally, at the moment of His death on the cross, the centurion which was in charge of the execution was moved to express his conviction that Jesus was actually the Son of God. "Now the centurion and they that were with him watching Jesus, having seen the earthquake and the things that were done, were sore afraid, saying: Indeed this was the Son of God."[13]

7. The fatherhood of God and Jewish teaching. All of this testimony was quite independent of the instruction offered by Jesus

---

7 Luke 1:32, 35.
8 Luke 2:11.
9 Matt. 4:3, 6; Luke 4:3, 9.
10 Luke 4:34; Mark 1:24.
11 Mark 3:2; Luke 4:41.
12 Luke 8:28; Mark 5:6; cf. Matt. 8:29.
13 Matt. 28:54; Mark 15:39.

Himself. Consequently it is not of immediate value as an indication of the content of His message regarding Himself, although it is interesting as showing how He was presented in these various ways to the people with whom He came into contact. Because it did not follow upon the teaching of Jesus Himself, there is nothing to indicate here that the title "Son of God" was used explicitly to designate the second Person of the Blessed Trinity. The fatherhood of God had been recognized in the Old Testament and insisted upon more strongly than before in the literature of the Jewish rabbis.[14] The line from the one hundred and second Psalm sums up perfectly the nature of this fatherhood. "As a father hath compassion on his children, so hath the Lord compassion on them that fear Him."[15] As Lebreton points out, the fatherhood of God was restricted in that portion of divine public revelation which was granted under the Old Testament to the people of Israel as a unit, or most to those individuals who were just and faithful within it. There was nothing of the tenderness of the message contained in the parable of the prodigal son,[16] in which the mercy of God is shown as applied to sinners, nor was there a distinct revelation of the natural sonship of the second Person of the Blessed Trinity. Consequently, at the most, we can see in the indications of the divine Sonship of Jesus, made by those men who had not come under the influence of His teaching, an exalted notion of the messianic dignity. However, it is well to note that the term "Son of God" was not applied to the Messiah, at least in the popular terminology. On the occasion when Jesus was greeted enthusiastically on His entrance into Jerusalem that first Palm Sunday, He was hailed by the populace as the Son of David, but not as the Son of God.[17]

8. The attitude of the Apostles. More important, then, are the words of the Apostles and the other disciples of Jesus, recorded in the synoptic gospels. Before his definitive vocation as an Apostle, St. Peter had responded to the miraculous draft of fishes by speaking to Jesus as "Lord." "Depart from me, for I am a sinful man, O Lord."[18]

---

14 Cf. Jules Lebreton, *Histoire du Dogme de la Trinité des Origines au Concile de Nicée*, TomeI, 8 ed. (Paris, 1927), pp. 257–261.
15 Ps. 102:13.
16 Luke 15:11–32.
17 Matt. 21:9; Mark 11:9–10; Luke 14:38.
18 Luke 5:8.

However, after hearing His teaching and after having witnessed the miracle of His walking upon the water of the Sea of Galilee, the disciples who were in the boat together "came and adored Him saying: Indeed Thou art the Son of God."[19] Quite similar is the reaction of the twelve to the miracle of the multiplication of the loaves and the fishes, the subsequent Eucharistic discourse, and the desertion of the unfaithful disciples which has been set down in the gospel according to St. John. "After this many of His disciples went back: and walked no more with Him. Then Jesus said to the twelve: Will you also go away? And Simon Peter answered Him: Lord, to whom shall we go: Thou hast the words of eternal life; and we have believed and have known that Thou are the Christ the Son of God."[20] It is interesting to note here that the received Greek text carries the words "the Holy One of God" rather than the formula given in the Vulgate.[21] In this instance the Greek reading would seem to be preferred, although the sense does not differ from that of the formula found in the Vulgate.

9. The confession of Peter. Much more solemn than any of the other pronouncements was that given by St. Peter in the name of the other disciples in the region of Caesarea Philippi. It is recorded that after Jesus had asked the Apostles concerning the current ideas relative to His identity, their responses brought Him to inquire of them, "But who do you say that I am. Simon Peter answered and said: Thou are Christ, the Son of the living God."[22] The whole tone of the narrative, showing the joy of Jesus occasioned by this confession of Peter, His insistence that this truth could only have been given to Him by God, and the promises which He made to the prince of the apostles, and through him to the Church which He was engaged in founding; all of these constitute a definite indication that the dignity which Peter had predicated of Him was something far greater than the mere messianic office.

The previous texts which have been cited and the narrative portion of the first chapter in the gospel according to St. John show us very clearly that the Apostles had, from the very beginning, been

---

19 Matt. 14:33.
20 John 6:67–70.
21 Cf. Vogels, *Novum Testamentum Graece*, 2 ed. (Dusseldorf, 1923), p. 263.
22 Matt. 16:15–16.

accustomed to consider their Master as the Messiah and as the king of Israel. The entire context of the narration which describes this event, not only in St. Matthew but also in the other two synoptics,[23] indicates very clearly that a new phase in the teaching process of Jesus had set in by reason of this confession. This truth, specially revealed by God, "Blessed art thou, Simon Bar-Jona: because flesh and blood hath not revealed it to thee, but My Father who is in heaven,"[24] was the statement that Jesus was distinctly the natural Son of the living God, a divine Person, whose relations with the Father were infinitely superior to those which could be enjoyed by any creature, even the most perfect.

The parallel passages in the other two synoptic gospels do not give the confession of St. Peter at the same length as does the verse of St. Matthew.[25] However, no serious critic at the present time calls the authenticity of the text in Matthew into question. It is perfectly consonant with the consequences which are described, both in this gospel and in the two others, in such a way that it is much easier to see and explain the completeness of Matthew in this instance than it can be to understand the brevity of the other two. In all three of these gospels the scene in Caesarea is attached to the prophecy concerning the sufferings and death of Jesus, which had not hitherto been clearly stated.[26] Likewise, in all of the three synoptics it is connected with a special insistence upon the necessity of following Jesus,[27] and the recital of the Transfiguration,[28] hence it is obvious that the confession of St. Peter was, in the minds of all three synoptic writers, an event of tremendous magnitude in the preaching of the Christian message. Certainly it could not have been so, were it merely a recognition of the messianic office of Jesus. The context of the entire gospel story shows that it must have been a profession of faith in His divinity.

10. The voice of the Father. The synoptic evangelists record that at the very outset of the public life of Jesus God Himself explicitly recognized in Jesus His well-beloved and only Son. At His baptism

---

23 Mark 8:27–30; Luke 9:18–21.
24 Matt. 16:17.
25 Mark 8:29; Luke 9:20.
26 Matt. 16:21–23; Mark 8:31–33; Luke 9:9–22.
27 Matt. 16:24–27; Mark 8:34–38; Luke 9:23–26.
28 Matt. 17:1–8; Mark 9:2–8; Luke 9:28–36.

by John the Baptist there came "a voice from heaven saying: This is My beloved Son in whom I am well pleased."[29] The same message was repeated in the presence of the three most privileged Apostles on the occasion of the Transfiguration, an event which all the three synoptic writers connect with the confession of St. Peter. "And lo a voice out of the cloud saying: This is My beloved Son, in whom I am well pleased: hear ye Him."[30] In each case the Greek word which is translated as "well beloved" carries with it the obvious connotation that Jesus is the Son of God in a way which is utterly unique and infinitely remote from the manner in which any creature whatsoever could be termed a child of God.

11. Jesus prepared His hearers for the doctrine of His divinity.

Naturally, from the point of view of apologetics, by far the most important testimony to Jesus' claim that He was divine is to be found in the words of the Master as these are recorded in the gospels. As a matter of fact the three synoptics insist upon this fact almost as clearly as does the gospel of St. John itself. The teaching of the divinity of Jesus forms a central theme, apart from which the texts themselves would be utterly pointless. The insistence of Jesus upon the fact that He was God is shown in the attitude which He manifested toward His heavenly Father and in the comparisons which He drew between Himself and creatures. It is shown in His assumption of the prerogatives and the attributes of the divinity and in His explicit declaration that He was the only-begotten Son of God.

It is a matter of record that Jesus insisted upon the fact of His divinity much more clearly and in a more public manner during the latter portion of His public life than He had at the beginning. To explain this some modern writers have invented the myth of a "growing divine consciousness in Jesus." Actually the same reasons which motivated a gradual revelation of the messianic dignity were such as to influence a still more deliberate manifestation of the divinity of Jesus. The absolute monotheism of the Jews, coupled with official distrust of a Man who declared Himself as the Messiah while rejecting the appurtenances which the Jewish tradition had ascribed to the messenger of God, would obviously prevent an effective

---

29 Matt. 3:17; Mark 1:11; Luke 3:22.
30 Matt. 17:5; Mark 9:7; Luke 9:35.

announcement of the divinity of Jesus to those who were unprepared to receive that announcement. The fact of the matter is that there is absolutely no basis in the text of the four gospels for the assertion that Jesus only gradually came to believe that He was the Son of God. Any attempt, therefore, to read such a meaning into these documents must run counter to all of the demands of critical science.

12. The glorification of the Father. The synoptic gospels recount five occasions on which Jesus explicitly declared Himself to be the only-begotten Son of God. In the first place, there is the striking passage which describes the glorification which Jesus rendered to the Father after the seventy-two disciples had returned to Him, joyous over the successful accomplishments of the mission which He had entrusted to them. "At that time Jesus answered and said: I confess to Thee, O Father, Lord of heaven and earth, because Thou hast hid these things from the wise and prudent, and hast revealed them to little ones. Yea, Father: for so hath it seemed good in Thy sight. All things are delivered to Me by My Father. And no one knoweth the Son but the Father: neither doth any one know the Father but the Son, and he to whom it shall please the Son to reveal to Him."[31] It is easy to see that in this statement, recorded as having been made to the intimate circle of the disciples, we have as clear an indication of the divinity of Jesus as in any passage which is to be found in the fourth gospel. In this passage the Son is described as fully equal to the Father, and moreover as the bearer of that revelation in the light of which man can find the only knowledge of the Father which is available to him in this world.

13. The Parable of the Evil Husbandmen. The second explicit declaration of the divine Sonship of Jesus is to be found in the parable of the vineyard and the husbandmen. Jesus intended this story as a striking rebuke to His enemies, and it is recounted that they were not slow to see its meaning. After Jesus had told of the many servants sent by the Lord of the vineyard to the husbandmen for the purpose of receiving from these husbandmen the fruits of His own property, He said: "Therefore having yet one Son, most dear to Him: He also sent Him unto them last of all, saying: They will reverence My Son. But the husbandmen said one to another: This is the Heir: come, let

---

31 Matt. 11:25–27; Luke 10:21–22.

The Trinity and the Incarnation

us kill Him: and the inheritance shall be ours."[32] The chief priests and the Pharisees knew at once that this story applied to them. They knew, too, that in making this declaration, Jesus was stating explicitly that His position with reference to God was quite distinct from that of the prophets and the just men of long ago, the "servants" whom the Lord of the vineyard had sent to mankind. As the only-begotten and dearly beloved Son of God He was obviously claiming divine honors and dignity. It was for this reason that they sought to lay hands upon Him, and would have done so but for the multitude who reverenced the Master as a prophet.[33]

14. The End of the World. The third explicit declaration of Jesus to the effect that He was the Son of God which is recorded on the pages of the synoptics is to be found in His teaching on the time of the end of the world. "But of that day or hour no man knoweth, neither the angels in heaven nor the Son, but the Father."[34] At first sight it might appear that this text speaks of a certain inequality between the Son and the Father, and implies an inferiority of the former with respect to the latter. The Arian heretics used this text in their futile attempt to demonstrate that the Son of God was merely a creature. The point of the matter is, however, that in this text, as in the others which have been cited, Jesus names Himself as the Son precisely with reference to the heavenly Father. The obvious implication, in the light of the previous declarations of Jesus, was that this department of knowledge belonged in a special way to the Father since it did not constitute a portion of that message which the Son was authorized to bring to men. A comparison with the first set of texts which have been alleged in this section[35] should make this very clear. Furthermore, as Lebreton notes, we must not allow the controversial background of such texts to blind us to the paramount fact that they express the relation of the Son of God to His eternal Father.

15. Before Caiphas. The fourth and by far the most striking statement of the divinity of Jesus to be recorded in the synoptics is to

---

32 Mark 12:6–7; Matt. 21:37–38.
33 Matt. 21:46; Mark 12:12.
34 Mark 13:32.
35 Matt. 11:27; Luke 10:22.

be found in the solemn response of Jesus to His accusers before the court of the high priest in Jerusalem the night before He died. The gospel according to St. Luke tells us that there were two explicit questions put to Jesus, the first of which obviously had reference to His messianic office and the second to His divinity. His condemnation followed upon His response to the second question. "And as soon as it was day, the ancients of the people, and the chief priests and scribes came together, and they brought Him into their council, saying: If Thou be the Christ, tell us. And He said to them: If I shall tell you, you will not believe Me: And if I shall also ask you, you will not answer Me, nor let Me go. But hereafter the Son of man shall be sitting on the right hand of the power of God. Then said they all: Art Thou the Son of God? Who say, that I am."[36]

We learn from the first and second gospels that Jesus was condemned on the charge of blasphemy. This charge could not have been incurred if He had merely ascribed to Himself the dignity and the office of the Messiah. As a matter of fact there were others both before and after His time who assumed this title and who were certainly not punished for blasphemy by the Sanhedrin. The count against Him was that He had made Himself God, and for that reason the unbelieving enemies of Jesus willed that He should die and found the cause for His condemnation. The first gospel tells us that the question was put to Jesus in the form of an adjuration by the leader of the Jewish community, the high priest himself. "And the high priest said to Him: I adjure Thee by the living God, that Thou tell us if Thou be the Christ, the Son of God?"[37] No question could have been more solemn nor more explicit. The response of Jesus was clear. In the face of the most horrible death which the perverted ingenuity of man has been able to devise, He affirmed solemnly and under oath that He was the Son of that God who was worshiped in Israel.

16. The commission of the Apostles. The final assertion by Jesus of His own divine sonship is to be found in the formula for that baptism in which the believers in His teaching are to find regeneration. "Going therefore teach ye all nations: baptizing them in

---

36 Luke 22:66–70. Cf. also Matt. 28:63–66; Mark 14:61–62.
37 Matt. 26:63.

the name of the Father, and of the Son, and of the Holy Ghost."[38] On this occasion it was obvious, as it was on the others we have mentioned, that the Son to whom Jesus referred was none other than Himself. In inserting His name into the baptismal formula, Jesus was teaching His followers that His role in the work of regeneration was equal to that of the Father and the Holy Ghost. The work of rebirth in the spiritual order was, according to the continued teaching of Jesus, something which could be brought about only through the divine power. In this baptismal formula He teaches that the Son, as a distinct Person, has the same divinity as the Father Himself.

17. Jesus claimed the attributes of God. The same truth, that of the divine sonship and the divinity of Jesus, is strongly implied in many another passage of the synoptic gospels. In the first place, Jesus indicated in the question which He put to the Jews concerning the descent of the Messiah from David the king that actually He enjoyed a dignity far greater than any which could be derived by the fact of descent from the great ruler of Israel.[39] The fact that David called Him Lord was an indication that He was the Son of One far greater than even David.

Furthermore, Jesus attributed to Himself obvious attributes proper to God alone, properties which a mere man could never claim for himself without incurring the guilt of blasphemy. First of all, He claimed for Himself superiority to everything which the Jews of His time regarded as sacred and most excellent. Solomon was thought to be almost the embodiment of human wisdom, the recipient from God of a knowledge which surpassed that conceded to any other creature. Yet openly Jesus asserted that He was "greater than Solomon."[40] Jonah the prophet was, as such, admittedly the bearer of the divine message, a man who was privileged and called by God to bring His teaching to the children of men. Jesus clearly claimed that He was "greater than Jonah."[41] He reminded the Jews that David himself had regarded his descendant who was to be the Messiah as his own superior, something which most certainly would not have

---

38 Matt. 28:19.
39 Matt. 22:42–45; Mark 12:35–37; Luke 20:41–44.
40 Matt. 12:42.
41 Matt. 12:41.

been true if he had owed his position to his generation from the head of the dynasty. It was the contention of Jesus that John the Baptist was a prophet, and even more than a prophet, by far the greatest in that long series of heralds sent by God to announce the coming of the Messiah. And yet Jesus declared that even the least in His own kingdom was superior to John.[42]

The dignity of Jesus, which He attributed to Himself as a part of that message which He proposed to man as divinely revealed, is far greater than that of the very angels of God. He speaks of the angels as His own, His ministers or servants whose function it will be to assist Him in the work of the judgment.[43] As the Lord of the angels, obviously Jesus attributed to Himself a position and a dignity far superior to that which could be enjoyed by any mortal. For in the Old Testament the angels had been termed the servants of God Himself. They were of God, and as a result the individual who constituted Himself as their Lord and Master was actually and plainly claiming a divine dignity.[44]

Openly Jesus proclaimed that He was greater than the temple of God in Jerusalem, by far the holiest of those elements which entered into the worship of God among the Jews. Moreover, He announced Himself as the Lord of the Sabbath, and thus the Master of that law by which the Sabbath itself had been instituted, the law of God Himself. "But I tell you that there is here a greater than the temple. . . . For the Son of man is Lord, even of the Sabbath."[45]

18. The love due to God is demanded by Jesus. In the synoptic writings as well as in the fourth gospel, Jesus of Nazareth is represented as demanding from man a love, obedience, and loyalty far surpassing those manifested to even the most cherished and worthy among human superiors. He demands that loyalty to Him should supersede even that love which is lavished upon a man's parents. It is obvious that only the love of the living God could be objectively more intense than that which is meant to be shown to the members of one's own family. Furthermore, He demands, as the manifestation

---

42 Luke 7:24–28; Matt. 11:7–14.
43 Matt 16:27. Cf. Mark 8:38; Luke 9:26; Matt. 13:39.
44 Cf. Gen. 16:7, 9; Exod. 23:33; 32:34 seq.
45 Matt. 12:6, 8.

The Trinity and the Incarnation 213

of the love which men have for Him, a life of abnegation of self and real suffering. The words of Christ are hard, and are meant to be so, since there never has been a man in the history of the world who has demanded of his friends that which Jesus expects of those who love Him, and who are to receive from Him the gift of eternal life. "If any man come to Me, and hate not his father, and mother, and wife, and children, and brethren and sisters, yea, and his own life also, he cannot be My disciple. And whosoever doth not carry his cross and come after Me can not be My disciple."[46] Jesus insisted time and time again on the absolute primacy of that love which His followers are to give Him, and He made the strength of that love the condition of the reward which He was to give to the disciples. "And Peter began to say unto Him: Behold we have left all things, and have followed Thee. Jesus answering said: Amen I say to you, there is no man who hath left house, or brethren or sisters, or father or mother, or children or lands for My sake and for the gospel, who shall not receive a hundred times as much, now in this time: houses and brethren and sisters and mothers and children and lands, with persecutions, and in the world to come, life everlasting."[47]

In the line with this demand for supreme love, of the sort which could be given only to God, Jesus coupled a statement that He was actually the center and the object of the religious life. Profession of faith in Him is declared essential for the attainment of eternal life, while a denial of Him and of His teaching will result inevitably in spiritual ruin. "Every one therefore that shall confess Me before men, I will also confess Him before My Father who is in heaven. But he that shall deny Me before men, I will also deny him before My Father who is in heaven."[48] According to the explicit teaching of Jesus, the man who follows Him will save his soul and thus accomplish the one essential task for which he is placed in this world. "Then Jesus said to His disciples: If any man will come after Me, let him deny himself, and take up his cross, and follow Me. For he that will save his life, shall lose it; and he that shall lose his life for My sake, shall find it.

---

46 Luke 14:24–27; Matt. 10:37–38. Cf. John 12:25; Matt. 16:24–27; Mark 8:34–38; Luke 9:23–26.
47 Mark 10:28–30; Luke 18:28–30; Matt. 19:27–29.
48 Matt. 10:32–33; Luke 12:8–9. Cf. also Matt. 16:27; Mark 8:38; Luke 9:36.

For what doth it profit a man, if he gain the whole world, and suffer the loss of his own soul? Or what exchange shall a man give for his soul?"[49] It is interesting to note that in the parallel passage in the second gospel the reward is promised to the man who will lose his life for the sake of the gospel. Now the gospel, in the terminology of Jesus, was precisely that message which He proposed to men as divinely revealed. Consequently the words of Jesus, as reported by the evangelists, tell us that He placed Himself on the same level with that communication which He professed to give to mankind. The doctrine was something in defense of which a man might properly give up his life, because the doctrine was divine. The reward of eternal life is promised in the teaching of Jesus, not only to the man who follows the law of God in general but precisely to the one who is willing to leave all things rather than to forsake Him.

19. The function of Jesus at the last judgment. The synoptic writers tell, as clearly as does St. John himself, the function of Jesus at the last judgment. It is clear then that He attributed to Himself a work which was clearly divine in all of its implications, the actual judgment of all men on the last day. According to the actual teaching of Jesus, as set down on the pages of St. Matthew, "Then shall appear the sign of the Son of man in heaven: and then shall all of the tribes of the earth mourn: and they shall see the Son of man coming in the clouds of heaven with much power and majesty."[50] Jesus spoke of the men of this world as responsible to Him and to be judged by Him in His own right. This contention would have been absolutely unthinkable unless He had claimed for Himself divine honors and dignity.

20. Jesus and the divine law. Furthermore, it is obvious that Jesus claimed to act as the supreme Lawgiver of the universe. On His own responsibility and by His own power He claimed to change and perfect the ordinances which were admittedly divine in their origin, in spite of the fact that some of the precepts which He rejected were those merely human in their nature, prescriptions which had been introduced by the tradition of the elders among the Jewish people. In altering the divine positive precepts, He put Himself on exactly the same level as the God of the Old Testament. "You have heard

---

49 Matt. 16:24–26; Mark 8:34–36; Luke 9:23–25.
50 Matt. 24:30; Mark 13:27; Luke 21:27. Cf. Matt. 16:27; Mark 8:38; Luke 9:26.

that it was said to you of old. . . . But I say to you."⁵¹ Clearly in these instances Jesus claimed for Himself the divine dignity.

21. Jesus and the forgiveness of sin. Another power which He claimed for Himself was that of remitting offenses which had been committed against God Himself. When His enemies stated that the forgiving of sin was distinctly a divine prerogative, He made no effort to deny this assertion, but performed a miracle in order to demonstrate to them, and to all men, that He possessed this power. "And when Jesus had seen their faith, he saith to the sick of the palsy: Son, thy sins are forgiven thee. And there were some of the scribes sitting there, and thinking in their hearts: Why doth this man speak thus? He blasphemeth. Who can forgive sins but God only? Which Jesus presently knowing in His spirit, that they so thought within themselves, saith to them: Why think you these things in your hearts? Which is easier to say to the sick of the palsy: Thy sins are forgiven thee: or to say: Arise, take up thy bed, and walk? But that you may know that the Son of man hath power on earth to forgive sins (He saith to the sick of the palsy), I say to thee: Arise, take up thy bed, and go into thy house. And immediately he arose: and taking up his bed, went his way in the sight of all, so that all wondered, and glorified God, saying: We never saw the like."⁵² Again in the house of Simon the Pharisee, Jesus forgave the sins of the repentant woman who came to Him to pour ointment upon Him and to manifest the sorrow she felt for the sins she had committed in the past. "And He said to her: Thy sins are forgiven thee. And they that sat at meat with Him began to say within themselves: Who is this that forgiveth sins also? And He said to the woman: Thy faith hath made thee safe: go in peace."⁵³

Jesus also claimed, on His own authority and by His own right, to communicate the power of forgiving sins to others, who were His followers. On His own authority He promised this power, both to Peter as an individual and later to the members of the apostolic college. "And I will give to thee (Peter) the keys of the kingdom of heaven. And whatsoever thou shalt bind upon earth, it shall be bound

---

51 Cf. Ch. IX.
52 Mark 2:5–12; Luke 5:20–26; Matt. 9:2–8.
53 Luke 7:48–50

also in heaven: and whatsoever thou shalt loose on earth, it shall be loosed also in heaven."[54] "Amen I say to you, whatsoever you shall bind upon earth, shall be bound also in heaven and whatsoever you shall loose upon earth, shall be loosed also in heaven."[55] "He said to them: Receive ye the Holy Ghost: Whose sins you shall forgive, they are forgiven them: and whose sins you shall retain, they are retained."[56]

22. Jesus performed miracles by His own power. Jesus also evidently claimed divine power, the power which is proper to God, when He acted to perform miracles in His own name and by His own authority. It is to be noted that elsewhere in the sacred books, where there is evidence of the performance of a miracle, this work is done explicitly by the power and with the authority of God Himself. The wonders which Moses performed before the king of Egypt were done in accordance with the specific directions which he had received from God. "And the Lord said to Moses and Aaron: When Pharao shall say to you: Show signs: thou shalt say to Aaron: Take thy rod and cast it down before Pharao, and it shall be turned into a serpent. So Moses and Aaron went in unto Pharao, and did as the Lord had commanded. And Aaron took the rod before Pharao and his servants, and it was changed into a serpent."[57]

Throughout the Old and the New Testaments, those who are represented as working miracles for the sake of the true doctrine are always shown as acting under the direct instructions of God or at least as calling upon God for the fulfillment of their design. Actually the miracles performed by the Apostles and their successors were performed in the name and by the power of Jesus Himself, as was the healing of the lame man in the Beautiful Gate of the temple in Jerusalem. "But Peter said: Silver and gold I have none: but what I have, I give thee: In the name of Jesus Christ of Nazareth, arise and walk."[58]

Only in the case of Jesus Himself do we find a different mode of procedure. As He had altered the divine law in His own name and by

---

54 Matt. 16:19.
55 Matt. 18:18.
56 John 20:22–23.
57 Gen. 7:8–10. The narrative as a whole is contained in this book, Chs. VII–XII.
58 Acts 3:6.

The Trinity and the Incarnation

His own authority, He considered Himself able to control the physical laws of the created universe without having reference to anyone else. He taught the Apostles that one species of diabolical possession was to be overcome only through the employment of prayer and fasting, but it is not recorded that He Himself made any special preparation of the expulsion of this devil.[59] The only time He is represented as having spoken to the Father before the performance of a miracle, He stated explicitly that this was done not because any prayer was needed but for the sake of the people who stood about. "Jesus, lifting up His eyes, said: Father, I give Thee thanks that Thou hast heard Me; and I knew that Thou hearest Me always, but because of the people who stand about have I said it: that they may believe that Thou hast sent Me."[60] Customarily, as the text of the gospels shows very clearly, Jesus performed miracles by a simple word of command. The fact that He went about His work in this way constituted a manifest indication that He considered Himself endowed with the divine power as His own. Unlike others who had worked miracles, Christ did so by his own power.

23. The mission of the Holy Ghost. Again the fourth gospel shows that Jesus of Nazareth taught His divine dignity by the fact that He is recorded as promising to send the Holy Ghost, Himself obviously a divine Person according to the teaching of Jesus. "But when the Paraclete cometh whom I will send you from the Father, the Spirit of truth, who proceedeth from the Father, He shall give testimony of Me."[61]

24. Jesus was adored as God. Finally, Jesus of Nazareth accepted from men the adoration which is licitly given only to God Himself.[62] More than that, He actually answered the entreaties of those who approached Him in this way. "And behold a leper came and adored Him, saying: Lord, if Thou wilt, Thou canst make me clean. And Jesus stretching forth His hand, touched him saying: I will. Be thou

---

59 Matt. 17:18–21; Mark 9:25–29; Luke 9:41–43.
60 John 11:41–42.
61 John 25:26.
62 The disciples of Christ steadfastly refused such adoration as did Paul and Barnabas at Lystris, Acts 14:7–17. Cf. also the Revelation 22:8–9 when the angel refuses this type of honor as belonging to God alone.

made clean. And forthwith the leprosy was cleansed."[63] He accepted the adoration of Mary Magdalen, with the holy women associated with her,[64] and of the entire group of the disciples, including those who hitherto had not believed the fact of His Resurrection.[65]

25. The divinity of Christ and the fourth gospel. However, it is to the fourth gospel that we must go for the most extensive report of the teaching of Jesus to the effect that He was God. The theme of this gospel was summed up by St. John in the very first verse. "In the beginning was the Word, and the Word was with God, and the Word was God."[66] The fourth gospel recounts that John the Baptist testified of Jesus that "of His fullness we all have received,"[67] insisting that the spiritual life which men are privileged to live is something which they derive from that One who is its principle and cause, the One who possesses by right that sort of activity which others have only by the favor of the Most High. St. John the Evangelist, who was a disciple of John the Baptist before he was privileged to follow Jesus, reports that the great precursor himself had announced that Jesus is the Son of God. "And I saw: and I gave testimony, that this is the Son of God."[68] It was thus that Nathanael greeted Jesus when he was called to the presence of the Master by his friend Philip. "Nathanael answered Him, and said: Rabbi, Thou art the Son of God, Thou art the King of Israel."[69]

Jesus spoke of the temple of God in Jerusalem as being in a special way the house of His Father, a house over which He had charge. "And to them that sold doves, He said: Take these things hence, and make not the house of My Father a house of traffic."[70] To Nicodemus, a disciple who never abandoned Him, although he feared to walk openly with Jesus at the outset of His preaching, the Master said, "Amen, amen I say to thee, that we speak what we know, and we testify what we have seen, and you receive not our testimony."[71] The

---

63 Matt. 8:2–3; Mark 1:40–42; Luke 5:12–13.
64 Matt. 28:9.
65 Matt. 28:17. In this case the critically accepted Greek text is clearer than the Vulgate.
66 John 1:1.
67 John 1:16.
68 John 1:34.
69 John 1:49.
70 John 2:16. See also Matt. 21:12–13; Mark 11:15–17; Luke 19:45–46.
71 John 3:2.

content of the preaching which Jesus gave to His fellow countrymen was obviously a doctrine about God Himself. In the interview with Nicodemus He asserted that this truth was something which He possessed by reason of evidence. It was something manifest to Him. It was clear enough to all of the Jews, with their insistence upon the spirituality of the one God, that this God could be seen by no mere man, with the natural operation of his faculties at least. Consequently the claim by Jesus that He had seen God was in itself, in view of the background in which the statement was made, a clear indication that He was a divine Person.

In the same interview, Jesus insisted upon His pre-existence, a condition which is quite incompatible with the natural status of a creature. According to His teaching, He had descended from heaven. "And no man hath ascended into heaven, but He that descended from heaven, the Son of man who is in heaven."[72] The most striking feature of this instruction was Jesus' assertion that He was the only-begotten Son of God, a divine Person who had come into the world for the purpose of saving it, and in whom men would have to have faith if they would achieve the goal of eternal happiness. "For God so loved the world, as to give His only-begotten Son: that whosoever believeth in Him, may not perish, but may have life everlasting."[73] When Jesus spoke of Himself as the *only-begotten Son,* He brought out the infinite distance which separated His relation to the heavenly Father from that of other men who might still speak of God as their Father. His sonship was unique, according to His own teaching. It is noteworthy that, during the course of His public life, He spoke of the living God as His own Father and as the Father of those who were His disciples. Yet He never spoke of our Father except on that occasion when He taught the Apostles the use of the Lord's Prayer. Then, of course, the words were not meant to be used by Him, but only by those who were to petition the Father in His name, and in that petition win the reward which God intended to give them. As far as His own terminology was concerned, God was "My Father and your Father." In this way He carried throughout His preaching

---

[72] John 3:13.
[73] John 3:16.

and instruction the truth which He enunciated so clearly during this interview He granted to Nicodemus.

26. The Jews persecuted Jesus because they understood Him to claim divine dignity. St. John records that the Jews first persecuted Jesus because of His violation of those edicts which they had inserted into the fabric of the divine law itself, and because of His authoritative altering of those portions of the moral code of the Old Testament which were to be perfected in the new dispensation. But very soon their hatred of the Master was to be motivated by an even stronger reason. "But Jesus answered them: My Father worketh until now, and I work. Hereupon therefore the Jews sought the more to kill Him, because He Hid not only break the Sabbath, but also said God was His Father, making Himself equal to God. Then Jesus answered and said to them: Amen, amen I say unto you: the Son cannot do anything of Himself, but what He seeth the Father doing: for what things soever He doth, these the Son also doth in like manner. For the Father loveth the Son, and showeth Him all things which Himself doth: and greater works than these will He show Him, that you may wonder. For as the Father raiseth up the dead, and giveth life: so the Son also giveth life to whom He will. For neither doth the Father judge any man: but hath given all judgment to the Son. That all men may honor the Son, as they honor the Father: he who honoreth not the Son, honoreth not the Father who hath sent Him."[74]

No indication could possibly be clearer. In the face of those who sought His life because He made these statements, Jesus of Nazareth openly declared Himself to be the Son of God, the equal of the Father, One who was able to perform all of those works which the Father Himself could accomplish. Furthermore, according to His express teaching, it is the intention and the will of God that the Son should be honored by men in the same way as the Father Himself. Far from implying any inferiority of the Son with reference to the Father, the passage clearly indicates that the Second Person of the Blessed Trinity proceeds from the First. The enemies of Jesus hated Him too much to be confused about the direction of His teaching. They knew, as well as did His disciples, that He had openly proclaimed Himself as divine.

---

74 John 5:17–23.

The Trinity and the Incarnation

In the discourse which followed upon the feeding of the five thousand, Jesus stated the fact that He was the Source of the supernatural life by which men might live in blessedness with God forever. "Labor not for the meat which perisheth, but for that which endureth unto life everlasting, which the Son of man will give you. For Him hath the Father sealed."[75] The cause of eternal life was precisely the gift of the Son, and certainly the Son could not present as a gift that which was not His by right. He had stated, before however, in a previous discourse to the Jews, that the very life of the Father was His as something which He had received from the Father and which He enjoyed as did the Father Himself. "For as the Father hath life in Himself: so He hath given to the Son also to have life in Himself."[76]

It was the contention of Jesus that a knowledge of Himself was actually a knowledge of God the Father and therefore that He was of the selfsame essence with the Father. "They said therefore to Him: Where is Thy Father? Jesus answered: Neither Me do you know, nor My Father: if you did know Me, perhaps you would know My Father also."[77] He told of His own relation to the Father. "From God I proceeded and came: for I came not of Myself, but He sent Me."[78] This procession from God is eternal rather than temporal. "Jesus said to them: Amen, amen, I say to you, before Abraham was made, I am."[79]

To the Jews who questioned Him while He walked in the portico of Solomon, Jesus indicated very clearly that He was consubstantial with the Father. "I and the Father are One."[80] When they took steps to stone Him to death for blasphemy, Jesus upbraided them for their objection to the term "son of God," which was quite in conformity with the usage of the Old Testament. However, He made it clear that others were not entitled to be designated by that term in the same way as was Himself. Furthermore, He appealed to the miracles which He performed for the justification of His claims. "The Jews then took up stones to stone Him. Jesus answered them: Many good works I have showed you from My Father. For which of those works do you

---

75 John 6:27.
76 John 5:26.
77 John 8:18.
78 John 8:42.
79 John 8:58
80 John 10:30.

stone Me? The Jews answered Him: For a good work we stone Thee not, but for blasphemy, and because that Thou being a man, makest Thyself God. Jesus answered them: Is it not written in your law: I said, you are gods? If He called them gods to whom the Word of God was spoken, and the Scripture cannot be broken: Do you say of Him whom the Father hath sanctified and sent into the world: Thou blasphemest: because I said, I am the Son of God? If I do not the works of My Father, believe Me not. But if I do: though you will not believe Me, believe the works, that you may know and believe that the Father is in Me, and I in the Father."[81]

27. Jesus consubstantial with the Father. The episode of the fatal sickness of Lazarus, which was to terminate in his being raised from the dead by Jesus, was described by the Master as "not unto death, but for the glory of God, that the Son of God may be glorified by it."[82] Clearly, then, He indicated Himself as the recipient of that glory which belongs to God alone and thereby acknowledged Himself as a divine Person. He asserted that to see Him was actually to see the eternal Father Himself.[83]

He acknowledged the propriety of the title "Lord" with which the Apostles customarily greeted Him, and therefore claimed for Himself a title which was conceded to the Father Himself among the Hebrew people. "You call Me Master and Lord: and you say well, for so I am."[84] Solemnly He informed His followers that He actually was the life and the truth, and not merely the bearer of the good tidings to men. "I am the way and the truth and the life: no man cometh to the Father, but by Me."[85] The fact of consubstantiality with the Father is repeated to the disciples ever more emphatically. "If you had known Me, you would without doubt have known My Father also: and from henceforth you shall know Him, and you have seen Him. Philip saith to Him: Lord, show us the Father, and it is enough for us. Jesus saith to him: So long a time I have been with you: and you have not known Me? Philip, he that seeth Me, seeth the Father also: How sayest thou:

---

81 John 10:32–38. Jesus referred to Ps. 81:6.
82 John 11:4.
83 John 12:45. Cf. John 14:9.
84 John 13:13.
85 John 14:6.

The Trinity and the Incarnation

Show us the Father? Do you not believe that I am in the Father, and the Father in Me? The words that I speak to you, I speak not of Myself. But the Father who abideth in Me, He doth the works."[86]

Jesus insisted that both He and the Father exercised, in the same way, the functions of the inhabitation of the Blessed Trinity in the souls of the just. "If any one love Me, he will keep My word, and My Father will love him, and We will come to him, and will make our abode with him."[87] According to His doctrine, hatred of Him involved hatred of the heavenly Father Himself. "He that hateth Me: hateth My Father also."[88] He stated that He had truly proceeded from the Father. "I came forth from the Father, and am come into the world: again I leave the world, and I go to the Father."[89] Finally, the object of His sacerdotal prayer to the Father was a unity among His disciples which should be modeled upon and caused by the unity of the divine Persons themselves. In that unity they are to see the glory of God, which is the glory which Jesus Himself possessed before the creation of the universe. "And now glorify Thou Me, O Father, with Thyself, with the glory which I had, before the world was, with Thee."[90] "That they all may be one, as Thou, Father, in Me, and I in Thee, that they also may be one in Us: that the world may believe that Thou hast sent Me."[91]

Thus there can be no question, after an examination of the reliable historical sources which are at our disposal, that Jesus of Nazareth preached a definite religious doctrine that was not a part of the teaching current among the people among whom He lived and preached.[92] He taught that He was God, a divine Person really distinct from the Father, although consubstantial with Him. It was His teaching that

---

[86] John 14:7–10.
[87] John 14:23.
[88] John 15:23.
[89] John 16:28.
[90] John 17:5.
[91] John 17:21.
[92] Both the intense realism of our own times and the structural exigencies of apologetics as a science militate against any consideration here of the far-fetched and fanciful suppositions of men like Frazer and Reinach, who considered the Christian mysteries as adaptations of those same folk legends current in pagan doctrine. The pagan "Incarnate gods" and "trinities" bear little resemblance to and have no ascertainable connection with the doctrine of Jesus.

the Father actually existed in Him and He in the Father. He asserted that He proceeded from the Father and that He possessed the title of Son of God from all eternity, in a way in which this title could never be possessed by one who was a creature of God.

28. The divinity of the Holy Ghost in the teaching of Jesus. The teaching of Jesus on His own divinity is completed by what He taught about the reality and the divinity of the Third Person of the Blessed Trinity and Holy Ghost. According to the teaching of Jesus, the Holy Ghost is a Person at once distinct from the Father and Son and coequal with both of them in their divinity. He is named, with the Father and with the Son in the baptismal formula, composed by Jesus Himself as an indication and as a cause of the spiritual regeneration in men. "Going therefore teach ye all nations: baptizing them in the name of the Father, and of the Son, and of the Holy Ghost."[93] Baptism involved the forgiveness of sin, and, as we have seen, Jesus acted upon the knowledge of His contemporaries that this was essentially a function of the living God. It involved spiritual regeneration, the giving of a life which was utterly superior to that which is natural to the children of men. As a result the Persons in the name of Whom it is given must be those who have the right and the power to bestow it. They are the Persons who possess this life in themselves, and in the formula composed by Jesus Himself, the Holy Ghost is named as One of these Persons. The formula would be absolutely devoid of meaning if the Holy Ghost were not actually a divine Person, distinct both from the Father and from the Son.

The divinity of the Holy Ghost is brought out with singular clarity in a formula which is to be found, with very slight variations, in all three of the synoptic gospels. "Amen I say to you, that all sins shall be forgiven unto the sons of men, and the blasphemies wherewith they shall blaspheme: But he that shall blaspheme against the Holy Ghost, shall never have forgiveness, but shall be guilty of an everlasting sin."[94] A blasphemy is certainly a sin against God. It would be blasphemous to say that a sin against a creature could receive forgiveness while one committed against God could not. The open meaning of this statement by Jesus is that the Holy Ghost is certainly a divine

---

93 Matt. 28:19.
94 Mark 3:28–29; Matt. 12:31–32; Luke 12:10.

Person, and that a sin against Him of the sort which He had found in those who claimed, against all evidence, that He was possessed of an unclean spirit, was a sort of offense involving a hardness of heart ordinarily not amenable to penance.

29. The personality of the Holy Ghost. In the teaching of Jesus the Holy Ghost is certainly presented as a Person and not merely as the personification of power or wisdom. Definite works, which could not be accomplished other than through the causality of a person, are attributed to Him. He is described as bringing about in a supernatural way the conception of Jesus in the womb of the Virgin Mother. "And the angel answering said to her: The Holy Ghost shall come upon thee, and the power of the Most High shall overshadow thee. And therefore also the Holy which shall be born of thee, shall be called the Son of God."[95] The conception of Jesus is described in the same way in the first gospel. "Now the generation of Christ was in this wise: When His mother Mary was espoused to Joseph, before they came together, she was found with child, of the Holy Ghost. Whereupon Joseph her husband, being a just man, and not being willing publicly to expose her: was minded to put her away privately. But while he thought on these things, behold the angel of the Lord appeared to him in his sleep, saying: Joseph, son of David, fear not to take unto thee Mary thy wife: for that which is conceived in her, is of the Holy Ghost."[96]

The Holy Ghost is represented as abiding in the soul of Simeon, the just man who prophesied about the infant Jesus when Mary and Joseph brought Him to the temple for the first time. "And behold there was a man in Jerusalem named Simeon, and this man was just and devout, waiting for the consolation of Israel, and the Holy Ghost was in him. And he had received an answer from the Holy Ghost, that he should not see death, before he had seen the Christ of the Lord."[97] In this passage the Holy Ghost is described as answering what could only have been a prayer to the God of Israel. Furthermore, in the same context the meeting of Simeon with Jesus and Mary and Joseph, and, by implication at least, the prophesy which he gave on

---
95 Luke 1:35.
96 Matt. 1:18–20.
97 Luke 2:25–26.

this occasion, is ascribed to the work of the Holy Ghost, the Third Person of the Blessed Trinity.

All four of the gospels describe the Holy Ghost as indicating, in a visible manner, the presence and the dignity of Jesus on the occasion of His baptism by John the Baptist. "Now it came to pass when all the people were baptized, that Jesus also being baptized and praying, heaven was opened: And the Holy Ghost descended in a bodily shape as a dove upon Him: and a voice came from heaven: Thou art My beloved Son, in Thee I am well pleased."[98] The fourth gospel carries the testimony of John the Baptist about the same event. "And John gave testimony saying: I saw the Spirit coming down as a dove from heaven, and He remained upon Him. And I knew Him not: but He, who sent me to baptize with water, said to me: He upon whom thou shall see the Spirit descending and remaining upon Him, He it is that baptizeth with the Holy Ghost. And I saw, and I gave testimony that this is the Son of God."[99]

The implication of this text is clarity itself. The Holy Ghost is obviously represented as a Person, One qualified to indicate with full authority the presence of another divine Person. Furthermore, He is described as performing acts which are not attributed to the Father and the Son. The voice which pointed out Jesus as the Son could certainly not have been that of the Holy Ghost, but that of the Father. The One indicated by the voice, and by the descent of the dove was certainly none other than the Son. (It goes without saying that in this account there is no trace of anthropomorphism. The voice of the Father did not belong to Him in the way that the voice of a man is described to the person who possesses it. God is a Spirit, and the bodily organs which produce the sound of a voice have no part in Him. But, because He is the First Cause of the universe, it lies absolutely within His competence to assume corporeal forms in order to teach men a lesson which will be brought home to them more effectively through the use of these signs.) The three synoptics also depict John the Baptist stating that Jesus was to baptize in the Holy Ghost and fire."[100]

---

98 Luke 3:21–22. Cf. also Matt. 3:16–17; Mark 1:10–11.
99 John 1:32–34.
100 Matt. 3:11; Mark 1:8; Luke 3:16.

The Trinity and the Incarnation

30. The Holy Ghost and the message of Jesus. Jesus attributed the sayings of the Holy Scriptures to the Holy Ghost. Now, as these were considered as the Word of God, it follows that the Person who is said to be responsible for them as the inspirer of the human author must be considered to be divine. Thus when Jesus stated that the Holy Ghost was the source of the statement contained on the pages of the psalms, He was equivalently declaring Him to be a divine Person. "For David himself saith by the Holy Ghost: The Lord said to my Lord, sit on My right hand, until I make Thy enemies Thy footstool."[101]

According to the express promises of Jesus, the Holy Ghost was to exercise the indubitably personal function of telling the Apostles what they were to answer to the questions of those who were to persecute them out of a hatred for the Master. "For the Holy Ghost shall teach you in the same hour what you must say."[102] It was also to be the function of the Holy Ghost so to act upon the disciples that, after the death and the ascension of Jesus, they would recall and understand the message which He had taught them. "But the Paraclete, the Holy Ghost? Whom the Father will send in My name, He will teach you all things, and bring all things to your mind, whatsoever I shall have said to you."[103]

According to Jesus, the Holy Ghost proceeds from the Father and is sent by the Son. "But when the Paraclete cometh whom I will send you from the Father, the Spirit of Truth, who proceedeth from the Father, He shall give testimony of Me."[104] Actually the Holy Ghost "has received" from the Son. "But when He, the Spirit of truth is come, He will teach you all truth: For He shall not speak of Himself: but what things so ever He shall hear, He shall speak: and the things that are to come, He shall show you. He shall glorify Me: because He shall receive of Mine, and shall show it to you."[105]

Clearly, then, in the central mysteries of the Trinity and the Incarnation, Jesus of Nazareth taught a definite doctrine of a

---

101 Mark 12:26. The citation is from Ps. 109:1.
102 Luke 12:12; Mark 13:11. In Matt. 10:20 He is called the Spirit of your Father.
103 John 14:26.
104 John 15:26.
105 John 16:13–14.

religious nature. It is obvious enough that this teaching, as it stood, had not been put forward by any other teacher. It is His own, and it is a doctrine for which He might well appeal to motives of credibility in order to show that this definite teaching was actually what He claimed it to be, a message supernaturally communicated by God to man.

Chapter 12

THE DOCTRINAL CONTENT IN THE MESSAGE OF JESUS

Part III:
The Redemption and the Church

1. Background of the chapter. It is the business of the apologist, in dealing with this section of his science, to demonstrate from the reliable historical records at his disposal that Jesus of Nazareth actually preached a religious doctrine which was not the same as that which was accepted among the Jewish people of His own time. He does this in order that he may be able to show with clarity and certitude that Jesus could actually appeal to motives of credibility in order to prove the authenticity of a definite doctrine as divine revelation, and then in order to manifest the full efficacy of the motives which can be alleged in favor of the preaching of Jesus.

In the pursuance of this end we have already seen briefly and for the most part from the evidence of the four canonical gospels considered as historical documents rather than as divinely inspired books, the relation of the doctrine of Jesus to the section of divine public revelation which had already been made manifest in the preaching of the prophets and the patriarchs who were His heralds. We have then recounted some of the texts which illustrate what Jesus taught about the central mysteries of Christianity, the Trinity and the Incarnation. It remains for us to consider two sections of His teaching which are intimately connected with these two mysteries, namely, the statements which He made about the redemption and the Church.

2. Importance of teaching on redemption and the Church in modern apologetics. In the teaching of Jesus, the work of the redemption is given as the reason for the Incarnation itself. Moreover, the Church which He organized and of which He is the perpetual

Head is a society essentially devoted to the carrying out of the work of the redemption. Insistence upon the reality of the Church is an absolute requisite for the effective use of scientific apologetics. It so happened that Jesus promised that His Church would itself be a motive of credibility, a work which is evidently such as to be beyond the power of any creature, actual or possible to institute or even to continue. In the science of apologetics we use the Catholic Church itself as a criterion of revelation. Thus it is essential to show that Jesus can be shown to have intended to found such an organization and then actually to have brought it into being.

Furthermore, the objectors against the doctrine of Jesus most prominent and powerful in our own time stress their denial of any foundation of an organized Church by Jesus.[1] When we look into the background of the many assertions to the effect that Jesus did not offer any religious teaching which was not then accepted and known by every well-educated Jew in His own time, we find that opponents of Catholicism are far more concerned with that portion of the doctrine of the Master which deals with the kingdom or the Church than they are with the sections which treat of strictly speculative verities. If they could succeed in proving that Jesus never organized a definite religious society which was meant to exist until the end of time, or at least in creating the assumption that no scientifically acceptable demonstration could be made in contradiction to their teachings, then they would have achieved their purpose. They would have put an obstacle in the way of a successful demonstration of credibility as applied to Catholic dogma.

3. The salvific mission of Jesus. At the very outset of His public life, in the interview which He granted to Nicodemus, Jesus spoke of the redemption of man as the purpose of the Incarnation itself, and indicated the manner in which this redemption was to be brought about. "And as Moses lifted up the serpent in the desert; so must the Son of man be lifted up: that whosoever believeth in Him, may not perish, but may have life everlasting. For God so loved the world, as to give His only-begotten Son: that whosoever believeth in Him, may

---

[1] Among the adversaries of Catholicism savants like Moore and popularizers like Browne agree that the Church was merely an afterthought instituted in apostolic times by reason of conditions not foreseen by Jesus.

The Redemption and the Church

not perish, but may have life everlasting. For God sent not His Son into the world to judge the world, but that the world may be saved by Him."[2]

When He first preached at Nazareth, Jesus utilized a dramatic and effective tactic to assure His fellow townsmen that He was actually the Saviour and Redeemer, as well as the Prophet, charged with the mission of bringing the divine message to the children of men. "And He came to Nazareth where He was brought up: and He went into the synagogue according to His custom on the Sabbath day, and He rose up to read, And the book of Isaiah the prophet was delivered unto Him. And as He unfolded the book, He found the place where it was written: The Spirit of the Lord is upon Me: wherefore He hath anointed Me, to preach the gospel to the poor He hath sent Me, to heal the contrite of heart, to preach deliverance to the captives, and sight to the blind, to set at liberty them that are bruised, to preach the acceptable year of the Lord, and the day of reward. And when He had folded the book, He restored it to the minister, and sat down. And the eyes of all in the synagogue were fixed on Him. And He began to say to them: This day is fulfilled this scripture in your ears."[3] The Messiah described by Isaiah was one destined to accomplish a mission which was salvific as well as doctrinal. He was expected to heal and liberate men, as well as to preach to them the doctrine of God. Thus, in claiming the fulfillment of this prophecy, Jesus explicitly asserted that He was a Saviour.

4. The work of Jesus for sinners. According to His own teaching, the mission of Jesus was not for those who were actually just in the sight of God, but rather to those who were averted from their Creator by sin. Furthermore, it was to result in the conversion of these sinners and their regaining of the life of grace which had been lost to them. "I came not to call the just, but sinners to penance."[4] He rebuked the headstrong reaction of the Apostles against the Samaritans who had refused to receive them, with the statement, "The Son of man came not to destroy souls, but to save."[5] Again He insisted that the

---

2 John 3:14–17.
3 Luke 4:16–21.
4 Luke 5:32; Matt. 9:13; Mark 2:17.
5 Luke 9:55.

beneficiaries of His salvific work were those who were actually lost. "For the Son of man is come to save that which was lost.... Even so it is not the will of your Father, who is in heaven, that one of these little ones should perish."[6]

5. The redemptive death of Jesus in His teaching. The process of saving the world involves the death of Jesus the Redeemer. "Even as the Son of man did not come to be ministered unto, but to minister, and to give His life a redemption for many."[7] He expressed this same doctrine in the analogy of the Good Shepherd. "I am the Good Shepherd. The Good Shepherd giveth His life for His sheep."[8] Jesus announced the manner in which His sacrifice was to be made. "Behold we go up to Jerusalem, and the Son of Man shall be betrayed to the chief priests and the scribes, and they shall condemn Him to death. And shall deliver Him to the gentiles to be mocked, and scourged, and crucified, and the third day He shall rise again."[9] However, the sacrifice of His life is to be entirely voluntary on the part of Jesus, who possesses superhuman control over His bodily life. "Therefore doth the Father love Me: because I lay down My life, that I may take it up again. No man taketh it away from Me: but I lay it down of Myself, and I have power to take it up again. This commandment have I received from My Father."[10]

This doctrine was so strange to those who had been imbued all during their lives with the rabbinical doctrines then in vogue, that the disciples themselves were not able to understand how One who had proclaimed Himself the Messiah and the Son of God could thus suffer ignominiously and die. "And they understood none of these things, and this word was hid from them, and they understood not the things that were said."[11] The rejection and the death of the Messiah had been clearly foretold in that section of the prophecy of Isaiah which deals with the servant of God.[12] However, this concept did not

---

6 Matt. 18:11, 14.
7 Matt. 20–28; Mark 10–45.
8 John 10:11.
9 Matt. 20:18–19; Matt. 18:22–23; Luke 18:31–33; 9:43–45; Mark 10:33–34; 9:30–32; 8:31; John 12:23–24.
10 John 10:17–18
11 Luke 18:34.
12 Isa. 53 in toto.

fit into the politico-national concept of the messianic dignity which had been elaborated by the rabbis, independently of revealed truth. Since His own followers did not understand this teaching because of its strangeness, it is quite obvious that this portion of the teaching of Jesus could not be termed merely a restatement of truths already accepted by all of the well-educated Jews of His own time.

Finally, at the last supper, in the very institution of the Blessed Eucharist, Jesus pointed out that His blood was to be the price for the redemption of man. "And whilst they were at supper, Jesus took bread and blessed, and broke, and gave to His disciples, and said: Take ye, and eat, this is My body. And taking the chalice He gave thanks: and gave to them saying: Drink ye all of this. For this is My blood of the New Testament which shall be shed for many unto the remission of sins."[13]

6. Jesus and the messianic kingdom. According to the teaching of Jesus, as this is contained in His own words in the canonical gospels, the fruits of His sacrificial death on Calvary were to be communicated to men through the agency of a definite religious society of which He was to be the Founder and the Head. The concept of this religious society is intimately bound up with the notion of that messianic dignity which Jesus obviously claimed for Himself. It was a commonplace in Old Testament teaching that the Messiah, upon His arrival, was to bring about a renovation and perfection in the lives of individual men and in the conduct of society as a whole. As a result the notion of the kingdom had become correlative with that of the Messiah, since a person could not possibly act as the promised deliverer unless in some way or other he acted of that society or nation which belonged intimately to God.

Jesus, then, was not faced with the task of telling His fellow countrymen that there would have to be a kingdom. The whole force of His instructions on this matter could be, and had to be, concentrated on the work of explaining to them what sort of society this kingdom was meant to be. The opposition which He encountered was based upon His contention that His kingdom was to be a spiritual society rather than a temporal state; a society which enjoined a perfect and stringent moral code and the acceptance of a

---

[13] Matt. 26:26–28; Mark 14:22–24; Luke 22:19–20; 1 Cor. 11:24–25.

definite and difficult set of dogmas, while at the same time it was to include within its membership even those who were not of the nation of Israel, according to the flesh at least.

7. The true Israel. According to the testimonies of the four gospels, the first announcement of this kingdom or church was that it would constitute the true Israel. The angel Gabriel announced to Mary that her Son was to possess the throne of David and rule over the house of Jacob, thus commanding the messianic kingdom. "He shall be great, and shall be called the Son of the Most High, and the Lord God shall give unto Him the throne of David His Father, and He shall reign in the house of Jacob forever and of His kingdom there shall be no end."[14] The assertion that the reign of Jesus was to be absolutely perpetual was another indication that this was meant to be the rule promised by God to the descendant of David who was to be the Saviour of the human race. The control of this society is promised by God not to a dynasty but to an individual. This one reign is to close the epic of the divine commerce with men.

The same consciousness of the kingdom as the continuation of the Israelitic state is evident in the words and the actions of those magi who came to acknowledge the royalty of the infant Jesus. "When Jesus therefore was born in Bethlehem of Juda, in the days of King Herod, there came wise men from the east to Jerusalem, saying: Where is He that is born King of the Jews? For we have seen His star in the east, and are come to adore Him."[15] Nathanael, called to follow Jesus by his friend Philip, also acknowledged that the rule of Jesus was to be over the true Israel. "Nathanael answered Him and said: Rabbi, Thou art the Son of God, Thou art the King of Israel."[16]

8. Carnal descent from Abraham is not the necessary condition for entrance into the kingdom. However, Jesus Himself made it very plain that entrance into His kingdom was not merely by the fact of birth. In order to achieve membership in this society men had to be reborn in the regeneration of baptism. "Jesus answered: Amen, amen I say to thee, unless a man be born again of water and the Holy

---

14 Luke 1:32–33.
15 Matt. 8:1–2.
16 John 1:49.

Ghost, he can not entered into the kingdom of God."[17] According to the teaching of Jesus, it was in and through this kingdom that men were meant to achieve that everlasting life which God wills them to possess, and which they attained through belief in the Son of Man who is to be crucified for their sake.[18]

9. The preaching of the kingdom. The evangelists give as the occupation of Jesus, during the years of His public life, the preaching of the gospel of the kingdom. "And after that John was delivered up, Jesus came into Galilee, preaching the gospel of the kingdom of God, and saying: The time is accomplished and the kingdom of God is at hand: repent, and believe in the gospel."[19] To the laggard disciple whom He favored with His vocation, He pointed out the announcement of the kingdom as the task to which he was called. "But He said to another: Follow Me. And he said: Lord, suffer me first to go, and to bury my father. And Jesus said to him: Let the dead bury their dead: but go thou and preach the kingdom of God."[20] The commission given to the twelve Apostles for their mission throughout the country of the Jews was to preach the gospel of the kingdom and to perform miracles which were meant to show the credibility of their message. "These twelve Jesus sent: commanding them, saying: Go ye not into the way of the gentiles, and into the cities of the Samaritans enter ye not: But go ye rather to the lost sheep of the house of Israel. And going preach, saying: The kingdom of heaven is at hand. Heal the sick, raise the dead, cleanse the lepers, cast out devils: freely have you received, freely give."[21] It was the will of God that the doctrines of the kingdom should first be preached to the Jews alone. Only after they had refused the benefit which God offered to them was the benefit to come to the gentiles.

Moreover, when Jesus sent the seventy-two disciples on their mission, their business was announcing the proximity of this same kingdom. "And after these things the Lord appointed also other seventy-two; and He sent them two and two before His face into

---

17 John 3:5.
18 Cf. John 3:14–18.
19 Mark 1:14–15; Matt. 4:7, 23; Matt. 9:35; Luke 8:1.
20 Luke 9:59–60.
21 Matt. 10:5–8; Luke 9:1–2.

every city and place whither He Himself was to come."[22] The essential charge which Jesus gave to these men was, "Heal the sick that are therein, and say to them: The kingdom of God is come nigh unto you."[23] Actually Jesus gave the preaching of the kingdom as the reason for His work during the public life. "To other cities also must I preach the kingdom of God: for therefore am I sent."[24]

10. Membership and perfection in the kingdom. Jesus asserted that His kingdom was to *belong* to those who practiced the acts of moral perfection which He taught them. Moreover, the beatitudes show, in their completeness, the qualities of those who will be citizens in the kingdom and the rewards which will accompany this membership. "Blessed are the poor in spirit: for theirs is the kingdom of heaven. Blessed are the meek, for they shall possess the land. Blessed are they that mourn: for they shall be comforted. Blessed are they that hunger and thirst after justice: for they shall have their fill. Blessed are the merciful: for they shall obtain mercy. Blessed are the clean of heart: for they shall see God. Blessed are the peacemakers: for they shall be called the children of God. Blessed are they that suffer persecution for justice sake: for theirs is the kingdom of heaven."[25] The basic moral law of the Old Testament, as well as its doctrinal content, held within the perfection of this kingdom. But, according to Jesus, the person whose justice was not definitely superior to that of the contemporary leaders of the Jewish nation would have no part in it. "He therefore that shall break one of these least commandments, and shall so teach man, shall be called the least in the kingdom of heaven. But he that shall do and teach, he shall be called great in the kingdom of heaven. For I tell you, that unless your justice abound more than that of the scribes and the Pharisees, you shall not enter into the kingdom of heaven."[26] Obedience to the law of God is a condition requisite for admittance to this kingdom. "Not every one that saith to Me, Lord, Lord, shall enter into the kingdom of heaven: but he that

---

22 Luke 10:1.
23 Luke 10:9.
24 Luke 4:4.
25 Matt. 5:3–10; Luke 6:20–22.
26 Matt. 5:19–20.

doth the will of My Father who is in heaven, he shall enter into the kingdom of heaven."[27]

The obvious implication of these statements is that membership in the kingdom of heaven is not lost by an offense against God. For the person who acts against the divine precepts and teaches improperly is said to be the least within the kingdom. He retains his membership even though he fails to profit by it. However, even the justice of the scribes and the Pharisees was purely external, and it certainly did not include the perfection of faith which is requisite for entrance into the realm of Jesus. Furthermore, it is the will of the Father, often cited by Jesus, that men should believe in His name. Thus the man who elicits an act of faith in order to enter into the kingdom, to that extent at least obeys the mandate of the Father. The person who acknowledges the sovereignty of Jesus merely in a mechanical way has not performed the act which is necessary for incorporation into this kingdom.

Membership in this organization which is the kingdom of heaven is an incomparable good, since it places a man in a better position before God than even that occupied by the great St. John the Baptist. "Amen I say to you, there hath not risen among them that are born of women a greater than John the Baptist: yet he that is the lesser in the kingdom of heaven is greater than he."[28] This good is to be looked upon as a prize to secure which men must do violence to the forces of evil which oppose them. "And from the days of John the Baptist until now, the kingdom of heaven suffereth violence, and the violent bear it away."[29]

Obviously, according to the teaching of Jesus, the citizens of this church or kingdom He preached were actually His followers. He asserted that these individuals, by the fact of their adherence to Him, acquired a definite dignity springing from relationship to Him. "And stretching forth His hand towards His disciples, He said: Behold My mother and My brethren. For whosoever shall do the will of My Father, that is in heaven: he is My mother and sister and brother."[30]

---

27 Matt. 7:21.
28 Matt. 11:11.
29 Matt 11:12.
30 Matt. 12:49–50; Mark 3:34–35; Luke 8:21.

11. The nature of a parable. A great deal of the instruction which Jesus gave to the populace about the kingdom of heaven was set forth in the form of parables. The parable was an instrument of teaching commonly employed and known in ancient times. Socrates used them so frequently in his instructions that Aristotle, in his *Rhetoric*, designated this figure as "Socratic." Plato has recorded many of them in his dialogues, and one of them, taken from the Phaedrus, will serve to show how the great Athenian utilized the parable: "And I wish that you would let me ask you a question: Would a husbandman who is a man of sense, take the seeds, which he values and which he wishes to be fruitful, and in sober earnest plant them during the heat of the summer, in some garden of Adonis, that he may rejoice when he sees them in eight days appearing in beauty (at least he does that, if at all, only as the show of a festival); but those about which he is in earnest he sows in fitting soil, and practices husbandry, and is satisfied if in eight months they arrive at perfection?"[31]

Aristotle lists parables among the instruments available in rhetoric for utilizing the common belief of men to explain the nature of the characteristics of the object the teacher is attempting to manifest. "It remains for us now to expound those forms of procedure which are common to all types of oratory, since we have finished speaking about the specialized kinds. There are two types of these common forms, the example and the enthymeme, since the maxim is a kind of enthymeme. And first we shall speak about example, for example is like induction, and induction is a beginning.

"There are two sorts of examples. For the speaker uses one kind of example when he refers to things which have actually taken place, and another when he makes up a story himself. Of this latter type of example, one form is the parable and another a fable, like those of Aesop or of the Libyans."[32] According to the examples which Aristotle gives, the fable differs from the parable in that it is a complete story out of which a definite lesson can be derived, while the parable brings out, in a situation which is clear to the hearer, a

---

31 *The Phaedrus of Plato*, translation of Jowett, The Dial Press. The Works of Plato, New York, Vol. 3, p. 444.
32 Aristotle, *Rhetoric*, Book 3, Ch. 20. In the edition of Sylvester Maurus, republished under the direction of Cardinal Ehrle in Paris, 1885, Ch. 21, numbers 1–2.

point directly parallel to that which the speaker wishes to manifest in the object of which he is treating.

12. The reason for Jesus' use of parables in preaching the doctrine of the kingdom. This point has its importance in apologetics when we consider the teaching of Jesus relative to His church. For the parable, as a distinct and useful instrument of teaching and persuasion, was frequently employed in the descriptions of that church which Jesus gave to the people. Jesus utilized them for the sake of effectiveness, because the temper and the dispositions of the people were not such as to allow a more direct exposition of the nature of the messianic kingdom. To the disciples, who were more closely united to Him and who were thus better prepared to bear the tremendous force of His teaching, Jesus stated clearly the meanings which He had placed in the illustrations the multitudes had heard. If the populace itself did not understand these lessons, it was not due to the obscurity of the means which Jesus employed. It was rather the fault of their predispositions for a worldly and political realm of the type which their rabbis had led them to expect. Jesus brought out the reason for His teaching the multitudes by means of parables very clearly when He was interrogated on this point by the Apostles. "And His disciples came and said to Him: Why speakest Thou to them in parables? Who answered and said to them: Because to you it is given to know the mysteries of the kingdom of heaven: but to them it is not given. For he that hath, to him shall be given, and he shall abound: but he that hath not, from him shall be taken away that also which he hath. Therefore do I speak to them in parables: because seeing they see not, and hearing they hear not, neither do they understand: And the prophecy of Isaiah is fulfilled in them, who saith: By hearing you shall hear, and shall not understand: and seeing you shall see, and shall not perceive. For the heart of this people is grown gross, and with their ears they have been dull of hearing, and their eyes have been shut: lest at any time they should see with their eyes, and hear with their ears, and understand with their heart, and be converted, and I should heal them. But blessed are your eyes, because they see, and your ears, because they hear. For amen I say to you, many prophets and just men have desired to see the things that you see, and have not seen them: and to hear the things that you hear and have not heard them."[33]

The meaning of the text is quite clear. Jesus taught the people by means of parables precisely because these people were too hardened and obtuse to profit by the direct type of teaching which He gave to the Apostles. In no way is there any intimation that the parable was an instrument which was not intended by Jesus to be effective and out of which the people could not derive that knowledge which He declared to be so necessary for them.

Voste, a modern authority upon the interpretation of the parables in the gospel text, lists twenty-two distinct examples as referring to dogmatic teaching about the church or the kingdom of God.[34] Eight of these have to do with the nature of the kingdom, and tell of its origin in the preaching of Jesus and of His Apostles, its worth, its growth, and its composition. Seven treat of the membership in this kingdom, establishing the reprobation of the Jews and the calling of the gentiles. Seven more deal with the final status of this kingdom in the eternal glory which is to accompany the second advent of Jesus Himself.

13. The parable of the sower. The first of these parables which refer to the nature of the kingdom is that of the sower. "And He spoke to them many things in parables, saying: Behold the sower went forth to sow. And whilst he soweth some fell by the way side, and the birds of the air came and ate them up. And other some fell upon stony ground, where they had not much earth: and they sprung up immediately, because they had no deepness of earth. And when the sun was up, they were scorched: and because they had no root, they withered away. And others fell among thorns, and the thorns grew up and choked them. And others fell upon good ground: and they brought forth fruit, some a hundredfold, some sixtyfold, and some thirtyfold."[35] We are privileged to know the interpretation or explanation of this parable which Jesus gave to the disciples themselves. It is recorded in all three of the synoptic gospels.

---

33 Matt. 13:1–17. Cf. Mark 4:10–12; Luke 8:9–10.
34 *Parabolae Selectae Domini Nostri Jesu Christi*, Interprete R. P. Jacobo—M. Voste, O.P. (Rome, 1933), 2 vols.
35 Matt. 13:3–81. Cf. Mark 4:3–9; Luke 8:5–8.

"Hear you therefore the parable of the sower. When any one heareth the word of the kingdom, and understandeth it not, there cometh the wicked one, and catcheth away that which was sown in his heart: this is he that received the seed by the wayside. And he that received the seed upon stony ground: this is he that heareth the word, and immediately receiveth it with joy. Yet hath he not root in himself, but is only for a time; and when there ariseth tribulation and persecution because of the word, he is presently scandalized. And he that received the seed among thorns, is he that heareth the word, and the care of this world and the deceitfulness of riches choketh up the word, and he becometh fruitless. But he that received the seed upon good ground, this is he that heareth the word, and understandeth, and beareth fruit, and yieldeth the one a hundredfold, and another sixty, and another thirty."[36] The obvious implication of this parable, as explained by Jesus, is that the individual's entrance into and profit from the kingdom of God must depend in some way upon his own personal dispositions. The kingdom of heaven is meant to be composed of those who accept the Word of God and who do not allow earthly considerations and spiritual enemies to obstruct the workings of divine grace.

14. The growth of the kingdom. Yet, according to the instructions of Jesus, the kingdom is meant to be an organization which develops swiftly, unnoticed by mankind as a whole. "And He said: So is the kingdom of God, as if a man should cast seed into the earth, And should sleep and rise, night and day, and the seed should spring, and grow up whilst he knoweth not. For the earth of itself bringeth forth fruit, first the blade, then the ear, afterward the full corn in the ear, And when the fruit is brought forth, immediately he putteth in the sickle, because the harvest is come."[37]

This same greatness of the kingdom, as an institution which is meant to grow from inconspicuous beginnings, is brought out in the parable of the mustard seed. "The kingdom of heaven is like to a grain of mustard seed, which a man took and sowed in his field. Which is the least indeed of all seeds: but when it is grown up, it is

---

36 Matt. 13:18–23. Cf. Mark 4:13–20; Luke 8:11–15.
37 Mark 4:26–29.

greater than all herbs, and becometh a tree, so that the birds of the air come, and dwell in the branches thereof."[38]

15. The worth of the kingdom. Furthermore, the kingdom was such as to transform the lives of all those who were to be privileged with citizenship within it. "The kingdom of heaven is like to leaven, which a woman took and hid in three measures of meal, until the whole was leavened."[39]

In the teaching of Jesus, the kingdom was announced as a precious good for which men should be willing to sacrifice all that is otherwise dearest to them. He brought out this aspect of the church in the parables of the hidden treasure and of the pearl. "The kingdom of heaven is like unto a treasure hidden in a field: which a man having found, hid it, and for joy thereof goeth, and selleth all that he hath, and buyeth that field."[40] "Again the kingdom of heaven is like to a merchant seeking good pearls. Who, when he had found one pearl of great price, went his way, and sold all that he had, and bought it."[41]

16. Membership in the kingdom. However, Jesus warned that this kingdom, during the first period of its existence, was to have as members those who were evil as well as those who were good. As He explained it, the first period of the existence of the kingdom was to be brought to an end with the end of the world as men know it now. After this event, the kingdom is to exist in an eternally perfect felicity, including only those within its membership who shine as friends of the living God. Jesus set this truth forth in the parables of the cockle, and of the net cast into the sea. "The kingdom of heaven is likened to a man that sowed good seed in his field. But while men were asleep, his enemy came and oversowed cockle among the wheat, and went his way. And when the blade was sprung up, and had brought forth fruit, then appeared also the cockle. And the servants of the good man of the house coming said to him: Sir, didst thou not sow good seed in thy field? Whence then hath it cockle? And he said to them: An enemy hath done this. And the servants said to him: Wilt thou that we go and gather it up? And he said: No, lest perhaps gathering

---

38 Matt. 13:31–32; Mark 4:30–32; Luke 13:20–21.
39 Matt. 13:33; Luke 13:20–21.
40 Matt. 13:44.
41 Matt. 13:45–46.

The Redemption and the Church 243

up the cockle, you root up the wheat also together with it. Suffer both to grow until the harvest, and in the time of the harvest I will say to the reapers: Gather up first the cockle, and bind it into bundles to burn, but the wheat gather ye into my barn."[42]

This was one of those parables which Jesus explained to the disciples in words which have been recorded on the pages of the canonical gospels. "Then having sent away the multitudes, He came into the house: and His disciples came to Him, saying: Expound to us the parable of the cockle of the field. Who made answer and said to them: He that soweth the good seed is the Son of man. And the field is the world. And the good seed are the children of the kingdom. And the cockle are the children of the evil one. And the enemy that sowed them is the devil. But the harvest is the end of the world. And the reapers are the angels. Even as the cockle therefore is gathered up, and burnt with fire: so shall it be at the end of the world. The Son of man shall send His angels, and they shall gather out of His kingdom all scandals, and them that work iniquity: And shall cast them into the furnace of fire: There shall be weeping and gnashing of teeth. Then shall the just shine as the sun in the kingdom of their Father."[43]

The same lesson is brought out in the parable of the net cast into the sea. "Again the kingdom of heaven is like to a net cast into the sea, and gathering together all kind of fishes. Which, when it was filled, they drew out, and sitting by the shore, they chose out the good into vessels but the bad they cast forth. So shall it be at the end of the world: the angels shall go out, and shall separate the wicked from among the just, And shall cast them into the furnace of fire; there shall be weeping and gnashing of teeth."[44]

In dealing with the membership in the kingdom of heaven which He preached as assiduously, Jesus insisted that not all of those who were members of the Jewish nation should be counted as citizens with His realm. "But whereunto shall I esteem this generation to be like? It is like to children in the market place: who, crying to their companions, say: We have piped to you, and you have not danced: we have lamented, and you have not mourned. For John came, neither

---

42 Matt. 3:24–30.
43 Matt. 13:36–43.
44 Matt. 13:47–50.

eating nor drinking, and they say: He hath a devil. The Son of man came, eating and drinking, and they say: Behold a man who is a glutton and a wine drinker, a friend of publicans and sinners. And wisdom is justified by her children."[45] The kingdom was presented to people who were indisposed to receive this ineffable benefit. They manifested themselves as equally prejudiced against any manner of presentation.

Those who enter into the kingdom of heaven through the acceptance of the divine teaching are able to find there remission of the sins which they have committed against God. Furthermore, the condition of a sinner who repents and enters into this kingdom is far better than that of the respectable man who refuses to heed the testimony of Jesus, according to His own teaching. "A certain man had two sons, and coming to the first he said: Son, go work today in my vineyard. And he answering said: I will not. But afterwards, being moved with repentance, he went. And coming to the other he said in like manner. And he answering said: I go, sir, and he went not; Which of the two did the father's will? They say to Him: The first. Jesus saith to them: Amen I say to you, that the publicans and the harlots shall go into the kingdom of God before you. For John came to you in the way of justice, and you did not believe him; but the publicans and the harlots believed him: but you seeing it, did not even afterwards repent, that you might believe him."[46]

17. Those who reject the kingdom. Jesus insisted that those who rejected His teaching and sought to encompass His defeat would not receive the privilege of membership in the kingdom of God. He brought this out with matchless clarity in the parable of the faithless husbandmen, addressed to the leaders among His enemies. "A certain man planted a vineyard and made a hedge about it, and dug a place for the wine vat and built a tower and let it to husbandmen, and went into a far country. And at the season he sent to the husbandmen a servant to receive of the husbandmen of the fruit of the vineyard. Who having laid hands on him, beat him, and sent him away empty. And again he sent to them another servant; and him they wounded in the head, and used him reproachfully. And again he sent another,

---

45 Matt. 11:16–19; Luke 7:31–35.
46 Matt. 21:28–32.

The Redemption and the Church

and him they killed: and many others, of whom some they beat and others they killed. Therefore having yet one son, most dear to him; he also sent him unto them last of all, saying: They will reverence my son. But the husbandmen said one to another: This is the heir; come, let us kill him; and the inheritance shall be ours. And laying hold on him, they killed him; and cast him out of the vineyard. What therefore will the Lord of the vineyard do? He will come and destroy those husbandmen; and will give the vineyard to others. And have you not read this scripture, The stone which the builders rejected, the same is made the head of the corner: By the Lord this has been done, and it is wonderful in our eyes. And they sought to lay hands on Him, but they feared the people; for they knew that He spoke this parable to them."[47]

Jesus made it abundantly clear that men possessed the tragic power to reject the preaching of the kingdom, and that those who refused to accept it would not participate in its benefits. "When one of them that sat at table with Him had heard these things, he said to Him: Blessed is he that shall eat bread in the kingdom of God. But He said to him: A certain man made a great supper, and invited many. And he sent his servant at the hour of supper to say to them that were invited, that they should come, for now all things are ready. And they began all at once to make excuse. The first said to him: I have bought a farm, and I must needs go out and see it: I pray thee, hold me excused. And another said: I have bought five yoke of oxen, and I go to try them: I pray thee, hold me excused. And another said: I have married a wife, and therefore I cannot come. And the servant returning told these things to his lord. Then the master of the house being angry, said to his servant: Go out quickly into the streets and lanes of the city, and bring in hither the poor and the feeble and the blind and the lame. And the servant said: Lord, it is done as thou hast commanded, and yet there is room. And the lord said to the servant: Go out into the highways and hedges, and compel them to come in, that my house may be filled. But I say unto you, that none of those men that were invited, shall taste of my supper."[48]

---

[47] Mark 12:1–12; Matt. 21:33–46; Luke 20:9–19.
[48] Luke 14:15–24.

The previous parables had made it evident that, according to the doctrine of Jesus, the gentiles were to be admitted to the kingdom of God because the Jews, to whom the invitation had first been proffered, had rejected it. However, He insisted also that not all of those who actually entered into the kingdom and enjoyed its benefits were to be found worthy of sharing in its eternal glory. Those who manifested themselves ungrateful to God were to be ejected on the last day. Thus membership in the kingdom was not, by itself, a guarantee of eternal salvation, although, of course, it was requisite for the eternal life which Jesus came to give. This fact was brought out in the parable of the wedding feast.

"And Jesus answering spoke again in parables to them, saying: The kingdom of heaven is likened to a king, who made a marriage for his son. And he sent his servants to call them that were invited to the marriage, and they would not come. Again he sent other servants, saying: Tell them that were invited: Behold, I have prepared my dinner, my beeves and fatlings are killed, and all things are ready: come ye to the marriage. But they neglected, and went their ways, one to his farm, and another to his merchandise. And the rest laid hands on his servants, and having treated them contumeliously put them to death. But when the king had heard of it, he was angry; and sending his armies, he destroyed those murderers and burned their city. Then he saith to his servants: The marriage indeed is ready, but they that were invited, were not worthy. Go ye therefore into the highways, and as many as you shall find, call to the marriage. And his servants going forth into the ways, gathered together all that they found, both bad and good; and the marriage was filled with guests. And the king went in to see the guests, and he saw there a man who had not on a wedding garment. And he saith to him: Friend, how cameth thou hither not having on a wedding garment? But he was silent. Then the king said to the waiters: Bind his hands and feet, and cast him into the exterior darkness: there shall be weeping and gnashing of teeth. For many are called, but few are chosen."[49]

18. The reward of the kingdom. Brilliantly Jesus pointed out, in the parable of the laborers in the vineyard, that the essential reward of those who were to work within the kingdom was one. In spite of

---

49 Matt. 22:1–14.

the fact that there are to be degrees of power and of excellence within that kingdom (for Jesus spoke of the "least" within it, and He gave to some of its members powers not enjoyed by others), He was at pains to show that the efforts expended for God within the kingdom would find an ample and supernaturally effective reward in eternal life. Thus other goods, which were of the temporal order, could not be claimed as the wage due in justice for meritorious activity.

"The kingdom of heaven is like to a householder who went out early in the morning to hire laborers into his vineyard. And having agreed with the laborers for a penny a day, he sent them into his vineyard. And going out about the third hour, he saw others standing in the market place, idle. And he said to them: Go you also into my vineyard, and I will give you what shall be just. And they went their way. And again he went out about the sixth and the ninth hour, and did in like manner. But about the eleventh hour he went out and found others standing, and he saith to them: Why stand you here all the day idle? They say to him: Because no man hath hired us. He saith to them: Go you also into my vineyard. And when evening was come, the lord of the vineyard saith to his steward: Call the laborers and pay them their hire, beginning from the last even to the first. When therefore they were come that came about the eleventh hour, they received every man a penny. But when the first also came, they thought that they should receive more, and they also received every man a penny. And receiving it they murmured against the master of the house, saying: These last have worked but one hour, and thou hast made them equal to us, that have borne the burden of the day and the heats. But he answering said to one of them: Friend, I do thee no wrong: didst thou not agree with me for a penny? Take what is thine, and go thy way: I will give also to this last even as to thee. Or, is it not lawful for me to do what I will? Is thy eye evil because I am good? So shall the last be first, and the first, last; for many are called, but few chosen."[50] In this parable Jesus makes it clear that the benefit of the kingdom is a matter of mercy as well as of justice. God is under no obligation to restrict His gifts to those who, like the Jews, had been in His service for a longer time than others.

---

50 Matt. 20:1–16.

19. Many would refuse the kingdom and its reward. Jesus taught that the kingdom thus presented and constituted would be sought and won by a comparatively few men. At least the number is small in comparison with the number of those who should enjoy the benefits of the church. Furthermore, it was announced explicitly that strangers should be with the patriarchs in the glory of the kingdom, while those who were actually descendants of Abraham would find themselves rejected. Surely this was not a doctrine familiar to the well-educated Jew of the time of Jesus. "And a certain man said to Him: Lord, are they few that are saved? But He said to them: Strive to enter by the narrow gate; for many, I say to you, shall seek to enter, and shall not be able. But when the master of the house shall be gone in, and shall shut the door, you shall begin to stand without, and knock at the door, saying: Lord, open to us. And he answering shall say to you: I know not whence you are. Then you shall begin to say: We have eaten and drunk in thy presence, and thou hast taught in our streets. And he shall say to you: I know not whence you are: depart from me all ye workers of iniquity. There shall be weeping and gnashing of teeth, when you shall see Abraham and Isaac and Jacob, and all the prophets in the kingdom of God, and you yourselves thrust out. And they shall come from the east and the west and the north and the south and shall sit down in the kingdom of God. And behold they are last that shall be first, and they are first that shall be last."[51]

20. The consummation of the kingdom. Other parables of Jesus cast light upon the consummation of this kingdom. Jesus foretold that this world would end, and that its ending would be preceded by definite signs. Once the world had come to an end, there would take place a final separation of the evil from the good, and only these latter would enjoy the benefits of the kingdom of God. However, men were to look for the signs which Jesus had indicated and stand in absolute readiness for the judgment.

What Jesus taught about the termination of this world is bound up closely in the text of the synoptics with His prophecy on the destruction of Jerusalem. As a matter of fact the teaching contained in the twenty-fourth chapter of St. Matthew is given as the response to one question which demanded two distinct replies. "And when

---

51 Luke 13:23–30.

He was sitting on Mount Olivet, the disciples came to Him privately, saying: Tell us when shall these things be? And what shall be the sign of Thy coming, and of the consummation of the world?"[52] Jesus had been speaking about the forthcoming destruction of the Temple of Jerusalem, and thus "these things" mentioned in the text have reference to the events which He foretold would accompany the final ruin of that great edifice. However, He replied to both elements which had entered into the question of the disciples, and the gospel text brings the statements which entered into both portions of the answer into close contact. For this reason it is imperative that we should examine into the context of the parables, and the other teachings which have reference to either of these two matters in order that we may realize which one of them is being considered.

Jesus used the parable of the budding fig tree to show the coming of the kingdom as heralded by the signs that He foretold. "And He spoke to them a similitude: See the fig tree, and all the trees: When they now shoot forth their fruit, you know that summer is nigh. So you also when you shall see these things come to pass, know that the kingdom of God is at hand. Amen I say to you, this generation shall not pass away, till all things be fulfilled. Heaven and earth shall pass away, but My words shall not pass away."[53] This parable obviously refers to what may be described as the opening event in the long series which is to precede the second coming of the kingdom on the day of judgment. Jesus declared that the great temple itself was to be ruined in the lifetime of those who actually listened to Him. Furthermore, the response of the Christian community at the time of the Jewish wars offers sufficient evidence that this parable of Jesus was thus understood by His followers.[54]

21. The requisite watchfulness. The final coming of the kingdom is to be unexpected, even though all of these signs have preceded it. It is something for which the followers of Jesus are meant to be prepared. "But of that day and hour no man knoweth, neither the angels in heaven nor the Son, but the Father. Take ye heed, watch and pray. For ye know not when the time is. Even as a man going into

---

52 Matt. 24:3.
53 Luke 21:29–33; Matt. 24:32–35; Mark 13:28–31.
54 Cf. Eusebius, *The Ecclesiastical History*, Book 3, Ch. 5.

a far country left his house, and gave authority to his servants over every work, and commanded the porter to watch. Watch ye therefore (for you know not when the lord of the house cometh: at even, or at midnight, or at the cock crowing, or in the morning). Lest coming on a sudden, he find you sleeping. And what I say to you, I say to all: Watch."[55] Furthermore, Jesus showed this same truth in the parable of the thief in the night. "Watch ye therefore, because you know not what hour your Lord will come. But this know ye, that if the good man of the house knew at what hour the thief would come, he would certainly watch, and would not suffer his house to be broken open. Wherefore be you also ready, because at what hour you know not, the Son of man will come."[56]

The reward of the vigilant servant of the Lord and the punishment which will be meted out to the negligent is depicted in another parable. "Who, thinkest thou, is a faithful and wise servant, whom his lord hath appointed over his family, to give them meat in season? Blessed is that servant, whom, when his lord shall come, he shall find so doing. Amen I say to you, he shall place him over all his goods. But if that evil servant shall say in his heart: My lord is long a coming: And shall begin to strike his fellow servants, and shall eat and drink with drunkards: The lord of that servant shall come in a day that he hopeth not, and at an hour that he knoweth not: And shall separate him, and appoint his portion with the hypocrites; there shall be weeping and gnashing of teeth."[57]

Jesus made it perfectly plain that some of these improvident individuals who are to be reproved on the last day will be citizens of the kingdom here on earth. "Then shall the kingdom of heaven be like to ten virgins, who taking their lamps went out to meet the bridegroom and the bride. And five of them were foolish, and five wise. But the five foolish, having taken their lamps, did not take oil with them: But the wise took oil in their vessels with the lamps. And the bridegroom tarrying, they all slumbered and slept. And at midnight there was a cry made: Behold the bridegroom cometh, go ye forth and meet him. Then all those virgins arose and trimmed their lamps. And the fool-

---

55 Mark 13:32–37; Luke 12:35–38.
56 Matt. 24:42–44; Luke 12:39.
57 Matt. 24:44–51; Luke 12:42–48.

ish said to the wise: Give us of your oil, for our lamps are gone out. The wise answered saying: Lest perhaps there be not enough for us and for you, go you rather to them that sell, and buy for yourselves. Now whilst they went to buy, the bridegroom came: and they that were ready went in with him to the marriage, and the door was shut. But at last came also the other virgins, saying: Lord, Lord, open to us. But He answering said: Amen I say to you, I know you not. Watch ye therefore, because you know not the day nor the hour."[58]

These parables made it clear that the kingdom would receive men according to the condition in which they were to be found at the time of the judgment itself. Naturally the lessons contained in these parables applied equally well to the particular and to the general judgment. By still other figures, Jesus stressed the necessity of utilizing the temporal and spiritual assets of the individual, if that individual is to receive the reward of the kingdom at the second coming. "For even as a man going into a far country, called his servants, and delivered to them his goods. And to one he gave five talents, and to another two, and another one, to every one according to his proper ability: and immediately he took his journey. And he that had received the five talents went his way, and traded with the same, and gained other five. And in like manner he that had received two, gained other two. But he that had received the one, going his way, digged into the earth, and hid his lord's money. But after a long time, the lord of those servants came, and reckoned with them. And he that had received the five talents coming, brought other five talents, saying: Lord, thou didst deliver to me five talents. Behold I have gained other five over and above. His lord said to him: Well done good and faithful servant, because thou hast been faithful over a few things, I will place thee over many things. Enter thou into the joy of thy lord. And he also that had received the two talents came and said: Lord, thou deliveredst two talents to me: behold I have gained other two. His lord said to him: Well done good and faithful servant: because thou hast been faithful over a few things, I will place thee over many things, enter thou into the joy of thy lord. But he that had received the one talent came and said: Lord, I know that thou art a hard man, thou reapest where thou hast not sown, and gatherest where thou hast not strewed. And

---

[58] Matt. 25:1–13.

being afraid I went and hid thy talent in the earth: behold here thou hast that which is thine. And his lord answering said to him: Wicked and slothful servant, thou knowest that I reap where I sow not, and gather where I have not strewed. Thou oughtest therefore to have committed my money to the bankers, and at my coming I should have received my own with usury. Take ye away therefore the talent from him, and give it him that hath ten talents. For to every one that hath shall be given, and he shall abound: but from him that hath not, that also which he seemeth to have shall be taken away. And the unprofitable servant cast ye out into the exterior darkness. There shall be weeping and gnashing of teeth."[59]

22. Rulers in the kingdom. While it was to exist in this world, prior to the second coming of Jesus, this church or kingdom was to be ruled by responsible officials. The Master confided the supreme stewardship of this organization to Peter, the prince of the Apostles. "And Jesus answering said to him: Blessed art thou, Simon Bar-Jona: because flesh and blood hath not revealed it to thee, but My Father who is in heaven. And I say to thee, that thou are Peter, and upon this rock I shall build My Church, and the gates of hell shall not prevail against it. And I will give to thee the keys of the kingdom of heaven. And whatsoever thou shalt bind upon earth, it shall be bound also in heaven: and whatsoever thou shalt loose on earth, it shall be loosed also in heaven."[60] Furthermore, the command which was promised to Peter as a reward for the profession of faith which he made that day "in the quarters of Caesarea Philippi," was actually conferred upon him by Jesus after the Resurrection. "When therefore they had dined, Jesus saith to Simon Peter: Simon son of John, lovest thou Me more than these? He saith to Him: Yea Lord, Thou knoweth that I love Thee. He saith to him: Feed My lambs. He saith to him again: Simon son of John, loveth thou Me? He saith to Him: Yea Lord, Thou knowest that I love Thee. He saith to him: Feed My lambs. He said to him the third time: Simon son of John, lovest thou Me? Peter was grieved because He had said to him the third time, Lovest thou Me? And he said to Him: Lord, Thou knowest all things: Thou knowest that I love Thee. He said to him: Feed My sheep."[61]

---

59 Matt. 25:14–30; Luke 19:12–27.
60 Matt. 16:17–19.
61 John 21:15–17.

The Redemption and the Church

The use of the imperative mood by Jesus shows that these words constituted an actual commission. From that day forward Peter, and, of course, the men who were to succeed him in this office, were to be placed in charge over all of those who followed the teachings of Jesus. The sheep remain those of Jesus rather than those of Peter. But Peter is to watch over them and to command them as the vicar of the Master Himself. The same thought is present in the promise made in Caesarea Philippi. The kingdom of heaven remains, of course, the kingdom of God. But the keys are delivered to Peter as to a steward from whom an accounting can and will be demanded.

According to the express teaching of Jesus, this primacy of Peter was to extend to the realm of doctrine as well as to that of jurisdiction in the legal sense. "And the Lord said: Simon, Simon, behold satan hath desired to have you that he may sift you as wheat: But I have prayed for thee that thy faith fail not: and that thou, being once converted, confirm thy brethren."[62] Thus, according to the outright claims of Jesus, the community of the followers of Jesus, or the kingdom of heaven, was the object of a special malevolence on the part of the chief enemy of God. The attacks of Satan were to be frustrated by the faith of Peter which was not to fail in itself, and which was to be the source out of which the belief of the others could be confirmed. This was a clear indication of the doctrinal infallibility which was to be the prerogative of Peter and of his successors, and at the same time of the authority through which the prince of the apostolic college could oversee and direct the teaching of the universal church. However, the terms of the text show us that this doctrinal authority is given not for the sake of Peter as an individual person but rather for the sake of the kingdom as a whole. That which Satan seeks to encompass is the ruin of the Church and in particular of the apostolic college. This tentative is to be brought to failure by the doctrinal power of an individual conferred upon him by reason of His prayer.

However, the society over which Peter was placed in charge was not meant by Jesus to be a purely monarchical institution. The power of Peter was absolute and ultimate, but a definite jurisdiction and power were both promised and granted to the other members of

---

62 Luke 22:31–32.

the apostolic college. "Amen I say to you, whatsoever you shall bind upon earth, shall be bound also in heaven: and whatsoever you shall loose upon earth, shall be loosed also in heaven."[63] The power thus promised was conferred upon the Apostles, and thus, by reason of the perpetuity of the Church and her mission, upon their successors by Jesus after His Resurrection. "He said therefore to them again: Peace be to you. As the Father hath sent Me, I also send you. When He had said this, He breathed on them: and He said to them: Receive ye the Holy Ghost. Whose sins you shall forgive, they are forgiven them: and whose sins you shall retain, they are retained."[64]

23. The visible Church. Naturally a society which has a visible authority and which possesses a group of men competent to forgive sins would be a visible society in the strictest sense of the term. However, Jesus made it clear that this kingdom or church was an organization before which an offender could be cited and a society which had authority to reject a man from its membership. "But if thy brother shall offend against thee, go and rebuke him between thee and him alone; if he shall hear thee, thou shalt gain thy brother. And if he will not hear thee, take with thee one or two more, that in the mouth of two or three witnesses every word may stand. And if he will not hear them: tell the church; and if he will not hear the church: let him be to thee as the heathen and the publican."[65]

This Church is meant, according to the doctrine of Jesus, to endure until the end of the world. No other organization is to displace it, as it had taken the position once occupied by the nation of the Jews. "And Jesus coming spoke to them saying: All power is given to Me in heaven and in earth. Going therefore teach ye all nations, baptizing them in the name of the Father and of the Son and of the Holy Ghost. Teaching them to observe all things whatsoever I have commanded you: and behold I am with you all days, even to the consummation of the world."[66]

---

63 Matt. 18:18.
64 John 20:21–23. This is the very point controverted by as conservative a writer as Ernest F. Scott, *The Nature of the Early Church* (New York, 1941), p. 6.
65 Matt. 18:15–17.
66 Matt. 28:18–20; Mark 16:15–18; Luke 24:44–49.

Because its King and Shepherd exercised a function quite distinct from that of earthly potentates, the Church was to be a spiritual rather than a temporal organization. Furthermore, it was to perform a definite sacrificial act, the commemoration of the Passion of Jesus in the Eucharist, as a characteristic and central rite. "Do this in commemoration of Me."[67] Finally, this society was, according to the announcement of Jesus Himself, to be opposed by the world and by the spirit of evil which was to animate the world. "But beware of men. For they will deliver you up in councils and they will scourge you in their synagogues. And you shall be brought before governors and before kings for My sake, for a testimony to them and to the gentiles."[68]

Nothing, then, could be clearer from a consideration of the teaching of Jesus Himself than that He taught a definite doctrine for which He could claim the dignity of divine revelation. However, in order to complete this portion of apologetics, it is imperative that we should consult other reliable historical documents in our possession and investigate whether or not the first disciple of Jesus actually understood Him to preach such a doctrine and to make such claims. Once we have established that such was their understanding, we have only to investigate the Christian appeal to the motives of credibility and to see how this doctrine, and this alone, has been authenticated by these evidences of divine origin.

---

[67] Luke 22:19.
[68] Matt. 10:17, 18; Mark 13:9. Cf. also John 15:18–24.

Chapter 13

THE APOSTOLIC WITNESS

1. Reasons for studying the apostolic teaching. In this section of the proof of credibility, which is the essential task of scientific apologetics, we are interested in the doctrine of the Apostles and of the earliest Christians insofar as it has a bearing on the claims and the doctrine of Jesus. We have already seen that there is ample and perfectly certain historical evidence to the effect that Jesus of Nazareth actually claimed to be the Messiah, and as such the bearer of a divine message to man. It is plain, furthermore, that He proposed a definite religious teaching, a doctrine not at all common to the other religious systems existing in His own time, and consequently something for which He could appeal to the authenticating evidence of motives of credibility. For, if Jesus merely restated doctrines which had been accepted prior to His preachings by all of those men who were interested in the worship of the living God, there would be no sense in attempting to show that any system of religious teaching was credible as divine revelation precisely insofar as it pertained to Jesus of Nazareth. This, however, is precisely the contention or the claim advanced by that Catholic dogma, the rational credibility of which in terms of divine revelation we seek to demonstrate in the science of apologetics. The proofs which have been advanced have tended to show that, from this angle at least, nothing prevents an appeal being made to motives of credibility in favor of a distinctly Christian revelation.

Thus demonstration will not be complete until we have been able to ascertain what the immediate disciples of Jesus thought of His claims and of His teaching. Naturally these men were in a better position than anyone else to know what Jesus said and what He did. If it can be shown that these men realized that Jesus had asserted that

He was the Messiah, and that He had preached as divinely revealed a doctrine with reference to the Old Law to the moral order, and to the various mysteries of the kingdom, then we shall have obtained the best possible historical evidence that Jesus really proposed this teaching and that He could appeal to motives of credibility in favor of the claims advanced for His own teaching.

Within the complex framework of modern apologetics, there is still another reason for considering the historical evidence about the teaching of the Apostles relative to the claims of Jesus. It so happens that one of the great motives of credibility, which, as we shall see, was appealed to by Jesus Himself, and by His disciples from the time of the earliest apologists down to the Vatican Council itself, is the Church which Jesus founded. It can be shown that this Church constitutes an effect which is manifestly beyond the natural competence of any creature, actual or possible, to produce or to maintain. In order to utilize this social miracle in favor of the teachings of Jesus, we must first be certain, from an historical point of view, that the teachings advanced by this Church as divine revelation are actually those which were proposed as such by Jesus of Nazareth.

2. Doctrinal unity in the primitive Church. The first factor which we must consider in the arrangement of this proof is the evident and indubitable doctrinal unity of the early Christian community. One of the most pathetic fallacies current in the twentieth century was that which pictured the primitive followers of Jesus as gentle souls, unconcerned about matters of dogma, going about doing good in a vague sort of way and manifesting a doctrinal tolerance, similar to that professed by modern liberals. As a matter of fact these first Christians were intensely, even violently, interested in preserving the purity of that teaching which they claimed to have received from Jesus through the apostolic college. The penalty for diverging from the unity of this doctrine was always separation from the community of the Christians. That penalty was inflicted upon an individual man or upon a group of men. The number made no difference. The fact of the matter was that no person could remain as a member of the Christian body if he professed a belief other than that which was the common teaching within the Church.

3. The Catholic epistles. Evidences of this fierce devotion to doctrinal unity and purity abound in the books of the New Testament, and, of course, in the writings of the early Fathers. In Revelation the Angel of the Church in Pergamus is bitterly reproved because he had retained in his communion men who held one set of false teachings. "So hast thou also them that hold the doctrine of the Nicolaites."[1] The angel, or actually the bishop of the place is not reproved as a heretic, but he stands condemned for not doing what the Christians regarded as his obvious duty and casting the heretics out of the Church.

St. John made it abundantly clear in his epistles that he and the Christian community whose attitude he expressed considered deviation from the actual teaching of Jesus an offense which separated a man from communion with God. "Whosoever revolteth, and continueth not in the doctrine of Christ, hath not God: he that continueth in the doctrine, the same hath both the Father and the Son. If any man come to you, and bring not this doctrine, receive him not into the house, nor say to him, God speed you. For he that saith unto him: God speed you, communicatee with his wicked works."[2]

St. John again, like the rest of the apostolic college, made it abundantly clear that he considered the acceptance of Christ's messianic dignity and mission, and the implied statement of His divine messengership as the fundamental teaching of Jesus. "Who is a liar, but he who denieth that Jesus is the Christ? This is Antichrist, who denieth the Father and the Son. Whosoever denieth the Son, the same hath not the Father; he that confesseth the Son, hath the Father also. As for you, let that which you have heard from the beginning, abide in you: If that abide in you which you have heard from the beginning, you also shall abide in the Son, and in the Father. And this is the promise which He hath promised us, life everlasting."[3] St. Jude points out this conviction about the teaching of Jesus with matchless clarity and vigor. "Dearly beloved, taking all care to write unto you concerning your common salvation, I was under a necessity to write unto you: and to beseech you to contend earnestly for the faith once

---

1 Rev. 2:15.
2 2 John 1:9–11.
3 1 John 2:21–25.

delivered to the saints. For certain men are secretly entered in (who were written of long ago unto this judgment) ungodly men, turning the grace of our Lord God unto riotousness and denying the only sovereign Ruler, and our Lord, Jesus Christ."[4] St. James refers to the belief of Christian people as "the faith of our Lord Jesus Christ of glory,"[5] thus expressing his conviction that Jesus was the Messiah.

St. Peter, the prince of the apostolic college, makes frequent reference to the doctrine of Jesus in the two canonical epistles he has left us. In the first place he refers to Jesus as the Christ, thereby showing that he and the universal society over which he had been placed in charge considered our Lord as a divine messenger and as the bearer of a communication which men are obliged to accept with the assent of divine faith. He speaks of the Resurrection of Jesus as the foundation of those high hopes entertained by those who are privileged to be His followers, and considered that the acceptance of Jesus' teaching would bring a man to the achievement of that glory which He promised and which is to be manifest at His second coming. "Blessed be the God and Father of our Lord Jesus Christ, who according to His great mercy hath regenerated us unto a lively hope by the Resurrection of Jesus Christ from the dead. Unto an inheritance incorruptible and undefiled and that cannot fade, reserved in heaven for you, who by the power of God are kept by faith unto salvation ready to be revealed in the last time. Wherein you shall greatly rejoice, if now you must be for a little time made sorrowful in divers temptations: That the trial of your faith (much more precious than gold which is tried by fire) may be found unto praise and glory and honor at the appearance of Jesus Christ: whom, having not seen, you love; in whom also now, though you see Him not, you believe: and believing shall rejoice with joy unspeakable and glorified; receiving the end of your faith, even the salvation of your souls."[6]

Manifestly then the Vicar of Christ taught the first members of the Church to accept the entire content of that message which Jesus had preached. The end of that belief is the eternity of perfect happiness

---

4 Jude 1:3–4.
5 James 2:1.
6 1 Pet. 1:3–9.

which the Master Himself had announced. Like his fellow Apostles he asserted that Jesus was God and that He had redeemed mankind through His sacrificial death on Calvary. In every instance the doctrine which the gospels record as having been proposed by Jesus is the same teaching set forth by the Apostles and firmly received by their followers.

4. The witnesses of Christ. Nowhere is the content of apostolic teaching demonstrated more effectively than is the historical narrative of the Acts of the Apostles. From the very outset the eleven regarded themselves primarily as "witnesses." They were the men who had been privileged to associate with Jesus. They were qualified to testify as to His teaching and with respect to those signs which He had invoked to show its inherent credibility. In the address to the followers of Christ on the occasion of the choice of Matthias to fill the place of the traitor, Judas Iscariot, Peter, the prince of the apostolic college, made that point clear. "Wherefore of these men who have companied with us all the time that the Lord Jesus came in and went out among us, beginning with the baptism of John until the day wherein He was taken up from us, one of these must be made a witness with us of His Resurrection."[7] On the day of Pentecost, Peter announced clearly to the assembled Jews, many of whom had been directly responsible for the murder of Jesus, "Therefore let all the house of Israel know most certainly, that God hath made Him both Lord and Christ, this same Jesus, whom you have crucified."[8] When some from the crowd who had heard this first Christian missionary sermon asked Peter for directions, he indicated the procedure and promised the results which Jesus had already pointed out. "Do penance, and be baptized every one of you in the name of Jesus Christ, for the remission of your sins: and you shall receive the gift of the Holy Ghost."[9]

Explaining the miraculous cure of the lame man in the Beautiful Gate of the Temple, the prince of the Apostles clearly stated to the Jewish people that Jesus was God. "The God of Abraham, and the God of Isaac, and the God of Jacob, the God of our fathers hath glorified His Son Jesus, whom you indeed delivered up and denied

---

7 Acts 1:21–22.
8 Acts 2:36.
9 Acts 2:38.

before the face of Pilate, when he judged He should be released. But you denied the Holy One and the Just, and desired a murderer to be granted unto you. But the Author of life you killed, whom God hath raised up from the dead, of which we are witnesses."[10] Furthermore, at this time, as on every other occasion when the Apostles had the opportunity to preach before the Jewish people, St. Peter insisted that the prophecies concerning the deeds and the sayings of the Messiah had been clearly fulfilled in Jesus, whose second coming would finally accomplish the predictions which God had given to the chosen race. "But those things which God before hath showed by the mouth of all the prophets, that His Christ should suffer, He hath so fulfilled. Repent therefore and be converted, that your sins may be blotted out. That, when the times of refreshment shall come from the presence of the Lord, and He shall send Him who hath been preached unto you, Jesus Christ, whom heaven indeed must receive until the times of the restitution of all things, which God hath spoken by the mouth of His holy prophets from the beginning of the world. For Moses said: A Prophet shall the Lord your God raise up unto you of your brethren, like unto me: Him you shall hear according to all things whatsoever He shall speak to you."[11]

Thus throughout the preaching of these witnesses, as it is recorded in the Acts of the Apostles, the same current of thought is manfest. They taught exactly what the four gospels record as the doctrine of Jesus Himself. They insist upon His messianic dignity and upon His divinity. They show His teaching on the Blessed Trinity, His assertion that He is the true Son of God, eternally generated from the Father, and His insistence that the Holy Ghost is a third divine Person, proceeding from the Father and from Himself. The Apostles taught, as did their Master, that men were called to do penance, to believe the doctrine which He had set forth, and to receive that baptism which He had instituted as a means of entrance into the kingdom of heaven. They claimed that the men who obeyed the mandates of Christ would be associated with God in this world to enjoy Him forever in heaven. They insisted upon the unity of faith and of charity in that organized society which they ruled by His authority.

---

10 Acts 3:13–15.
11 Acts 3:18–22, citing Deut. 18:15.

There was once a fashion, set by the critic Baur, of considering the teaching of St. Paul as something quite distinct from that of Peter and the other members of the original apostolic college. It was a bizarre point of view, destined to be ruined by any sort of critical examination into the narrative of the Acts or the epistles of St. Paul himself. In the first place, it is manifest from the Acts that Peter, the visible head of the universal Church, and James, the head of the society in Jerusalem itself, freely and manifestly received Paul and associated him in their own ministry. In the letter of "the Apostles and ancients, brethren, to the brethren of the Gentiles that are at Antioch and in Syria and Cilicia,"[12] the rulers of the church explicitly rejected objections which had been raised against the doctrine of St. Paul and of his friend and associate, St. Barnabas. "Forasmuch as we have heard that some going out from us have troubled you with words: subverting your souls, to whom we gave no commandment: It hath seemed good to us, being assembled together, to choose out men, and to send them unto you with our well-beloved Barnabas and Paul, men that have given their lives for the name of our Lord Jesus Christ."

The men who gave this testimonial of fidelity to Paul were the very witnesses who insisted upon absolute fidelity to the original message of Jesus. In giving this commendation they clearly acknowledged that the doctrine of St. Paul was the very teaching which they had been commissioned to present to the world.

A further testimony to the identity of the Pauline message with the teachings of the other Apostles and thus with that of Jesus Himself is to be found in the order of the synoptic gospels. Eusebius makes it abundantly clear that the gospel according to St. Mark is nothing more or less than a written expression of the actual teaching of St. Peter.[13] At the same time it is manifest that St. Luke, the author of the third gospel, was the friend and the companion of St. Paul[14] who approved of this writing as an expression of his own teaching.[15] Now this third gospel agrees so perfectly with those written by SS.

---

[12] Acts 15:23–29.
[13] Eusebius, *The Ecclesiastical History*, Book 2, Ch. 15, citing Clement of Alexandria; Book 3, Ch. 39, citing Papias; Book 5, Ch. 8; Book 6, Ch. 25, citing Origen.
[14] Eusebius, *a.c.* Book 3, Ch. 4; Book 3, Ch. 24; Book 1, Ch. 8; Book 6, Ch. 25, "The gospel commended by Paul."
[15] Cf. 2 Cor. 8:18.

Matthew and Mark that the three together are called synoptics. The Scripture scholars have long devoted themselves to an explanation of the striking resemblance of these three documents which for the most part describe the same sermons and accomplishments of Jesus. Quite obviously, from this point of view, the message of Paul was exactly that propounded by his fellow laborers in the apostolate arid thus identical with the actual doctrine of the Master.

5. The testimony of St. Paul. St. Paul presented the teaching of Jesus in a different manner from that employed by the four evangelists. These latter expressed their doctrine in the actual words of Jesus, and thus framed their message in the background of the Master's life and death. St. Paul, on the other hand, wrote to definite Christian communities, instructing them on those doctrinal points on which they were in danger of being led astray and cautioning them against the concrete betrayals of Christian morality to which they were tempted. Nevertheless the teaching is exactly the same in content. We can gain a sufficient appreciation of this identity by examining what St. Paul had to say with reference to the central portions of that message which Jesus of Nazareth had set forth.

In the first place St. Paul insisted upon the doctrine of the Blessed Trinity, which Jesus had clearly enunciated and which had formed the central mystery in the Master's teaching. He taught that there is only one true God, the Source of all those supernatural consolations which come to the followers of Christ. "Is He the God of the Jews only? Is He not also of the gentiles? Yes, of the gentiles also. For it is one God that justifieth circumcision by faith and uncircumcision through faith."[16] However, the Apostle of the Gentiles preached that there are three divine persons, really distinct one from the other and equal in their consubstantiality. He makes this point abundantly clear in the blessing which he suffixes to the Second Letter to the Corinthians. "The grace of our Lord Jesus Christ, and the charity of God, and the communication of the Holy Ghost be with you all. Amen."[17] Obviously this is a blessing in the strictest sense of the term, a prayer or petition that the favor of God should be given to those whom the Apostle loved. Yet there are three distinct persons

---

16 Rom. 3:29–30. Cf. 1 Cor. 8:6; Eph. 4:6; 1 Tim. 2:5.
17 2 Cor. 13:13.

recognized as qualified to send the divine dispensations of which the Corinthians stood in manifest need.

We can recognize the same teaching in his first letter to the church at Corinth. "Now there are diversities of graces, but the same *Spirit*: and there are diversities of ministries, but the same *Lord*, and there are diversities of operations, but the same *God*, who worketh all in all."[18] St. Paul attributes to each one of these three consubstantial divine persons a distinct contribution to the economy of human salvation. "For whosoever are led by the Spirit of God, they are the sons of God. For you have not received the spirit of bondage again in fear, but you have received the spirit of adoption of sons, whereby we cry: Abba (Father). For the Spirit Himself giveth testimony to our spirit, that we are the sons of God. And if sons, heirs also; heirs indeed of God, and joint heirs with Christ."[19]

St. Paul insists upon the reality of the Incarnation and the Redemption, indeed this latter fact is the master idea that pervades all of his epistles. No more concise statement of his central concern can be found than this announcement to the Galatians: "But when the fullness of the time was come, God sent His Son made of a woman, made under the law, That He might redeem them who were under the law, that we might receive the adoption of sons."[20] According to the Apostle of the Gentiles, the Church which Jesus Christ had founded was meant to be obedient to the commands of that Founder. Furthermore, the perfection of that Church is measured insofar as its members are meant to be conformed to and united with the Son of God. St. Paul wrote to the Christians of Ephesus that God "gave some Apostles, and some Prophets, and other some Evangelists, and other some pastors and doctors, for the perfecting of the saints, for the work of the ministry, for the edifying of the body of Christ: Until we all meet into the unity of faith and of the knowledge of the Son of God, unto a perfect man, unto the measure of the age of the fullness of Christ."[21] According to his teaching, as according to the doctrine of Jesus Himself, the Church is definitely subject to

---

18 1 Cor. 12:4–6.
19 Rom. 8:14–16. Cf. also Gal. 4:4–8; Tit. 3:4–6; 2 Cor. 1:21–22; Rom. 15:15–16.
20 Gal 4:4–5.
21 Eph. 4:11–13.

our Lord. St. Paul insisted upon this point. "Let women be subject to their husbands as to the Lord: Because the husband is the head of the wife, as Christ is the Head of the Church. He is the saviour of his body. Therefore as the Church is subject to Christ, so also let the wives be to their husbands in all things."[22]

The Apostle of the Gentiles held that the Church was a definite and hierarchical society, in which the divinely constituted leaders were expected to use their authority for the good of the people over whom they were placed. "We are God's coadjutors: you are God's husbandry, you are God's building."[23] "If also I should boast somewhat more of our power, which the Lord hath given us unto edification and not for your destruction; I should not be ashamed."[24] This power, claimed by St. Paul as the minister or ambassador of Christ, the actual authority which Jesus Himself had conceded to His Apostles[25] was executive and judicial. "What will you? Shall I come to you with a rod, or in charity, and in the spirit of meekness?"[26] "I indeed, absent in body, but present in spirit, have already judged, as though I were present, him that hath so done."[27]

Just as the Saviour had announced a Church which was to be visibly one, holy, catholic, and apostolic, St. Paul preached that the Christian society in which he was privileged to labor should be marked by the same characteristics. In the first place, St. Paul made it clear that the society with which he was concerned was actually undivided. "We being many are one body."[28] "You are all one in Christ Jesus."[29] "One body and one spirit: as you are called in one hope of your calling. One Lord, one faith, one baptism. One God and Father of all."[30]

The Church was, according to his doctrine, essentially a holy organization. "He chose us in Him before the foundation of the

---

22 Eph. 5:22–24.
23 1 Cor, 3:9. Cf. 2 Cor. 5:20.
24 2 Cor. 10:8.
25 Matt. 10:40.
26 1 Cor. 4:21.
27 1 Cor. 5:3.
28 1 Cor. 10:17.
29 Gal. 3:28.
30 Eph. 4:4–6

world, that we should be holy and unspotted in His sight in charity."[31] Furthermore, the Church and the gospel which it presented was meant for the entire human race, and thus the society itself was catholic. "The gospel is come unto you, as also it is in the whole world."[32] Finally, this organization as described by St. Paul is clearly apostolic. "You are fellow-citizens with the saints, built upon the foundations of the Apostles and prophets, Jesus Christ Himself being the chief Corner Stone."[33]

St. Paul characterized the Church as infallible, thereby repeating the instructions given by Jesus. He spoke of it as "The house of God, which is the Church of the living God, the pillar and ground of the truth."[34] Furthermore, he asserted that this society was made up of men who were elevated by the dignity of brotherhood with Jesus. "Whom He foreknew. He also predestined to be made conformable to the image of His Son: That He might be the First Born amongst many brethren."[35]

There is no need to continue those texts which witness the absolute identity in the content of St. Paul's message with that doctrine which had been announced by Jesus of Nazareth, and which was presented in His name by the original apostolic college. The Acts of the Apostles record that St. Paul "went through Syria and Cilicia, confirming the churches: commanding them to keep the precepts of the Apostles and the Ancients."[36] These precepts, as we have already seen, were given together with an explicit commendation of SS. Paul and Barnabas by the Apostles to the churches which these laborers for Christ had founded. The men who were vitally concerned, the remnants of the Twelve and the later Apostles could see the absolute identity of their own teaching. All the devices of misinformed moderns will never be sufficient to explain that salient fact away.

6. The living tradition. The successful conduct of scientific apologetics demands recognition of another obvious reality. The doctrine preached by Jesus of Nazareth and proposed in His name

---

31 Eph. 1:4; 5:25–27; Tit. 2:14.
32 Col. 1:6.
33 Eph. 2:19–20.
34 1 Tim. 3:15.
35 Rom. 8:29. Cf. also Prat, *La Theologie de St. Paul.*
36 Acts 15:41.

by the original Apostles and by St. Paul is the very teaching which the Catholic Church holds and teaches today as her own dogma. Steadfastly and practically this Church has acclaimed the truths contained in sacred Scripture and in divine tradition as verities revealed by God to be accepted by all men with the assent of divine faith.[37] Furthermore, it has been her intention "to conserve in the Church by removing errors the purity of that Gospel which, having been promised before through the prophets and in Holy Scripture, our Lord Jesus Christ, the Son of God, first promulgated in His own instruction and then ordered to be preached to every creature by His Apostles as the source of every salutary truth and of moral discipline."[38] The Vatican Council meant "to profess and to declare the salutary doctrine of Christ."[39]

The Catholic Church is manifestly apostolic, in such a way that its identity as that organization over which the twelve Apostles were placed constitutes one of the visible characteristics by which it may be recognized as the kingdom or society founded by Jesus of Nazareth. Its teaching is demonstrably that of the twelve and that of their crucified Master. It accepts with the assent of divine faith all of those statements and only those statements which it received from the Apostles as the message from God to man. Furthermore, the Church holds these doctrines in the same sense and with exactly the same meaning which they possessed when the Apostles and Jesus Himself enunciated them.

Realizing this fact, we close the second portion of scientific apologetics. As we have already seen, it is the business of this portion of sacred theology to demonstrate, or to manifest, the credibility of Catholic dogma as divine revelation. The first section of apologetics must then be devoted to an explanation of what this attribute of divine revelation, claimed for the body of Catholic dogma, actually means. Only after this question has been solved can we consider profitably the demands of that discernibility or credibility actually pertinent to this teaching. The second section investigates the background of Catholic dogma, and ascertains that it is, from the historical point

---

37 The Vatican Council. The Constitution, *Dei Filius,* Ch. 3 (Denzinger, 1792).
38 The Council of Trent, Session IV (Denzinger, 1783).
39 Denzinger, 1781.

of view at least, exactly what it claims to be, a definite system of instruction which Jesus of Nazareth proposed to men as a message of universal import communicated by God to the world through Him. Since this preliminary work has been done, we can proceed to the study of those demonstrations offered in support of the claims attached to this living and historical teaching.

Chapter 14

THE HOLINESS AND WISDOM OF JESUS

1. The two functions of the intrinsic motives. The exigencies of scientific procedure compel us to consider first of all that motive of credibility which consists in the intellectual and moral characteristics of that Man who announced Himself to the world as the Son of God. Furthermore, the peculiar temper of modern religious controversy makes exactly the same demand. For there would be absolutely no need to take seriously the claims set forth by an individual who was mentally unbalanced or morally dishonest, and thus we must seek naturally attainable evidence of sanity and uprightness in Jesus. Actually the opponents of Christianity whose vocal acerbity far surpasses their sense of historical criticism have uttered challenges which make the investigation absolutely imperative for an effective presentation of Christian credibility. However, the result of serious study on this matter shows very clearly that Jesus of Nazareth was not only demonstrably sane and righteous, but that His moral and intellectual goodness were of such an order that they could never be explained merely by the unaided forces of human nature. In other words, the holiness and the wisdom of Jesus are visibly miracles of the intellectual and moral order, manifestly attached to the teaching He presented to the world. As such they are *positive* indications that this doctrine is rationally credible as divine revelation.

The mere sanity and moral goodness visible in Jesus, as He is known through the reliable historical documents telling of His words and works, constitute a *negative* motive of credibility. It would be rash in the extreme to accept as a divine message some body of teaching which had been set forth by an individual suffering from delusions or hallucinations. It would be folly rather than virtue to take seriously claims to divine messengership advanced by a person who lived in violation of the moral law. When we show, as we are able easily to do, that Jesus of Nazareth was manifestly sane and righteous, we have demonstrated that there is nothing to stand in the way of a serious and scientific consideration of those signs which He claimed as indicative of the divine origin of that message which He presented to the world.

Naturally we must look to the life, as well as to the doctrine of Jesus for evidence of this moral and intellectual integrity. In this case the actions and the doctrines must be considered together. The moral and mental wholeness of the man, as manifested in His deeds and in His teaching, constitutes the negative motive of credibility with which we are first concerned. However, the miraculous holiness and wisdom of Jesus, as manifest in His conduct and in His teaching, constitutes one definite positive criterion of revelation while the manifestly supernatural attitude of the message itself can be considered as a distinct sign, indicating the divine approbation for the claim that this teaching was a message sent by God.

2. Denials of righteousness and wisdom in Jesus. We must not allow ourselves to imagine that challenges against the sanity of Jesus have ceased in the literary and critical world in which we live. They were set forth by a few grubby, pretentious sciolists of the past century with an eruditional apparatus which made up in technical terminology what it lacked in scientific solidity. To a certain extent, however, the men who made such charges against Jesus of Nazareth were consistent. Logically a man who rejects the message which Jesus set forth as divinely revealed must have some semblance of reason for his action. He can take the ordinary course, and assert that the documents which purport to tell about the Master's words and actions are not historically reliable and that we have no adequate evidence to show that Jesus actually claimed the prerogatives of divine revelation for the message He preached. Or he can close his eyes to the obvious meaning contained in these documents, and by dint of "critical" editing, arrange a gospel text in which there is no special mention of a distinctively divine communication, and then conclude that the claim of divine revelation was a mere adventitious accretion to Christian doctrine. But if a man is realistic enough to acknowledge the manifest fact that the words of Jesus recorded in the canonical gospels are

The Holiness and Wisdom of Jesus

genuine, then he has the alternative of accepting this message at the valuation which Jesus Himself placed upon it or declaring that He was either mistaken or a deliberate deceiver.

3. Attacks in the name of psychiatry. Because the matter involved is so tremendously important, deception in this line would imply a radical madness or outstanding villainy on the part of a person thus mistaken. An occasional trespasser on the field of New Testament criticism has hazarded the conjecture that Jesus Himself was mentally unwell. The melancholy distinction of having been the first in comparatively modern times to have set forth this conclusion seriously belongs to a Danish candidate for the ministry, one Emil Ramussen.[1] A German, Dr. Georg Lomer[2] who wrote under the pseudonym of de Loosten, and the prominent French psychiatrist, Dr. Binet-Sangle,[3] also attempted to convince their contemporaries that Jesus of Nazareth had been insane. Far more important for Americans is the fact that one of our own writers, Professor McCown,[4] alleges that many students think that only a paranoiac could make the statement "I and the Father are One," which the gospel according to St. John puts into the mouth of Jesus.

Modern literature abounds in passages wherein writers manifest their naïve pleasure in playing with technical terms properly employed in the vocabulary of psychiatry itself. The books to which we have referred are expressions of this same amusing trend. Ramussen attempted to show that not only Jesus Himself, but also the prophets of the Old Testament as a group were victims of epilepsy. The inanity of his reasoning is shown by any examination of the portrait of Jesus as it is presented on the pages of the four-canonical gospels. The error is too far removed from truth to demand or profitably to receive any detailed explanation. Suffice it to say that none of the accounts about the life of Jesus could possibly give rise to the rational conjecture that

---

[1] An excellent account of these attacks, and a detailed refutation may be found in Felder, *Christ and the Critics*, Vol. 2, pp. 18–72. Ramussen's book is translated as *Jesus: A Comparative Psycho-Pathological Study* translated and published by Arthur Rothenburg (Leipzig, 1905).

[2] *Jesus Christus vom Standpunkte des Psychiaters* (1905).

[3] *La Folie de Jesus*, 2 vols. (Paris, 1910).

[4] *The Search for the Real Jesus*, p. 163. A man of vast erudition, Dr. McCown ruins his work by his manifest anxiety to establish a point rather than to examine evidence.

the writers were describing an epileptic. Lomer's book pictured Jesus as a degenerate, and the work as a whole moves in an atmosphere of depraved billingsgate rather than of scientific inquiry. Binet-Sangle tried to make it appear that those closest to Jesus considered Him mentally unwell, and that the actions and words of the Master manifested definite and recognizable paranoiac tendencies.

4. The reaction of Christ's friends. The passage which all of these men fastened upon is contained in the second gospel. "And when His friends had heard of it, they went out to lay hold on Him. For they said: He is become mad."[5] In itself, of course, this verse might seem to lend telling weight to the contentions of Ramussen, Lomer, Binet-Sangle, and their ilk. If this were the only fact that we knew about Jesus of Nazareth, or even if it stood as absolutely an isolated narration, there might be some grounds for supposing that they should be taken seriously. Unfortunately for their system, however, the passage is not alone. It happens to record the reactions of one particular group to a phenomenon which certainly appeared distressing to those who had the comfort and the merely material well-being of Jesus at heart. The Pharisees, the dominant political and religious faction of Judea and in Galilee, had recently allied themselves with the followers of Herod, otherwise their despised and bitter enemies, for the express purpose of destroying Him.[6] Merely human prudence demanded that a man thus marked should keep himself in absolute retirement. However, in defiance of all their ill-will and menaces, He had openly gone about His work of preaching, had actually selected the twelve men destined to be His witnesses and His official companions, and had now gathered a very considerable crowd around Him to hear those very doctrines which had enraged his enemies.[7] This group included the scribes themselves, and these officials of the Jewish Gestapo manifested a reaction to the same situation quite different from that shown by the timid friends of the Master. "And the scribes who were come down from Jerusalem, said: He hath Beelzebub, and by the prince of devils He casteth out

---

5 Mark 3:21.
6 Mark 3:16.
7 Mark 3:7–20.

devils."[8] Jesus reproved, in logical and concise form, their impudent conceit.[9]

5. The attitude of Christ's enemies. There is no need to go beyond the examination into the reactions of those frustrated foes of Jesus for an appreciation of that system elaborated by our gentlemen of psychopathic predilection. There is nothing more evident in all the course of gospel history than the fact that the Jewish leaders as a group, in spite of certain very honorable exceptions, pursued the person and the doctrine of Jesus with unrelenting and fanatical hatred. They were very efficient individuals, and they did not rest until they had finally encompassed their design of inflicting upon Him the most humiliating and frightful death that the savage ingenuity of the ancient world could devise. Their ferocity extended to His message and to His followers who continued to broadcast that teaching even after their Master had been murdered. They exploited every resource at their disposition to discredit His person and His teaching. They charged that He was possessed by a devil,[10] that He was a Samaritan,[11] and thus a member of a race hated and despised by the inhabitants of Galilee and of Judea. They told Pilate that He had attempted to turn the people away from the civil obedience which they owed to the Roman emperor.[12] Yet in no case did they even attempt *seriously* to insinuate that He was not of sound mind. Once it is recounted that they used this term in reviling Jesus, after the discourse that followed upon His reception of the man to whom He had given sight. "A dissension rose again among the Jews for these words, and many of them said: He hath a devil, and is mad: why hear you Him? Others said: These are not the words of one that hath a devil: can a devil open the eyes of the blind?"[13] The contempt with which the defenders of Jesus treated this charge and the constant direction of the attacks made by His enemies show that the word was simply used as invective. In their serious practical councils, the Jews never spoke of Jesus in this manner.

---

8 Mark 3:22.
9 Mark 3:23–30.
10 Cf. Matt. 9:34; 12:24; Mark 3:22; Luke 11:15; John 7:20; 8:52.
11 John 8:48.
12 Luke 32:2; John 19:12.
13 John 10:19–21.

The ignorant masses might possibly have been misled into thinking that Jesus acted with diabolic rather than with divine power if the Master Himself had not confuted this charge with masterly and triumphant logic. The crowd in Jerusalem might have imagined for a moment that He was a foreigner, but Jesus disdained to reply to an accusation which would melt away when any Galilean in the group recognized Him as a fellow countryman. Pilate as a Roman civil official had no touch with Jewish religious affairs, and he might well have been misled had Jesus not informed him about the spiritual nature of that kingdom which He commanded. But no man who saw and heard Jesus could possibly be deluded into thinking that He was a madman, and the Pharisees were far too efficient and deadly in their hatred to set forth a charge which would be so manifestly ludicrous. It is safe to say that their knowledge of Jesus' intellectual health was somewhat superior to that of Ramussen and his allies.

Simply as an indication of the futility which characterizes such charges against Jesus of Nazareth, it is well for us to note that paranoia is a definite type of psychic malady and paranoiacs are a well-defined class of maladjusted and recognizably unfit individuals. Paranoia itself is generally defined as a chronic systematized delusional state, of gradual development, arising from internal causes and without the occurrence of hallucinations.[14] Those who suffer delusions of persecution suffer from this malady, which is considered an aspect of psychic degeneration. The delusions of the true paranoiac case render any effective adjustment to society absolutely impossible.

6. The social acceptability of Jesus. Jesus of Nazareth appears to us, on the pages of those reliable historical documents which give information about Him, as a man of definite social charm, perfectly adjusted to the society in which He lived. He chose a group of twelve companions and assistants. He held their affection as a group until the end of their lives and of His own earthly career. One of them betrayed Him to His enemies, but was so overcome by remorse that he hurled back the fruits of his treason to the authors of it and then went out and destroyed himself. The remaining eleven were willing to abandon their possessions and their homes, and to devote the rest

---

14 Cf. *A Text Book of Psychiatry for Students and Practitioners,* by Henderson and Gillespie, 4 ed., New York, p. 235.

of their lives to His service, even when that work meant to them the frenzied opposition of their own religious and racial leaders. He was kind and gracious to others not of this intimate circle, and the pages of the canonical gospels do not record even one instance where He refused to help those who were suffering or in real need. Not only men, but women also were attracted to Him, and met with a response which motivated them to become His followers.

He was sought after as a guest by ambitious and lion-hunting hosts. He was courteous to all, and on one occasion at least keenly alive to the niceties of politeness in a way that must have been disconcerting to a gentleman who had invited Him to table but who had been intolerably careless about His reception.[15] When He called Matthew to the work of the apostolate, the former publican could think of no better way to celebrate his good fortune than by inviting Jesus and His disciples, with a group of his erstwhile associates in the business of tax gathering to a banquet. The enemies of the Master did not approve of this highly social conduct. However, the three synoptic gospels record that Jesus accepted the invitation. St. Luke called the affair a "great feast" and the party was an unquestioned success.[16] Only the most extravagant pedant could find in such conduct evidence, of all things, of paranoia.

7. Jesus and His mother. In His relations with His mother, Jesus displayed all the characteristics of a normal dutiful Son. In spite of the fact that, even at the age of twelve, He was definitely conscious of His dignity and of His mission, St. Luke tells us that He was an obedient and submissive Son to Mary and to St. Joseph.[17] Jesus was invited to the wedding feast of Cana, along with Mary and the disciples. When His mother asked Him, in the insinuating way that mothers have always had, to perform a miracle in order to relieve the embarrassment of their hosts, His response was that which the normal and affectionate young man would naturally make. He did two things. He pointed out the manifest untimeliness of her petition and then He fulfilled it. The story is one of the most beautiful and typically normal accounts of natural affection ever set down in history.

---

15 Luke 7:36–50.
16 Luke 5:27–32; Mark 2:13–17; Matt. 9:9–13.
17 Luke 2:51.

"There was a marriage in Cana of Galilee: and the mother of Jesus was there. And Jesus also was invited, and His disciples, to the marriage. And the wine failing, the mother of Jesus saith to Him: They have no wine. And Jesus saith to her: Woman, what is that to Me and to thee? My hour is not yet come. His mother saith to the waiters: Whatsoever He shall say to you, do ye. Now there were set there six waterpots of stone, according to the manner of the purifying of the Jews, containing two or three measures apiece. Jesus saith to them: Fill the waterpots with water. And they filled them up to the brim. And Jesus saith to them: Draw out now, and carry to the chief steward of the feast. And they carried it. And when the chief steward had tasted the water made wine, and knew not whence it was, but the waiters knew who had drawn the water; the chief steward calleth the bridegroom, and saith to him: Every man at first setteth forth good wine: and when men have well drank, then that which is worse. But thou hast kept the good wine until now. This beginning of miracles did Jesus in Cana of Galilee; and manifested His glory, and His disciples believed in Him."[18]

There have been opponents of Christianity who have professed to see in the words of Jesus to His mother an unnatural harshness which indicated an abnormal mental state on His part. Unfortunately there have even been Catholic publicists who have taken some sort of scandal out of what they regard as the asperity of the text, and have gone to every length, even to that of gross mistranslation, to read into this response some saccharine sentiment. It is very difficult to reason with men of this type, precisely because they seek the perfection, not of a normal young man with a dutiful affection for his mother, but of some idealized marionette. They forget that the gospel pages record the life and the sayings of a male human being. They lose sight of the fact that the doctrine of the Incarnation, one of the central mysteries of Christian teaching, assures us that the Second Person of the Blessed Trinity assumed a human nature, not in an abstract and idealized condition, but of a man with all the tendencies which have characterized normal male activity since the inception of the human race. The words of St. John do not depict a plaster saint, but a perfectly adjusted and affectionate young man who pleased His

---

18 John 2:1–11.

mother far more than He would have had He acted according to the fantastic and unreal lights of quibblers.

In this historical episode, Mary acted as a typical mother, conscious of and grateful for the real and normal affection of her Son. "They have no wine." The words themselves might express a mere observation, but Jesus who loved her so well was quite aware that they meant far more than that to Him. No woman worthy of her salt would demean herself to explain accurately and logically exactly what she desired. Mary was definitely cognizant of the fact that Jesus understood what she meant.

"Woman, what is that to Me and to thee? My hour is not yet come." This is the normal response of an obedient and affectionate son. Any man who has at least the cherished memory of a beautiful and gracious mother knows very well what that answer signifies and implies. Jesus told her plainly that in itself the situation was not one in which He would have interfered. He spoke in exactly the same way that normal and affectionate sons have spoken to their mothers from time immemorial. And thereby He gave joy to Mary's heart in a way that these dry-as-dust critics could never comprehend. For He made her understand that this favor was done for her sake. If she had not spoken, there would have been no miracle that day in Cana of Galilee. This response in itself, and not in some softened translation, was a message of affection to her.

As He was dying in agony on the cross of Calvary, Jesus thought of His mother. He confided the charge of caring for her to St. John, the beloved disciple. He commanded her to think of John as a son, and thus to find her place and her adjustment in the world.[19] Certainly there was nothing subnormal in this relation.

His very enemies recognized His popularity. Indeed, apart from that expression of perfect adjustment to society, they would never have bothered to persecute Him at all. "The Pharisees therefore said among themselves: Do you see that we prevail nothing? Behold, the whole world is gone after Him."[20] The world does not go after paranoiacs.

---

19 John 19:26–27.
20 20 John 12:19.

8. The Jewish legends. The Jewish legends which have crystallized in the Talmud depict Jesus of Nazareth as a deceiver, utilizing stage tricks of magic to delude His people. The same legends were known and used by Celsus, the erudite and forceful opponent of Christianity so decisively beaten by the peerless Origen. As a matter of fact the enemies of Christ made that charge against Him after He was dead, in petitioning the Roman governor for a guard around His tomb. "And the next day, which followed the day of preparation, the chief priests and the Pharisees came together to Pilate, saying: Sir, we have remembered that that Seducer said, while He was yet alive: After three days I will rise again."[21] Actually, of course, there was little else that men in their position could say. They chose freely and culpably to reject the teaching and the claims which Jesus had set forth. Since they did not have the comfortable alternative, familiar to critics of the past hundred years, of asserting that the discourses attributed to Him were not historical, they were constrained to insist that He was either a seducer or a paranoiac. His memory was far too fresh among them and among their fellow Jews who had frequently seen Jesus triumph over them in debate to allow practical men like themselves the luxury of claiming that He had been mentally unbalanced. Obviously then the only course open to them was to assert that He had deliberately set out to deceive and mislead His fellows.

Now there is only one standard by which the aptness of their designation may properly be computed. That standard is, of course, objective truth itself. If in reality Jesus of Nazareth was not what He claimed to be, and if the message He preached was not actually a message which the living God had communicated to man in a supernatural way, then He would have been far more guilty than even the frenzied rage of His enemies attempted to make Him appear. And, if He was inculpably mistaken on this point, His teaching would have been the most catastrophic delusion in all the history of the human race. However, since His message was truly divine revelation, and precisely because He was what He professed Himself to be, the charges of his enemies, both ancient and modern, are false and baseless.

---

21 Matt. 27:62–63.

9. The way of temperance. An occasional hater of Jesus and His teaching takes advantage of one statement He made in order to assert that He lacked something of ascetical perfection. In rebuking the men of His own time for their manifest unwillingness to receive His teaching in a body, He declared that they quibbled against every form in which the divine message had come to them. "But whereunto shall I esteem this generation to be like? It is like to children sitting in the market place, who, crying to their companions, say: We have piped to you, and you have not danced: we have lamented, and you have not mourned. For John came neither eating nor drinking, and they say: He hath a devil. The Son of man came eating and drinking, and they say: Behold a man that is a glutton and a wine drinker, a friend of publicans and sinners. And wisdom is justified by her children."[22]

It is obvious both from the text and the context of this apostolic narrative that Jesus did not mean to imply that He had been guilty in any way of intemperance with regard to eating and drinking. It is clear enough that the charge was leveled against Him. Indeed the banquets He attended, on the occasion of Matthew's call to the apostolate, in the house of Simon the Pharisee and in the home of Simon the leper among others show us very clearly that He was not at all averse to attending affairs where men enjoyed each other's company and the taking of nourishment. However, the very formation of the passage in question makes it abundantly clear that the reproaches cast in His direction for this reason were as manifestly false and baseless as was the accusation of diabolical possession aimed at John the Baptist.

As a matter of fact the texts of the gospels show that it was precisely amidst the convivial and pleasant surroundings of the banquet table that Jesus found the opportunity to inculcate some of the most beautiful and profound portions in all the content of His teaching. Moreover, His conduct in associating with His friends fulfills all the requirements of the virtue of friendship described by Aristotle himself and recognized as the characteristic of a morally good man.[23] The virtue of temperance in itself in no way demands complete abstinence from alcoholic drink. Such complete abstinence is laudable and sometimes even necessary where a good work which

---

22 Matt. 11:16–19.
23 Cf. Aristotle, *The Nichomachean Ethics*, Books 8 and 9.

a man is bound to perform, would be impeded or prevented through the use of what is in itself a definite and useful good to humanity. As a matter of fact the work which Jesus of Nazareth set out to accomplish was one which would have been hampered rather than aided by a refusal on his part to mix on ordinary terms in his own contemporary society. He presented Himself as the Chief Prophet of public revelation, charged with the duty of bringing God's message as effectively as possible to the people who stood in need of it. The first recipients of that communication according to His teaching were to be the children of Israel themselves.[24] He refused to neglect any agency by which He could instruct these people at all properly.

10. The direction of holiness. There was nothing in the character or in the operations of Jesus to prevent His being taken seriously in claiming to be the Bearer of a divine communication to men. But, from the moral point of view, the life of Jesus constitutes not merely a negative, but distinctly a positive motive of credibility in favor of that doctrine which He advanced or revealed by God. For, as He is described in the reliable historical documents which are available to us, it becomes evident that He possessed a singular holiness, a nearness to God which is manifestly beyond the natural competence of man as such, and which therefore was in Him by reason of a divine operation distinct from and superior to those forces which operate on the level of created nature. Thus God testified to the authenticity of the claims advanced in favor of the teaching which Jesus Himself proposed to men. Consequently the teaching of Jesus is credible as divine revelation insofar as it is freely and manifestly signed by God in this way.

Specifically the holiness which Jesus obviously possessed, and which men were and still are able to observe in Him, consists in a firm adherence to God together with a constant aversion from moral evil. As such it is far more than mere passing moral rectitude. Any individual *act* of a human being is reckoned as morally good insofar as it is concerned with a righteous object, ordered to a good end and not vitiated by evil circumstances. A *man* is said to be morally good when the course of his activity is directed toward God, or when, in other words, he does good things for the sake of God. Holiness implies

---

24 Matt. 15:24; Matt. 10:5–6.

perfection and firmness. A man, or for that matter a thing, is said to be holy in the measure that he is devoted to God and absolutely removed from moral evil. This is the characteristic manifest in Jesus of Nazareth to a miraculous degree.

11. Holiness and the love of God. In treating of this sign of divine revelation, clearly manifest in the conduct and in the very life of Jesus, we must not, even for a moment, abandon the point of view of strictest realism. The fact of the matter is that God exists, and that He is the Pure Act, the infinitely perfect, immutable, omniscient, eternal, and sovereignly free Creator of the universe. Again it is reality that man owes God a tribute of service and love. If that tribute is not paid, then, despite the other qualifications with which an individual may be endowed, he is a distinct failure in the moral order. Conversely the love of God, a real affection of benevolence, constitutes the basic motive in a life which is morally acceptable. Jesus of Nazareth manifested a sincere love and service of God in every department and aspect of His activity. That love influenced Him toward the loftiest heights of moral perfection in His dealings with men and in the government of His own life. In this activity, guided and crowned by a supreme affection for God, lies the evident sanctity of Jesus of Nazareth.

Now holiness is primarily an internal affair. The love for God is an act of the human will, an act which in itself cannot be observed or described through the sensible activities of other men. But a sincere and real affection for God will inevitably reveal itself in the manifest activity of the person who possesses it, and thus the men of His time and those of our own day have an infallible indication of this sanctity, even while the love which motivates it remains in itself invisible.

It is important that we understand, once and for all, how and why a sincere affection for God, and the sanctity which results from such love, can be naturally visible to the eyes of men. The key to the explanation lies in the nature of that love and service which men really owe to the living God. A real love of benevolence involves the intention to do that which is good for the object of that affection. When we love a creature in this way, we sincerely propose to do whatever is within our power in order to bring him the happiness and perfection he is capable of receiving. When, on the other hand, we possess a real and sincere love of benevolence for God, we know at once that there is nothing which we can do to add in any way whatsoever to His infinite perfection and felicity.

However, we can understand, even from a purely natural point of view, that this Pure Act, who is the Creator and the End of the created universe, has actually brought all things distinct from Himself into being for the sake of His own eternal and ineffable glory. Using the natural powers of our minds alone, we are quite competent to realize that this glory of God is the only motive which would be adequate and proper for the creation of a finite universe on the part of the infinitely perfect Creator. Now the glory of God consists in our appreciative knowledge of His goodness, a knowledge manifestly demanding and resulting in praise for the divine perfection. As a result a true and sincere love of benevolence for God involves an effective desire to realize the divine glory by furthering and expressing a realistic appreciation of His existence, His nature, and His attributes.

It is essential for us to realize that, although no additional good accrues to the Creator out of any activity of an individual creature, or for that matter out of the corporate operation of the universe as a whole, there is a definite benefit received by the intellectual creature who gives glory to God. In willing His own glory, God intends by that very fact that His intellectual creatures should know Him well enough to recognize His goodness and perfection. It happens that knowledge itself is a kind of possession. As a matter of fact it is the only way in which a spiritual being can be possessed. Consequently in willing that He Himself should be glorified, God intends that His intellectual creatures should possess Him, and that in this possession they should enjoy the only ultimately satisfactory blessedness man is capable of acquiring. For happiness consists in the firm possession of an ultimate good, and no being less than God Himself is competent to satisfy all the longings of the human heart.

12. Holiness a positive sign of divine revelation. It is easy to see the manifestation of a true love of benevolence for God. The man who has this affection expresses it in recognizing and praising the Creator in his own life, and then in directing his activity in such a way that by means of it others will come to glorify their Creator and thus enjoy the one finally adequate object of human felicity. It is true that there can be, and there most certainly are other means available

The Holiness and Wisdom of Jesus

for testing the reality of a love of God which is meant to be used by other men as a guide in their own activity. Actually the Catholic Church demands and receives adequate authentication of the sanctity attached to those persons whom she canonizes as saints through legally attested miracles. Likewise, the sanctity of Jesus Himself, visible as such, is confirmed and as it were witnessed by the other motives of credibility which attach themselves to the doctrine which He proposed to men as divinely revealed.

It would be unscientific and totally at variance with the manifest tradition of Christian apologetics to consider the various motives of credibility which substantiate the claims of Jesus as so many disconnected and unrelated entities. Really the sanctity of Christ, the miracles and prophecies, the social miracle that is the Church, and the wondrously satisfactory character of the Christian message in itself all stand as various organized parts in the one visibly divine seal, testifying to the credibility of the Christian message as divine revelation. All of these may be considered in themselves. Each motive of credibility has its own force, and the miracles and prophecies especially are competent to give us an objectively certain appreciation of Christian credibility. However, the full power and perfection of the divine attestation is visible only when we see the combined evidence of all these signs.

13. Jesus and affection for God. We may, however, consider the sanctity of Jesus Christ by and in itself. It is strikingly evident that the Jesus of Nazareth described in the four canonical gospels was a man of the highest degree of holiness, a holiness which is manifestly supernatural in origin when we consider it in its own light, but is still more extraordinary if we compare it with the moral qualities of other men who have founded historical religious doctrines or who have been intimately identified with other religious cults. Mohammed,[25] and long before him men like Epictetus[26] and Marcus Aurelius[27] have expressed beautiful sentiments of affection for God. Yet a man could never say fairly that the love of God was the sole or even the outstanding interest of these men. The prophet of Islam most

---

25 Cf. the Koran.
26 Cf. particularly "The Discourses of Epictetus," by Arrian.
27 Cf. the *Meditations*.

definitely arranged his life in such a way as to gain a tremendous amount of material wealth and sensual pleasure for himself. The two great Stoic philosophers made even the love of God a means for the aggrandizement of their own pride.

As a twelve-year-old boy in the temple at Jerusalem, Jesus of Nazareth had uttered a statement which was to be the keynote of His entire life. "I must be about My Father's business."[28] Again He could state, without fear of contradiction, at the height of His public career and in the face of His most bitter enemies, "I seek not My own will, but the will of Him that sent Me."[29] Finally, as He was preparing for the Passion, in the prayer to His Father which concludes the last address to the Apostles, He could declare with confidence, "I have glorified Thee on the earth."[30]

14. The manifest beneficence of Jesus. His entire public life was spent in an unremitting effort to teach a doctrine about God, a system of truth that was meant to bring men to an eternal and ineffable possession of their Creator. He had manifested for God the strong and perfect affection of a Son. He had been obedient to His Father, following every prescription of the natural law and every precept of that mosaic code which governed the activity of the children of Israel. This conformity with the divine injunction on His part was a matter so well known among His fellow Jews that He was able to offer successfully the most striking challenge a man has ever been able to set before his accusers. "Which of you shall convince Me of sin?"[31]

In His contacts with the people of His own time this miraculous holiness stands out still more clearly. Almost alone among the men of this world, Jesus manifestly aided and perfected every human being who was willing to receive His influence. He cared for the material wants of the people, frequently bringing to their assistance the miraculous powers with which He was equipped. The miracles of Jesus of Nazareth were not like the tricks jugglers perform in a theater, merely intended to amuse or to astound the populace. In every

---

28 Luke 2:49.
29 John 5:30.
30 John 17:4.
31 John 8:46.

one of them a definite benefit, one which under the circumstances at least would not have been accorded by the use of purely natural means, was conceded to some individual or group of individuals. His commands and counsels were always manifestly such as to make the persons who followed them really better men and women than they would have been otherwise.

On the other hand, no harm or evil came to the children of men through the preaching or the activity of Jesus. He did not seek to advance His doctrine by means of violence. No man suffered hurt, no family was left indigent because He had sought acceptance of His teaching. A sincere love of benevolence for God carries with it the intention of doing good for those who are called upon to glorify God for all eternity. No words can express the beneficent attitude of Jesus toward His fellow men better than those in which He expressed His own sentiments in this regard, "Come to Me, all you that labor and are burdened, and I will refresh you."[32] He regarded His fellow men as having been confided to His care by the heavenly Father, and He considered that His function demanded that they be led to God in and through Him. "I have manifested Thy name to the men whom Thou hast given Me out of the world: Thine they were, and to Me Thou gavest them: and they have kept Thy word."[33]

Finally, His love for God, manifest and expressed in His affection for His fellow men, was strong and perfect enough to influence Him freely to undergo the most horrible torment and death that the sins of men might be forgiven and that God might be eternally glorified by the individuals thus redeemed. He saw the Passion and death He was about to undergo as something willed by the Father, and consequently as an affliction which He would accept in order to accomplish the divine mandate. "My Father, if it be possible, let this chalice pass from Me; nevertheless not as I will but as Thou wilt."[34] Furthermore, He was cognizant of the fact that His death and the shedding of His blood would be ineffably beneficial to those whom He loved in God the Father. "This is My blood of the New

---

32 Matt. 11:28.
33 John 17:6.
34 Matt. 26:39. Cf. Mark 14:36; Luke 22:42.

Testament which shall be shed for many unto remission of sins."[35] Thus in the case of Jesus, the love of God which is the root and the foundation of all true holiness was demonstrated and made manifest for all men in the most difficult and heroic act a man can be called upon to perform.

15. Freedom from sin. The real and sincere affection of Jesus for the living God is likewise manifest in His utter and constant removal from all sin. In spite of the fact that He was readily accessible to men and women whom the Jewish populace recognized as sinners, there was no trace of an offense against the living God in His activity. As a matter of fact both the followers and the enemies of Jesus were compelled to admit that there was no shadow of fault in Him. St. Peter in his first epistle took definite cognizance of this fact. He was able to commend the example of Jesus to His followers without qualification or apology. According to the prince of the Apostles, Jesus of Nazareth lived perfectly in accordance with the doctrine which He propounded. Thus a Christian would be a perfect man, and would achieve that sanctity requisite in an adopted son of God precisely insofar as He imitated the life of Jesus. "For unto this are you called: because Christ also suffered for us leaving you an example that you should follow His steps: Who did not sin, neither was guile found in His mouth."[36] St. Paul insisted upon exactly the same fact. "Him that knew no sin, for us He hath made sin: that we might be made the justice of God in Him."[37] "For we have not a high priest who cannot have compassion on our infirmities: but one tempted in all things such as we are, without sin."[38] The beloved disciple, St. John the Apostle and evangelist, who had known the Master even more intimately than had his associates, was able to assure the Christians that Jesus had been utterly without moral fault. "And you know that He appeared to take away our sins: and in Him there is no sin."[39]

16. Discernibility of Christ's holiness. Now there are two facts of salient importance which must be taken into consideration when we deal with the manifestly superhuman holiness of Jesus. In the first

---

35 Matt. 26:28. Cf. Mark 14:24; Luke 22:20.
36 1 Pet. 2:21–22.
37 2 Cor. 5:21.
38 Heb. 4:15.
39 1 John 3:5.

The Holiness and Wisdom of Jesus

place His life was not lived in rural obscurity, nor was He privileged with the privacy and adulation which naturally fall to the lot of the rich and powerful. Again His was a moral goodness which has served as an effective guide and exemplar to those men who have lived most successfully according to the moral code from that day to our own. Only when we recall these two truths can we gain anything like an accurate and fitting recognition of this motive of credibility.

The background against which Jesus of Nazareth moved and preached was anything but sympathetic and gullible. Shortly after the outset of His public career, He gained for Himself the bitter hostility of three very influential groups of men. The Herodians, retainers and courtiers in the houses founded by Herod the Great took up arms against Him. Once they joined with the disciples of the Pharisees in a design to discredit Jesus before the people.[40] Again, with these same Pharisees, they entered into a definite conspiracy to destroy Him. "And the Pharisees going out immediately made a consultation with the Herodians against Him, how they might destroy Him."[41] Herod II, the leader of the family in the time of Jesus, murdered John the Baptist and threatened to kill Jesus Himself. The response of Jesus, when He was brought news of Herod's menace, shows the contempt in which the Master held this plotter. "That same day there came some of the Pharisees, saying to Him: Depart and get thee hence, for Herod hath a mind to kill Thee. And He said to them: Go, and tell that fox: Behold I cast out devils, and do cures today and tomorrow, and the third day I am consummated."[42] Secondly He acquired the undying hatred of the chief priests, members, most of them at least, of the sadducee school. These men were most interested in retaining the good will of the Romans, for it was by their favor that they continued in their influential and highly lucrative offices. The members of this group were of necessity in the background during most of the active campaigning against Jesus. Yet it was one of their number, Joseph Caiphas, who made the definite motion for the death of Jesus in the conciliabulum summoned to decide His fate. "The chief priests therefore and the Pharisees gathered a council, and said:

---

40 Matt. 22:16.
41 Mark 3:6.
42 Luke 12:31–32.

What do we, for this man doth many miracles? If we let Him alone so, all will believe in Him: and the Romans will come, and take away our place and nation. But one of them named Caiphas, being the high priest that year, said to them: You know nothing, neither do you consider that it is expedient for you that one man should die for the people, and that the whole nation perish not."[43] It was this same Caiphas who called for the verdict of death against Jesus, and then handed Him over to the Romans.[44]

Yet, even more persistent and venomous than these in their hostility to the Master were the Pharisees. These nationalists and zealots for the Jewish tradition which was afterward to crystallize in the Talmud, written by their successors, were engaged in every activity which was set up against Jesus and His teaching. From this group were drawn most of the scribes, the clerical officials of the Jewish commonwealth. As a class these scribes are frequently marked as distinct enemies of Jesus, along with the other members of the pharisaic organization to which they belonged.

Two individual members of this sect of Pharisees are recorded as having been on friendly enough terms with Jesus to have invited Him to their houses.[45] However, in each instance the man displayed a lack of courtesy at the dinner he gave, and Jesus did not fail to chide them for it. When they are mentioned as a group, invariably they appear as bitter and unrelenting enemies, determined at any cost to ruin the influence of Jesus upon the people and to encompass His death. St. Matthew has set down the most terrible denunciation Jesus ever uttered against a class of men.[46] It was directed expressly against the scribes and the Pharisees.

Now their hostility against Jesus stands as the most perfect guarantee of His miraculous holiness. These individuals were as thorough and despicable in their methods as the OGPU or the Gestapo of our own days. We have already seen that they sent emissaries to Galilee to investigate the teaching and the conduct of Jesus. We know of the labored and exact bureaucratic process by which they endeavored to

---

43 John 11:47–50.
44 Matt. 26:65; Mark 14:63.
45 Luke 8:36; 11:37.
46 Matt. 23:13–36.

influence a man whom He had cured of blindness to testify that He was a sinner.[47] They watched Him to see whether or not He would heal the ailing on the sabbath day, and they found that He preferred to answer the call of holiness rather than to follow their ridiculous hypocrisy.[48] They were not only spies themselves, but they attempted to influence the entire populace to trail and observe Jesus.[49]

Now if there had been even the least remarkable lapse from perfect holiness, it would never have escaped the attention of this lynx-eyed and contemptible group. The final accusations which they brought to bear against Jesus were manifestly false, and were in effect nothing but twisted versions of a prophecy which He had made before the people. "And the chief priests and all the council sought for evidence against Jesus, that they might put Him to death, and found none. For many bore false witness against Him: and their evidence did not agree. And some rising up, bore false witness against Him, saying: We heard Him say: I will destroy this temple made with hands, and within three days I will build another not made with hands. And their evidence did not agree."[50] At the end of the three years of intensive spying this was the best that the enemies of Jesus could adduce against Him. The silly futility of their charges is the most eloquent witness that the moral conduct of Jesus must have been not merely above reproach but miraculous in its purity and prudence.

17. The creative sanctity of Jesus' life. However, the final and convincing evidence that the holiness of Jesus was actually a moral miracle must be sought in the creative nature of that sanctity. We can say with strict scientific accuracy that all which has been best in the line of holiness among men since the time of Jesus has been modeled, expressly and laboriously, on the moral perfections easily recognizable in His conduct. The heroic St. Paul, whose preaching brought the message of Christ to the gentiles through all the plots and oppositions raised against it, called upon the Christian to imitate his activity, and at the same time proudly professed that his own conduct had followed the example of Jesus. "Wherefore I beseech

---

47 John 9.
48 Luke 6:7.
49 John 11:56.
50 Mark 14:55–59.

you, be ye imitators of me, as I also am of Christ."[51] St. Ignatius of Antioch, in writing to the Romans, saw in the very martyrdom he was about to undergo a final step toward conformity with the life of his Master, and thus he desired this immolation as a seal of that perfection which he recognized in Jesus.[52] As a matter of fact the "Imitation of Christ" has always been and will ever be the only road to true moral perfection open to the men of this world.

Now there would be nothing specifically miraculous in the fact that the virtues of one individual served as exemplars in the moral life of another person living under much the same set of circumstances as himself. However, we are keenly aware of the fact that the natural competence and influence of a man is bound to be limited. By the very force of things, the individual person exercises attraction and serves as a model within a definitely circumscribed area, for a definite period of time, and within the confines of a definite racial or occupational group. The kind of influence which is effectively exercised without respect for any natural boundary whatsoever is manifestly something which belongs to that One who alone is competent to create and to direct the universe as a whole. Upon this salient and unmistakable fact rests the application of the sanctity of Jesus as a positive motive of credibility in the full and strict sense of the term. For we do not show that the holiness of Jesus was miraculous merely because it was outstanding as human perfection. In the probity and fullness of His moral conduct, Jesus of Nazareth manifested a force which was evidently beyond the capacity of any creature, actual or possible. He showed men a power of goodness which stands as a definite and recognizable seal of divine approval upon His claim that the doctrine He set forth as revealed by God really was all that He claimed it to be.

Since this holiness, by reason of its potent universality, is something which belongs to God, and could not possibly pertain on natural grounds to any creature whatsoever, it follows evidently that God has given it to the Person who actually possesses it. Now this gift of God, like every other dealing of the Creator with men, is something which He has obviously given freely and intelligently. God is freely the Source of that holiness which we find in Jesus of Nazareth in the sense

---

51 1 Cor. 4:16; 11:1; Phil. 3:17; 1 Thess. 1:6.
52 St. Ignatius, *To the Romans*, Ch. 6.

that no man has a natural claim to such universal and thus unlimited influence in any way whatsoever. Furthermore, in giving it, God was perfectly cognizant of all the circumstances which surrounded the conferring of this favor. As a result, if He had granted this manifestly supernatural moral perfection to a man who was using it to back up a false claim of divine origin for a doctrine he was propounding, God would have performed an act similar to that perpetrated by a man who attaches his signature to a document he knows to be false. God would not and could not be party to such deception. Consequently we are perfectly assured that a teaching offered as divine revelation, and signed with an evident seal which could only be that of the Creator, is definitely and rationally credible as a communication made to men by the living God.

We cannot insist too strongly upon this evidently supernatural universality in the holiness of Jesus. He has been an effective model for sanctity in persons of every condition, of every age, of every nation, and of both sexes. St. Louis of France could imitate the virtues of Christ in ruling a nation or in leading an army in the thirteenth century. Kateri Tekakwitha could model her life on that same holiness as a little girl among the savage Mohawks. There is no age so advanced, no country so distant, no condition so highly specialized, but that in their circumstances men may achieve full moral perfection in building their lives according to the manifest exemplar in Jesus.

18. Unlimited holiness in the teaching of Jesus. We must keep the same principle of effective universality in mind when we consider the miraculous holiness apparent in the doctrine of Jesus. Naturally the term holiness has the same basic meaning when it is applied to a man and when it is predicated of a teaching. It always involves closeness to God and absolute removal from evil. Now the sanctity which characterizes the doctrine set forth by Jesus of Nazareth is clearly manifest in its utter aversion from evil of any sort whatsoever, and in its insistence upon an effective closeness to the Creator in any possible set of circumstances. In other words, the teaching of Jesus is visibly holy insofar as it offers an accurate teaching about the living God, a correct notion of the place and function of man in the created universe, and finally a real appreciation of the activity by which man achieves and lives according to the norm of holiness. The fact that it can produce models of sanctity in every race and age attests the miraculous character of that holiness.

First of all there could be no such thing as a really holy doctrine which was not based upon an accurate natural knowledge about God. It so happens that sanctity is an affair which may be recognized by the effects which it brings about in the visible universe. Jesus of Nazareth was quite insistent upon this point. "Beware of false prophets, who come to you in the clothing of sheep, but inwardly they are ravening wolves. By their fruits you shall know them. Do men gather grapes of thorns, or figs of thistles? Even so every good tree bringeth forth good fruit, and the evil tree bringeth forth evil fruit. A good tree cannot bring forth evil fruit: neither can an evil tree bring forth good fruit."[53] A man will be holy insofar as he loves God with a true and constant love of benevolence which, in its turn, motivates the acts of all the moral virtues. The moral virtues themselves depend upon a recognition of the true and living God. The doctrine of Jesus is basically and recognizedly holy in as much as it offers an objective and exact understanding of what we can know naturally about the existence and the attributes of the Creator.

There could be no such thing as a real affection for God unless He is presented and recognized for what He is, a Being infinitely perfect, merciful, wise, and just, and thus ineffably deserving of all the affection which man is at all capable of showing Him. Actually Jesus of Nazareth presented such a doctrine about the Creator at a time when Jewish sacred studies had degenerated into an obscure zeal for rabbinical traditions and while the pagan writers and teachers were attributing to the deities of their pantheon a series of vices which would disfigure and pervert even purely human activity. That doctrine about the divine nature and attributes laid the groundwork for a perfect instruction on the place and the operation of those virtues in the exercise of which man achieves the ideal of holiness. As a result, the doctrine itself, both from a practical and from a speculative point of view, was recognizably holy.

19. Uncompromising opposition to sin, the doctrine of Jesus. Even from a negative aspect, the teaching of Jesus manifests a real

---

53 Matt. 7:15–18.

and splendid sanctity. He gave no directions for compromising with evil. He did not point out a standard of mere utilitarian respectability. There was no limit beyond which He did not wish the holiness of His followers to extend. After having concluded the first injunctions which He laid upon His disciples in the Sermon on the Mount, Jesus showed them the only ultimate standard in the light of which human perfection and holiness must be evaluated. "Be you therefore perfect as also your heavenly Father is perfect."[54]

In order to achieve this perfection, man must perform certain acts and omit others. For example he must love God and his neighbor, and he must refrain from adultery and murder. In this field Jesus gave His followers definite and inescapable commandments, disobedience to which meant loss of perfection. But there were certain conditions which, while not in themselves necessary for all men, were still mightily helpful to man in his essential task of advancing in perfection. Jesus advised those who were able to do so to utilize these conditions. Thus we have the evangelical counsels of poverty, chastity, and obedience. The ultimate exemplar of that perfection depicted in the teaching of Jesus remains the ineffable goodness of the divine nature itself. In a unique sense, His is the teaching of absolute sanctity. The doctrine is miraculously holy in that it betrays none of that limitation which must naturally condition all of the purely natural efforts of man.

20. The holiness of Jesus is manifestly beyond the natural competence of creatures. The effects of this doctrine clearly indicate its absolute lack of limitation. The great figures of holiness within the world since the time of Jesus have imitated Him in accordance with the directions contained in that doctrine which He presented as divinely revealed. The results of His doctrine have been lives of holiness and perfection incomparably beyond anything which the world has ever seen outside of His influence. The doctrine has been absolutely effective in producing sanctity despite all obstacles of temperament and background on the part of the persons who have accepted it, and against every sort of interference brought to bear against it. It has been unlimited in its scope, producing miracles of holiness in martyrs and virgins, in doctors and confessors of the Church, in men and women of every age and of every walk of life. Such a doctrine, with

---

54 Matt. 5:48.

its unrestricted efficacy, could never have been evolved or produced by creatures of limited competence. It is manifestly an argument for the claims advanced in its own favor.

21. The historical background of the motive of holiness. We must not allow ourselves to imagine that this argument from holiness was merely an historical afterthought, a demonstration adduced in later ages by brilliant students of that teaching which Jesus offered to the world. As a matter of fact this, like every other motive of credibility which has ever been properly advanced to show that Catholic dogma can reasonably and prudently be accepted as divine revelation, was specifically mentioned by Jesus of Nazareth Himself. Apologetics would be neither scientific nor effective if it were not treated as what it really is, an integral part of that highly unified discipline which we know by the name of sacred theology. Now it is the essential function of sacred theology to explain, and to state, efficaciously, clearly, and without equivocation, the actual meaning conveyed in the deposit of that revelation which God has given to the world in the preaching of Jesus, and which is requisite for all men. Jesus stated explicitly that His message was to be *carried* to the body of humankind. "Going therefore teach ye all nations: baptizing them in the name of the Father, and of the Son, and of the Holy Ghost. Teaching them to observe all things whatsoever I have commanded you: and behold I am with you all days, even to the consummation of the world."[55] He intended that every available resource of human ingenuity should be expended in the all-important task of bringing this communication to men. St. Paul took cognizance of this intention in his instructions to Timothy. "I charge thee before God and Jesus Christ, who shall judge the living and the dead, by His coming and His kingdom: Preach the word, be instant in season, out of season: reprove, entreat, rebuke in all patience and doctrine."[56]

22. Jesus Himself appealed to His manifest holiness as a criterion of revelation. Now that doctrine was meant to be given to men as Jesus Himself had formulated it. He had confided it to the care of the Apostles and of the Catholic Church of which they were the very foundation stones as a teaching which was evidently credible

---

55 Matt. 28:19–20; Mark 16:15.
56 2 Tim. 4:1–2.

The Holiness and Wisdom of Jesus 297

in its claim as divine revelation. Moreover, He had shown the very points on which the evident credibility of this teaching was manifest. One of those points was holiness, His own manifest sanctity and that of the doctrine He preached.

Jesus indicated His own visible and miraculous sanctity, along with miracles and prophecies, as a true and compelling motive of credibility in that mysterious and powerful discourse which He addressed to the Jews in the Temple of Jerusalem on Solomon's porch. "The Jews therefore came round about Him, and said to Him: How long dost Thou hold our souls in suspense? If Thou be the Christ, tell us plainly. Jesus answered them: I speak to you, and you believe not: the works that I do in the name of My Father, they give testimony of Me. . . . If I do not the works of My Father, believe Me not. But if I do, though you will not believe Me, believe the works, that you may know and believe that the Father is in Me, and I in the Father."[57] Now we happen to know very well, from the explanation given by Jesus Himself, exactly what He considered "the works of the Father," the characteristic divine signature that guaranteed the message He proposed as a true communication from God to man. The Master had already given a summary list of these "works" to the disciples of John the Baptist, who had sent what we might term the official inquiry to ascertain the identity of Jesus as the Messiah, and thus as the divinely appointed Messenger who was to bear the teaching of God to His fellow men. "Now when John had heard in prison the works of Christ, sending two of his disciples, He said to Him: Art Thou He that art to come, or look we for another? And Jesus making answer said to them: Go and relate to John what you have heard and seen. The blind see, the lame walk, the lepers are cleansed, the deaf hear, the dead rise again, the poor have the gospel preached to them. And blessed is he that shall not be scandalized in Me."[58]

The response as a whole appeals to the motives of credibility, not as separate and unrelated entities, but as constituting a coordinated and unified signature of divine approval for that doctrine which Jesus was preaching to the children of men. Naturally apologetics, as a part or function of sacred theology, intends to bring out the exact meaning

---

57 John 10:24, 25, 36, 38.
58 Matt. 11:2–6; Luke 7:18–23.

of Jesus in His very claims to credibility. Thus it must, in order to accomplish its task effectively, look to the manifest and miraculous holiness of Jesus and of His teaching as motives which are intimately related to the other signs of divine revelation, and meant to cooperate with them in showing the evident credibility of His doctrine as divine revelation.

In this answer of Jesus, there is a manifest reference to the prophecy of Isaiah. Twice this great herald of God had foretold the very phenomena which Jesus of Nazareth recounted on this occasion. In the thirty-fifth chapter of his book we read of the beneficent physical and social miracles which are to characterize the work of the coming Messiah.[59] Later, however, he distinctly refers to miracles of charity, which are to be accomplished by the same Person and in the same set of circumstances. Isaiah speaks in the name and the person of the divine Messenger, whose coming he predicts. "The Spirit of the Lord is upon Me, because the Lord hath anointed Me: He hath sent Me to preach to the meek, to heal the contrite of heart, and to preach a release to the captives, and deliverance to them that are shut up. To proclaim the acceptable year of the Lord, and the day of vengeance of our God: to comfort all that mourn: To appoint to the mourners of Sion, and to give them a crown for ashes, the oil of joy for mourning, a garment of praise for the spirit of grief. And they shall be called in it the mighty ones of justice, the planting of the Lord to glorify Him."[60]

Thus the great prophet of the Hebrews foretold explicitly that effective holiness was to characterize the workings of the Messiah. The sanctity of the Messiah, as described by Isaiah, was to be clear and evident enough to enable the people to recognize the Person who manifested it as the promised Messenger from God. As a result it could be of no common order. Evidently there were to be great and good men in Israel between the time of Isaiah and that of the promised Messenger. But there would be, and there could be no man apart from Him, who would manifest the evidently miraculous and unlimited effective holiness which was to characterize the Messiah. The work of this chief Prophet of God was to be summed up in

---

59 Isa. 35:5–6.
60 Isa. 61:1–3.

The Holiness and Wisdom of Jesus 299

the accomplishment of delivering a saving truth about God to those who stood most clearly in need of it. It was to the "meek," those who habitually restrain their impulses to anger, that the Messiah was to bring His teaching. These meek are the captives, the enclosed, the all but forgotten men of this world. They are the poor in spirit, the men who, whether they possess a measure of this world's goods or not, recognize the radical insufficiency of all material wealth. Naturally the greater number among them do not possess this wealth in any considerable quantity.

The miracle of holiness to be manifest in the Messenger from God was to be, according to Isaiah, shown in the effective relief of these people through a presentation to them of a saving truth about the living God. We can recognize a work of true benevolence as a measure of human moral value. We know very well that a man who devotes himself to assuaging the ills of others and to heaping benefits upon those who stand in need of them is clearly a morally good individual. Obviously the excellence or degree of this moral goodness is to be measured by the worth of the benefit conferred, by the perfection manifest in the intention of the benefactor, and finally by the extent of the benefaction itself.

23. The beneficence of holiness. In this case the *benefit* to be conferred upon the human race by the promised Messiah, the good which Jesus of Nazareth really brought to men and that to which He referred as an evident sign when He mentioned the poor having the gospel preached to them, is the most ineffably valuable possession which the children of men can attain. It is nothing more or less than truth by which man can receive the accurate notion of God, with all of the necessary cultural and moral implications flowing from this concept. It is a definite teaching through which men may have an eternity of perfect and ineffable happiness and avoid a never ending frustration and failure. The gift that the promised Messiah was to offer, the holy teaching which Jesus of Nazareth actually set forth, is something apart from which man cannot have the final felicity which he seeks. Apart from it there will be no concept of God available to all men and requisite for the full enjoyment and perfection of that social life which men are expected to live in this world. As a result the presentation of this truth to men constitutes an act of benevolence and is thus a characteristic of holiness.

In our own times men are prone to forget or to ignore the actual fact that a correct doctrine about the living God constitutes a blessing of incalculable magnitude for mankind. They will, as a rule at least, gaily concede that an individual who has managed to acquire some hitherto undiscovered truths in the field of medicine or of technology and who takes the trouble to communicate this information to those of his fellow men who are in a position to utilize it, is a benefactor of the human race. The real favor done to society and to the individuals who compose it in the publication of information about God and about the eternal destiny of man is fully as actual and as evident. After all the standard used is that of human welfare, in the absolute sense of the term. The knowledge of the physician or of the chemist is a benefit to mankind in the sense that it can prolong human life, intensify the enjoyment of those goods which should be utilized in the full and perfect living of this life and prevent suffering. Insofar as man has contributed to the attainment of these ends, he is rightfully considered as a benefactor of the human race.

The correct natural teaching about the living God constitutes the necessary keystone for all the cultural and moral doctrine that lends dignity to human life. In giving this knowledge to his fellows, a teacher makes it possible for them to live with realistic and intelligent happiness in the midst of a world they understand. It preserves them against the dangers of ignorance in the cultural and in the moral order. The revelation which Jesus of Nazareth presented to the world, the "gospel" mentioned in the book of Isaiah, is actually information which makes it possible for a man to enjoy an eternity of perfect felicity. Thus human welfare is advanced far more by this "good tidings" (for thus the word evangelium or gospel should be defined) than by any contribution which can be made in purely secular fields. That is reality. It is the business of the apologist so to explain his matter that his hearers may observe this reality.

24. The intention of Jesus. The second norm which we can apply in discerning the miraculous holiness of Jesus, as evident in His presentation of that doctrine which we mean to establish as rationally credible, is the *intention* manifest in His preaching. He Himself averred that His message was delivered to the poor. The passage of Isaiah the prophet mentions the meek, the captives, and men who are under restraint as the recipients of that teaching. The implication is clear enough. In the first place it was the purpose of Jesus to benefit those who stood in the greatest and most obvious need of His doctrinal ministrations. Secondly, those for whom He worked were precisely those in no position to gain for Him any material or social emoluments. The only motive which could influence such activity was manifestly a love for men as such, for men insofar as they are called upon to be the adopted children of the living God. Ultimately, then, the motive was an effective and benevolent affection for God Himself. This love constitutes the essential and requisite basis for all true holiness.

Now it is evident that the performance of an act based upon the love for God is heroically good when it is carried on in the face of opposition and when no return is received from the beneficiaries at all commensurate with the benefit which is conferred upon them. In the case of Jesus of Nazareth we find such opposition. We find that He did not seek any sort of a material reward. His preaching was carried on despite the most stupendous instances of ingratitude and malevolence manifested in His own regard. A preacher like Mohammed might make his teaching the means for acquiring a civic regal state, for himself and for his family. Gautama might find that his own doctrine brought him a central position in a pleasant group of men devoted to the practice of prayerless meditation. Jesus of Nazareth paid with tortures and with His own death for His work of evangelizing the poor.

25. The extent of that holiness manifest in the preaching of Jesus. The third standard by which the holiness manifest in preaching may be discerned is that of *extent*. Naturally and obviously a work which is beneficial for a larger group of men is greater, *positis ponendis,* than that which is of service only to a few. The sanctity of Jesus was clearly heroic and miraculous in that He intended to give and actually presented a teaching of invaluable worth to all men. The limitless beneficence of the Christian message is something which any man, willing to consider real facts, can readily observe. As a result this effective and absolutely unlimited favor to humanity stands as a striking indication that the man who presented it and the doctrine itself are miraculously holy. The love for God manifest in the beneficent and holy activity of a creature as such could not possibly be endowed with this absolutely universal perfection. Thus the holiness of Jesus, to which He appealed in His response to the messengers of John the Baptist, and which He set as the keynote of His lifework when He cited the prophecy of Isaiah in the synagogue at Nazareth, is a valid mark of God's approval for the claim of divine origin set forth in favor of the Christian message.[61] The infinitely wise and veracious Creator would never freely have given such holiness to a man who was engaged in presenting a spurious divine message.

26. The appeal to wisdom. There was likewise manifest in the doctrine and in the life of Jesus a *wisdom* or intellectual perfection evidently quite superior to anything which might be found in the natural mental equipment of any man. Wisdom consists in the knowledge of all things in their ultimate cause. In the speculative order it is described best as that perfection of the mind in which it grasps the meaning of the universe as a whole. In the practical order wisdom is that consummate prudence, in the light of which man knows how to act in such a way as to manifest the dignity and perfection of a true child of God under every set of circumstances which may befall.

The practical wisdom of Jesus is manifest in the miraculous holiness which characterized His life. The fact that he acted always and perfectly in the capacity of a holy man, and that He could face every set of circumstances which can affect the morality of human acts without ever deviating from the line of the most perfect moral conduct is evidence that He possessed an intellectual quality not naturally present in the human mind. It was something of divine origin, something which God presented to Him and which would never have been obtained by any individual who appealed to miraculous sanctity, among other signs, as an indication of divine origin in that message which He presented to the world as a communication from the living God.

At the moment we are most concerned with the miraculous speculative wisdom manifest in the teaching of Jesus, insofar as that

---

61 Cf. Luke 4:16–21.

teaching has been set down faithfully in reliable historical works at our disposal. It so happens that the message of Jesus, considered as a unit, is presented as intrinsically supernatural. As a result it stands as a body of doctrine which men could never ascertain by the merely natural exercise of their own cognitive faculties. Furthermore, even after men have accepted it with the certain and unwavering assent of divine faith once it has been revealed, they are still unable, as long as they remain in this life, to see and observe this doctrine as something evidently true.[62] Thus there is no direct way to make it naturally certain that there are three divine Persons, or that the Second Person of the Blessed Trinity became incarnate.

Indirectly, however, we have two means at our disposal for distinguishing this intrinsically supernatural Christian message as a doctrine of naturally manifest miraculous wisdom. In the first place we can compare the mysteries themselves with those truths which we can ascertain through the purely natural powers of human reason. Secondly, we may examine the concepts or terms in which the intrinsically supernatural propositions were and still are expressed. These terms were explained and defined insofar as they entered into the statement of the Christian mysteries. We have it within our power to judge whether or not the definitions of these terms, or what we sometimes know as the preambles of Christian faith, were in accordance with the dictates of natural intelligence. It will be to our advantage to consider first the miraculous wisdom as manifest in the formation of these preambles.

27. The mysteries taught by Jesus. We must not allow ourselves to overlook the fact that while the truths presented as mysteries in the doctrine of Jesus are thus set forth as absolutely beyond the natural competence of the unaided human mind, the terms in which these mysteries are couched are quite obviously within the realm of reason. Jesus had said "The Father and I are one."[63] The truth which He stated is obviously one which no man could possibly demonstrate by any merely natural process whatsoever. It is stated as a fact about the intimate life of God Himself. As a result only one who sees the intimate life of God can possibly have evidence of its verity. The only

---

62 The Vatican Council, The Constitution, *Dei Filius* (Denzinger, 1796).
63 John 10:30.

way in which such a statement can be accepted with objective and satisfactory certitude is in the definite assent of divine faith.

However, the terms which go to make up this proposition are words which any man can understand naturally. We know very definitely what the significance of "Father" and of "One" is in this particular statement. By far the most important term in all the doctrinal message of Jesus is the word "God." Jesus stated that His Father was God, the One who had always been adored by the Jews themselves. "Jesus answered: If I glorify Myself, My glory is nothing. It is My Father that glorifyeth Me, of whom you say that He is your God."[64] He took very good care that the people to whom He addressed His message should understand what He meant by the term "God." Thus His teaching, as we have already seen, abounds in explanations about the existence, the attributes, and the creative activity of God. In exactly the same way He sketched a picture of the world and of man. He stated truths which are in themselves within the natural competence of human reason in order that there might be ground for neither error nor ambiguity in accepting the mysteries properly so called.

As a result the teachings of Jesus have come into intimate contact with the body of that human wisdom which we know by the name of philosophy. Thus we are at liberty to compare at least this portion of it with the writings and the teachings of those men who have been the outstanding philosophers of all time. Plato and Aristotle, Porphyry, Epictetus and Marcus Aurelius from olden times have all left to the world well-articulated doctrines about God and man. Utterly apart from and independent of their entire current and tradition is that teaching which Jesus of Nazareth offered. The world has learned to know and to appreciate the cultural competence of the ancient seekers after wisdom. Yet, with the passage of time it has found that the teachings of any individual, or for that matter of the entire body of the great philosophers, is incomparably and visibly inferior to the wisdom of Jesus as manifest even in those teachings within the natural realm of reason. It is obvious that His intellectual perfection is of an order entirely above that of which human nature is itself capable.

28. The unlimited wisdom manifest in the preaching of Jesus. Again the most effective standard available to us for the purpose of

---

64 John 8:54.

comparison is that of universality. We know from experience, and we can demonstrate from rigorous metaphysical principles that the perfections of any creature are necessarily limited. This limitation, of course, extends to the field of wisdom itself. A man can easily obtain a grasp of reality sufficient for himself or for his own time and culture. Furthermore, if his exposition is at all complete and effective, his teachings may be highly beneficial for students of all subsequent ages. But there is not and there obviously cannot be one man or one group of men who can lay down a definite, complete, and coherent body of natural wisdom which can serve as a wholly competent guide to the human beings of all times and of all cultures, acting with even the full force and competence of human nature alone. This, however, is exactly what Jesus of Nazareth has done, and what He continues to do, in even the naturally ascertainable portion of His doctrine. So it is that He manifests an intellectual perfection of the divine rather than of the merely created order. Thus He offers one added guarantee that the message which He presented to the world as divinely revealed was actually of divine origin, for God could never possibly have conceded such an evidently supernatural wisdom as something to be utilized in bolstering up the claims of a spurious revelation.

It is quite easy to recognize this transcendent universal perfection in the teachings of Jesus. There is no necessary point of doctrine about God or man which He did not expose with manifest accuracy. He did not utilize the traditions of any of the powerful philosophical or rabbinical schools extant and flourishing, during the period in which He lived. Yet while the members of all these schools have left us the sort of incomplete and sometimes even erroneous doctrine which we may expect from the natural activity of any creature, Jesus of Nazareth, acting as an independent Teacher, gave the world a system of natural truth which remains a marvel of fullness and accuracy even to our own day. As a matter of fact His influence upon the progress of philosophy has been such that the men of our time have come to recognize the appropriateness of "Christian" as the characteristic designation of those philosophical systems which embody the naturally ascertainable truths which He set forth.

29. Limitation manifest in man's intellectual accomplishments. The wisdom of Plato or Aristotle or Epictetus, to mention only three of the best-known ancient philosophers, may have more than a mere historic interest to the students of our own time. Speculative and moral philosophers can and should derive valuable information from consulting the books which the first two wrote, and the volumes which set for the teaching of the latter. But no man in his right mind today could consider himself fully and completely the disciple of any of them. Some of these ancient writers mingled a good many serious errors with the truths which they presented to the world, while all of them are definitely limited in their immediate efficacy as teachers. No one of them presented a clear, unequivocal, and accurate natural knowledge about God definitely available to all men without exception. That is precisely what Jesus of Nazareth has manifestly done, and it is in this that we find the obviously supernatural and unlimited nature of His wisdom.

We must not lose sight of the fact that we are dealing with matters which can be checked up and verified just as clearly as any problem in the fields covered by chemistry or physics. When a man makes a statement about the nature or the attributes of God, insofar as these can be learned from an examination of the proofs by which we know of His existence, we can subject that statement to rigorous analysis and find with perfect certainty either its truth or falsity. Furthermore, when a man presents a systematic teaching about God, man, and the universe, we have it within our power to examine the completeness and accuracy of the system. We can see if there is some lacuna that definitively prevent some organized teaching which might otherwise be considered as an adequate guide for all men. The wisdom of Jesus as an intellectual miracle is very clear indeed in this field.

Most of those men who are charged with the expression of Christian teaching had high regard for Plato. Yet they were quite well aware that the founder of the Academy condoned certain forms of unnatural vice and actually taught that the best elements in society should possess women, not in the natural bonds of matrimony, but in common.[65] The philosophy of Aristotle is recognized as the most accurate expression in all the ancient tradition, yet the great Stagyrite had a very low concept of divine providence, and failed to see the conjunction of his own argument from motion with the absolute

---

65 *The Republic*, Book 5.

mercy of God.[66] Philo disfigured his philosophy with the description of an entity placed between God and the created universe. Epictetus had no idea whatsoever of the divine mercy, and considered the men who followed his teaching in some way equal to God Himself. Marcus Aurelius Antonius begins his *Meditations* with a prayer which would remind the reader of the gospels of the declaration by the Pharisee in the parable of the Pharisee in the publican.

30. A means of comparison. We must realize that the best basis for comparison is the reading of the canonical gospels with the books which contain the thought of these philosophical masters of antiquity. We cannot help admiring the genius of these non-Christian authors, but the very excellence of their production fades into insignificance in comparison with the teaching of Jesus. They were brilliant, and their brilliance enlightened not only certain men of their own nations and generations, but also a good number of their successors. Yet in every case theirs is essentially a talent of the schools. Scholars could achieve a certain serenity of conduct through the reading of Plato or Epictetus. But they could never begin to appeal to all men without exception. Aristotle could bring man of mature and trained judgment to acknowledge the existence of an unmoved First Mover. But he could never begin to refresh the body of mankind by pointing out that this First Cause was the tender and merciful Father of mankind. Epictetus could speak of the fatherhood of God, but even a glance at his teaching in this regard shows infinite distance by which the doctrine of Jesus surpasses it.

The fact of the matter is that the smallest child who learns the doctrine of Jesus through the little traditional Baltimore catechism has a far more perfect recognition of God than any cognizance these masters of non-Christian thought ever achieved. That child is matched by the little ones of China and Poland, by the boys and girls of Brazil and of Italy. The genius of St. Augustine and of St. Thomas Aquinas, the erudition of the Sylvius or Petavius, have all been expended in examining the teaching of Jesus. Every one of these men has acknowledged that the task of explaining the doctrine which the Nazarene set forth as divinely revealed was one which surpassed whatever intellectual perfection they may have possessed.

---

[66] *The Physics*, Books 7 and 8; *Metaphysics*, Book 12 on Lombda.

Truly history has been the great standard for showing forth the sublime supernatural wisdom of Jesus.

Now this teaching has never suffered from a dearth of opponents. From the very time of Jesus until this present day there have always been able and distinguished men who have been willing to utilize every resource at their disposition to discredit Jesus and His message. Yet we find that there never has been one item in all the naturally attainable doctrine set forth by Jesus which these men have been able successfully to controvert. In some ways, of course, this negative testimony is difficult to handle. Yet the fact that the enemies of Christ have no single point on which they can claim an intellectual victory over His teaching constitutes the strongest possible evidence of its divine origin. It would be absurd to attempt such a defense in favor of any other teaching which has been brought to men in the history of the world.

31. Examination of the mysteries reveals their transcendent wisdom. With reference to the mysteries themselves, the procedure is, of course, quite different. When an enemy of the faith attempts to deny or to disprove some naturally attainable truth and enunciated by Jesus, we can offer satisfactory and intellectually compelling evidence in favor of that truth itself. But when someone chooses to controvert a mystery, like the Trinity or the Incarnation, we can only point out that any argument which might tend to show the falsity of these statements is itself faulty and inconclusive. In other words, we can and have established in the inaccuracy of the real objections which have been urged during the centuries against the central dogmas of our faith. At the same time, however, we know very well that it is utterly beyond our competence to demonstrate these mysteries in anyway whatsoever. Still the fact that they have withstood the onslaughts of able foeman for upward of nineteen centuries is an indication that here, too, we find a more than natural wisdom. It would be a greater wonder than all the mysteries if an obscure Palestinian Jew could have fabricated as divinely revealed mysteries certain statements, admittedly beyond the capacity of the human mind to demonstrate, and then have submitted these forgeries to a serious but unsuccessful attack for nearly two millennia. The hard commonsense of mankind knows very well the utter impossibility of such a hypothesis.

An even greater tribute to and indication of the miraculous wisdom contained in the doctrine of Jesus is to be found in the attitude of His followers toward the mysteries themselves. During the more than nineteen hundred years which have elapsed since the death of Jesus, the cultural and social conditions of the world have been in a continual state of flux. Theory has succeeded theory in realms scientific. Portions of the earth which were absolutely unknown to the men of Jesus' time have been found and inhabited. The technical advance has been tremendous. Yet in spite of all these changes, the doctrine which was enunciated in the valley of the Jordan by Jesus of Nazareth retains its validity, and what is more its vitality. Origen could defend this teaching against the "modern" objections of Celsus in the third century, and could gain an immortal triumph. Peter the Lombard could state them clearly and unequivocally in the twelfth with such signal success that his admittedly literal statement of the Master's teachings could animate the culture of an era. In the midst of the scientific and cultural activities of our own times, Garrigou-Lagrange and Walshe can present the same doctrines as fresh and totally in accordance with the modern needs and knowledge. Obviously no merely human doctrine could expect to receive such unlimited success.

The post-Christian Jews saw their pharisaical traditions crystallize into the Talmud. In spite of the fact that a great people remains to this day animated by the spirit of this somewhat extensive document, no educated Hebrew of our own time would venture to defend every statement contained in this compilation. As a matter of fact the more brilliant Jewish scholars have always shown a tendency to veer away from the strict acceptance of this teaching. That tendency was manifest in Spinoza. It is manifest in men like Adler in our own day. The Mohammedan scholars began with the idea of commenting on the Koran. The most ingenious among them invariably ended as suspect at least by reason of the necessity which they found of avoiding or denying some of its content. Only with the wisdom of Jesus do we find traditionalism and brilliance combined. Those Catholic scholars who have done most for the thought of the world have been precisely men like Sylvius, Suarez, and Vitoria, writers who held and defended every statement which is set down in reliable documents as having been taught by Jesus of Nazareth.

Jesus Himself appealed to the obvious wisdom and truth in His message as an indication of the divine guarantee for the credibility of the mysteries themselves "But if I say the truth, you believe Me not. Which of you shall convince Me of sin? If I say the truth to you, why do not believe Me? He that is of God, hearest the words of God. Therefore you hear them not because you are not of God."[67]

32. Jesus Himself appealed to the manifest wisdom of His teaching. It is obvious that the Master appealed to this wisdom or truth of His doctrine directly. It was manifest to the Jews themselves, that in those portions of His teaching which were within the natural competence of human reason, He had spoken correctly. As a result He was justly indignant with them for rejecting the message as a whole. The God of heaven and earth could never allow His truth to be prostituted to the service of a false revelation. The fact that Jesus had been truthful, and that His wisdom was of the miraculous order, stands as evident divine signature, attesting to the credibility of the teaching which He presented as revelation from God.

The Samaritans in whose village Jesus stopped for two days accepted His teaching as a divine message and used the miraculous wisdom manifested in His discourse as a principal motive of credibility. "So when the Samaritans were come to Him, they desired Him that He would tarry there. And He abode there two days. And many more believed in Him because of His own words. And they said to the woman: We now believe, not for thy saying: for we ourselves have heard Him, and know that This is indeed the Savior of the world."[68] Those who take the trouble to investigate the teachings of Jesus, seeking for the truth rather than for mere dispute, will ever recognize the same ineffable intellectual perfection.

However, the clearest appeal of Jesus to the obviously supernatural wisdom of His teaching is described in the first and third gospels. This is an unmistakable assertion that the manifestly supernatural perfection of His discourses was sufficient evidence of their divine origin. He made this statement when a group of the scribes and Pharisees, ignorant of the true nature of miracles and their efficacy as indications of the divine approbation, asked Him to perform a

---

67 John 8:45–47.
68 John 4:40–42.

The Holiness and Wisdom of Jesus

wonder for their own amusement or edification. "Then some of the scribes and Pharisees answered Him, saying: Master, we would see a sign from Thee. Who, answering said to them: An evil and adulterous generation seeketh a sign: and a sign shall not be given it, but the sign of Jonah the prophet. For as Jonah was in the whale's belly three days and three nights; so shall the Son of man be in the heart of the earth three days and three nights. The men of Niniveh shall rise in judgment with this generation, and shall condemn it: because they did penance at the preaching of Jonah. And behold a greater than Jonah here. The queen of the south shall rise in judgment with this generation, and shall condemn it: because she came from the ends of the earth to hear the wisdom of Solomon, and behold a greater than Solomon here."[69]

In this assertion we find a clear prophecy of the Resurrection. At the same time we have the unequivocal statement that the wisdom manifest in His teaching, as obviously superior to the legendary intellectual perfection of Solomon the king, should have drawn the men of Judea and Galilee to recognize the fact that God himself was speaking to them in the discourses of Jesus. Jesus said that the force manifest in the preaching of Jonah had been sufficient evidence for the powerful and corrupt Ninivites of the divine origin of that message which he proposed to them. His own teaching, rejected by His compatriots, carried in itself far more striking manifestation of the divine approbation.

---

69 Matt. 12:38–42; Luke 11:29–32.

Chapter 15

THE TESTIMONY OF MIRACLES

1. The reality of those miracles attributed to Jesus. In this chapter we must answer a series of questions pertinent to the credibility of Catholic dogma as divine revelation. In the first place we must find out whether or not we have historical evidence to say that Jesus of Nazareth actually performed miracles. Then we must learn what sort of deeds are ascribed to him on the pages of reliable historical documents as signs and wonders. From this we must ascertain whether the actual works which are attributed to Jesus of Nazareth actually support His contention that the doctrine He preached was really a message from the living God, meant to be accepted by all men with assent of divine faith. In this regard we should look into the connection between the miracles of Jesus and the ancient messianic prophecies in which these were foretold. Finally, it is our business to learn of the way in which Jesus Himself appealed to these miracles and in which the apologists of the Catholic Church have followed the example of their Master.

To the man who approaches this question from an unbiased and scientific historical point of view, nothing can be more evident in all the long career of the human race than the fact that Jesus of Nazareth worked miracles. We have the unanimous testimony of the four Gospels, the Acts of the Apostles, and the epistles of St. Paul to this effect, and all of these work stand as absolutely reliable historical documents. The testimony of the friends and followers of Jesus is fully corroborated by that of His most deadly enemies. We have at our disposal ancient writings, from Christian and non-Christian sources alike, all united in the contention that the life of this man abounded works which are obviously beyond on the natural competence of any creature whatsoever.

2. The gospels as sources of our knowledge about miracles.
Obviously the most important sources from which we can learn about the miracles of Jesus are the four canonical gospels themselves. Arranging the gospel narrative according to the biographical order taught by the most eminent scripture scholar of our own days, Father M. J. Lagrange, O.P.,[1] we find no less than forty-eight occasions on which Jesus is said to have performed manifestly miraculous acts. Many of these accounts tell of a great series of such acts, others describe individual healings or wonders in detail. The recountal of these miracles obviously enters into the intimate fabric of the gospel narratives themselves. In the acknowledgement of these miraculous activities, the four gospels preserve exactly the same historical narrative style that they manifest in telling about any other accomplishments of Jesus.

The gospels not only recount the series of miracles and individual wonders performed by Jesus of Nazareth, but they also tell of the reaction to the signs on the part of His friends and His enemies. His disciples as a group are said to have believed in Him after His first public miracle, the changing of water into wine at the wedding feast at Cana in Galilee. "This beginning of miracles did Jesus in Cana of Galilee: and manifested His glory, and His disciples believed in Him."[2] The dignitary whose son He cured by mere word believed, and brought all of his dependents to the faith once he learned of the miracle.[3] The first four Apostles, Peter, Andrew, James, and John, accepted the definitive call to the ministry of Jesus once they had witnessed the miraculous draught of the fishes.[4] Those who learned of the resurrection of the widow's son at Naim recognized in Jesus who had performed the miracle a great Prophet whom God had raised up among the people.[5] The men who witnessed the first multiplication

---

[1] We have used the "Synopse des Quatres Évangiles en Francois d'apres la Synopse Grecque du R.P. M.J. Lagrange, O.P., par le R.P.C. Lavergne, O.P."; 20th thousand (Paris, 1934). In this work Father Lavergne modifies the order of the Greek synopsis only where the more mature studies of Father Lagrange, manifest in his masterly *L'Evangile de Jesus-Christ*, 11th thousand (Paris, 1930), have shown the way.
[2] John 2:11
[3] John 5:43.
[4] Matt. 4:20–22; Mark 1:18–20; Luke 5:11.
[5] Luke 7:16.

The Testimony of Miracles

of the loaves and fishes actually wished to seize upon Him and to acknowledge their acceptance of His divine messengership by giving Him the temporal royalty which they mistakenly considered an adjunct to that office.[6] The men who were on the ship with Him when He calmed the tempest acknowledged that He was truly the son of God.[7] The Galileans who heard of His healing of the deaf-mute acknowledged that "He had done all things well."[8]

However, the evangelists are careful to state that a considerable number of those who had been privileged to see His miracles refused to believe in Jesus. The raising of Lazarus from the dead, with all of its explicit and direct appeal as a motive of credibility, brought many of those who witnessed it to believe and left others so unmoved that they were willing to betray Him to His enemies. "Many therefore of the Jews who were come to Mary and Martha, and had seen the things that Jesus did, believed in Him. But some of them went to the Pharisees and told them the things that Jesus had done. The chief priests therefore and the Pharisees gathered a council and said: What do we, for this man doth many miracles? If we let Him alone so, all believe in Him: the Romans will come and take away our place and nation."[9]

3. The enemies of Christ and His miracles. Cold-blooded, vicious, but intensely realistic, the enemies of Jesus never attempted to deny His miracles. They considered them as effective signs, performed by the sort of man who is worthy of credence by reason of His intellectual and moral integrity. It was precisely because they were effective and real that they meant to take definitive action against Him. It would have been the easiest thing in the world, from their point of view, to indicate to the people who reverenced and follow them that the hated Nazarene had never performed any miracles at all. The fact that these tireless spies and inquisitors did not do this is most certain evidence that the supernatural character of Jesus' works was so manifest as to render such instructions ludicrous. The men of the Sanhedrin felt that they could not afford to let Jesus alone. Still

---

6 John 6:15.
7 Matt. 14:32.
8 Mark 8:37.
9 9 John 11:45–48.

less could they afford to make themselves a laughingstock before the people by denying the reality of His signs.

4. The case of Nicodemus. Some of the leaders among the Jewish people were sufficiently free from passion and prejudice to acknowledge both the reality of His miracles and their demonstrative value. Nicodemus was one of these. At the same time he was well enough aware of the dire consequences which would follow upon association with Jesus to come to Him by night for his first interview. The words of this clear-thinking man show one common response to the works of Jesus. "And there was a man of the Pharisees, named Nicodemus, a ruler of the Jews. This man came to Jesus by night, and said to Him: Rabbi, we know that Thou art come a Teacher from God, for no man can do these signs which Thou dost, unless God be with him."[10] Contact with Jesus evidently confirmed the judgment which Nicodemus had drawn from observing His miracles, for we find on the other two occasions in which he appears in the gospel narrative that he later braved the wrath of his fellow Sanhedrinites in defending Jesus against their attacks,[11] and finally that he was definitively numbered among the disciples.[12] In all the history of Christian apologetics no one has expressed the reality and the probative force of those miracles which Jesus wrought with more perfect accuracy than did this amicable and cultured leader.

5. An official investigation. The actual enemies of Jesus did not take his miracles on mere hearsay. They were witnesses to a good many of them, and we have seen how they sent investigators into Galilee from Jerusalem itself in order to observe His works and His teaching.[13] Moreover, the entire ninth chapter in the fourth gospel is given over to the account of one of the most striking miracles Jesus ever performed and the relentless inquisition which the Sanhedrin set up to discredit it if possible. The miracle was the giving of sight to a man born blind. The work was occasioned by a question the disciples themselves put to Jesus. "And Jesus, passing by, saw a man who was blind from his birth: And His disciples asked Him: Rabbi, who hath

---

10 John 3:1–2.
11 John 7:50–51.
12 John 19:39–41.
13 Cf. Mark 2:6, 16, 24, 3:6, 7:1; Matt. 9:3, 11, 12:2, 14, 15:1; Luke 5:21, 30, 6:2, 11.

sinned, this man or his parents, that he should be born blind?"[14] The answer of Jesus was an indication of the nature of a miracle as such, and the assertion that this man's affliction was something which God had ordered to His own glory. "Jesus answered: Neither hath this man sinned, not his parents; but that the works of God should be manifested in him."[15] What was to be performed would be precisely and evidently a divine work.

Then came the action of granting sight to this man who had been born blind. This time Jesus did not act as He did in the performance of most of His other miracles and bring about the effect merely by the pronouncement of a command or through touching the afflicted person. He made use of natural means, but of means manifestly incapable of restoring sight by their own power. Again, as happened on a few of the other occasions mentioned in the gospel histories, the actual effect was not produced in the sight of those who were with Jesus at the time. "When He had said these things, He spat on the ground and made clay of the spittle, and spread the clay upon his eyes. And said to him: Go, wash in the pool of Siloe (which is interpreted, Sent), He went therefore and washed, and he came seeing."[16]

The people who were acquainted with this man were naturally astounded at the wonderful turn of events. When they ascertained that the miracle had been wrought by Jesus, they brought the man to the Pharisees, knowing well that they would object to the work because the man had been given his sight on the Sabbath. "The neighbors therefore and they that had seen him before, that he was a beggar, said: Is not this he that sat and begged? Some said: This is he. But others said: No, but he is like him. But he said: I am he. They said therefore to him: How were thy eyes opened? He answered: That man that is called Jesus made clay and anointed my eyes, and said to me: Go to the pool of Siloe and wash. And I went, I washed, and I see. And they said to him: Where is He? He saith: I know not. They bring him that had been blind to the Pharisees. Now it was the sabbath when Jesus made the clay and opened his eyes."[17]

---

14 John 9:1–2.
15 John 9:3.
16 John 9:7–8.
17 John 9:8–14.

The subsequent conduct of the Jewish rulers makes it evident that they could not be accused of any kind credulity. They made three distinct official inquiries, questioning the man that had been cured twice and his parents once. They learned to their own satisfaction that the man had been blind since birth, and that Jesus had actually given him his sight by using a simple ointment of mud on the helpless eyes and by enjoining upon the man a bath in one of the pools around Jerusalem. By every device within their power they attempted to bring the recipient of this miraculous favor to turn against his Benefactor. At every turn they were met and confuted by an irresistible appeal to facts. Their inquisition served to confirm, rather than to becloud, the fact that this cure was actually a miracle. The rigid character of their inquiry can be best shown by an examination of the gospel narrative itself. "Again therefore the Pharisees asked him how he had received his sight. But he said to them: He put clay on my eyes, and I washed, and I see. Some therefore of the Pharisees said: This man is not God who keepeth not the Sabbath. But others said: How can a man that is a sinner do such miracles? And there was a division among them. They say therefore to the blind man again: What sayest thou of Him that hath opened thy eyes? And he said: He is a prophet. The Jews then did not believe concerning him that he had been blind and had received his sight, until they called the parents of him that had received his sight: And asked them, saying: Is this your son, who you say was born blind? How then doth he now see? His parents answered them and said: We know that this is our son, and that he was born blind: But how he now seeth, we know not: or who hath opened his eyes, we know not: ask himself: he is of age, let him speak for himself. These things his parents said because they feared the Jews: for the Jews had already agreed among themselves, that if any man should confess Him to be Christ, he should be put out of the synagogue. Therefore did his parents say: He is of age: ask him.

"They therefore called the man again that had been blind, and said to him: Give glory to God; we know that this man is a sinner. He said therefore to them: If He be a sinner I know not: one thing I know, that whereas I was blind, now I see. They said then to him: What did He do to thee? How did He open thy eyes? He answered them: I have told you already, and you have heard: why would you hear it again? Will you also become His disciples? They reviled him therefore and said: Be thou His disciple: but we are the disciples of Moses. We know that God spoke to Moses: but as to this man, we know not from whence He is. The man answered and said to them: Why, herein is a wonderful thing that you know not from whence He is, and He hath opened my eyes: Now we know that God doth not hear sinners: but if a man be a server of God, and doth His will, him He heareth. From the beginning of the world it hath not been heard that any man hath opened the eyes of one born blind. Unless this man were of God, He could not do anything. They answered and said to him: thou wast wholly born in sins, and dost thou teach us? And they cast him out."[18]

The reality of the miracle of which he had been the beneficiary so affected the man who had been born blind that He acknowledged the divinity of Jesus by an act of adoration which was reserved for the living God. "Jesus heard that they had cast him out: and when He had found him He said to him: dost thou believe in the Son of God? He answered and said: Who is He, Lord, that I may believe in Him? And Jesus said to him: Thou hast both seen Him, and it is He that talketh with thee. And he said: I believe, Lord. And falling down he adored Him."[19] Knowing that his own cure was a miracle in the strictest sense of the term, the man who had been cured recognized it for what it was, an indubitable indication of the divine messengership belonging to the man who had performed that miracle. Jesus tested that reaction by revealing to him the central mystery in all His teaching, the fact of His own divine Sonship. This Jew, convinced of the divine unity as were all his countrymen, and upright enough to have braved the wrath of his national leaders rather than betray the truth, instantly manifested his acceptance of this teaching as a divine message. His words and his actions expressed his belief in the divine Sonship of Jesus, and his acceptance of the Healer's message on the authority of God Himself.

6. Miracles performed on the Sabbath. The Jewish leaders objected to many of the miracles of Jesus precisely because He had performed them on the Sabbath day. They claimed to see in this

---

18 John 9:15–34.
19 John 9:35–38.

failure to observe the rigor of their human traditions a transgression of the divine law itself, and thus an indication that the healings of Jesus proceeded from some supernatural force other than that of God. We have already seen how the council of the Pharisees objected to the giving of sight to the man born blind. Similar reclamations are found in the Jewish leaders' injunction to the man whom Jesus healed at the pond called Probatica, not to carry his bed as Jesus commanded him.[20] In this instance it is said explicitly that the persecution suffered by Jesus at the time was caused by the fact that His miracle was performed on the sacred day of rest. "Therefore did the Jews persecute Jesus, because He did these things on the sabbath."[21] On this occasion Jesus replied to their contentions by stating that the miracle was the work of God, His own Father.

In a similar situation, when the master of the synagogue where a miracle of healing was performed inveighed against Jesus because He had acted on the Sabbath day, the Master retorted *"ad hominem et ad nationem"* by pointing out that their concern for the Lord's day was in reality much less heroic than they would have had it appear. The gospel narrative simply states that His enemies were put into confusion by the miracle and by their own unmasking.[22] Furthermore, it is recounted that Jesus was aware of the resentment of His enemies when, in the house of one of the leading Pharisees, He miraculously cured a man who was ill of the dropsy on the Sabbath day.[23]

7. Admission of miracles as superhuman acts. We have already seen that, in their railing against Jesus, the Jews shrieked that He was mad, and possessed by a devil.[24] The epithet of madman was evidently a mere expression of unthinking rage. However, His enemies seem to have made something of a deliberate and organized effort to convince themselves and the multitude who were subject to this influence that the miracles of Jesus were actually brought about by the power of the devils. This charge was brought forward particularly on those occasions when Jesus used His supernatural force to cast out the evil

---

20 John 5:1–16.
21 John 5:16.
22 Luke 13:10–17.
23 Luke 14:1–6.
24 John 10:19–21.

spirits who possessed certain individuals. "But the Pharisees said: By the prince of devils, He casteth out devils."[25]

The fact that the scribes and the Pharisees attributed the cures of Jesus to a diabolical power rather than to a divine power is the surest indication possible that these individuals were convinced, much against their will, that He was performing works far beyond the natural competence of any human being. They were evil men, but they definitely and obviously were not stupid. They hated Jesus, and they much preferred the comfortable security and leadership they enjoyed at the moment to membership in a kingdom that demanded penance and humility. There were two manifest facts which they had to take into very practical consideration. In the first place they were not going to acknowledge His authority. Secondly they were faced with their own realization, and that of the people, that works obviously beyond the capacity of human nature were being effected by Jesus. To be consistent with their own stand, they had to declare that these works were accomplished by the spiritual enemy of God, rather than by God Himself. When Jesus triumphantly refuted their claim, most of them persevered in making it. This was the one stand harmonious with their frantic hatred for Jesus, and the voice of logic is faint indeed in the ears of aversion like their own.

8. Witnesses of miracles. The conduct and the words, both of the friends and of the enemies of Jesus, clearly and evidently attests the reality of those miracles He performed. In the first place we can bring forward a recognized and authoritative historical document which recounts the events that took place immediately after the ascension of Jesus, and the first missionary activity of the Church which He had founded during His life on earth. This book is the Acts of the Apostles, the fifth and last of those historical books included in the canon of the New Testament. It is convincing evidence that those who had known Jesus of Nazareth most intimately were perfectly convinced, even after His death, that He had actually performed works over and above the natural competence of any creature. It recounts the actual words of the followers of Jesus, spoken to the people who had seen and known Him. The tenor of those words and the effect they produced make it abundantly clear that those

---

25 Matt. 9:34; Mark 3:23–7; Luke 11:17–23.

in a position best to know Jesus and His acts realized that He had performed true miracles, genuine motives of credibility.

In the first place, when the Apostles gathered to choose a man who would take the place left vacant by the suicide of Judas Iscariot, the betrayer of Jesus, they judged that their work consisted in acting as "witnesses of the resurrection," the greatest and the most important of all the miracles of Jesus. "Wherefore of those men who have companied with us, all the time that the Lord Jesus came in and went out among us, beginning from the baptism of John until the day wherein He was taken up from us, one of these must be made a witness with us of His Resurrection."[26] These were the words of Peter.

The same prince of the apostolic college was able confidently to appeal to the fact that the Jews to whom he spoke on that first Pentecost had firsthand knowledge of the miracles performed by Jesus. "Ye men of Israel hear these words: Jesus of Nazareth a man approved by God among you by miracles and wonders and signs, which God did by Him in the midst of you, as you also know."[27] We must note that on this occasion St. Peter adverted not only to the existence of true miracles, manifestly performed by his Master, but to the demonstrative value of these signs as well. The Man who had worked these wonders was "approved by God," and obviously approved for what He claimed to be, the bearer of a message from God to man which all men are to accept with the certain and unwavering assent of divine faith. The reaction to this assertion on the part of the Jews showed that they, as a group, were perfectly cognizant with the reality of those miracles, particularly the Resurrection itself, to which St. Peter had appealed. "Now when they had heard these things, they had compunction in their heart, and said to Peter and to the rest of the Apostles: What shall we do, men and brethren. But Peter saith to them: Do penance and be baptized, every one of you, in the name of Jesus Christ for the remission of your sins: and you shall receive the gift of the Holy Ghost. For the promise is to you and to your children, and to all that are far off, whomsoever the Lord our God shall call. And with many other words did he testify and exhort them saying: Save yourselves

---

26 Acts 1:21–22.
27 Acts 2:22.

form this perverse generation. They therefore that received his word were baptized, and there were added in that day about three thousand souls. And they were persevering in the doctrine of the Apostles, and in the communication of the breaking of bread and in prayers."[28] In this case we have a clear acknowledgment of the fact that Jesus had performed supernatural acts, an admission expressed in the only truly adequate and congruous way possible, the acceptance of His teaching as a true message from the living God.

Again St. Peter was able to assert publicly that Jesus had risen from the dead after he and St. John had miraculously given the power to walk to the lame man who was a beggar in the Beautiful Gate of the temple. "But the Author of life you killed, whom God hath raised from the dead, of which we are witnesses."[29] The same statement was made without fear of contradiction to the leaders of the Jewish nation after the two Apostles had been arrested and examined by reason of the tumult which the miracle in the Beautiful Gate had occasioned. "Be it known to you all, and to all the people of Israel: that by the name of our Lord Jesus Christ of Nazareth, whom you crucified, whom God hath raised from the dead, even by Him this man standeth here before you whole."[30] As far as the science of apologetics is concerned, the most important aspect of these narratives is to be found in the fact that within a few weeks after the crucifixion of Jesus, the Apostles who were interested in bringing as many as possible to accept His message as divine revelation could speak publicly and appeal without fear or danger of contradiction to public wonders done by their Master.

9. The response of the Sanhedrin. Since Jesus Himself no longer appeared among them, the leaders of the Jewish race had no reason to allow these claims to go unchallenged unless they realized that the miracles had actually been performed, and unless furthermore they were fully aware that the populace itself knew about their reality. The Apostles repeated their statement that Jesus of Nazareth had risen miraculously from the dead when the high priest himself called them before him on the charge of disobeying the orders of the Sanhedrin.

---

28 Acts 2:37–42.
29 Acts 3:15.
30 Acts 4:10.

"But Peter and the apostles answering said: We ought to obey God rather than men. The God of our fathers hath raised up Jesus, whom you put to death, hanging Him upon a tree. Him hath God exalted with His right hand to be Prince and Saviour, to give repentance to Israel, and remission of sins; and we are witnesses of these things, and the Holy Ghost whom God hath given to all that obey Him."[31] Actually the words of the Apostles so angered the chief priests that they were ready to put them to death, and actually would have done so had it not been for the prudent judgment of Gamaliel in their behalf. They administered the cruel and degrading punishment of scourging, in order obviously to lessen the influence of the Apostles upon the people of Jerusalem. But they did not and could not take what would have been otherwise the easiest means of attaining their objectives and putting an end to the party of Jesus, by offering some sort of refutation against the public assertion that He had shown a divine commission by performing works which were manifestly beyond the competence of any created nature whatsoever. The fact that they did not do so indicates very clearly their own conviction that the miracles of Jesus were indeed real, and that, despite all evidence of divine approbation given to Him, they intended to continue their opposition.

10. Paul and the Resurrection. The idea of one miracle of Jesus, the most striking and by all means the most effective as a motive of credibility pervades all the teaching of St. Paul, recorded in the Acts of the Apostles and in his epistles. This miracle is, of course, the glorious Resurrection. The manner in which he refers to this miracle in one of the first of his doctrinal letters shows very clearly the kind of certitude he possessed about the reality of this supernatural act. "Now I make known unto you, brethren, the gospel which I preached to you, which also you have received and wherein you stand. By which also you are saved: if you hold fast after what manner I preached unto you, unless you have believed in vain. For I delivered unto you first of all, that which I also received: how that Christ died for our sins according to the scriptures: And that He was buried, and that He rose again the third day according to the scriptures: After that He was seen by Cephas, and after that by the eleven: Then He was seen by more

---

31 Acts 5:29–32.

than five hundred brethren at once: of whom many remain until this present, and some are fallen asleep. After that, He was seen by James, then by all the apostles: And last of all He was seen also by me, as by one born out of due time."[32] The implication of this statement is clear enough. St. Paul staked all the claims of Christianity on the reality of God's approbation as manifest in the motives of credibility, and ultimately on this one most effective motive, which was the Resurrection itself. He points out that the very man with whom the Corinthians are most familiar has been privileged to witness this most powerful of all signs which to attest the veracity of those claims advanced in favor of the Christian message. The Apostles as a group, and then the most prominent among them, Peter, James, and Paul, are all cited as having seen the Master alive after He had really died in the horrible torments of crucifixion. Writing to a body of believers in the great commercial port of Corinth, a place where the news of the world would be received and dispensed most effectively, St. Paul clearly stated that five hundred men had seen the risen Jesus less than twenty-five years ago, and that a great number of these men were still alive. Naturally, if no such men existed, the Corinthians would very well know the falsity of this claim. The fact that he dared to make this assertion to such a group is the best possible indication that St. Paul knew very well that he could substantiate every element and aspect of this proof.

11. The testimony of Quadratus. It is interesting to note that, years later, Quadratus, the first of the glorious company of Catholic apologists, was able to set forth a like assertion in a letter to the Roman emperor, Hadrian. Eusebius of Caesarea, the father of Church history, has recorded the following statement from the apology of Quadratus, a book which has unfortunately been lost during the course of the centuries. "But Trajan having held the sovereignty for twenty years, wanting six months, is succeeded in the imperial office by Aelius Adrian. Quadratus addressed a discourse to him as an apology for the religion that we profess; because certain malicious persons attempted to harass our brethren. The work is still in the hands of some of the brethren, as also in our own. From it anyone may see evident proof both of the man's understanding

---

32 1 Cor. 15:1–8.

and of his apostolic faith. This writer shows the antiquity of the age in which he lived in these passages. 'The deeds of our Saviour,' he says, 'were always before you, for they were true miracles. Those that were healed, those that were raised from the dead, were seen, not only when healed and when raised, but were always present. They remained living a long time, not only while our Lord was on earth, but likewise when He had left the earth. Thus some of them have also lived to our own times.' Such was Quadratus."[33]

12. Celsus. Perhaps the most eloquent testimony to the reality of Jesus' miracles is to be found in the writings of His enemies themselves. Celsus in his book, *The True Discourse*, written during the early years of the third century uses the device of citing typically Jewish attacks against the Master as the contention of a fictitious Jew whom he pictures as reviling Jesus Himself. This personage attacks the Master as One who "having hired Himself out as a servant in Egypt, on account of His poverty, and having there acquired some miraculous powers, on which the Egyptians greatly pride themselves, returned to His own country highly elated on account of them, and by these means proclaimed Himself a God."[34] Origen points out very shrewdly that in formulating this accusation, Celsus, like all the other instructed adversaries of Christianity, implicitly admits the historical accuracy of the canonical gospels themselves. The invective of the fictitious Jew is an obvious twisting of facts set forth by St. Matthew.[35] Moreover, the great apologist remarks that Celsus is here "admitting somehow the miraculous works done by Jesus, by means of which He induced the multitude to follow Him as the Christ."[36]

13. The list of miracles. There can be no room for any reasonable doubt that Jesus of Nazareth was and is known to history as One who performed miracles. Knowing that He actually did these things, it remains for us to investigate in some detail the actual works which man has always recognized and designated as wonders. The four canonical gospels record forty-eight distinct individual or group

---

33 Eusebius, *The Ecclesiastical History,* Book IV, Ch. 3.
34 Origen, *Contra Celsum,* Book I, Ch. 28. The *True Discourse* of Celsus has come down to us only insofar as it is cited by Origen.
35 Matt. 2:13–22.
36 Origen, *a.c,* Book II, Ch. 38

miracles as brought about by Jesus of Nazareth. The synopsis of Lagrange-Lavergne distributes them in the following order:

1. Cana in Galilee, the changing of water into wine at the marriage feast (John 2:1–11).

2. Again at Cana, the restoration to health of a boy who was at the point of death. The boy's father, a dignitary from Capernaum, received this favor of Jesus in Cana, where he had gone to entreat the Master to come to the lakeside city and cure his son. The boy recovered in Capernaum at the moment when Jesus granted the petition to his father, some fifteen miles away (John 4:46–54).

3. At Capernaum, the casting out of an impure spirit from a man possessed. The demon recognizes Jesus as "the Holy one of God," but He forbade any further mention of His dignity by this unworthy being (Mark 1:23–27; Luke 4:33–36).

4. At Capernaum, the mother-in-law of St. Peter cured of a fever (Matt. 8:14,15; Mark 1:29–31; Luke 4:38, 39).

5. At Capernaum, the curing of all the sick and infirm who were brought to Jesus (Matt. 8:16; Mark 1:32–34; Luke 4:40).

6. At Capernaum, casting out of devils (Mark 1:34; 3:11; Luke 4:41).

7. The towns of Galilee outside Capernaum, many cures and healings (Matt. 4:23).

8. On the Sea of Galilee, a miraculous draught of fish (Luke 5:1–11).

9. In an unnamed town in Galilee, the cleansing of a leper (Matt. 8:1–3; Mark 1:40, 41; Luke 5:12, 13).

10. Capernaum, before a crowd that included Pharisees from every part of Galilee, from Judea and from Jerusalem; the cure of a paralytic. This miracle was used by Jesus as a demonstration of the fact that He was competent to perform the divine work of forgiving sins (Matt. 9:2–7; Mark 2:1–12; Luke 5:18–26).

11. Capernaum, the same day, other cures which are not described in detail (Luke 5:17).

12. A synagogue in Galilee, the restoration of a withered hand, a miracle performed on the Sabbath, in the presence of scribes and Pharisees. Jesus read the thoughts of these men and confuted their objections (Matt. 12:9–13; Mark 3:1–5; Luke 6:6–10).

13. Capernaum, a servant, about to die was restored to health. Jesus commended the faith of his master, a centurion, who acknowledged

that the Master could heal the servant at a word, without actually going to see and touch him (Matt. 8:5–13; Luke 7:1–10).

14. Nairn, a young man who had died, and whose body was being carried out for burial was restored to life (Luke 7:11–16).

15. Place and time unknown, seven devils cast out from Mary Magdalen (Mark 16:9).

16. The Sea of Galilee, the calming of a tempest at the word of Jesus (Matt. 8:18–27; Mark 4:35–41; Luke 8:22–25).

17. Near Gerasa, southeast of the Sea of Galilee, the casting out of many devils from a possessed man. These demons recognized Jesus and hailed Him as the Son of God. They asked to be sent into a herd of swine grazing near the site. Their request was granted and the swine plunged from a cliff into the sea and were drowned. The Gerasians, struck with terror, asked Jesus to leave their country (Matt. 8:28–34; Mark 5:1–20; Luke 8:26–39).

18. Galilee on the return from Gerasa, the healing of a woman who had been under medical care for an incurable issue of blood for twelve years. She was relieved of her infirmity on touching the garment of Jesus (Matt. 9:20–22; Mark 5:25–34; Luke 8:43–48).

19. Galilee, the same day, the daughter of Jairus, a ruler of the synagogue in a Galilean town was raised from the dead. It was while He was on the way to perform this miracle, at the request of the girl's father, that the incident recorded under 18 took place (Luke 8:51–56; Matt. 9:23–26; Mark 5:35–43).

20. Nazareth, a few sick persons were restored to health by Jesus through the laying on of His hands. Both evangelists who mention this incident remark that the number of these miracles was comparatively small because of the unwillingness of the Nazarenes to believe (Matt. 13:58; Mark 6:5).

21. Galilee, the twelve Apostles, acting as the agents and heralds for Jesus, cast out demons and cured the sick by anointing them with oil as He had commanded them to do (Mark 6:13; Luke 9:6).

22. Near Bethsaida of Galilee, the first multiplication of loaves and fishes. Five loaves of bread and two fishes were sufficient to satisfy the hunger of a crowd of about five thousand men, not counting the women and children. Twelve baskets were filled with what remained of the food after this banquet (Matt. 14:15–21; Mark 6:35–44; Luke 9:12–17; John 6:1–15).

23. Near Bethsaida, healing of sick brought to Jesus (Matt. 14:14).

24. The Sea of Galilee, Jesus walks on the surface of the water. The storm which had agitated the boat in which His Apostles were sailing ceased when He came aboard. St. Matthew recounts that Peter asked for the favor of walking on the sea with Jesus. His petition was granted, but he began to sink when he lost confidence. Jesus rescued him (Matt. 14:22–32; Mark 6:45–52; John 16–21).

25. Genesareth, on the shore of the Sea of Galilee, Jesus healed all the infirm who were brought to Him (Matt. 14:34–36; Mark 6:53–56).

26. Jerusalem, at the pool called Probatica, the healing, on the Sabbath day of a man who had been an invalid for thirty-eight years. The Jewish leaders persecuted Jesus because of this act of mercy (John 5:1–18).

27. In the territory of Tyre and Sidon, north of Galilee on the eastern shore of the Mediterranean, the daughter of a Syro-Phoenician woman relieved of diabolical possession. Her mother begged this favor of Jesus who at first would not grant it because His mission was primarily to those of the Jewish race. The humble perseverance of the mother won both the commendation of the Master and the favor she petitioned (Matt. 15:21–28; Mark 7:24–30).

28. In the region of Decapolis, the "ten cities" occupied the territory east of the Jordan River and to the southeast of the Sea of Galilee, here Jesus cured many infirm. St. Matthew mentions that there were several lame, with mangled or withered hands, blind and deaf-mutes, as well as numerous other afflicted individuals. St. Mark tells in some detail the granting of speech and hearing to one deaf-mute. Jesus put His fingers into the ears of the sufferer, then, spitting, touched his tongue and gave the command "Open." St. Mark records that the newly relieved man spoke correctly (Matt. 15:29–31; Mark 7:31–37).

29. On the shore of the Sea of Galilee, probably near the site of the previous miracle, a second multiplication of loaves and fishes. This time there were seven loaves and a few small fish. A crowd that counted four thousand men, besides women and children were filled with this meal. Seven full baskets of leavings were gathered up (Matt. 15:32–39; Mark 8:1–10).

30. Bethsaida on the northern shore of the Sea of Galilee, sight was given to a blind man who had been brought to Jesus by the peo-

ple. St. Mark, the only evangelist to record this incident, states that, unlike the other works of Jesus, this healing was first partially then completely effected. Jesus took the man out of the town, spat on his eyes and then laid His hands upon the afflicted individual. When He asked whether the man could see, the beneficiary of the miracle informed Him that he could see "men like trees, walking." Then Jesus laid hands on him again and from this time on his sight was perfect (Mark 8:22–26).

31. On a high mountain, apart from the cities, a strong and constant tradition, which finds literary expression as early as the fourth-century writings of St. Cyril of Jerusalem fixes the site as Mount Tabor, a high elevation near and almost directly east of Nazareth and roughly southeast of Cana, the transfiguration of Jesus before Peter, James and John, the Apostles. This comforting vision was inseparably connected, in the minds of all three synoptic evangelists, with the profession of faith by St. Peter in Caesarea Philippi and the consequent prediction of the Passion and Resurrection which had taken place six days previously (Matt. 17:1–8; Mark 9:2–8; Luke 9:28–36).

32. In the midst of the crowd which had gathered at the foot of the mountain upon which Jesus had been transfigured, the relief and cure of a boy who was afflicted with epilepsy and possessed of a devil. The father of the boy recounted to Jesus that the Apostles who were left with the crowd had tried to cure the sufferer, but had failed. Jesus ascertained that the boy had been stricken since his infancy. The father gave evidence of his own faith. Jesus cast out the devil from the boy, who then gave every appearance dying. The Master then took him by the hand and restored him to his father, alive and well. Later He informed the Apostles that demons of this type could be cast out only after prayer and fasting. Furthermore, He stressed the ineffable power of faith (Matt. 17:14–20; Mark 9:14–29; Luke 9:37–43).

33. Jerusalem, near the temple in which the Jews had just attempted to stone Jesus, Jesus gave sight to a man born blind. This work was investigated by the Pharisees as described above in this chapter (John 9:1–38).

34. On the road from Capernaum, Jesus gave sight to two blind men. He touched their eyes after having asked whether they believed that He could cure them (Matt. 9:27–30).

35. Place not given, but this work is connected in the account of St. Matthew with the miracle mentioned above, the relief of a possessed man who was also stricken with dumbness. The Jews attributed this miracle to the power of the prince of devils (Matt 9:31–34).

36. Place not given, another distinct miracle in which relief was given to a man who was both deprived of speech and possessed of a devil. SS. Matthew and Luke describe this work, and St. Mark, while not mentioning the work itself, recounts the comment of the Jews which is also set down in the books of his fellow synoptic evangelists. The enemies of Jesus claimed that this miracle as the other wonders wrought by Jesus were done by the power of Beelzebub, prince of the devils (Matt. 12:22–24; Luke 11:14–16; see also Mark 3:22).

37. In the synagogue of an unnamed town, on the Sabbath day, the cure of a woman who had been an invalid for eighteen years. Jesus confuted the insolence of the synagogue-master who blamed Him for this work of mercy on the Sabbath (Luke 12:10–17).

38. In the house of one of the leaders among the Pharisees, on the Sabbath day, the cure of a man sick with the dropsy. The doctors of the law and the Pharisees refused to express their opinion on the legality of this cure when they were challenged by the Master (Luke 14:1–6).

39. In a town near the border between Galilee and Samaria, the cleansing of ten lepers. Jesus bade them to go and show themselves to the priest. The cure took place while they were on the way. One only of the ten, a Samaritan, returned to thank Jesus (Luke 17:12–19).

40. In Bethany, near Jerusalem, Jesus raised Lazarus, His friend, to life after he had been buried for four days. The body gave evidence of corruption. Jesus explicitly thanked His Father before the miracle took place for having heard Him always. He announced that the divine power was manifest for the sake of those who were present, that they might know that God had sent Him. It is the clearest possible claim to divine messengership, a claim substantiated by the miracle that followed. The Jews made this miracle the immediate occasion for their final and effective design to put Jesus to death (John 11:1–53).

41. Near Jericho, Jesus gave sight to two blind men. The second and third evangelists mention only one beneficiary, whom St. Mark calls Bar Timaeus (Matt. 20:29–34; Mark 10:46–52; Luke 18:35–49).

42. On the road from Bethany to Jerusalem, a fig tree which did not bear fruit withered and died the very day that Jesus cursed it for its idleness (Matt. 21:18–22; Mark 11:12–21).

43. In the garden called Gethsemani outside of Jerusalem, Jesus restored the ear of the servant Malchus, who had been struck with a sword by St. Peter. All four of the evangelists record the blow, but only St. Luke tells of the miraculous cure (Matt. 26:51; Mark 14:47; Luke 22:50, 51; John 18:10).

44. Gethsemani, that same night, the cohort which had come to arrest Jesus fell to the ground when He announced His identity (John 18:6).

45. Jerusalem, at the hour when Jesus died, the temple veil was torn, there was an earthquake. Tombs were opened and, after the Resurrection of Jesus, many of the dead appeared to the inhabitants of Jerusalem. A terrible and unnatural darkness covered the earth. These events were enough to convince the centurion who had been placed in charge of the execution that Jesus was a just man and the true Son of God (Matt. 27:51–54; Mark 15:38, 39; Luke 23:45–47).

46. The Holy Sepulcher, the first Easter, the triumphant Resurrection of Jesus (Matt. 28:1–10; Mark 16:1–11; Luke 24:1–9; John 26:1–18). The various appearances which Jesus made, even entering a room while the doors were closed (John 20:26) are rightly considered as manifestations of the Resurrection itself.

47. The shore of the Sea of Galilee, another miraculous draught of fishes (John 21:6).

48. The Hill near Bethany, the Ascension (Luke 24:50–52; Acts 1:9–11).

Such were the wonders which history attributes to Jesus of Nazareth. These works, perfectly attested as they are by the friends and enemies of Jesus, stand as perfect indications of the divine power. Individually or taken as a group they obviously surpass the natural capacity of any creature, actual or possible. Furthermore, they are in harmony with what we knew and can demonstrate rigidly about the divine nature itself.

14. The demonstrative force of the individual miracles. Considered individually, every one of these works was such that no creature could possibly perform them by natural power alone. We must not lose sight of the fact that a creature, as such, is a definitely limited being. One of the obvious manifestations of this limitation is the inclusion of the creature within the single plan of divine providence. Now we do not see that plan as it exists in the mind of God. However, we can know its accomplishment insofar as it applies to the fixed physical laws of the material universe. We know very well that there is a cycle that runs from birth to maturity and to death, and we can see that no agency within the created universe has the power to reverse this cycle. Furthermore, we know very well certain obvious qualities of inanimate nature.

The surface of a lake will not support a man who walks upon it. Earth and saliva will not immediately quicken an atrophied optic nerve. The sound of a man's voice will not restore a hand that is withered, nor will it call back to life a man whose body is already rotting in the grave. Most important of all, a man whose body has been torn by every torment known to the perverse ingenuity of his fellows and who has died cannot and will not return to life because he wishes to do so. Yet these precisely are the actions which Jesus of Nazareth performed.

We might search into the realm of absolute possibility and conjure up the figure of some creature to whom works of this type would be natural. Yet, by the most manifest and rigorous scientific demonstration we can show that such a figure would be merely a figment of the imagination. The basis of this effective proof is, of course, the accurate naturally attainable knowledge about God Himself. We can know God as the necessary First Cause of all the reality contained within the created universe. This First Cause is obviously the Lord and Master of all things distinct from Himself. As a result we shall find activity which is manifestly characteristic of God whenever we see operation which is clearly unlimited by any of the confines which circumscribe the effectiveness of created beings. Quite clearly the activity which Jesus of Nazareth performed was of this type. No creature actual or possible could act as the Lord of the universe any more than it could operate and exist as the necessary First Cause. Hence the works which we recognize as having been performed by Jesus of Nazareth are quite obviously operations of which God Himself is the principal Cause.

15. The cumulative power of the miracles as a motive of credibility. We see this truth very clearly first of all when we consider the works of Jesus altogether. There was no type of creature with which He was not perfectly at home and with respect to which He was not absolutely the Master. He showed His mastery over the inanimate matter which abounds in the universe by walking on the water in the sight of all. His control over vegetative life was manifest in the destruction of the fig tree. He made sensible manifestation of His power over the realm of pure spirits by casting out innumerable demons that infected and possessed the souls of so many among His countrymen.

Most frequently, however, we find Him working miraculous effects upon the human body itself. At times, as in the cure of St. Peter's mother-in-law, He produced an effect which might naturally have been brought about even in this particular subject, but which most certainly could never have been produced naturally in the manner in which He brought it into being. A person may very well recover from an ordinary fever, but only an individual who controls the order of nature itself can cure a fever merely by commanding it to leave the one who is ill[37] or by taking the hand of the sufferer."[38]

Most frequent, and for that matter the most spectacular among the miracles Jesus performed were those in which He brought about effects which nature itself is able to produce, but which it manifestly could not have caused in those definite subjects upon which He worked. Nature, or to be more concrete, a created being by its natural power can produce the act of vision, but most obviously it can never produce this act in an eye that has been darkened since birth. The power of created beings is sufficient to produce the acts of life, but certainly these acts will not be brought about in a body already moldering in the grave. In His activity, Jesus of Nazareth showed an unlimited ability to perform works of this type. He manifestly cured diseases like leprosy which are incurable. He gave not mere prolongation of life, but absolute freedom from the disfiguring characteristic of the disease itself. He gave sight to the blind, speech to the dumb, hearing to the deaf, and the power of locomotion to those who had

---

37 E.g., Luke 4:39.
38 E.g., Matt. 8:15; Mark 1:31.

lost the use of their legs. His accomplishments were manifestly those of One who is not in any way limited by the physical laws themselves, but who has control of the material universe, as the omnipotent Lord and Creator of that universe. Thus they were manifestly works beyond the natural power of any creature, actual or possible, acts freely performed by an infinitely wise and veracious God.

The risen Jesus clearly showed operations which physical nature is entirely unable to produce in any subject whatsoever. For example the Apostles gathered in the upper chamber at Jerusalem could see that Jesus entered a room that was entirely closed off. This necessitated, on His part, a miraculous compenetration of matter. His body passed through solid wall without disturbing the substance of which the wall was composed. Likewise, He left the sepulcher in the garden without moving the stone which sealed it. These were manifestly works which could not be performed other than with the divine power.

16. The miracles of Jesus and the divine attributes. Moreover, all of these miracles were eminently consonant with what we know naturally about the divine attributes. God is infinite perfection and goodness. As a result we would at once recognize as spurious a work attributed to Him, when that work resulted in real harm, and particularly in moral ruin to the individuals upon whom it was accomplished. Judged by this standard the works of Jesus are clearly in harmony with the divine nature. The overwhelming majority of His miracles gave life, health, and bodily integrity to men. Demons who impelled men toward degrading activity were cast out so that the resultant conduct of these individuals was good. In no case was a person harmed by these miracles. As a matter of fact, Jesus firmly refused to make use of the divine power which He enjoyed in order to destroy His enemies.[39]

God is infinitely Holy. As a result His works would not be performed like tricks which conjurers do on the stage to amuse a group of onlookers. Jesus of Nazareth upheld the divine dignity in the performance of His works. We know that He refused to gratify the curiosity of the Nazarenes who wished to see Him duplicate in their city the wonders He had previously wrought in Capernaum.[40]

---

39 Matt. 26:53.
40 Luke 4:23.

The men who had witnessed the first multiplication of the loaves and fishes had the temerity to ask Him for another sign by which they could recognize the reality of His mission and reasonably believe the doctrine He propounded, in this instance the sublime teaching on the Eucharist. He was unwilling, of course, to accede to a request based upon hardness of heart and mere curiosity.[41] He would not make the ostentatious entry into Jerusalem performing idle wonders as His relatives suggested.[42] The fiery sons of Zebedee could not persuade Him to use His power to destroy the Samaritan village which refused them hospitality.[43] When the Pharisees and the sadducees, both knowing His deeds very well by reason of their constant spying upon His movements, asked Him for a sign from heaven, He would not accede to their request and flatter their vanity, but instead gave them the somber prediction of His own death and the glorious prophecy of His own Resurrection.[44] Herod was curious about Jesus, and wished to witness a miracle, but Jesus would not oblige him even while He stood before the tetrarch's tribunal.[45] As He hung on the cross of Calvary, the enemies who had encompassed Him taunted Him and challenged Him to come down. He did not prostitute His wondrous power to answer these blasphemous insults. Manifestly, then, there is nothing in the accounts of these miracles to justify the least reasonable doubt about their character as divine works.

17. Jesus appealed to His miracles as motives of credibility. However, we see the full probative force of the miracles wrought by Jesus only when we realize that He appealed explicitly to them as evidence for the credibility of that teaching which He proposed to the world as a message from God. Here again the power of the demonstration depends upon an accurate natural concept of God Himself. The omnipotent Creator, who is infinitely just and all seeing, could not affix what is manifestly His seal of approval on a spurious divine revelation. Even an honest man would refuse to affix his signature to a statement he knew to be false. Because it is historically

---

41 John 6:30.
42 John 7:2–8.
43 Luke 9:54–55.
44 Matt. 12:38–41; 16:1–4; Mark 7:11–12.
45 Luke 23:8–11.

certain that Jesus performed real miracles, and because these signs were given precisely as a seal of divine approbation that His doctrine was from God, we have perfect and unwavering certitude that this teaching is credible for what it claims to be.

The four canonical gospels abound in statements showing that Jesus appealed to miracles and actually performed them precisely to demonstrate His position as a messenger from God. He cured the paralytic in Capernaum in order that His hearers might know "that the Son of man hath power on earth to forgive sins."[46] Obviously in this case Jesus claimed for Himself a divine power. The miracle was testimony that He could offer a divine act to show that He was empowered to do what only God can accomplish, a forgiveness of sin in His own name. But the greater dignity includes the lesser. Showing Himself as a divine Person, Jesus demonstrated that it was reasonable to accept the message He proposed as divine revelation, and to hold it with the certainty of divine faith.

When the disciples of John the Baptist came to Him for a definitive and official declaration of His messianic character, and consequently for His office as the bearer of a message from the living God, Jesus pointed explicitly to His miracles. "Now when John had heard in prison the works of Christ, sending two of his disciples, he said to Him: Art Thou He that art to come, or look we for another? And Jesus making answer to them: Go and relate to John what you have heard and seen. The blind see, the lame walk, the lepers are cleansed, the deaf hear, the dead rise again, the poor have the gospel preached to them. And blessed is he that shall not be scandalized in Me."[47] In this instance Jesus appealed to the miracles He had performed, precisely insofar as these had been *prophesied* by Isaiah and insofar as they were joined with and confirmed by the manifest sanctity of His conduct. Seen in this light they offer man absolutely incontrovertible evidence that God approved with His own signature the claim that the message of Jesus was divine.

A very practical way in which Jesus attached miraculous works as evidences of credibility to His own doctrine is to be found in His granting of miraculous powers to the Apostles. He chose these men

---

46 Matt. 9:6–7; Mark 2:11–12; Luke 5:24–25.
47 Matt. 11:2–6; Luke 7:18–23.

that "They might be with Him: and that He should send them to preach. And He gave them power to heal sicknesses and to cast out devils."[48] The Apostles exercised that power both before and after the death of their Master.[49] Furthermore, He allowed others to perform miracles in His name, even though these were not members of the apostolic college.[50] The seventy-two disciples received a like commission and attained the same results.[51] Jesus then deemed the miracles as a requisite seal for His own doctrine. His control of the divine power was complete. He could effectively grant men the authority to perform these miraculous works as His agents. The actual performance of these wonders testified to the reality of His control and the genuineness of His claim.

Before the Jewish leaders who persecuted and hated Him, alleging as a motive the puerile excuse that He performed manifestly divine acts on the Sabbath, Jesus stated clearly that His miracles demonstrated that He was a messenger from God, and that consequently the doctrine He preached was actually divine revelation which men were bound to accept with the certain assent of divine faith. He added that the power to perform these miracles was His own, as the natural and consubstantial Son of the living God. Unquestionably a just God could not have allowed further miracles to be performed unless the doctrine as a whole, and this claim of divine Sonship in particular, had been really a truth communicated by God to man. The account in the gospel according to St. John follows the story about the cure of the sick man by the pool called Probatica. The man had reported to the Jews that Jesus was the One who had cured him. "Therefore did the Jews persecute Jesus because He did these things on the Sabbath. But Jesus answered them: My Father worketh until now, and I work. Hereupon, therefore, the Jews sought the more to kill Him: because He did not only break the Sabbath, but also said God was His Father, making Himself equal to God. Then Jesus answered and said to them: Amen, amen, I say unto you: the Son cannot do anything of Himself, but what He seeth the Father doing: for what things soever

---

48 Mark 3:14, 15. Cf. Matt. 10:1; Mark 6:7; Luke 9:1, 2.
49 Matt. 11:1; Mark 6:12; Luke 9:6; Acts 3:6–8.
50 Mark 9:38–40; Luke 9:49, 50.
51 Luke 10:9, 17.

He doth, these the Son also doth in like manner. For the Father loveth the Son, and showeth Him all things which Himself doth: and greater works than these will He show Him, that you may wonder. For as the Father raiseth up the dead and giveth life: so the Son also giveth life to whom He will."[52] The meaning is clear. Jesus acknowledges His own work as a true miracle and thus as a genuine motive of credibility. He asserts that the work is done by His own power.

However, in this same discourse, Jesus showed that His own teaching had been manifested as credible by works of sufficient clarity. "The works which the Father hath given Me to perfect: the works themselves which I do, give testimony of Me that the Father hath sent Me: And the Father Himself who hath sent Me, hath given testimony of Me."[53] The composite statement is clear. The actual miracles which He had performed up to that time are alleged as sufficient evidence for the divine origin of His teaching. At the same time He promised that other and greater works, likewise authentic and certain signs of divine revelation, would follow. There could be no more perfect and effective joining of an actual divine signature to a doctrine than that which was manifested here by Jesus of Nazareth.

We find the same conclusion, that His miracles were meant to indicate the divine origin of the doctrine of Jesus in His triumphant refutation of those Pharisees and scribes who had attributed His casting out of devils to the power of Beelzebub. "But if I by the Spirit of God cast out devils, then is the kingdom of God come upon you."[54] He had shown that His work was directly opposed to that of the powers of evil. The prince of devils would not destroy his own achievements. Furthermore, the effect produced by the exorcisms of Jesus was similar to that brought about by those Jews who used the name of the living God to cast out devils. The conclusion was inescapable. His work was a divine operation. The implication was sure also. Since the miracle was performed by One who claimed to present a divine message, the message was authentic and credible. The kingdom had arrived because its Leader and Prince was on the scene. Furthermore, their rejection of His miracle was, according to

---

52 John 5:16–21.
53 John 5:36, 37.
54 Matt. 12:28; Luke 11:20.

Jesus, a sin against that Spirit of God by whose power the devils were cast out.[55] The miracle, then, was considered as a divine sign by Jesus.

Again He asserted that He, by virtue of His Resurrection, would be a sign to mankind. He claimed to be a greater and more effective sign than Jonah had been by reason of his miracle, or Solomon because of his wisdom. The effect of these lesser signs had been the belief of those men to whom they were directed. Jesus bitterly blamed the men of His own generation for their unwillingness to believe Him.[56] Here we have the clearest indication that Jesus considered His miracles as true motives of credibility and appealed to them as such.

At the Feast of the Dedication in Jerusalem, in the Temple, on Solomon's porch "The Jews therefore came round about Him, and said to Him: How long dost Thou hold our souls in suspense? If Thou be the Christ, tell us plainly. Jesus answered them: I speak to you, and you believe Me not. The works that I do in the name of My Father, they give testimony of Me."[57] The works to which Jesus refers are the miracles themselves. Explicitly He appeals to them as indicating His divine mission.

However, by far the most striking appeal recorded as having been made by Jesus to an individual miracle as a motive of credibility is found in the account of the raising of Lazarus from the dead. Standing in the midst of a crowd before the tomb in which the body of His friend was already rotting away, Jesus thus spoke to God. "Father, I give Thee thanks that Thou hast heard Me. And I knew that Thou hearest Me always, but because of the people who stand about have I said it: that they may believe that Thou hast sent Me."[58] He invoked and used the divine power and performed the miracle precisely so that men might recognize Him as an envoy sent from God and might thus be led to accept His teaching as divine revelation.

Finally, Jesus asserted, in that solemn discourse that followed the Last Supper, that the evidence of His works was so clear and unique that those who were aware of them and still refused to accept His teaching were guilty of serious moral fault. The words resume all the

---

55 Matt. 12:31, 32; Mark 3:28, 29; Luke 12:10.
56 Matt. 12:39–42. Cf. Luke 11:29, 32.
57 John 10:24–25.
58 John 11:41–42.

The Testimony of Miracles

subsequent theological teaching on the demonstrative force of Jesus' miracles. "If I had not done among them works that no other man hath done, they would not have sin. But now they have both seen and hated both Me and My Father."[59] The words echo the terrible warning He gave to the Pharisees before that time. "Therefore I said to you that you shall die in your sins; for if you believe not that I am He, you shall die in your sin."[60] The sin of the Jews consisted in rejecting the manifest testimony of God in the miracles of Jesus, as He told His enemies after they had blasphemously refused to believe after they had seen the evidence in the cure of the man born blind. "Jesus saith to them: If you were blind, you should not have sin. But now you say: We see. Your sin remaineth."[61]

The miracles of Jesus have a tremendous cumulative force as motives of credibility. As He declared they were truly works such as no other man has ever done in all history. Long ago Arnobius[62] remarked that the miracles of Jesus surpassed in number all of the wonders attributed to the various pagan gods. Performed in every field of reality, innumerable, foretold in prophecy, and joined with His manifestly supernatural goodness and wisdom, the miracles of Jesus offer not some proof, but actual overwhelming evidence that His teaching is a message from God which all men are bound to accept as divine revelation. Incontestably they demonstrate the genuineness of the divine good He offered to mankind.

---

59 John 15:24.
60 John 8:24.
61 John 9:41.
62 Arnobius, *Adversus Nationes*, Book 1, Ch. 43.

Chapter 16

THE RESURRECTION

1. Supreme moment of the Resurrection as a criterion of revelation. Jesus of Nazareth died. He was buried. He lived and walked again. This incontrovertible truth constitutes the supreme evidence for the reliability of His teaching as divine revelation. So intimately is the fact of the Resurrection bound up with the credibility of divine faith, that St. Paul could state that the acceptability of the Christian message as such depended upon it. "But if there be no resurrection of the dead, then Christ is not risen again. And if Christ be not risen again, then is our preaching vain, and your faith is also vain. Yea, and we are found false witnesses of God: because we have given testimony against God, that He hath raised up Christ, whom He had not raised up, if the dead rise not again. For if the dead rise not again, neither is Christ risen again. And if Christ be not risen again, your faith is vain, for you are yet in your sins. Then they also that are fallen asleep in Christ are perished. If in this life only we have hope in Christ, we are of all men most miserable. But now Christ is risen from the dead, then first fruit of them that sleep."[1]

Since the Resurrection of Jesus from the dead occupies this position of unique importance as a motive of credibility, it is essential that scientific apologetics should take special cognizance of the naturally available information about it. We must first examine the historical evidence about the reality of the death, the burial, and the Resurrection. Then we can analyze this datum and understand exactly why it constitutes the outstanding seal of God's approval for the claim that the message of Jesus was actually divine revelation.

---

1 1 Cor 15:13–20.

2. The gospel accounts of the Resurrection. The most important documents on this matter are the four canonical gospels. We shall examine, side by side, the independent accounts given by the evangelists of those events which were of primary importance in world history.

St. Matthew 27	St. Mark 15	St. Luke 23	St. John 19
50. And Jesus again crying with a loud voice, yielded up the ghost.	37. And Jesus having cried out with a loud voice, gave up the ghost.	46. And Jesus crying with a loud voice, said: Father into Thy hands I commend My spirit. And saying this, He gave up the ghost.	30. Jesus therefore when He had taken the vinegar, said: It is consummated. And bowing His head, He gave up the ghost.
51. And behold the veil of the temple was rent in two from the top even to the bottom; and the earth quaked, and the rocks were rent.	38. And the veil of the temple was rent in two from the top to the bottom.	45. And the sun was darkened and the veil of the temple was rent in the midst.	
52. And the graves were opened: and many bodies of the saints that had slept, arose.			
53. And the coming out of the tombs after His resurrection, they came into the holy city and appeared to many.			
54. Now the centurion and they that were with him watching Jesus, having seen the earthquake and the things that were done, were sore afraid, saying: Indeed this was the Son of God.	39. And the centurion who stood over against Him, seeing that crying out in this manner He had given up the ghost, said: Indeed this man was the Son of God.	47. Now the centurion seeing what was done, glorified God, saying, Indeed this was a just man.	

St. Matthew 27	St. Mark 15	St. Luke 23	St. John 19
55. And there were many women afar off who had followed Jesus from Galilee, ministering unto Him:	40. And there were also women looking on afar off: among whom was Mary Magdalen, and Mary the Mother of James the less, and of Joseph and Salome.	48. And all the multitude of them that were come together to that sight, and saw the things that were done, returned striking their breasts.	
56. Among whom was Mary Magdalen, and Mary the mother of James and Joseph, and the mother of the sons of Zebedee.	41. Who also when He was in Galilee, followed Him and ministered to Him, and many other women that came up with Him to Jerusalem.	49. And all His acquaintance, and the women that Had followed Him from Galilee, stood afar off beholding these things.	
	42. And when evening was now come (because it was the Parasceve, that is the day before the sabbath).		31. Then the Jews (because it was the Parasceve), that the bodies might not remain upon the cross on the sabbath day (for that was a great sabbath day) besought Pilate that their legs might be broken, and that they might be taken away.

The Resurrection

St. Matthew 27	St. Mark 15	St. Luke 23	St. John 19
			32. The soldiers therefore came: and they broke the legs of the first, and of the other that was crucified with Him.
			33. But after they were come to Jesus, when they saw that He was already dead, they did not break His legs.
			34. But one of the soldiers with a spear opened His side, and immediately there came out blood and water.
			35. And he that saw it hath given testimony: and his testimony is true. And he knoweth that he saith true: that you also may believe.
			36. For these things were done that the Scripture might be fulfilled: You shall not break a bone of Him.
			37. And again another Scripture saith: They shall look on Him whom they pierced.

St. Matthew 27	St. Mark 15	St. Luke 23	St. John 19
57. And when it was evening, there came a certain rich man of Arimathea, named Joseph, who also himself was a disciple of Jesus. 58. He went to Pilate and asked the body of Jesus. Then Pilate commanded that the body should be delivered.	43. Joseph of Arimathea a noble counsellor, who was also himself looking for the kingdom of God, came and went in boldly to Pilate and begged the body of Jesus. 44. But Pilate wondered that He should already be dead. And sending for the centurion, he asked him if He were already dead. 45. And when he had understood it by the centurion, he gave the body to Joseph.	50. And behold there was a man named Joseph, who was a counsellor, a good and just man. 51. (The same had not consented to their counsel and doings); of Arimathea, a city of Judea; who also himself looked for the kingdom of God. 52. This man went to Pilate, and begged the body of Jesus.	38. And after these things Joseph of Arimathea (because he was a disciple of Jesus, but secretly for fear of the Jews) besought Pilate that he might take away the body of Jesus. And Pilate gave leave. He came therefore and took away the body of Jesus. 39. And Nicodemus also came, he who at first came to Jesus by night, bringing a mixture of myrrh and aloes, about a hundred pounds weight.
59. And Joseph taking the body, wrapped it up in a clean linen cloth; 60. And laid it in his own	46. And Joseph buying fine linen and taking Him down, wrapped Him up in the fine linen and laid	53. And taking Him down, he wrapped Him in fine linen, and laid Him in a sepulcher that was hewed	40. They took therefore the body of Jesus, and bound it in linen cloths with the spices, as the

The Resurrection

St. Matthew 27	St. Mark 15	St. Luke 23	St. John 19
new monument, which he had hewed out in a rock. And he rolled a great stone to the door of the monument and went his way.	Him in a sepulcher which was hewed out of a rock, and he rolled a stone to the door of the sepulcher.	in stone, wherein never yet any man had been laid.	manner of the Jews is to bury. 41. Now there was in the place where He was crucified a garden: and in the garden a new sepulcher wherein no man had yet been laid.
		54. And it was the day of the Parasceve, and the sabbath drew on.	42. There, therefore, because of the Parasceve of the Jews, they laid Jesus, because the sepulcher was nigh at hand.
61. And there was there Mary Magdalen and the other Mary sitting over against the sepulcher.	47. And Mary Magdalen and Mary the mother of Joseph beheld where He was laid.	55. And the women that were come with Him from Galilee, following after, saw the sepulcher, and how the body was laid.	
62. And the next day, which followed the day of preparation, the chief priest and the Pharisees came together to Pilate,			
63. Saying: Sir, we have remembered that that seducer said, while He was yet alive: After three days I will rise again.			

St. Matthew 27	St. Mark 15	St. Luke 23	St. John 19
64. Command therefore the sepulcher to be guarded until the third day; lest perhaps His disciples come and steal Him away, and say to the people He is risen from the dead: and the last error shall be worse than the first.			
65. Pilate said to them: You have a guard: Go, guard it as you know.			
66. And they departing, made the sepulcher sure, sealing the stone, and setting guards.			

St. Matthew 28	St. Mark 16	St. Luke 24	St. John 20
1. And in the end of the sabbath when it began to dawn towards the first day of the week, came Mary Magdalen, and the other Mary to see the sepulcher.	1. And when the sabbath was past, Mary Magdalen and Mary the mother of James, and Salome, brought sweet spices, that coming they might anoint Jesus.	1. And on the first day of the week, very early in the morning they came to the sepulcher, bringing the spices which they had prepared.	1. And on the first day of the week, Mary Magdalen cometh early, when it was yet dark, unto the sepulcher.
	2. And very early in the morning, the first day of the week, they came to		

The Resurrection

St. Matthew 28	St. Mark 16	St. Luke 24	St. John 20
2. And behold there was a great earthquake. For an angel of the Lord descended from heaven: and coming, rolled back the stone and sat upon it. 3. And his countenance was as lightning, and his raiment as snow. 4. And for fear of him the guards were struck with terror, and became as dead men. 5. And the angel answering said to the women: Fear not you: for I know that you seek Jesus who was crucified. 6. He is not here: for He is risen, as He said. Come, and see the place where the Lord was laid.	the sepulcher, the sun being now risen. 3. And they said one to another: Who shall roll us back the stone from the door of the sepulcher? 4. And looking they saw the stone rolled back. For it was very great. 5. And entering into the sepulcher, they saw a young man sitting on the right side, clothed with a white robe: and they were astonished. 6. Who saith to them: Be not affrighted: You seek Jesus of Nazareth who was crucified. He is not here, behold the place where they laid Him. 7. But go, tell His disciples and Peter that He goeth before you into Galilee: there you shall see Him as He told you.	2. And they found the stone rolled back from the sepulcher. 3. And going in, they found not the body of the Lord Jesus. 4. And it came to pass, as they were astonished in their mind at this, behold two men stood by them in shining apparel. 5. And as they were afraid and bowed down their countenance towards the ground, they said unto them: Why seek you the living with the dead? 6. He is not here, but is risen: Remember how He spoke	

St. Matthew 28	St. Mark 16	St. Luke 24	St. John 20
7. And going quickly tell ye His disciples that He is risen: and behold He will go before you into Galilee: there you shall see Him. Lo, I have foretold it to you. 8. And they went out quickly from the sepulcher, with fear and great joy, running to tell His disciples. 9. And behold, Jesus met them, saying; All hail. But they came up and took hold of His feet, and adored Him. 10. Then Jesus said to them: Fear not, go, tell my brethren that they go into Galilee, there they shall see Me. 11. Who when they were departed, behold some of the guards came into the city, and told the chief	8. But they going out fled from the sepulcher: for a trembling and fear had seized them: and they said nothing to any man: for they were afraid.	unto you, when He was yet in Galilee, 7. Saying: The Son of man must be delivered into the hands of sinful men, and be crucified, and the third day rise again. 8. And they remembered his words. And going back from the sepulcher, they told all these things to the eleven and to all the rest.	

The Resurrection

St. Matthew 28	St. Mark 16	St. Luke 24	St. John 20
priests all things that had been done. 12. And they being assembled together with the ancients taking counsel, gave a great sum of money to the soldiers, 13. Saying: Say you, His disciples came by night and stole Him away when we were asleep. 14. And if the governor shall hear of this, we will persuade him, and secure you. 15. So they, taking the money, did as they were taught: And this word was spread abroad among the Jews even unto this day.	9. But He rising early the first day of the week, appeared first to Mary Magdalen, out of whom He had cast seven devils. 10. She went out and told	9. And going back from the sepulcher, they told all these things to the eleven: and to all the rest. 10. And it was Mary Magdalen, and Joanna, and Mary of	2. She ran therefore and cometh to Simon Peter and to the other disciple whom Jesus loved, and said to them: They have taken away the Lord out of the sepulcher, and we

St. Matthew 28	St. Mark 16	St. Luke 24	St. John 20
	them that had been with Him, who were mourning and weeping. 11. And they hearing that He was alive and had been seen by her, did not believe.	James, and the other women that were with them who told these things to the apostles. 11. And these words seemed to them as idle tales, and they did not believe them. 12. But Peter rising up ran to the sepulcher: and stooping down he saw the linen cloths laid by themselves, and went away wondering in himself at that which was come to pass.	know not where they laid Him. 3. Peter therefore went out and that other disciple, and they came to the sepulcher. 4. And they both ran together, and that other disciple did outrun Peter, and came first to the sepulcher. 5. And when he stooped down, he saw the linen cloths lying, but yet he went not in. 6. Then cometh Simon Peter following him, and went into the sepulcher and saw the linen cloths lying. 7. And the napkin, that had been about His head, not lying with the linen cloths, but apart, wrapt up in one place.

The Resurrection

St. Matthew 28	St. Mark 16	St. Luke 24	St. John 20
			8. Then that other disciple also went in, who came first to the sepulcher: and he saw and believed.
9. For as yet they knew not the Scripture, that He must rise again from the dead.
10. The disciples therefore departed to their home.

3. Details of the appearance to Mary Magdalen.

John 20:11–18 (cf. Mark 16:9). 11. But Mary stood at the sepulcher without, weeping. Now as she was weeping, she stooped down, and looked into the sepulcher. 12. And she saw two angels in white sitting, one at the head and one at the feet, where the body of Jesus had been laid. 13. They say to her: Woman, why weepest thou? She saith to them: Because they have taken away my Lord: and I know not where they have laid Him. 14. When she had thus said, she turned herself back, and saw Jesus standing: and she knew not that it was Jesus. 15. Jesus saith to her: Woman, why weepest thou? Whom seekest thou? She thinking that it was the gardener saith to Him: Sir, if thou hast taken Him hence, tell me where thou hast laid Him: and I will take Him away. 16. Jesus saith to her: Mary. She turning saith to Him: Rabboni (which is to say, Master). 17. Jesus saith to her: Do not touch Me, for I am not yet ascended to My Father. But go to My Brethren and say to them: I ascend to My Father and to your Father, to My God and to your God. 18. Mary Magdalen cometh and telleth the disciples: I have seen the Lord, and these things He said to me.

4. The appearance to the Disciples at Emmaus.

St. Mark 16	St. Luke 24
12. And after that He appeared in another shape to two of them walking, as they were going into the country. 13. And they going told it to the rest: neither did they believe them.	13. And behold, two of them went that same day to a town which was sixty furlongs from Jerusalem, named Emmaus. 14. And they talked together of all these things which had

happened. 15. And it came to pass that while they talked, and reasoned with themselves: Jesus Himself also drawing near went with them. 16. But their eyes were held that they should not know Him, 17. And He said to them: What are these discourses that you hold, one with another as you walk, and are sad? 18. And one of them, whose name was Cleophas, answering, said to Him: Art Thou only a stranger in Jerusalem, and hast not known the things that have been done there in these days? 19. To whom He said: What things? And they said: Concerning Jesus of Nazareth, who was a Prophet, mighty in work and word before God and all the people. 20. And how our

chief priests and princes delivered Him to be condemned to death, and crucified Him. 21. But we hoped that it was He that should have redeemed Israel. And now besides all this, today is the third day since these things were done. 22. Yes, and certain women also of our company affrightened us, who, before it was light, were at the sepulcher, 23. And not finding His body came, saying that they had also seen a vision of angels, who say that He is alive. 24. And some of our people went to the sepulcher, and found it so as the women had said, but Him they found not. 25. Then He said to them: O foolish and slow of heart to believe in all things which the prophets have spoken! 26. Ought not Christ to have suffered these things, and so to enter into His glory? 27. And beginning at Moses and all the prophets, He expounded to them in all the scriptures the things that were concerning Him. 28. And they drew nigh to the town whither they were going: and He made as though He would go farther. 29. But they constrained Him, saying: Stay with us, because it is towards evening, and the day is now far spent. And He went in with them. 30. And it came to pass, whilst He was at table with them, He took bread, and blessed, and broke, and gave to them. 31. And their eyes were opened, and they knew Him: And He vanished out of their sight. 32. And they said one to the other: Was not our heart burning within us, whilst He spoke in the way, and opened to us the scriptures? 33. And rising up the same hour they went back to Jerusalem: and they found the eleven gathered together, and those that were with them, 34. Saying; The Lord is risen indeed, and hath appeared to Simon. 35. And they told what things were done in the way: and how they knew Him in the breaking of bread.

5. The appearance to the disciples in the absence of Thomas.

St. Luke 24	St. John 20
36. Now whilst they were speaking these things, Jesus stood in the midst of them and saith to them: Peace be to you: it is I. Fear not. 37. But they being troubled and frighted, supposed that they	19. Now when it was late that same day, the first of the week: and the doors were shut, where the disciples were gathered together for fear of the Jews, Jesus came, and stood in the midst,

saw a spirit. 38. And He said to them: Why are you troubled, and why do thoughts arise in your hearts? 39. See My hands and feet, that it is Myself: handle and see: for a spirit hath not flesh and bones as you see Me to have. 40. And when He had said this, He showed them His hands and feet. 41. But while they yet believed not and wondered for joy, He said: Have you here any thing to eat? 42. And they offered Him a piece of a broiled fish, and a honeycomb. 43. And when He had eaten before them, taking the remains, He gave to them.

and said to them: Peace be to you. 20. And when He had said this, He showed them His hands and His side. The disciples therefore were glad, when they saw the Lord. 21. He said therefore to them again: Peace be to you. As the Father hath sent Me. I also send you. 22. When He had said this, He breathed on them: and He said to them: Receive ye the Holy Ghost: 23. Whose sins you shall forgive, they are forgiven them: and whose sins you shall retain, they are retained.

6. The appearance to the eleven in the presence of Thomas.

St. Mark 16	St. John 20
14. At length eleven He appeared to them as they were at table: and He upbraided them with their incredulity and hardness of heart: because they did not believe who had seen Him risen again.	24. Now Thomas, one of the twelve who is called Didymus, was not with them when Jesus came. 25. The other disciples therefore said to him: We have seen the Lord. But he said to them: Except I shall see in His hands the print of the nails, and put my hand into His side, I will not believe. 26. And after eight days, again His disciples were within:

and Thomas with them. Jesus cometh, the doors being shut, and stood in the midst, and said: Peace be to you. 27. Then He saith to Thomas: Put in thy finger hither and see My hands, and bring hither thy hand, and put it into My side: and be not faithless but believing. 28. Thomas answered, and said to Him: My Lord and my God. 29. Jesus saith to Him: Because thou hast seen Me, Thomas, thou hast believed. Blessed are they that have not seen, and have believed.

7. The appearance on the shore of Galilee.

St. John 21. 1. After this Jesus showed Himself again to the disciples at the sea of Tiberias. And He showed Himself after this manner. 2. There were together Simon Peter, and Thomas who is called Didymus, and Nathanael who was of Cana in Galilee, and the sons of Zebedee, and two others of His disciples. 3. Simon Peter said to them: I go a fishing. They say to him: We also come with thee. And they went forth and entered into the ship: and that night they caught nothing. 4. But when the morning was come, Jesus stood on the shore: yet the disciples knew not that it was Jesus. 5. Jesus therefore said to them: Children have you any meat? They answered Him: No. 6. He saith to them: Cast the net on the right side of the ship: and you shall find. They cast therefore: and now they were not able to draw it for the multitude of fishes. 7. That disciple therefore whom Jesus loved, said to Peter: It is the Lord. Simon Peter when he heard that it was the Lord, girt his coat about him (for he was naked) and cast himself into the sea. 8. But the other disciples came in the ship: (for they were not far from the land, but as it were two hundred cubits) dragging the net with the fishes. 9. As soon then as they came to land, they saw hot coals lying, and a fish laid thereon, and bread. 10. Jesus saith to them: Bring hither of the fishes which you have now caught. 11. Simon Peter went up, and drew the net to land, full of great fishes, one hundred fifty-three. And although there were so many, the net was not broken. 12. Jesus saith to them: Come and dine. And none of them who were at meat durst ask Him: Who art Thou? knowing it was the Lord. 13. And Jesus cometh and taketh bread and giveth them, and fish in like manner. 14. This is now the third time that Jesus was manifested to His disciples, after He was risen from the dead. 15. When therefore they had dined, Jesus saith to Simon Peter, Simon son of John, lovest thou Me more than these? He saith to Him: Yea, Lord, Thou knowest that I love Thee. He saith to him: Feed My lambs. 16. He saith to him again: Simon, son of John, lovest thou Me? He saith to Him: Yea, Lord, Thou knowest that I love Thee. He saith to him: Feed My lambs. 17. He saith to him the third time: Simon, son of John, lovest thou Me? Peter was grieved because He had said to him the third time: Lovest thou Me? And he said to Him: Lord, thou knowest all things; thou knowest that I love Thee. He said to him: Feed My sheep. 18. Amen, amen I say to thee: When thou wast younger, thou didst gird thyself, and didst walk where thou wouldst: but when thou shalt be old, thou shalt stretch forth thy hands, and another shall gird thee, and lead thee whither thou wouldst not. 19. And this He said, signifying by what death he should glorify God. And when He had said this, He saith to him: Follow Me. 20. Peter turning about, saw that disciple whom Jesus loved, following, who also leaned on His breast at supper, and said: Lord, who is he that shall betray Thee? 21. Him therefore when Peter had seen, he saith to Jesus: Lord and what shall this man do? 22. Jesus saith to him: So I will have him to remain till I come, what is it to thee? Follow thou Me. 23. This saying therefore went abroad among the brethren, that that disciple should not die. And Jesus did not say to him: He should not die; but: So I will have him to remain until I come, what is it to thee?

8. The appearance on a hill in Galilee.

St. Matthew 28	St. Mark 16
16. And the eleven disciples went into Galilee, unto the mountain where Jesus had appointed them. 17. And seeing Him they adored, but some doubted. 18. And Jesus, coming, spoke to them, saying: All power is given to Me in heaven and in earth: 19. Going therefore teach ye all nations: baptizing them in the name of the Father, and of the Son, and of the Holy Ghost: 20. Teaching them to observe all things whatsoever I have commanded you. And behold I am with you all days, even to the consummation of the world.	15. And He said to them: Go ye, into the whole world, and preach the gospel to every creature. 16. He that believeth and is baptized, shall be saved: but he that believeth not, shall be condemned. 17. And these signs shall follow them that believe. In My name they shall cast out devils. They shall speak with new tongues. 18. They shall take up serpents. And if they shall drink any deadly thing, it shall not hurt them. They shall lay their hands upon the sick, and they shall recover.

9. The last appearance in Jerusalem.

St. Luke 24. 44. And He said to them: These are the words which I spoke to you while I was yet with you, that all things must needs be fulfilled which are written in the law of Moses and in the Prophets and in the Psalms concerning Me. 45. Then He opened their understanding, that they might understand the scriptures. 46. Then He said to them: Thus it is written, and thus it behooved Christ to suffer, and to rise again from the dead the third day. 47. And that penance and remission of sins should be preached in His name unto all nations beginning at Jerusalem. 48. And you are witnesses of these things. 49. And I send the promise of My Father upon you; but stay you in the city till you be endued with power from on high.

10. The ascension.

St. Mark 16

19. And the Lord Jesus, after He had spoken to them, was taken up into heaven, and sitteth on the right hand of God. 20. But they, going forth, preached everywhere, the Lord working withal, and confirming the word with signs that followed.

St. Luke 24

50. And He led them out as far as Bethania, and lifting up His hands, He blessed them. 51. And it came to pass whilst He blessed them, He departed from them, and was carried up to heaven. 52. And they adoring went back into Jerusalem with great joy. 53. And they were always in the temple praising and blessing God. Amen.

Acts 1

1. The former treatise I made, O Theophilus, of all things which Jesus began to do and to teach. 2. Until the day on which giving commandments by the Holy Ghost to the apostles whom He had chosen, He was taken up: 3. To whom He also showed Himself alive after His Passion, by many proofs, for forty days appearing to them and speaking of the kingdom of God. 4. And eating together with them, He commanded them that they should not depart from Jerusalem, but should wait for the promise of the Father, which you have heard (saith He) by My mouth. 5. For John indeed baptized with water, but you shall

be baptized with the Holy Ghost not many days hence. 6. They therefore who were come together asked Him, saying: Lord, wilt Thou at this time restore again the kingdom to Israel? 7. But He said to them: It is not for you to know the times or the moments which the Father hath put in His own power: 8. But you shall receive the power of the Holy Ghost coming upon you. And you shall be witnesses unto Me in Jerusalem, and in all Judea and Samaria, and even to the uttermost part of the earth. 9. And when He had said these things, while they looked on, He was raised up: and a cloud received Him out of their sight. 10. And while they were beholding Him going up to heaven, behold two men stood by them in white garments. 11. Who also said: Ye men of Galilee, why stand you looking up to heaven? This Jesus who is taken up from you into heaven, shall so come as you have seen Him going into heaven. 12. Then they returned to Jerusalem from the mount that is called Olivet, which is nigh Jerusalem within a sabbath day's journey.

11. The purpose and the signature of St. John.

St. John 20. 30. Many other signs also did Jesus in the sight of His disciples, which are not written in this book. 31. But these are written that you may believe that Jesus is the Christ, the Son of God: and that believing you may have life in His name. St. John 21. 24. This is that disciple who giveth testimony of these things, and hath written these things: and we know that his testimony is true. 25. But there are also many other things which Jesus did: which, if they were written every one, the world itself, I think, would not be able to contain the books that should be written.

12. The appearances mentioned by St. Paul.

1 Corinthians 15. 1. Now I make known unto you, brethren, the gospel which I preached to you, which also you have received and wherein you stand, 2 by which also you are saved: if you hold fast after what manner I preached unto you, unless you have believed in vain. 3. For I delivered unto you first of all, that which I also received: how that Christ died for our sins according to the scriptures: 4. And that He was buried, and that He rose again the third day according to the scriptures: 5. And that He was seen by Cephas and after that by the eleven. 6. Then He was seen by more than five hundred brethren

at once: of whom many remain until this present, and some are fallen asleep. 7. After that He was seen by James, and then by all the apostles. 8. And last of all, He was seen also by me, as by one born out of due time.

13. The Resurrection in apostolic preaching. We have ample historical evidence to show that the Apostles spoke openly of the Resurrection in the city of Jerusalem before those very individuals who had been responsible for the murder of their Master and who now focused their attention on the task of preventing and discrediting the teachings of His followers. Had there been the slightest chance of disproving the apostolic assertions, the high priest and the Pharisees would have produced the body of Jesus, or at least shown what had happened to it, and thereby stopped the existence of that society which they hated. They never made any move in this direction. Thus the earliest preaching of the Apostles stands as an unshakable evidence for the reality of the Resurrection itself.

These Apostles considered themselves primarily witnesses to the Resurrection, and the successor to the traitor, Judas Iscariot, was meant to act in that same capacity. "Wherefore of these men who have companied with us all the time that the Lord Jesus came in and went out among us, beginning from the baptism of John until the day wherein He was taken up from us, one of these must be made a witness with us of His Resurrection."[2] These were the words of St. Peter.

The prince of the apostolic college showed very well what he meant by fulfilling the function of a witness to the Resurrection of Jesus in his pentecostal sermon to the Jews, delivered in Jerusalem a matter of only seven weeks after the event he describes. "Ye men of Israel, hear these words: Jesus of Nazareth, a man approved of God among you by miracles and wonders and signs, which God did by Him in the midst of you, as you also know: This same being delivered up by the determinate counsel and foreknowledge of God, you by the hands of wicked men have crucified and slain: Whom God hath raised up, having loosed the sorrows of hell, as it was impossible that He should be holden by it. For David saith concerning Him: I foresaw the Lord

---

2 Acts 1:21-22.

before My face always: because He is at my right hand that I may not be moved: For this my heart hath been glad, and my tongue hath rejoiced: moreover my flesh also shall rest in hope: Because Thou wilt not leave My soul in hell, nor suffer Thy Holy One to see corruption. Thou hast made known to Me the ways of life: and Thou shalt make Me full of joy with Thy countenance. Ye men, brethren, let me freely speak to you of the patriarch David, that he died, and was buried; and his sepulcher is with us to this present day. Whereas therefore he was a prophet, and knew that God had sworn to him with an oath that of the fruit of his loins One should "sit upon his throne: Foreseeing this, he spoke of the Resurrection of Christ, for neither was He left in hell, neither did His flesh see corruption. This Jesus hath God raised again, whereof all we are witnesses."[3]

We find the same positive and unquestioned statement of fact in the sermon of St. Peter, delivered to the throng that gathered when he and St. John the Evangelist healed the lame man in the Beautiful Gate of the temple at Jerusalem. "Ye men of Israel, why wonder you at this? Or why do you look upon us as if by our virtue or power we had made this man to walk? The God of Abraham, and the God of Isaac, and the God of Jacob, the God of our fathers, hath glorified His Son Jesus, whom you indeed delivered up and denied before the face of Pilate, when he judged He should be released. But you denied the Holy One and the Just, and desired a murderer to be granted unto you. But the Author of life you killed, whom God hath raised from the dead, of which we are witnesses."[4]

The prince of the Apostles made the same statement, unchallenged, before the Sanhedrin, the body which was officially responsible for the murder of Jesus. These rulers had thrown Peter and John into prison by reason of the miracle which they had performed, and which had resulted in the Christian community's so increasing in numbers that it then included more than five thousand men. "And as they were speaking to the people, the priests and the officer of the temple and the sadducees came upon them, being grieved that they taught the people, and preached in Jesus the Resurrection from the dead. And they laid hands upon them, and put them in hold, till the

---

[3] Acts 5:22-32.
[4] Acts 3:12-15.

next day: for it was now evening. But many of them who had heard the word, believed: and the number of men was made five thousand. And it came to pass on the morrow, that their princes, and ancients and scribes were gathered together in Jerusalem; and Annas, the high priest, and Caiphas and John and Alexander, and as many as were the kindred of the high priest. And setting them in the midst, they asked: By what power, or by what Name have you done this? Then Peter, filled with the Holy Ghost, said to them: Ye princes of the people and ancients, hear: If we this day are examined concerning the good deed done to the infirm man, by what means he hath been made whole, be it known to you all, and to all the people of Israel: that by the name of our Lord Jesus Christ of Nazareth, whom you crucified, whom God hath raised from the dead, even by Him this man standeth here before you whole."[5]

The reaction of the Sanhedrin constitutes an admission of the reality of the Resurrection itself. "Now seeing the constancy of Peter and John, understanding that they were illiterate and ignorant men, they wondered. And they knew them that they had been with Jesus. Seeing the man also who had been healed standing with them, they could say nothing against it. But they commanded them to go aside out of the council: and they conferred among themselves, saying: What shall we do to these men? For indeed a known miracle hath been done by them to all the inhabitants of Jerusalem. It is manifest and we cannot deny it. But that it may be no farther spread among the people, let us threaten them, that they speak no more in this Name to any man. And calling them, they charged them not to speak at all, nor teach in the name of Jesus. But Peter and John answering said to them: If it be just in the sight of God to hear you rather than God, judge ye. For we cannot but speak the things which we have seen and heard."[6]

The ordinary teaching of the Apostles was designated as witnessing to the Resurrection. "And with great power did the apostles give testimony of the Resurrection of Jesus Christ, our Lord: and great grace was in them all."[7] There was no possibility of deception. The men who spoke had seen and heard the risen Jesus, and the very

---

5 Acts 4:1-10.
6 Acts 4:13-20.
7 Acts 4:33.

enemies they confronted and sought to aid were men who were all too well aware that Jesus had died and lived again.

The first official instruction given to candidates for baptism who were not of the Jewish nation contains this same insistence upon the fact of the Resurrection. St. Peter spoke to Cornelius the centurion about "Jesus of Nazareth: how God anointed Him with the Holy Ghost, and with power, who went about doing good and healing all that were oppressed by the devil, for God was with Him. And we are witnesses of all things that He did in the land of the Jews and in Jerusalem, whom they killed, hanging Him upon a tree. Him God raised up the third day, and gave Him to be made manifest, not to all the people, but to witnesses preordained by God: even to us who did eat and drink with Him after He rose again from the dead."[8] A solemn assertion that Jesus really rose from the dead, an assertion strengthened by the fact that His official witnesses ate and drank with Him after the Resurrection.

The various sermons recounted in the Acts of the Apostles manifest the habitual mode of teaching employed by the earliest Christian teachers. We find that form exemplified in the instructions of St. Peter, which we have seen above. We see it again in the discourse of St. Stephen, the first martyr,[9] and in the recorded sermons of St. Paul. The Apostles taught the doctrine of Jesus in its proper historical perspective. His words are inserted into the context telling of His life, death, and Resurrection. This announcement in its turn is placed against its proper background when the earliest teachers of Christianity preface the recountal of God's dealings with the chosen people to the actual account of their Master's life and doctrine. Papias, Irenaeus, Clement of Alexandria and Origen and Eusebius all show us that the second gospel itself is a transcription of St. Peter's own instruction.[10] Thus we see the certitude which those who knew Jesus possessed about the Resurrection, and the great importance they attached to it.

14. The catechesis of St. Paul. In the Acts of the Apostles we have several examples of such teaching set forth by St. Paul. One of these, the sermon delivered by the Apostle of the gentiles in Antioch

---

8 Acts 10:38-41.
9 Acts 7:2-53.
10 Cf. Ch. 8.

of Pisidia manifests the reality of the Resurrection with special clarity. "Men, brethren, children of the stock of Abraham, and whosoever among you fear God, to you the word of this salvation is sent. For they that inhabited Jerusalem, and the rulers thereof, not knowing Him, nor the voices of the Prophets which are read every sabbath, judging Him have fulfilled them. And finding no cause of death in Him, they desired of Pilate that they might kill Him. And when they had fulfilled all things that were written of Him, taking Him down from the tree, they laid Him in a sepulcher. But God raised Him up from the dead the third day: Who was seen for many days by them who had come up with Him from Galilee to Jerusalem: who to this present are His witnesses to the people. And we declare unto you that the promise which was made to our fathers, this same God hath fulfilled to our children, raising up Jesus, as in the second Psalm is also written: Thou art My Son, this day have I begotten Thee. And to show that He raised Him up from the dead now not to return any more to corruption, He said thus: I will give You the holy things of David faithful. And therefore in another place also He saith: Thou shalt not suffer Thy Holy One to see corruption. For David, when he had served in his generation according to the will of God, slept: and was laid unto His fathers, and saw corruption. But He whom God hath raised from the dead, saw no corruption."[11]

So we have the open and unchallenged assertion of St. Paul that Jesus had died, had been buried, and had risen again. Like all of his fellow Apostles, he insisted that the risen Jesus was utterly incorruptible, immortal, and glorious. He stated plainly that a good number of those who had seen Jesus after the Resurrection were still living, and thus still competent to testify about the reality of His risen body. Like the other Apostles too, St. Paul insists that the greater number of those who were privileged to see Jesus after the Resurrection were those who had known Him best, and thus those best able to realize that the Person they saw was actually the Master they had long loved and followed.

15. The Resurrection in the apocryphal "Gospel of Peter." The earliest noncanonical account we possess about the Resurrection of Jesus is the fragmentary and apocryphal "Gospel of Peter,"

---

11 Acts 13:26-37.

most probably written a few years before AD 150. The work manifests Docetist tendencies in that it slides over the actual sufferings and death of the Master. In its own way, however, it is valuable as an indication that even those men who had broken away from the unity of Catholic faith were still certain that Jesus had risen from the grave. We shall cite the most pertinent parts. "Now it was noonday, and darkness prevailed over all Judea. . . . And many went about with lamps and some fell. And the Lord cried out aloud saying: My power, My power, thou hast forsaken Me. And when He had so said, He was taken up. And in the same hour was the veil of the temple of Jerusalem rent in two.

"And then they plucked the nails from the hands of the Lord and laid Him upon the earth; and the whole earth was shaken, and there came a great fear upon all.

"Then the sun shone forth, and it was found to be the ninth hour. And the Jews rejoiced, and gave His body unto Joseph to bury it, because he had beheld all the good things which He did. And he took the Lord and washed Him and wrapped Him in linen and brought Him unto his own sepulcher, which is called the Garden of Joseph.

"Then the Jews and the elders and the priests, when they perceived how great evil they had done themselves, began to lament and to say: Woe unto our sins: the judgment and the end of Jerusalem is drawn nigh.

"But I with my fellows was in grief, and we were wounded in our minds and would have hid ourselves; for we were sought after by them as malefactors, and as thinking to set the temple on fire. And beside all these things, we were fasting, and we sat mourning and weeping night and day until the sabbath.

"But the scribes and Pharisees and elders gathered one with another, for they had heard that all the people were murmuring and beating their breasts, saying: If these very great signs have come to pass at His death, behold how righteous He was. And the elders were afraid and came unto Pilate, entreating him and saying: Give us soldiers that we may watch the sepulcher for three days, lest His disciples come and steal Him away and the people suppose that He is risen from the dead, and do us hurt. And Pilate gave them Petronius the centurion with soldiers to watch the sepulcher: and the elders and scribes came with them unto the tomb; and plastered thereon seven seals; and they pitched a tent there and kept watch.

"And early in the morning as the sabbath dawned, there came a multitude from Jerusalem and the region round about to see the sepulcher that had been sealed.

"Now in the night whereon the Lord's day dawned, as the soldiers were keeping guard two by two in every watch, there came a great sound in the heaven, and they saw the heavens opened and two men descend thence, shining with a great light, and drawing near unto the sepulcher. And that stone which had been set on the door rolled away of itself and went back to the side, and the sepulcher was opened and both of the young men entered in. When therefore those soldiers saw that, they waked up the centurion and the elders (for they were also there keeping watch); and while they were yet telling them the things which they had seen, they saw again three men come out of the sepulcher, and two of them sustaining the other, and a cross following after them. And of the two they saw that their heads reached into heaven, but of Him that was led by them that it overpassed the heavens. And they heard a voice out of the heavens saying: Hast Thou preached unto them that sleep? And an answer was heard from the cross, saying: Yea.

"Those men therefore took counsel one with another to go and report these things unto Pilate. And while they yet thought thereabout, again the heavens were opened and a man descended and entered into the tomb. And they that were with the centurion, when they saw that, hastened to go by night unto Pilate, and left the sepulcher whereon they were keeping watch, and told all that they had seen, and were in great agony, saying: Of a truth He was the Son of God.

"Pilate answered and said: I am clear from the blood of the Son of God, but thus it seemed good unto you. Then they all came and besought him and exhorted him to charge the centurion and the soldiers that they should tell nothing of what they had seen. For they said, it is expedient for us to incur the greatest sin before God rather than to fall into the hands of the people and be stoned. Pilate therefore charged the centurion and the soldiers that they should say nothing.

"Now early on the Lord's day, Mary Magdalen, a disciple of the Lord, who being afraid because of the Jews, for they were inflamed with anger, had not performed at the sepulcher of the Lord those things which women are accustomed to do unto them that die and are beloved of them, took with her the women, her friends, and came unto the tomb where He was laid. And they feared lest the Jews should see them and said: Even if we were not able to weep and lament Him on that day whereon He was crucified, yet let us now do so at His tomb. But who will roll away for us the stone also that is set upon the door of the tomb, that we may enter in and sit beside Him and perform that which is due? For the stone was great and we fear lest any man see us. And if we cannot do so, yet let us cast down at the door these things which we bring for a memorial of Him, and we will weep and lament until we come unto our house.

"And they went and found the sepulcher open. And they drew near and looked in there, and saw there a young man sitting in the midst of the sepulcher, of a fair countenance and clad in very bright raiment, who said unto them: Wherefore are ye come? Whom seek, ye? Not Him that was crucified? He is risen and is departed: but if ye believe it not, look in and see the place where He lay, that He is not here. For He is risen and is departed thither whence He was sent. Then the women were affrighted and fled.

"Now it was the last day of unleavened bread, and many were coming forth out of the city and returning unto their own homes because the feast was at an end. But we, the twelve disciples of the Lord, were weeping and were in sorrow, and each one being grieved for that which had befallen, departed unto his own house. But I, Simon Peter, and Andrew my brother, took our nets and went unto the sea: and there was with us Levi, the son of Alphaeus, whom the Lord."[12]

16. The testimony from the enemies of Jesus. Actually the explanations offered by those who sought to discredit and to destroy the teachings of Jesus constitute a valuable indication of the reality of His Resurrection. Naturally enough these explanations would never have been set forth unless there had been definite and universally

---

12 Here the manuscript ends. The English text of the entire document may be studied in M. R. James's translation of the Apocryphal New Testament. Oxford, 1926 (2nd impression), pp. 91-94; and in the version of J. Armitage Robinson, found in the ninth volume of the "Ante Nicene Fathers" (New York).

manifest facts which the foes of Christ felt that they must interpret in their own way. The basic and what we may term the classical statement of the enemies of the Christians is that which St. Matthew recounts in his gospel. "And they being assembled together with the ancients, taking counsel, gave a great sum of money to the soldiers, saying: Say you, His disciples came by night and stole Him away while we were asleep."[13]

It is very important for the scientific apologist to realize how that identical claim was advanced during the next generations. Justin the Martyr alludes to it in his *Dialogue with Trypho* the Jew. "And though all the men of your nation knew the incidents in the life of Jonah, and though Christ said that He would give amongst you the sign of Jonah, exhorting you to repent of your wicked deeds at least after He rose again from the dead, and to mourn before God as did the Ninevites, in order that your nation and city might not be taken and destroyed, as they have been destroyed; yet you not only have not repented after you learned that He rose from the dead, but as I said before, you have sent chosen and ordained men throughout all the world to proclaim that a godless and lawless heresy had sprung from one Jesus, a Galilean deceiver, whom we crucified, but His disciples stole Him by night from the tomb where He was laid when unfastened from the cross, and now deceive men by asserting that He has risen from the dead and ascended to heaven."[14]

Even in the time of St. Justin, who died about AD 165, the Jews were far too close to the actual events which followed upon the death of Jesus to overlook the fact of the empty tomb. They were far too effective and realistic in their hatred of Christianity to pretend that Jesus had not died and had not been buried. Furthermore, they took cognizance of the manifest reality, that His body was no longer within the tomb where His disciples had placed it, and that it had disappeared a matter of hours after the inhumation itself, while the tomb was guarded. The men who watched over the sepulcher of Christ were not some hangers on of the temple, sent for the purpose by the Jewish leaders. They were Roman soldiers, under the command of an officer. Nevertheless the body of Jesus left that tomb, and

---

13 Matt. 28:12-13.
14 St. Justin Martyr, *Dialogue With Trypho*, Ch. 108.

the Jews were driven to assert that the poor frightened and ineffectual disciples had managed to overpower the legionaries.

Any denial of the Resurrection is and must be an attempt to explain away obvious facts. Yet the Jewish proclamation was less ineffective than later hypotheses in that it denied as few facts as possible.

It so happened that the very ferocity of His enemies constituted a means by which the men of all times may be perfectly certain that He rose again from the dead. In the first place the manner in which Jesus was afflicted by His enemies left no doubt whatsoever concerning the reality of His death. It would be perfectly possible for a false report to be spread abroad about the death of some person who lived remote from any crowd. Jesus of Nazareth was condemned to the ignominious death of the cross and actually suffered it. He died in the presence of official witnesses and before a throng gathered from the city of Jerusalem itself. He suffered on the chief feast day of the Jews, on a day when the city housed not only its own inhabitants but a tremendous throng of pilgrims from Palestine and even from the Diaspora. This tremendous crowd saw Him die on the cross and then observed the "coup de grace," the lance thrust of the Roman guard that opened His side.

Furthermore, they knew that His body had been taken down from the cross and buried, wrapped in linen cloths with a hundred pounds of spice. Both His friends and His enemies were aware that He had promised to rise from the dead after having undergone the torture of crucifixion which He had actually suffered. Consequently His enemies, wishing to forestall any argument in His favor from this source adopted the very course of conduct which rendered the reality of His Resurrection absolutely unmistakable to the men of their generation and for that matter to historians of all times. They set a guard around the sepulcher and sealed it, thus insuring themselves that no marauders would take away that body they feared so much. Obviously it was their intention, to point to that sealed tomb after the three days were over, and blast every attempt to preach the doctrine of Jesus with the evidence that He did not accomplish what He had promised and set out to do.

The position of the guard in those days carried a heavy responsibility. We know from the Acts of the Apostles what happened to the men who were placed in charge of St. Peter when he was awaiting the sentence of Herod. An angel had led the prince of the apostolic college out of the prison. The fate of those men who had been set to guard him shows us very well why those in similar positions took their duties seriously. "Now when day was come, there was no small stir among the soldiers, what was become of Peter. And when Herod had sought for him and found him not, having examined the keepers, he commanded that they should be put to death."[15] The guard at the tomb of Jesus was a serious affair. No man who is capable of forming an historical judgment would imagine that the disorganized and terrified disciples, who had fled from Jesus at His arrest, were ready or able to match their strength with the men of the legions.

In modern times there is a great deal of attention paid to an hypothesis that the body of Jesus was thrown into a common grave, together with the corpses of the malefactors who had been crucified with Him and by inference at least with the bodies of those who had previously suffered a like fate at the same place. Against this airy theory stands the solid rock of fact. The canonical gospels all assure us that, because of the interposition and influence of Joseph of Arimathea, this practice was not followed in the case of Jesus. History testifies with clarity and certitude that Joseph and Nicodemus, both wealthy and influential Jews, buried Jesus in a new stone vault, the property of Joseph himself. This was the vault which the soldiers guarded, and it was from this same tomb that Jesus rose triumphantly.

The tactic of the Jews more than a century after the crucifixion is the best possible extrinsic testimony of the historicity of our accounts about the burial of Jesus. Had the body of Christ merely been thrown into a common grave and left unattended, there would have been no possible reason for the anxiety of His enemies to spread the report that the body had been stolen. In a common pit the remains of any one man are tragically soon indistinguishable from those of any other. Soon there would be no evidence one way or another as to the presence of any particular body in such a place. Had such a procedure been followed, then it would have been to the advantage of the Jews simply to deny the reality of those appearances which Jesus made. There would have been no reason for stressing that the body had

---

15 Acts 12:18–19.

been removed surreptitiously had it not been for the all too manifest fact that there was a place where that body had been placed, and where it would have been, were it not that an Agency more powerful than all created force had intervened.

17. Hypotheses contradicting the verity of the Resurrection. During the nineteenth century, when imaginations ran wild on the subject of scriptural interpretation, some seriously advanced the hypothesis that the Sanhedrin itself spirited away the body of Jesus in order to prevent the Apostles from doing the same thing. This hypothesis attributes to the Jewish leaders a stupidity and weakness utterly at variance with what we know about their intellectual acumen. They would never have withheld evidence that would devastate forever the claims of their antagonists. We have already seen that the Apostles after that first Christian Pentecost continuously stressed the Resurrection as a chief motive of credibility before the people and before the assembled Sanhedrin itself. If the leaders could have shown the people where the body of Jesus actually was, no power on earth would have prevented them from doing so. Certainly they would have been not antagonists but proponents of Christianity had they sent envoys abroad to testify that the body was stolen while all the time they could have produced it themselves.

We must remember that the fact of the Resurrection assumed tremendous importance in the minds of those who knew something about the hatred of the Jews for Christianity. When Festus spoke to Agrippa and Bernice about his illustrious prisoner, Paul, he summed up the belief of the Apostle as an insistence upon the fact that Jesus had died and now lived again. The delegates of the Sanhedrin, he said "brought no accusation of things which I thought ill of: but had certain questions of their own superstition against him, and of one Jesus, deceased, whom Paul affirmed to be alive."[16] The Roman court gave every opportunity for the Sanhedrinites to produce the remains of Jesus, and thus to convict Paul of manifest perjury. The fact that no such evidence was received or even offered, disposes once and for all of any suggestion that the Sanhedrinites had smuggled away the body and knew of its whereabouts. However, the outstanding evidence for the Resurrection of Jesus is the fact that those men and women

---

16 Acts 25:18–19.

who had known Him and who had seen Him die, met Him, spoke with Him, and ate with Him after He had been buried, and after His body had disappeared from the tomb in which it was enclosed and sealed. From the earliest ages of Christianity, the enemies of Jesus have striven to prove that these apparitions were mere phantasms or visions, impressions recorded in the minds of those who claimed that they had seen Jesus, yet devoid of any real contact with external reality. We find this claim set down by Celsus in his *True Discourse*, a book which the peerless Origen refuted point by point, and which he has conserved for posterity in the process. The technique of Christ's opponents has not improved since the time of Celsus, as we can assure ourselves through examining this document and the works of our own times. Celsus seems to have been an able rhetorician. He set out to thoroughly discredit the teachings of Christianity. The first part of his volume contains the arguments against the Christian message which were set forth in the name of orthodox Judaism, while the remainder, and by far the larger portion of the work, is devoted to pagan attacks which seek to disprove the contentions of Christianity and of Judaism as well. In the first portion of the *True Discourse* he writes in the person of a Jew who inveighs against the doctrines and works of Jesus. When he comes to the question of the Resurrection and the recognition of Jesus with the marks of the crucifixion still upon Him, he says, "Who beheld this? A half-frantic woman, as you state, and some one also of those engaged in the same system of deception."[17] The implication is, of course, that it was at best a mere vision or dream of Jesus which the Apostles tried to palm off upon the world as an actual appearance of their risen master. Origen states that Celsus was speaking of a vision conjured up in the minds of certain followers of Christ during their waking hours.[18]

This hypothesis is as evidently untenable as that of the Sanhedrin's stealing away the body of Jesus. In the first place the disciples of the Lord had been so badly broken in spirit that they no longer looked for the accomplishment of the Resurrection. They refused to credit the stories told by Mary Magdalen and by those others who were first favored with a visit from their risen Lord, and for this they were

---
17 Origen, *Contra Celsum*, Book II, Ch. 49.
18 *Ibid.*, Ch. 50.

roundly and publicly upbraided when He came to them while they were gathered together. He ate with them and let them examine and consume the remains of His meal. He spoke to them and gave them definite and ordered directions. To satisfy the incredulity of St. Thomas, He commanded this reluctant Apostle to put his fingers into the imprints of the nails and to put his hand into the opening which the soldier's lance had made in His side. The Apostles were manifestly men who had to be convinced. After Jesus had appeared to them, they recognized Him just as well as any man or group of men has ever been able to know an intimate friend, gone away a few days ago and now returned.

18. The vision theories. Furthermore, and most important of all, visions are by their very nature individual experiences. Mary Magdalen, and Peter and James and Paul at least saw and recognized their Master alone while others were not with them, or, in the last case, while others did not see Him. But on some occasions the disciples as a group saw Jesus. The most striking apparitions occurred when Jesus spoke and ate with the disciples altogether, and answered, in the hearing of all, questions which individuals put to Him. In the forthright world of men, those disciples could never be said to have enjoyed a mere collective vision of Jesus. Either they saw and recognized their risen Master, or they did not. In the first case they told the truth; in the second they were the most gruesome deceivers and destructive falsifiers in the history of mankind.

Modern writers are unwilling to follow the impeccable logic of Celsus and of the Jews who opposed Christianity in the days of St. Justin the Martyr. These men refused to believe that the message of Jesus was divinely revealed. They rejected it as the teaching of the living God. They denied that Jesus had really risen from the dead. Since the Apostles said that He lived again, they stigmatized the Apostles as mendacious villains and their teaching as a godless deception. If Jesus had not really risen, then their contention would have been true. There is no room for the dreamy sentimentality of moderns who picture these same Apostles as having invented the story of the Resurrection out of the whole cloth while at the same time exonerating them of all formal guilt. The Apostles declared from one end of the world to the other that their Master had died and

The Resurrection

had risen again to die no more. They said that they had seen Him, and set themselves up explicitly as witnesses of that occurrence. No sane man could speak and act in this manner unless either the statement were literally true or he was an unrepentant scoundrel.

We cannot fully appreciate the full force of the historical certitude for the Resurrection of Jesus until we read the bald statement of modern infidel opinion on the subject. The manifest denial of scientific evidence needed for the rejection of the Resurrection constitutes a perfect demonstration of its reality. One of the most forcefully written modern accounts of the events described at the end of the canonical gospels is that of Lewis Browne. He speaks of the disciples after the death of Jesus. "Without their faith in him and his Messiahship, their own lives became empty, meaningless. Skulking there amid the rock-strewn hills outside Jerusalem, they realized as never before that they still had to believe in him—or die. . . . And, because believing in a corpse was too difficult, they began to believe that Jesus was still alive. They began to say that three days after his burial he had miraculously arisen from the dead. They even declared that they had actually seen him in the act of rising from the sepulcher, had seen him as he was taken up to Heaven, right up to the throne of glory. They began to tell how his spirit had actually walked and talked with them, had even broken bread with them. . . . It was not desire to deceive that impelled those disciples to tell such stories. They sincerely believed the stories themselves."[19]

In the charming never-never land where deniers of the Resurrection dwell, there can be no such thing as a plain blunt fact. Naturally this paragraph ignores the datum about the empty tomb. Of course, one of the striking features manifest in the historical treatise on the early Church is the fact that the disciples never claimed to have seen their Master emerging from the sepulcher. They found the tomb empty; they received, in a supernatural way, information that Jesus of Nazareth who had been dead now lived again. Then they saw Him. But such sober realities have no place in the denial of fact. Again no existent source speaks of the "spirit" of Jesus as having walked and eaten with the disciples. Certainly they never said that the "spirit" of their Master had come to them. They were insistent that

---

19 *This Believing World*, 4 ed. (New York, 1941), p. 273.

the Visitor had stated and had demonstrated precisely that He was not a mere spirit. But all this is accuracy, and accuracy has no place in these fanciful hypotheses.

Realistic men know very well that a person who is firmly convinced of the existence of some phantasm is deluded. They are also quite well aware that mass delusions of the type described by Mr. Browne and by the modern romanticists do not occur in the order of nature. Scattered through the various insane asylums around the world are unhappy and manifestly maladjusted individuals who sincerely believe themselves to be Napoleon. Conceivably there are others who claim to have talked with that famous conqueror. But there never has been a case in history where a battalion has come in and claimed to have seen and talked with their deceased commander and where each man offered himself as a witness of this event. Should such an occurrence be reported, the scientific modern man would never have recourse to mass delusion as an explanation. In such an instance there would be no middle ground between truth and criminal conspiracy. The conspiracy would obviously be all the more revolting if the falsehood involved loss of life and happiness to mankind.

If the sequence of events described by Mr. Browne actually took place, they would have constituted a wonder fully as striking as the Resurrection itself. They would be recognized as a miracle of incoherence and disorder. A number of lunatics all hitting upon the same delusion simultaneously, and encountering enemies fierce enough to kill them so as to stop their preaching and at the same time gentle enough not to expose their error—such a picture is utterly outside the bounds of reasonable reality. Yet these are the basic lines of the situation accepted as sober fact by the learned enemies of Christianity.

Still another hypothesis has been suggested to account for the events described as taking place after the death of Jesus. This is the famous "swoon theory" according to which Jesus of Nazareth never really died at all, but simply lost consciousness. While in this state He is said to have been buried. Later in the cool and quiet of the tomb He awoke, and simply walked out of the place. In the course of His wanderings He met several of His disciples who were of course astonished to see Him. Later, it is thought that He sickened and died from the wounds He had received that day on Calvary.

This hypothesis is interesting from a scientific point of view in showing the utter impossibility of finding an alternative to the manifest fact of the Resurrection which men have not sought out and tried to exploit. In the first place there is no fact in history better attested than the death of Jesus. Again, if He was not really dead when the people and the soldiers saw every evidence of death upon Him, He would most certainly have expired immediately as a result of the lance thrust which the Roman Soldier gave as a "coup de grace." Finally, any man, well or wounded, would have smothered to death in a matter of seconds, sealed in a tomb and wrapped up in a hundred pounds of spices.

The spectacle of a man who had undergone all of this, who had not tasted food or water for three days, walking out from a sealed tomb, rolling back a stone which a group of women confessed themselves unable to stir would be again as great a miracle as the Resurrection. Add to the story the essential ingredients of this man, with his poor pierced hands and feet, moving the stone and hurrying through an armed camp of Roman legionaries, and the thing enters the realm of absurdity. There is nothing in all the realms of history to justify a like conjecture.

19. The conditions of the risen Christ. One essential feature of the story witnessed by the Apostles is to be found in the characteristics of the risen Jesus. We must not forget that the disciples recognized their Master just as truly as any men have ever recognized one of their fellows. At the same time they saw that His body was radically in a different condition from that which had hitherto characterized it. Previously the body of Jesus had been amenable to suffering. Now the Apostle Thomas could put his finger into the frightful wounds of the hands, and could bring his hand into the opened side without causing pain or distress to the Master. Now Jesus appeared and disappeared as He would. The locked door of the upper room remained as it was. The Apostles gathered without Jesus, and while the door stayed locked, He came in to them. When He had completed the instructions He wished to give the disciples at Emmaus, He vanished from their sight. In other words, Jesus of Nazareth, risen from the grave, manifested a complete mastery over the laws which govern the created universe.

Those whom Jesus had raised from the dead previous to His own Resurrection did not manifest these qualities at all. Quadratus could very well assert that people whom Jesus had brought back to life had lived in his own time, but the implication is, of course, that finally they died. Jesus was the first to return to life glorious and immortal. His return, and the qualities He manifested, both constitute overwhelmingly ample evidence that the doctrine which He offered to the world as divine revelation actually was what He claimed it to be.

20. The Resurrection as prophesied. However, we would not have a complete understanding of the demonstrative force contained in the Resurrection of Jesus unless we realized that this event was clearly foretold by Him. On four distinct occasions Jesus informed His hearers that He would be put to death and would rise triumphantly from the dead on the third day. The first prediction took place immediately after the confession of St. Peter and the primacy in the Church made to him by Christ. "From that time Jesus began to show to His disciples that He must go to Jerusalem, and suffer many things from the ancients and scribes and chief priests, and be put to death, and the third day rise again."[20] The second time Jesus added the information that He would be betrayed to His enemies. "And when they abode together in Galilee, Jesus said to them: The Son of man shall be betrayed into the hands of men; and they shall kill Him, and the third day He shall rise again."[21]

Jesus predicted the Resurrection the third time when He refused to perform a miracle to satisfy the curiosity and to cater to the intellectual pride of the Pharisees. This prophecy is the famous sign of Jonah. "Then some of the scribes and Pharisees answered Him, saying: Master we would see a sign from Thee. Who answering said to them: An evil and adulterous generation seeketh a sign: and a sign shall not be given it, but the sign of Jonah the prophet. For as Jonah was in the whale's belly three days and three nights; so shall the Son of man be in the heart of the earth three days and three nights."[22]

---

20 Matt. 16:21; Mark 8:31; Luke 9:22.
21 Matt. 17:21–22; Mark 9:30–31; Luke 9:44.
22 Matt. 12:38–40; Luke 11:29–30.

The last time He foretold the Resurrection to His disciples was in the final journey toward Jerusalem. "And Jesus going up to Jerusalem, took the twelve disciples apart, and said to them: Behold we go up to Jerusalem, and the Son of man shall be betrayed to the chief priests and the scribes, and they shall condemn Him to death, and shall deliver Him to the gentiles to be mocked and scourged and crucified, and the third day He shall rise again."[23] There was, however, still another way in which Jesus spoke of His Resurrection. It was a cryptic announcement which He made at the very beginning of His public life in the temple at Jerusalem after He had cast out the men who bought and sold in that house of prayer. "The Jews therefore answered and said to Him: What sign dost Thou show unto us, seeing Thou dost these things? Jesus answered and said to them: Destroy this temple, and in three days I will raise it up. The Jews then said: Six and forty years was this temple in building, and wilt Thou raise it up in three days? But He spoke of the temple of His body."[24]

21. The results of the prophecies concerning the Resurrection. Long ago Celsus anticipated many of the claims made by modern enemies of Christ when he declared that the prophecies which Jesus had enunciated had been made up out of the whole cloth by the disciples after the events in question had already taken place. "The disciples of Jesus, having no undoubted fact on which to rely, devised the fiction that He foreknew everything before it happened."[25] In a less raucous form, this claim is repeated in practically every non-Christian treatise on the life of Jesus. Certainly the accepted historical facts known to us are such that there would be no reasonable explanation of them at all possible had there been no prophecy about the Resurrection made by Jesus of Nazareth. Two of the four accounts we possess about His trial in the court of the high priest tell that He was accused of threatening to destroy the temple. Furthermore, these chronicles tell us that the iniquitous judges themselves recognized the worthlessness of this charge. The words used by the false witnesses who assailed Jesus were nothing but misstatements of that first mysterious prophecy He had made within the temple precincts

---

23 Matt. 20:17–19; Luke 18:31–33; Mark 10:32–34.
24 John 2:18–31.
25 Cited by Origen, *Contra Celsum*, Book II, Ch. 15.

about His own Resurrection. "And some rising up, bore false witness against Him, saying: We heard Him say: I will destroy this temple made with hands, and within three days I will build another not made with hands. And their witness did not agree."[26]

However, they manifested their bad faith, and showed very clearly that they knew the existence and the meaning of Jesus' prophecy when they appealed to Pilate for a guard around His tomb. "The chief priests and the Pharisees came together to Pilate, saying: Sir we have remembered that that seducer said while He was yet alive: After three days I will rise again."[27] There would have been no reason for their placing a watch around the tomb of Jesus had they not realized that He had promised to return alive from death itself. They realized, before it happened, that the Resurrection precisely as the supreme miracle which Jesus had frequently and clearly foretold, would influence many men to accept His teaching as divine revelation. The whole procedure of the Pharisees at the trial and after the death of Jesus would be beyond understanding if there had been no public and widely understood prophecy about the Resurrection.

These prophecies had their own effect upon the apostolic college. St. John mentions their reaction to the fact that Jesus had foretold His own Resurrection in the verse that follows the prophecy about the temple which was the body of Christ. "When therefore He was risen again from the dead, His disciples remembered that He had said this, and they believed the scripture and the word that Jesus had said."[28]

The obvious reference is to those prophecies of the Old Testament which, as we know from the Acts of the Apostles, the first disciples of the Lord continually cited as evidence that His Resurrection had been foretold during the earlier dispensation. Once they had seen the risen Jesus, they recalled what He had said. In properly scientific language St. John the Evangelist confutes the fantastic theory that the words of Jesus and the faith of His disciples had produced the illusion of a Resurrection. After they had assured themselves that Jesus was risen, they recalled His own prophecies, and saw that these had been fulfilled. They believed the Scriptures in that they realized

---

26 Mark 14:57–60; Matt 26:60–61.
27 Matt. 27:62–63.
28 John 2:22.

that the promise of the Old Testament really referred to that Leader who died and rose again. Finally, they believed the word that Jesus had said. They utilized the Resurrection as the supreme miracle, foretold by Jesus Himself and announced in the Old Testament generations before them for what it was meant to be—the outstanding and all-sufficient motive of credibility.

The story of Christ's rising from the dead is something of a different order from those nature legends which entered into the fabric of Egyptian and Babylonian religion. In these stories there is an obvious personification of natural forces, the powers of fecundity and growth. The exploits of Jesus are on the contrary those of an historical personage. The figures that crowd the pages of the gospels, the acts and the epistles are known to us through other reputable historians of the same epoch. Pontius Pilate, Tiberius, Herod, Joseph Caiphas, Annas, Festus and Felix, all of these are men whom we know from other writers. The places are recognized historical localities. The actions of the Romans and of the Jews are those which history has taught us to expect from the men of their nations.

A man died and lived again as He had said that He would. He had promised this miracle as a proof that the teaching He proposed to men was actually what it claimed to be, the teaching of the living God. The Resurrection, as authenticated and prophesied, constitutes, a divine signature, which no man can begin effectively to counterfeit. This event, manifestly beyond the power of all created nature, is and should be for us the great sign that God has sent Jesus, and that the message which Jesus brought to the world is actually the teaching of the living God. Because Jesus of Nazareth rose from the dead, Catholic dogma is manifestly and rationally credible as divine revelation.

Chapter 17

THE WITNESS OF PROPHECY

1. Prophecy in modern Catholic apologetics. It was the studied contention of St. Thomas Aquinas[1] that the divine signature attached to the Christian message could best be recognized for what it is only when all of the motives of credibility are seen as cooperating for the achievement of a common end. In this way we best realize that God has guaranteed the authenticity of Catholic dogma as a divine message in that He has sealed it with works obviously beyond the natural competence of any creature, actual or possible, and moreover He has announced that these works would be accomplished precisely as testimony to the genuineness of a divinely revealed doctrine. When we see this picture as a whole, we can see at once that there could be no counterfeit motive of credibility effectively imitating those signs which God offers to man to show that His message is rationally acceptable. Thus prophecy, in the authentic and traditional background of Catholic apologetics, is not meant to be a motive of credibility entirely separated from those other divine works which guarantee the divine origin of a message.

There are two distinct types of prophecy which are used to indicate the divine mission of Jesus and the authenticity of His teaching as divine revelation. Some of these prophecies are declarations which He made Himself during the course of His earthly life. Others are statements about Him, made by the inspired prophets of God during the course of Old Testament history. Each of these types of prophecy constitutes a certain and reliable motive of credibility. Taken together, and in union with the other signs of divine revelation which are available to men, they make it strikingly evident that Catholic

---

[1] Cf. St. Thomas, *Summa Contra Gentiles*, Book I, Ch. 6.

dogma is a message which God has communicated to man in a way distinct from and superior to the natural mode in which man acquires his knowledge. They form a sign which a man can misinterpret only through his own fault and his own blindness.

By themselves prophecies, like miracles, are primary and powerful motives of credibility. They are of service to man in that they manifest the divine omniscience. Only God can possess certain and accurate knowledge of those actions which are not produced necessarily, but which depend upon the free activity of creatures. When such knowledge is manifest it is obviously a divine work. When this divine work is attached as a true signature to a doctrine which claims to be divine then the claim is justified.

However, for the people of our own time, we must be careful to bring out the full demonstrative value of prophecy as a motive of credibility. Prophecy has a tremendous probative force, a power valid in and valuable for the conditions of our own days. But it is fairly easy to waste that power by looking, as it were, in the wrong direction for the value of a prophecy.

We must not lose sight of the fact that a prophecy is always the foretelling of future events which depend upon the free and consequently the undetermined operation of rational beings. Clearly the prophecy receives its power as a motive of credibility at the moment it is fulfilled. Once men have seen that some event which obviously a created mind could never possibly know by its own natural light, but which has nevertheless been foretold with absolute confidence and certainty, they have a right to say that the knowledge manifest in the prediction was divine rather than merely human. And if this prophecy was uttered by or about a man who offers to the world a doctrine which he presents as divinely revealed, then it is evident that God Himself has communicated this truth to the man who uttered the prophecy, perfectly well aware that this expression of His own omniscience would be used as a motive of credibility.

2. The uses of messianic prophecies in apologetics. The messianic prophecies themselves fulfill a double function. They constitute a means by which we can recognize the character and content of the messianic office, as it belongs to Jesus of Nazareth, and at the same time they are a corporate intellectual miracle of the first order. Very briefly we have considered the first function in that section of this volume dealing with the messianic claims of Jesus. It is now our business to inquire into the second function. The messianic prophecies were set down in writing over a long period of time. Taken together they describe with tremendous accuracy and force the life, the works, the death, and the Resurrection of Jesus. It is easy enough to see that the doctrine contained in them constitutes a real intellectual miracle of the first order once we have examined them in some detail.

We must remember from the very outset that in order to have a real prophecy there must be a real description of some future event which no created mind could possibly know by its own natural power. Thus the statement in itself must refer to a future event, and must be so couched that men may understand its reference to coming times. However, as we might very well expect, the meaning of a prophecy becomes more apparent once it has been fulfilled. It is not necessary for the validity of a prophecy that man should have realized its full meaning from the very moment that it was made. However it is essential that we can know, from an examination of the statement itself, that it refers to some event or series of events which had not as yet taken place at the time that the assertion was made. Naturally it makes no difference for the probative force of the prophecy whether the statement is made in the future tense, or in the narrative present or past. The only thing requisite is that we be able to demonstrate that the assertion referred to the future and that it was accomplished to the letter in the career of Jesus. The Catholic apologist has at his hands scientifically reliable information to show that such statements were issued as prophecies long before the time of Jesus, and he can demonstrate that these prophecies were fulfilled in the life of the Master. From this point he can prove beyond the shadow of a reasonable doubt that these statements constitute a real and powerful motive of credibility in favor of Catholic dogma.

3. The existence of messianic prophecies. There is a tendency today, even among men of unquestioned scholarly achievements, to deny that there were any real prophecies about Jesus at all. Thus we find the eminent Harvard professor Nock writing, "Most churchgoing people have in the creed recited 'according to the Scriptures' as a phrase which has now little interest and meaning other than those which cling to a survival. It is a commonplace that the passages in the Old Testament which were thought to foretell the coming and death and rising of Christ can bear no such sense, that they refer to imminent or past events of an earlier time."[2] No semblance of a proof is attached to this assertion. The examination of those passages from the Old Testament cited by Jesus Himself and by His immediate followers will show its radical inaccuracy.

For, while the nonexistence of messianic prophecy may very well be a commonplace to Professor Nock and to certain moderns, it was most obviously not so to Jesus of Nazareth and to His contemporaries. The Jewish people as a whole were firmly convinced that their sacred books indicated the coming of a royal prophet who was to institute a victorious and everlasting kingdom. The sovereign proof that this conviction existed is to be found in the readiness of the Jews to accept even spurious claimants to this role. History has recorded for us the names of several of these imposters. We know Judas of Galilee and two distinct individuals, both named Theudas, who arose and led rebellions against the power of Rome within the lifetime of that generation in which Jesus lived. Bar Chochebas began his fierce rebellion in the year 132 crowned and anointed by one of the leaders in Israel and claiming to be the Messiah promised in the Scriptures. Certainly Jesus of Nazareth claimed to be *the* Messiah, and the people to whom His words were addressed knew very well what He meant, and what He claimed.

Both Jesus and His foes claimed to find in the inspired writings of the Old Testament the clear and unequivocal notice of a Saviour who was to come. No man among their hearers called the prophecies themselves into question, although the leaders refused to acknowledge that Jesus was the Christ. Obviously no such reaction could have occurred unless the Scriptures, as they were expounded to the people of that time, really designated the advent of a royal prophet. That was the way the people understood these divinely inspired books.

We must not lose sight of the fact that the Scripture or any other volume for that matter, can never be a dead text. The Jewish nation

---

2 A. D. Nock, *Conversion, The Old and the New in Religion From Alexander the Great to Augustine of Hippo* (Oxford, 1933), p. 237.

considered these divinely inspired words as their special property, and as embodying a message which God meant for them. This same racial group utilized rules of the most severe mechanical tradition to preserve intact the meaning which that message had conveyed to their forebears. It is perfectly true that the dominant pharisaical party came at long last to pay more attention to the rules which they had set up to guard the purity of the Scripture message than they did to the content of the message itself. Nevertheless they never attempted to tamper with the substantial meaning contained in the Bible. What they taught as the actual statement of Scripture was substantially what was contained in the books themselves. Jesus of Nazareth acknowledged this fundamental accuracy in their teaching, while at the same time He excoriated the hypocrisy by which they failed to conform their lives to the divine law. "Then Jesus spoke to the multitudes and to His disciples, saying: The scribes and the Pharisees have sitten on the chair of Moses. All things therefore whatsoever they shall say to you, observe and do. But according to their works do ye not: for they say and do not."[3]

4. The appeal to prophecy in the synagogue at Nazareth. The canonical gospels record several occasions on which Jesus appealed to ancient prophecies. One of the most interesting of these appeals was made in the synagogue of Nazareth. "And He came to Nazareth where He was brought up: and He went into the synagogue according to His custom on the sabbath day, and He rose up to read. And the book of Isaiah the prophet was delivered unto Him. And as He unfolded the book, He found the place where it was written: The Spirit of the Lord is upon Me: wherefore He hath anointed Me, to preach the gospel to the poor He hath sent Me, to heal the contrite of heart, to preach deliverance to the captives, and sight to the blind, to set at liberty them that are bruised, to preach the acceptable year of the Lord, and the day of reward. And when He had folded the book, He restored it to the minister and sat down. And the eyes of all in the synagogue were fixed on Him. And He began to say to them: This day is fulfilled this Scripture in your ears."[4]

---

3 Matt. 23:1–3.
4 Luke 4:16–21.

The passage which Jesus read is to be found in the first two verses in the sixty-first chapter of Isaiah. No one could possibly begin to appreciate the meaning of these verses until he looks at them in their proper background of the entire writing from Chapter 59, verse 20, to the end of the book. The passage is quite long, but an examination of its content from a scientific point of view will once and for all dispel the "commonplace" mentioned by Professor Nock. We cite the first portion.

Chapter 59

20. And there shall come a redeemer to Sion, and to them that return from iniquity in Jacob, saith the Lord. 21. This is My covenant with them, saith the Lord: My Spirit that is in Thee, and My words that I have put in thy mouth, shall not depart out of thy mouth, nor out of the mouth of thy seed, nor out of the mouth of thy seed's seed, saith the Lord, from henceforth and for ever.

Chapter 60

1. Arise, be enlightened, O Jerusalem: for thy light is come, and the glory of the Lord is risen upon thee. 2. For behold darkness shall cover the earth, and a mist the people: but the Lord shall arise upon thee, and His glory shall be seen upon thee. 3. And the gentiles shall walk in thy light, and kings in the brightness of thy rising. 4. Lift up thy eyes around about and see: all these are gathered together, they are come to thee: thy sons shall come from afar and thy daughters shall rise up at thy side. 5. Then shall thou see and abound, and thy heart shall wonder and be enlarged, when the multitude of the sea shall be converted to thee, the strength of the gentiles shall come to thee: 6. The multitude of camels shall cover thee, the dromedaries of Madian and Epha: all they from Saba shall come, bringing gold and frankincense, and showing forth praise to the Lord. 7. All the flocks of Cedar shall be gathered together unto thee, the rams of Nabainth shall minister to thee: they shall be offered upon My acceptable altar, and I will glorify the house of My majesty. 8. Who are these that fly as clouds, and as doves to their windows? 9. For the islands wait for Me, and the ships of the sea in the beginning, that I may bring thy sons from afar: their silver and their gold with them, to the name of the Lord thy God, and to the Holy One of Israel, because He hath glorified thee. 10. And the children of strangers shall build up thy

walls, and their kings shall minister to thee: for in My wrath have I struck thee, and in My reconciliation have I had mercy upon thee. 11. And thy gates shall be open continually: they shall not be shut day or night, that the strength of the gentiles may be brought to thee, and their kings may be brought. 12. For the nation and the kingdom that will not save thee, shall perish: and the gentiles shall be wasted with desolation. 13. The glory of Libanus shall come to thee, the fir tree and the box tree and, the pine tree together, to beautify the place of My sanctuary: and I will glorify the place of My feet. 14. And the children of them that afflicted Me shall come bowing down to thee, and all that slandered thee shall worship the steps of thy feet, and shall call thee the city of the Lord, the Sion of the Holy One of Israel. 15. Because thou wast forsaken and hated, and there was none that passed through thee, I will make thee to be an everlasting excellence, a joy unto generation and generation: 16. And thou shalt suck the milk of the gentiles, and thou shalt be nursed with the breast of kings: and thou shalt know that I am the Lord thy Saviour and thy Redeemer, the mighty One of Jacob. 17. For brass I will bring gold, and for iron I will bring silver: and for wood, brass, and for stones, iron: and I will make thy visitation peace, and thy overseers justice. 18. Iniquity shall no more be heard in thy land, wasting nor destruction in thy borders, and salvation shall possess thy walls, and praise thy gates. 19. Thou shall no more have the sun for thy light by day, neither shall the brightness of the moon enlighten thee: but the Lord shall be unto thee for an everlasting light, and thy God for thy glory. 20. Thy sun shall go down no more, and thy moon shall not decrease: for the Lord shall be unto thee for an everlasting light, and the days of thy mourning shall be ended. 21. And thy people shall be all just. They shall inhabit the land forever, the branch of My planting, the work of My hand to glorify Me. 22. The least shall become a thousand, and a little one a most strong nation. I the Lord will suddenly do this thing in its time.

Chapter 61

1. The Spirit of the Lord is upon Me, because the Lord hath anointed Me. He hath sent Me to preach to the Meek, to heal the contrite of heart, and to preach a release to the captives and deliverance to them that are shut up. 2. To proclaim the acceptable year of the Lord, and

the day of vengeance of our God: to comfort all that mourn: 3. To appoint to the mourners of Sion: and to give them a crown for ashes, the oil of joy for mourning, a garment of praise for the spirit of grief. And they shall be called in it the mighty ones of justice, the planting of the Lord to glorify Him. 4. And they shall build the places that have been waste from of old, and shall raise up ancient ruins, and shall repair the desolate cities, that were destroyed for generation and generation. 5. And strangers shall stand and shall feed your flocks: and the sons of strangers shall be your husbandmen, and the dressers of your vines. 6. But you shall be called the priests of the Lord. To you it shall be said: Ye ministers of our God. You shall eat the riches of the gentiles, and you shall pride yourselves in their glory.

5. The fulfillment of this prophecy in Jesus. This prophecy belongs to the second portion of Isaiah, beginning with the fortieth chapter and continuing until the end. Manifestly its immediate purpose is to instruct and to encourage the Jews during the Babylonian captivity. It was offered and received as the word of the living God, hence as a literally exact statement of the future. We must not forget that. In part this second portion of Isaiah refers explicitly to Cyrus, the ruler who liberated the Jews and gave them permission to return into Palestine. However it is perfectly obvious that the passage we have cited as well as most of the prophecies contained in this second part of Isaiah can have proper reference neither to Cyrus nor to any ordinary or imminent Jewish ruler. The men who accepted it as referring to a past age, or to a condition which was to follow through political and military change, simply would not and could not receive it as the Word of God. Applied to any merely political ruler, the statements could never be termed prophecies, but simply expression of a cross and deluded demagogy. The fact that the Jewish nation accepted them as divinely inspired is a clear indication that they accepted them for what they were meant to be, descriptions of the person, the function and the reign of one who wants to give perfect felicity to the true Israel.

It is not too difficult to see how this prophecy was fulfilled in Jesus of Nazareth. The personage described in the book of Isaiah is a ruler who brings about a status of perfect power and felicity in Israel, and who preaches the beneficial message of God to those who stand in need of it. No ruler, either from the outside or among the Jews themselves could begin to correspond to the outlines of that portrait. Jesus preached, and directed His doctrine to sinners, to the afflicted, in short to those who were ready and willing to profit by the consolation He offered. He proclaimed Himself a Ruler, and drew under His sway not only men of Jewish blood, but those from the gentiles who came under His direction to adore the God of Israel and to unite themselves in the Jerusalem of true believers. He exercised a power greater than that of any political king in that He manifested control over all the natural forces and finally overcame death itself. In short, if a man examines this testimony of Isaiah, he will find, beneath the typically oriental imagery, a true picture of Jesus. This is a portrait which could have been drawn only from the divine omniscience. No creature, actual or possible, could have made, on his own natural knowledge alone, the certain statement that such a leader would appear and live within the land of Israel.

6. The response to the disciples of John the Baptist. We have already alluded[5] to the gospel passage in which Jesus referred to the prophecies which foretold His miracles. "Go and relate to John what you have heard and seen: The blind see, the lame walk, the lepers are cleansed, the deaf hear, the dead rise again, to the poor the gospel is preached. And blessed is he whosoever shall not be scandalized in Me."[6] This passage is an obvious reference to Isaiah.

Chapter 35

1. The land that was desolate and impassable shall be glad, and the wilderness shall rejoice, and shall flourish like the lily. 2. It shall bud forth and blossom, and shall rejoice with joy and praise. The glory of Libanus is given to it, the beauty of Carmel and Saron. They shall see the glory of the Lord and the beauty of our God. 3. Strengthen ye the feeble hands and confirm the weak knees. 4. Say to the faint hearted: Take courage and fear not: behold your God will bring the revenge of recompense. God Himself will come and will save you. 5. Then shall the eyes of the blind be opened, and the ears of the deaf shall be unstopped. 6. Then shall the lame man leap as a hart, and the tongue of the dumb shall be free: for waters are broken out in the

---

5 Cf. Chapter 15.
6 Luke 7:22–23; Matt. 11:4–6.

desert, and streams in the wilderness. 7. And that which was dry land shall become a pool, and the thirsty land springs of water. In the dens where dragons dwelt before shall rise up the verdure of the reed and the bulrush. 8. And a path and a way shall be there, and it shall be called the holy way: the unclean shall not pass over it. And this shall be unto you a straight way, so that fools shall not err therein. 9. No lion shall be there, nor shall any mischievous beast go up by it nor be found there. But they shall walk there that shall be delivered. 10. And the redeemed of the Lord shall return, and shall come into Sion with praise: and everlasting joy shall be upon their heads. They shall obtain joy and gladness, and sorrow and mourning shall flee away.

When Jesus cited this passage to the disciples of John, He was of course claiming for Himself the office described in the prophecy of Isaiah. He utilized the prophecy in the same way that science of sacred theology has always employed these predictions in demonstrating to those who accept as true the teachings of the Old Testament that He was actually the leader foretold and described on its pages. At the same time, however, there is another way in which the scientific theologian can utilize the datum of prophecy. He can appeal to it as an intellectual miracle. He can show that it is a clear and certain prediction of events which no creature could possibly have foreseen by its own unaided natural power. In the chapter on miracles as seals testifying to the actual divine origin of the Christian message, we have seen how this prophecy can be effectively employed in the first way. Now it is our duty to inquire into its efficacy as a manifest intellectual miracle.

The chapter we have just seen describes the condition of Israel, the true Israel that is to say, when God Himself shall have come to the assistance of His people. There is to be life and fecundity over and above anything that was to be found in the kingdom of Judah as the writer and his contemporaries knew of it. Moreover there was to be a manifestation of the divine power through the frequent performance of miraculous cures. Now it is obvious that no such condition existed in the time of Isaiah or of his immediate disciples. Likewise it is perfectly clear that these men did not expect such a condition to eventuate through any purely political change to be brought about in the policy of Israel and Judah. As a result, since it was offered and accepted as the literally true Word of God, it is evident that it had reference to some status which God would bring about in the more or less remote future.

From the purely natural point of view these men had no more right than we have certainly to predict a widespread performance of miracles within the confines of their own territory. However such a state was foretold, and the career of Jesus attested the veracity of the prediction. Manifestly this certain knowledge could only belong to God, Who, in His infinitely perfect providence, foresees all the events that will take place in the universe until the end of time. The knowledge expressed in this chapter is manifestly supernatural. Its basic connection with the doctrines of Jesus affirms once again the divine origin of that doctrine which He proposed to the world as divinely revealed. The connection comes from the fact that He is evidently the One whose activity is foretold. Above all the men who have lived, Jesus was seen and recognized primarily as a worker of miracles, and then wonders were not the capricious and meaningless operations ascribed to the pagan magicians, but benefits conferred upon His fellows. Thus, at the end of the third century, Arnobius was able to taunt the enemies of Christianity with this challenge. "Can you specify and point out to me any one of all those magicians who have ever existed in past ages that did anything similar, in the thousandth degree, to Christ?"[7] The worker of miracles foretold in the book of Isaiah is precisely the Man who offered the world a doctrine which He proposed as divinely revealed. Furthermore, the prophecy declared that the Person who was destined to accomplish these wonders was God Himself. That Jesus declared Himself to be a divine Person we have already seen.

7. The prediction of a precursor for the Messiah. In the discourse which followed Jesus' announcement to the disciples of John, He cited a prophecy which stated that the Messiah would be preceded by a herald who would prepare the way for Him. He identified this herald as John the Baptist. "This is he of whom it is written: Behold I send My angel before Thy face, who shall prepare Thy way before Thee."[8] Of course, only God could have known

---

7 Arnobius, *Adversus Nationes*, Book I, Ch. 43.
8 Luke 7:27; Matt. 11:10.

that a Redeemer would actually come to Israel, to bring to men the benefits which God Himself wished to confer upon them. Obviously, too, no one but God Himself would have known the details which surrounded the advent of this Messiah, and the work of a precursor was one of these details. Now the whole tenor of the gospel narrative shows that John the Baptist announced Himself precisely as one who was to prepare the way for a greater Figure to follow him. "I indeed baptize you in water unto penance: but He that shall come after me is mightier than I, whose shoes I am not worthy to bear. He shall baptize you in the Holy Ghost and fire."[9] Explicitly John pointed out that the One who was to follow after him was Jesus of Nazareth. "The next day John saw Jesus coming to him, and he saith: Behold the Lamb of God. Behold Him who taketh away the sin of the world. This is He of whom I said: After me there cometh a man who is preferred before me: because He was before me. And I knew Him not. But that He may be made manifest in Israel, therefore am I come baptizing with water. And John gave testimony, saying: I saw the spirit coming down as a dove from heaven, and He remained upon Him. And I knew Him not: but He who sent me to baptize with water said to me: He upon whom thou shalt see the Spirit descending and remaining upon Him, He it is that baptizeth with the Holy Ghost. And I saw: and I gave testimony that this is the Son of God."[10] As a matter of fact John the Baptist himself appealed to the prophecy of Isaiah to explain his role as precursor to the Messiah when he was officially interrogated by the Pharisees. "They said therefore with him: Who art thou, that we may give an answer to them that sent us? What sayest thou of thyself? He said: I am the voice of one crying in the wilderness: make straight the way of the Lord, as said the prophet Isaiah. And they that were sent were of the Pharisees."[11]

Now both Isaiah and Malachi had foretold exactly the operation of a precursor before the Messiah who was to come. "Be comforted, be comforted My people, saith your God. Speak ye to the heart of Jerusalem, and call to her: for her evil is come to an end, her iniquity is forgiven. She hath received from the hand of the Lord double for

---

9 Matt. 2:11; Mark 1:7–8; John 1:26.
10 John 1:29–34. Cf. also Matt. 3:16; Mark 1:10; Luke 3:21–22.
11 John 1:22–24. Cf. also Matt. 3:3; Mark 1:2–4; Luke 3:3–4.

all her sins. The voice of one crying in the desert: Prepare ye the way of the Lord, make straight in the wilderness the paths of our God. Every valley shall be exalted, and every mountain and hill shall be made low, and the crooked shall become straight, and the rough ways plain. And the glory of the Lord shall be revealed, and all flesh together shall see that the mouth of the Lord hath spoken."[12] The prophecy of Malachi, cited by Jesus Himself, is fully as clear. "Behold I send My angel, and he shall prepare the way before My face. And presently the Lord whom you seek, and the Angel of the testament, whom you desire, shall come to His temple. Behold He cometh, saith the Lord of Hosts."[13]

In both of these instances we are obviously confronted with promises that deal with the future. In and through the oriental imagery in the context of the two writers we find the announcement that a Personage, long and ardently awaited by the Hebrew people will appear and will confer the benefits which it shall please God to render to men. Both insist that this Messiah will be preceded by an agent whose duty it will be to prepare the people for His coming. Neither could possibly apply to any merely political or military aid which might be brought to the service of Israel. The whole context of the documents stands out against any such interpretation. We are left with two descriptions, which could only have been made in function of the divine foreknowledge. The appearance of Jesus, preceded by John the Baptist clearly demonstrated that these had been true prophecies. As true prophecies, and consequently miracles in the intellectual order, they stand then as criteria in the light of which we may judge with certitude that the doctrine of Jesus was of God, as He claimed it to be.

8. The prediction about the use of parables. Jesus likewise appealed to a prophecy of Isaiah which testified that the coming Messiah was to teach through parables, in such a way that actually the people who heard His instructions would not profit from them. "And His disciples came and said to Him: Why speakest Thou to them in parables? Who answered and said to them: Because to you it is given to know the mysteries of the kingdom of heaven: but to

---

12 Isa. 40:1–5.
13 Mal. 3:1.

them it is not given. For he that hath, to him shall be given, and he shall abound: but he that hath not, from him shall be taken away that also which he hath. Therefore do I speak to them in parables: because seeing they see not, and hearing they hear not, neither do they understand. And the prophecy of Isaiah is fulfilled in them, who saith: By hearing you shall hear, and shall not understand: and seeing you shall see, and shall not perceive. For the heart of this people, is grown gross, and with their ears they have been dull of hearing, and their eyes they have shut: lest at any time they should see with their eyes, and hear with their ears, and understand with their heart, and be converted, and I should heal them."[14]

In the use which Jesus makes of this prophecy, we notice at once that the parable is not used as a teaching form in order that the hearers should refuse to believe. On the contrary, the hardness of heart found in those who were privileged to hear the instructions of Jesus made analogy the only form of statement which would be at all effective for them. Jesus then cites Isaiah as prophesying that the very persons who would receive the teaching of the Messiah would reject that teaching. Taken in its context with the prediction of innumerable miracles and other authentic signs by which the genuineness of His message might be recognized, the prophecy stands as a manifestly divine pronouncement.

In effect the composite picture given in the prophecies cited by Jesus is that of a divine Redeemer who comes among His own people, identifies Himself as a divine Messenger in the performance of tremendous and innumerable miracles, and then finds that people unwilling, and, because of the voluntary hardness of their hearts, unprepared to receive His teaching. Each separate prophecy shows another part or aspect of this portrait. Each part has its own demonstration value. However, the testimony of these prophecies as a whole manifestly understood by the people as divine oracles and as predictions about one Redeemer, possesses an unsurpassed force in demonstrating the rational credibility of that doctrine which Jesus offered as divine revelation. No created mind could naturally foretell the coming of a Redeemer at all. Moreover, granted that such information had been given, only God would be in a position to

---

14 Matt. 13:10–15; Mark 4:10–12; Luke 8:9–10. Cf. also John 12:39–41.

know with absolute certitude and assurance that His teaching would be rejected by those very individuals who were immediate witnesses of the competent proofs of authenticity brought forward in its favor.

The prophecy of Isaiah to which Jesus referred is this "And He said: Go, and thou shalt say to this people: Hearing hear and understand not, and see the vision and know it not. Blind the heart of this people, and make their ears heavy, and shut their eyes: lest they see with their eyes, and hear with their ears, and understand with their heart, and be converted and I heal them."[15] The prophecy, here issued in the form of a command, is manifestly fulfilled in Jesus of Nazareth and in no other. Although the Jewish people at times contended against Isaiah, and still more frequently reacted against Jeremiah and some of their successors in the prophetical office, they ultimately received all of them and incorporated the books in which their doctrines are set down into the canon of those books which they revered as divinely inspired. Jesus, whose teaching was certified by signs far more effective and spectacular than those which accompanied the doctrine of any among His heralds, they rejected flatly. Truly but solely in the sense that His teaching was too spiritual for them to receive, He could be said to have "blinded their hearts." The force of this prophecy strikes us when we consider the reaction of the false disciples to His eucharistic discourse, given in the synagogue at Capharnaum. "Many therefore of His disciples, hearing it, said: This saying is hard, and who can hear it."[16]

Such were the false notions entertained by the Jews with reference to the kingdom of God, that Jesus could not ordinarily speak openly about it without exasperating the very populace He meant to instruct. "All these things Jesus spoke in parables to the multitudes: and without parables He did not speak to them: That it might be fulfilled which was spoken by the prophet saying: I will open My mouth in parables. I will utter things hidden from the foundation of the world."[17] The words of the evangelist constitute a further development of that portrait of Jesus which existed in the prophecies. The psalmist begins his didactic poem on the dealings of God with His people with the

---

15 Isa. 6:9–10.
16 John 6:61.
17 Matt. 13:34–35.

words: "Attend, O My people, to My law: incline your ears to the words of My mouth. I will open My mouth in parables. I will utter propositions from the beginning.[18] The Jews considered this psalm, one inscribed "Understanding for Asaph" as a prophecy. "And Ezechias and the princes commanded the levites to praise the Lord with the words of David and Asaph the seer: and they praised Him with great joy, and bowing the knee, adored."[19] Asaph was recognized as a seer or prophet precisely insofar as he predicted the future. In the seventy-seventh psalm he speaks in the person of God Himself, and announces clearly that the divine message would come to the people in the form of parables. The words which are ascribed to him in the psalter manifest no characteristic use of parables. As a matter of fact the only one who used this form of teaching in such a way as to have it considered as it were proper to His presentation was Jesus of Nazareth.

Here we find a clear prediction that a definite and well known type of illustration will be utilized in teaching a religious message. The fulfillment of that prediction in the actual and observable preaching of Jesus could never have been known naturally to any created mind. When Jesus taught in parables, He conformed to one more aspect or portion of that picture which the divine foreknowledge had painted of the Messiah generations ago. He showed that the prediction was an act of the divine foreknowledge, and thus a certain and evident motive of credibility advanced in favor of His teaching.

9. The people among whom the Messiah was to live. Again Jesus cited a prophecy of Isaiah, this time not having reference to Himself but to those among whom His message was preached. "And the Pharisees and scribes asked Him: Why do not Thy disciples walk according to the tradition of the ancients, but they eat bread with common hands? But He answering said to them: Well did Isaiah prophesy of you hypocrites, as it is written: This people honoreth Me with their lips, but their heart is far from Me. And in vain do they worship Me, teaching doctrines and precepts of men. For leaving the commandment of God, you hold the tradition of men, the washing

---

18 Ps. 77:1–2.
19 2 Chron. 29:30.

of pots and of cups: and many other things you do like to these."[20] The words of the prophet were "And the Lord said: Forasmuch as this people draw near Me with their mouth, and with their lips glorify Me, but their heart is far from Me, and they have feared Me with the commandment and doctrines of men: Therefore behold I will proceed to cause an admiration in this people by a great and wonderful miracle. For wisdom shall perish from their wise men, and the understanding of their prudent men shall be hid."[21]

As the statement stands it cannot truthfully refer to Isaiah himself nor to any of those Hebrew prophets who followed him. None of these men were extraordinary in their power of miracles, as was Jesus of Nazareth. Furthermore, only the divine mind could have known with absolute certainty that the people who would be unwilling to accept an obviously marked Messiah, a people whose opposition was such as to compel Him to address them in parables rather than by a direct statement of doctrine, would be a group professing ardent worship of God. However unlikely such an eventuality might seem from a purely human point of view, Isaiah made this statement as a divine prophecy, and the people of Israel accepted it as such. The fulfillment of this prophecy in Jesus of Nazareth again showed that it was a true motive of credibility, attesting that the claims advanced in favor of His teaching were genuine and reliable.

10. The triumphant King. When Jesus entered triumphantly into Jerusalem on the first Palm Sunday, He acted in such a way as to fulfill expressly and manifestly a prophecy enunciated long before Zachariah. "Rejoice greatly, O daughter of Sion. Shout for joy, O daughter of Jerusalem. Behold thy King will come to thee, the just and Saviour. He is poor, and riding upon an ass, and upon a colt, the foal of an ass. And I will destroy the chariot out of Ephraim, and the horse out of Jerusalem, and the bow for war shall be broken. And He shall speak peace to the gentiles, and His power shall be from sea to sea, and from the rivers even to the end of the earth."[22]

Here we find a certain and unwavering declaration about the future. The scene described is manifestly one of which no creature could be

---

20 Mark 7:5–8; Matt. 15:1–3.
21 Isa. 29:13–14.
22 Zach. 9:9–10.

at all sure by the natural power of his own mind. A glorious King who is the Saviour shall ride into Jerusalem upon an ass. He will be poor, and at the same time ruler over all the earth. His power shall be acknowledged not only by the children of Israel but also by the gentiles themselves. History fails to record any other person to whom that prediction might apply. The political rulers of Judah might enter into Jerusalem in any way they pleased, but certainly none of them was ever considered poor in the financial sense of the term. Manifestly, too, none claimed nor enjoyed universal dominion. Jesus alone corresponded in every way to this prediction. "And when they drew nigh to Jerusalem, and were come to Bethphage unto Mount Olivet; then Jesus sent two disciples, saying to them: Go ye into the village that is over against you, and immediately you shall find an ass tied, and a colt with her: loose them and bring them to Me. And if any man shall say anything to you, say ye that the Lord hath need of them: and forthwith he will let them go. Now all this was done that it might be fulfilled which was spoken by the prophet, saying: Tell ye the daughter of Sion. Behold thy King cometh to thee, meek and sitting upon an ass and a colt, the foal of her that is used to the yoke. And the disciples going did as Jesus commanded them. And they brought the ass and the colt: and laid their garments upon them, and made Him sit thereon. And a very great multitude spread their garments in the way: and others cut boughs from the trees and strewed them in the way. And the multitudes that went before and that followed cried saying: Hosanna to the Son of David. Blessed is He that cometh in the name of the Lord. Hosanna in the highest."[23] Mark and Luke mention the incident without citing the prophecy.[24]

This occasion stood out in the minds of the Apostles only after the Resurrection of their Master. "These things His disciples did not know at the first: but when Jesus was glorified, then they remembered that these things were written of Him: and that they had done these things to Him."[25] The portrait of the Messiah in Zachariah the prophet was far too striking for the Apostles to overlook its conformity and fulfillment in Jesus.

---

23 Matt. 21:1–9; John 12:12–14.
24 Mark 11:1–10; Luke 19:29–38.
25 John 12:16.

The Witness of Prophecy

11. The Messiah to be rejected. Jesus took advantage of the parable about the evil husbandman to cite another prophecy foretelling that the Lord would be rejected by His own people. "Jesus saith to them: have you never read in the Scriptures: The stone which the builders rejected, the same is become the head of the corner? By the Lord this hath been done, and it is wonderful in our eyes. Therefore I say to you that the kingdom of God shall be taken from you, and shall be given to a nation yielding the fruits thereof. And whosoever shall fall upon this stone shall be broken. But on whomsoever it shall fall, it shall grind him to powder. And when the chief priests and Pharisees had heard His parables, they knew that He spoke of them."[26]

The first part of this composite prophecy cited by Jesus is found in Psalm 117.[27] It is a literal quotation. The second portion is found in Isaiah. "Sanctify the Lord of Hosts Himself, and let Him be your fear, and let Him be your dread. And He shall be a sanctification to you, but for a stone of stumbling and for a rock of offense to the two houses of Israel, for a snare and a ruin to the inhabitants of Jerusalem. And very many of them shall stumble and fall, and shall be broken in pieces, and shall be snared and taken."[28] The same idea is brought out in the prophecy of Daniel.[29]

Here we have a definite statement, made long before the time of Jesus, to the effect that the Lord Himself would be rejected by His own people and exalted by reason of their very refusal to accept Him. The statement is clear enough. The two houses of Israel, the northern and the southern kingdoms together, would reject this Redeemer who was to offer amply sufficient indication of His identity. The result of that rejection was to be the ruin and the reprobation of Israel itself. Again that prophecy was manifestly fulfilled in the rejection of Jesus, and in no other event recorded in history.

12. The Son of David. This is tremendously important for the purposes of apologetics on the various prophecies to which Jesus appealed in His encounter with the Pharisees in the temple on the Wednesday before He died. "And the Pharisees being gathered

---

26 Matt. 21:42–45; Mark 12:10–11; Luke 20:17–18.
27 Ps. 117:22–23.
28 Isa. 8:13–15.
29 Dan. 2:34–44.

together, Jesus asked them saying: What think you of Christ? Whose Son is He? They say to Him: David's. He saith to them: How then doth David in spirit call Him, Lord, saying: The Lord said to my Lord: sit on My right hand, until I make Thy enemies Thy footstool. If David then call Him Lord, how is He his Son? And no man was able to answer Him a word: neither durst any man from that day forth ask Him any more questions."[30]

The entire context of this passage shows us very clearly that Jesus of Nazareth made no effort to deny that, according to the universally accepted prophecy, the Messiah was to be a lineal descendant of that David whom God had raised up to replace Saul, the first king of Israel. He merely pointed out that David's own understanding of the Redeemer supposed that He was to be a divine Person, the equal of the omnipotent and eternal Father. In the conduct of scientific apologetics we can of course do no better than follow the line of procedure laid down by Jesus. The Master did not use the fact of His own divinity as a criterion of revelation. Quite on the contrary the fact of His divinity constituted one of the essential and central statements in that communication which He proposed to men as divinely revealed, and which He demonstrated as rationally credible through these manifestly divine seals, one of which is prophecy itself.

Now it is a fact that the Jewish people at the time Jesus taught were unanimous in their expectation of a Redeemer or Messiah, who was to be a lineal descendant of the royal patriarch, David. The prophecy was given to David by Nathan. "From the day that I appointed judges over My people Israel: and I will give thee rest from all thy enemies. And the Lord foretelleth to thee, that the Lord will make thee a house. And when thy days shall be fulfilled, and thou shalt sleep with thy fathers, I will raise up thy seed after thee, which shall proceed out of thy womb. I will establish his kingdom. He shall build a house to My name, and I will establish the throne of his kingdom forever. I will be to him a Father, and he shall be to Me a son: and if he commit any iniquity, I will correct him with the rod of men, and with the stripes of the children of men. But My mercy I will not take away from him, as I took it from Saul, whom I removed from before My face. And

---

30 Matt. 22:41–46; Mark 22:35–37; Luke 20:41–44.

thy house shall be faithful, and thy kingdom forever before thy face, and thy throne shall be firm forever."[31]

In this prophecy we can discuss very clearly certain statements which would apply to Solomon, David's son and his immediate successor upon the throne of Israel. However, there are other pronouncements which could never, by even the wildest stretch of the imagination, have reference to Solomon or to any of his royal followers. The people who received this as a divine oracle knew very well that the political rule had been taken away from the family of David long ago. Thus, when they accepted this message as absolutely true, they manifestly applied it to some ruler quite distinct from the line of kings who had already lost their power. That ruler was the Messiah, long awaited and promised as the descendant of Adam through Noah, Abraham, Isaac, and Jacob. Thus, when Jesus asked the Jewish leaders of His own time about the ancestry of that Messiah whom they all expected, they replied as they would have done to anyone who made a similar inquiry. They were perfectly assured that the Redeemer would be the lineal descendant of David the King.

Jesus of Nazareth conformed to this prophecy, as He did to all the others which had reference to the Messiah in His first coming. He was the Son of David, tracing His ancestry back by way both of legal and natural ancestry to the ancient and illustrious king of Israel. Here again, manifestly we have a fact which only the divine foreknowledge could apprehend during the centuries previous to the coming of Jesus. Briefly the Wonder-Worker who was to give ample and certain evidence of His divine mission was to be a member of a definite and known family. Jesus appeared, worked the wonders which had been foretold with perfect certainty, and manifested Himself as a member of this royal race. Thus He showed that the prediction was an act of the divine foreknowledge and consequently a true motive of credibility, testifying to the reliability of His claims in favor of His own teachings.

The probative force of that prophecy which described the Messiah as a descendant of David the king can be seen in its full extent only when we realize that this was only the final determination in a prophecy which had grown progressively clearer during all the years

---

31 2 Kings 7:11–16.

the Jews were receiving that message which they accepted as divinely revealed. According to this communication set down on the pages of the Old Testament, God had promised to our first parents that a descendant of Eve would undo the harm which had come to the human race through the offense of Adam. "And the Lord God said to the serpent: Because thou hast done this thing, thou are cursed among all cattle and beasts of the earth. Upon thy breast thou shalt go, and earth shalt thou eat all the days of thy life. I will put enmities between thee and the woman, and thy seed and her seed. She shall crush thy head, and thou shalt lie in wait for her heel."[32]

13. The Son of Abraham, Isaac, and Jacob. The Jews understood from this same message that the Messiah was to be a descendant of the patriarch Abraham. "And the Lord said to Abraham: Go forth out of thy country, and from thy kindred, and out of thy father's house, and come into the land which I shall show thee. And I will make of thee a great nation, and I will bless thee, and magnify thy name, and thou shalt be blessed. I will bless them that bless thee, and curse them that curse thee, and in thee shall all the kindreds of the earth be blessed."[33] The blessing was to come through the family of Isaac, the son of Abraham, according to a promise given to Isaac himself. "And the Lord appeared to him and said: Go not down into Egypt, but stay in the land that I shall tell thee. And sojourn in it, and I will be with thee, and will bless thee. For to thee and to thy seed I will give all these countries, to fulfill the oath which I swore to Abraham thy father. And I will multiply thy seed like the stars of heaven. And I will give to thy posterity all these countries. And in thy seed shall all the nations of the earth be blessed."[34] Again the promise of God was to be accomplished in the progeny of Isaac's son, Jacob. "And God appeared again to Jacob after he returned from Mesapotamia of Syria, and He blessed him, saying: Thou shalt not be called any more Jacob, but Israel shall be thy name. And He called him Israel, and said to him: I am God almighty. Increase thou and be multiplied. Nations and peoples of nations shall be from thee, and kings shall come out

---

32 Gen. 3:14–15.
33 Gen. 12:1–3.
34 Gen. 26:2–4.

of thy loins. And the land which I gave to Abraham and Isaac, I will give to thee and to thy seed after thee."[35]

Previously Isaac had conferred his prophetic blessing upon Jacob, giving to him rather than to his brother Esau the privilege of having the Redeemer among his descendants. "And immediately as he smelled the fragrant smell of his garments, blessing him he said: Behold the smell of my son is as the smell of a plentiful field which the Lord hath blessed. God give thee of the dew of heaven, and of the fatness of the earth, abundance of corn and wine. And let peoples serve thee, and tribes worship thee. Be thou lord of thy brethren, and let thy mother's children bow down before thee. Cursed be he that curseth thee: and let him that blesseth thee be filled with blessings."[36] Later Isaac renewed this blessing. "And God almighty bless thee, and make thee to increase, and multiply thee: that thou mayst be a multitude of peoples. And give the blessings of Abraham to thee, and to thy seed after thee, that thou mayst possess the land of thy sojournment which He promised to thy grandfather."[37] This blessing God Himself conferred upon Jacob, according to the doctrine which the Jewish people accepted as divine revelation. "And he saw in his sleep a ladder standing upon the earth, and the top thereof touching heaven: the angels also of God ascending and descending by it: And the Lord leaning upon the ladder saying to him: I am the Lord God of Abraham thy father and the God of Isaac. The land wherein thou sleepest, I will give to thee and to thy seed. And thy seed shall be as the dust of the earth. Thou shalt spread abroad to the west, and to the east, and to the north, and to the south. And in thee and thy seed all the tribes of the earth shall be blessed."[38]

Jacob prophesied that the promise of God would be fulfilled in the progeny of Judah, his son. "Judah, thee shall thy brethren praise: thy hand shall be on the necks of thy enemies: the sons of thy fathers shall bow down to thee. Judah is a lion's whelp: to the prey, my son, thou art gone up. Resting thou hast couched as a lion, and as a lioness. Who shall rouse him? The scepter shall not be taken away from

---

35 Gen. 35:9–12.
36 Gen. 27:27–29.
37 Gen. 28:3–4.
38 Gen. 28:12–14.

Judah, nor a ruler from his thigh, till He come that is to be sent, and He shall be the expectation of nations. Tying his foal to the vineyard, and His ass, O my son, to the vine. He shall wash His robe in wine, and His garment in the blood of the grape. His eyes are more beautiful than wine, and His teeth whiter than milk."[39]

In appealing to His own Davidic origin, Jesus of Nazareth implicitly referred to still another messianic prophecy which testified that the promised Redeemer would be an all-triumphant ruler. The prediction was made by Balaam, a prophet whom Balai the king had hired to curse the children of Israel during their peregrinations toward the Promised Land, but who found himself unable to give a message other than that which he received from God. The Jews received this blessing as divine revelation, and as a prophecy which would be fulfilled in the coming of the Messiah. "Therefore taking up his parable again, he said: Balaam the son of Beor hath said: The man whose eye is stopped up hath said: The bearer of the words of God hath said, who knoweth the doctrine of the Highest, and seeth the vision of the Almighty, who falling hath his eyes opened. I shall see Him, but not now: I shall behold Him, but not near. A star shall rise out of Jacob, and a scepter shall spring up from Israel: and shall strike the chief of Moab, and shall waste all the children of Seth. And he shall possess Idumea: the inheritance of Seir shall come to their enemies: but Israel shall do manfully. Out of Jacob shall He come that shall rule, and shall destroy the remains of the city."[40]

14. The family of David. The unspeakable impostor who is known to history as Bar Chochebas adopted that name, meaning Son of the star, to mislead his deluded countrymen into thinking that the prophecy of Balaam was fulfilled in his person. The success he achieved is the best possible indication that the Israelites, even long after the times of Jews, continued to be certain that the promised Messiah was an individual person, a ruler rather than the Hebrew nation or race as a whole. That attitude of the Jews was traditional. It expressed the meaning which the inspired writer had placed in the prophecy of Balaam, and the significance which the people had always found in all the predictions we have mentioned. Only in Jesus

---

39 Gen. 49:8–12.
40 Num. 24:15–20.

of Nazareth have we a figure conforming to this composite portrait. His Davidic origin was unquestioned. We have not only the testimony of the first and third gospels to this effect, but also an eloquent and independent later testimony. The passage is too beautiful and eloquent to be overlooked. "But when the same Domitian had issued his orders, that the descendants of David should be slain, according to an ancient tradition, some of the heretics accused the descendants of Judas, as the brother of our Saviour according to the flesh, because they were of the family of David and as such also were related to Christ. This is declared by Hegesippus as follows. 'There were yet living of the family of our Lord the grandchildren of Judas, called the brother of our Lord according to the flesh. These were reported as being of the family of David, and were brought to Domitian by the Evocatus. For this emperor was as much alarmed at the appearance of Christ as Herod. He put the question, whether they were of David's race, and they confessed that they were. He then asked them what property they had, or how much money they owned. And both of them answered that they had between them only nine thousand denarii. And this they had not in silver, but in the value of a piece of land containing only thirty-nine acres; from which they raised their taxes and supported themselves by their own labor. Then they also began to show their hands, exhibiting the hardness of their bodies, and the callosity formed by incessant labor on their lands, as evidence of their own labor. When asked also, respecting Christ and His kingdom, what was its nature and when and where it was to appear, they replied that it was not a temporal nor an earthly kingdom, but celestial and angelic; that it would appear at the end of the world, when coming in glory He would judge the quick and the dead, and give to everyone according to his works. Upon which Domitian despising them made no reply: but treating them with contempt, as simpletons, commanded them to be dismissed and by a decree ordered the persecution to cease. Thus delivered, they ruled the churches, both as witnesses and relatives of the Lord. When peace was established they continued living even to the times of Trajan.' Such is the statement of Hegesippus."[41]

---

41 Eusebius, *The Ecclesiastical History*, Book III, Chs. 19–20.

This Hegesippus, cited by Eusebius of Caesarea, was one of the most interesting and valuable Christian writers of the second century. Very well versed in the customs and laws of the Jews, and perfectly conversant with the traditions of the Christian Church in Palestine, he set down in his "Memorials" a digest of ecclesiastical lore. The incident he records is undoubtedly historical. We know far too much about the thoroughness of the informers who worked in the Roman Empire to imagine that either Domitian or his satellites would have bothered for one moment about a spurious claim of royal ancestry. When the Roman emperor received the descendants of Jesus' cousin as members of the Davidic family, we have a remarkable guarantee that the Master Himself conformed to the picture drawn in the prophecies, assuring us that these were genuine manifestations of the divine foreknowledge, and applying them as motives of credibility to the message He gave to the world.

We must not lose sight of the fact that the blessing given to Judah the patriarch stated clearly that the scepter would not be taken away from him until such time as the promised Messiah would arrive. This introduces a temporal element into that prophecy which Jesus invoked in His question to the Pharisees. As a matter of fact this element too was fulfilled in His coming. From the time of David until the days of Jesus Himself there were temporal rulers specifically over the house of Judah. Until the time of the Babylonian captivity these rulers were of the house of David himself. After the captivity there was a priestly rule, but these Aaronitic kings governed as rulers of Judah. The last of these Asmoneans was succeeded by Herod the Great. This adventurer was a foreigner whose kingdom was supported by and dependent upon the Roman Government. From the time of his death, however, his dominions were divided, and, after the short-lived kingly administration of Archelaus his son, Roman governors or prefects controlled Jerusalem and the surrounding territory. Jesus was born in the last days of Herod. The holy family returned from Egypt during the reign of Archelaus. Thus, even on this point the prediction made to Judah was accomplished. Only the divine mind could have foreseen with certainty that events would shape themselves in this way. That divine foreknowledge, manifest in the accomplished prophecy, named the One who was to come as the

Messiah, and thereby guaranteed the credibility of Jesus' teaching as divine revelation.

15. Prophecy of the betrayed. Jesus of Nazareth pointed out to His disciples that His own betrayal had been foretold in the Scriptures. Here again we find a prediction obviously applying to Him and again obviously beyond the natural competence of any creature, actual or possible. "I speak not of you all: I know whom I have chosen: but that the Scripture may be fulfilled: He that eateth bread with Me, shall lift up his heel against Me. At present I tell you before it come to pass: That when it shall come to pass, you may believe that I am He. Amen, amen, I say to you: He that receiveth whomsoever I send, receiveth Me: and he that receiveth Me, receiveth Him that sent Me."[42]

The implication is clear enough. According to Jesus Himself, the prophecy about His betrayal, cited by Himself that night at the last supper, was sufficiently clear. It constituted, according to His own claim, a definite and effective motive of credibility, valid in itself yet incalculably powerful when used together with the other pronouncements which foretold the Messiah.

The second portion of the fortieth psalm, from which Jesus of Nazareth quoted, has an obvious Messianic significance. "My enemies have spoken evils against Me: When shall He die and His name perish? And if he came in to see Me, he spoke vain things. His heart gathered together iniquity to itself. He went out and spoke to the same purpose. All my enemies whispered together against Me. They devised evils to Me. They determined against Me an unjust word: shall He that sleepeth rise again no more? For even the man of My peace in whom I trusted: who ate my bread, hath greatly supplanted Me. But Thou, O Lord, have mercy on Me and raise Me up again: and I will requite them. By this I know that Thou hast had a good will for Me: because My enemy shall not rejoice over Me. But Thou hast upheld Me by reason of My innocence, and hast established Me in Thy sight forever."[43]

16. Fulfillment of this prophecy in Jesus. Manifestly the person whom God had established in His sight forever was not David the king nor any of the other prophets who came to enlighten the land

---

42 John 13:18–20.
43 Ps. 40:6–13.

of Israel. David was truly a type, in the sense that the prophecy has an obvious reference to the plots engineered against him by Arbitophel and the other partisans of Absalom. But the full meaning of the statement could never be applied to the royal patriarchs. In the history of Jesus we find the full meaning of this prediction. The canonical gospels tell of four distinct plots against Him before the final conspiracy in which the traitor Judas Iscariot agreed to betray his Master. The first came after Jesus had miraculously healed the man with the withered hand and had triumphantly unmasked the hypocrisy of His enemies who objected against this miracle being performed on the Sabbath.[44] The second took the form of preparing stratagems to betray Him in His speech. The scribes and Pharisees took part in this plot after Jesus had excoriated their hypocrisy.[45] The third was still more ambitious. At first the Pharisees and the Herodians had conspired against Jesus in Galilee. Now the plotters included the chief priests, the scribes and the princes of the people.[46] The next day on the Tuesday of holy week, the chief priests and the Pharisees again laid snares for Him after He had unmasked their iniquity through the parable of the evil husbandmen.[47] The first and third gospels recount that the popularity of Jesus was such that the cowardly schemers despaired of any open attack upon Him.

On the following day, Wednesday, the Sanhedrinites entered into their infamous agreement with the traitor Apostle, Judas Iscariot.[48] Previously they had decided finally to encompass the death of Jesus.[49] Judas Iscariot partook of the last supper with his Master and then betrayed Him. The men who engineered those plots unconsciously and in spite of themselves filled out one more portion of that portrait which the inspired writers had drawn of the coming Messiah. Certainly only God Himself could have known that the Person who offered such compelling guarantees of a beneficent mission would be or could be the Victim of plotting and treachery on the part of those to whom He presented the divine message.

---

44 Matt. 13:14; Mark 3:6; Luke 6:11.
45 Luke 11:53.
46 Mark 11:18; Luke 19:47–48.
47 Matt. 11:45–46; Mark 12:12; Luke 20:19.
48 Matt. 26:14–16; Mark 14:10–11; Luke 22:3–6; John 13:2.
49 Matt. 26:1–5; Mark 14:1–2; Luke 22:2; John 11:47–53.

In the previous chapter we have seen that Jesus Himself predicted His Passion, death, and Resurrection. We must not forget that both before the last supper and after the Resurrection He appealed to prophecies in the Old Law relative to these events. "Then Jesus took unto Him the twelve and said to them: Behold we go up to Jerusalem, and all things shall be accomplished which were written by the prophets concerning the Son of man. For He shall be delivered to the gentiles, and shall be mocked and scourged and spit upon. And after they have scourged Him, they will put Him to death, and the third day He shall rise again."[50] At the same time the evangelist assures us that the Apostles did not understand the teaching of their Master in this regard. "And they understood none of these things, and this word was hid from them, and they understood not the things that were said."[51] Patently then the Apostles did not realize, in spite of the explicit declaration of their Master, that the prophetic announcements in the Old Testament described a Messiah who was to suffer and to die. We know very well that the rabbinical teachers of that time had distorted the portrait of the Messiah in the Old Testament oracles into the image of an all-conquering politico-religious hero. That misconception dulled the understanding of the Apostles themselves. Yet even a forgotten truth remained evident. The descriptions of the suffering Messiah abounded in the Old Testament writings, even when the teachers of the day chose to pass over the austere truth conveyed in these portraits. The prophecies in this regard were not less truly expressions of the divine and infinite foreknowledge simply because they ran counter to the popular errors.

Even at the last supper itself Jesus insisted that His forthcoming sufferings and death had been prophesied. "And the Son of man indeed goeth, as it is written of Him, but woe to that man by whom the Son of man shall be betrayed; it were better for him if that man had not been born."[52]

17. The messianic prophecies in the message of Jesus. Now it is clear enough that a considerable part of the instruction which Jesus gave to His disciples after the Resurrection had to do

---

50 Luke 18:31–33.
51 Luke 18:34.
52 Mark 14:21; Matt. 26:24; Luke 22:22.

with the verification of prophecies about Him contained in the Old Testament. The disciples on the road to Emmaus heard Him explain these predictions. "Then He said to them: O foolish and slow of heart to believe in all things which the prophets have spoken! Ought not Christ to have suffered these things, and so to enter into His glory? And beginning at Moses and all the prophets, He expounded to them in all the Scriptures the things that were concerning Him."[53] Thus we may expect to find the prophecies which Jesus cited used by the Church during the first period of her missionary activity. We have, moreover, in the canonical gospels themselves, certain quotations indicating the places in the Old Testament which Jesus alleged as predictions of His own Passion, death, and Resurrection.

When, after the last supper, Jesus made as it were a final effort to impress upon the minds of the Apostles the tremendous gravity of the situation they were about to face, He made use of a citation from Isaiah. "Then said He unto them: But now he that hath a purse, let him take it, and likewise a scrip: and he that hath not, let him sell his coat and buy a sword. For I say unto you, that this that is written must yet be fulfilled in Me: And with the wicked was He reckoned. For the things concerning Me have an end."[54] Moreover He contended that the unjust hatred which the Jewish leaders maintained against Him had been foretold in the Old Testament. "If the world hate you, know ye that it hath hated Me before you. If you had been of the world: the world would love its own. But because you are not of the world, but I have chosen you out of the world, therefore the world hateth you. Remember the word that I said to you: The servant is not greater than his master. If they have persecuted Me, they will also persecute you. If they have kept My word, they will keep yours also. But all these things they will do to you for My name's sake: because they know not Him that sent Me. If I had not come and spoken to them, they would not have sin. But now they have no excuse for their sin. He that hateth Me, hateth My Father also. If I had not done among them the works which no other man hath done, they would not have sin. But now they have both seen and hated both Me and My Father. But that the word may be fulfilled, which is written in their law: They hated Me

---

53 Luke 24:25–27.
54 Luke 22:36–37.

without cause."⁵⁵ Furthermore, He appealed to the prediction that the Apostles would scatter when their Master was attacked. "They went out unto Mount Olivet. Then Jesus saith to them: All you shall be scandalized in Me this night. For it is written: I will strike the shepherd, and the sheep of the flock shall be dispersed."⁵⁶

18. The messianic prophecies in primitive Christian teaching. St. John the Apostle, instructed as he was by Jesus Himself on the prophecies which concerned the Passion, cites one other prediction as verified in the sufferings of his Master. "The soldiers therefore, when they had crucified Him, took His garments (and they made four parts: to every soldier a part) and also His coat. Now the coat was without seam, woven from the top throughout. They said then one to another. Let us not cut it, but let us cast lots for it, whose it shall be. That the Scripture might be fulfilled saying: They have parted My garments among them: and upon My vesture they have cast lot. And the soldiers indeed did these things."⁵⁷

The same instruction on the fulfillment of the prophecies is manifest in the doctrine of Philip the deacon. "Now an angel of the Lord spoke to Philip, saying: Arise, go towards the south, to the way that goeth down from Jerusalem into Gaza: this is desert. And rising up he went and behold a man of Ethiopia, an eunuch of great authority under Candace the queen of the Ethiopians, who had charge over all her treasures, had come to Jerusalem to adore. And he was returning, sitting in his chariot and reading Isaiah the prophet. And the Spirit said to Philip: Go near, and join thyself to this chariot. And Philip, running thither, heard him reading the prophet Isaiah, and he said: Thinkest thou that thou understandest what thou readest? Who said: And how can I, unless some man show me? And he desired Philip that he would come up and sit with him. And the place of the Scripture which he was reading was this: He was led as a sheep to the slaughter: and like a lamb without voice before His shearer, so openeth He not His mouth. In humility His judgment was taken away. His generation who shall declare, for His life shall be taken from the earth? And the eunuch answering Philip said: I

---

55 John 15:18–25.
56 Matt. 26:30–31; Mark 14:27.
57 John 19:23–24.

beseech thee, of whom doth the prophet speak this, of himself or of some other man? Then Philip opening his mouth and beginning at this Scripture, preached unto him Jesus."[58] From these citations we have exact clues to the prophecies which Jesus of Nazareth declared to have been fulfilled in Him.

19. The prophecies to which Jesus appealed. The best way in which we can realize the import of these prophecies as motives of credibility is to examine the very passages to which the Christians and their Master appealed. If we find that these passages offer a description of events which no creature could naturally foretell, and which actually transpired, we may recognize them as an intellectual miracle, as expressions of the manifestly divine foreknowledge which serve to guarantee the divine origin of that definite doctrine Jesus brought to the world of man.

The prophecy to which Jesus referred when He predicted the confusion and dispersion of the Apostles is found in the book of Zachariah. "Awake, O sword, against My Shepherd, and against the man that cleaveth to Me, saith the Lord of Hosts. Strike the shepherd and the sheep shall be scattered: and I will turn My hand to the little ones."[59] When He spoke of His enemies as unjustly hating Him, and appealed to scriptural prophecies of this hatred, He pointed to actual and clear messianic declarations in the psalms. "Let not them that are My enemies wrongfully rejoice over Me: who have hated Me without cause, and wink with the eyes. For they spoke indeed peaceably to Me: and speaking in the anger of the earth, they devised guile. And they opened their mouth wide against Me. They said: Well done, well done, our eyes have seen it. Thou hast seen this, O Lord, be not Thou silent: O Lord depart not from Me."[60] The same prediction of a man despised and unjustly persecuted is conveyed in another of the songs of Israel. Nothing could be more striking than the picture drawn in the sixty-eighth psalm, a picture which obviously refers to the sufferings and death of Jesus. "They are multiplied above the hairs of My head, who hate Me without cause. My enemies have grown strong, who have wrongfully persecuted Me. Then did I pay that which I took

---

58 Acts 8:26–35.
59 Zach. 13:7.
60 Ps. 34:19–22.

not away... Because for Thy sake I have borne reproach: shame hath covered My face. I am become a stranger to my brethren, and an alien to the sons of My mother... thou knowest My reproach, and My confusion, and My shame. In Thy sight are all they that afflict Me. My heart hath expected reproach and misery. And I looked for one that would grieve together with Me, but there was none: and for one that would comfort Me, and I found none. And they gave Me gall for My food: and in My thirst they gave Me vinegar to drink."[61] Again the twenty-first psalm foretells the historically verifiable circumstances of the Passion, as well as the bestial hatred which influenced the Jewish leaders to encompass the death of Jesus. The first words of this psalm are those which Jesus recalled during His agony on the cross. "O God, My God, look upon Me: why hast Thou forsaken Me?... But I am a worm and no man, the reproach of men and the outcast of the people. All they that saw Me have laughed Me to scorn: They have spoken with the lips and wagged the head. He hoped in the Lord, let Him deliver Him. Let Him save Him, seeing He delighteth in Him... Depart not from Me, for tribulation is very near: for there is none to help Me. Many calves have surrounded Me. Fat bulls have besieged Me. They have opened their mouths against Me, as a lion ravening and roaring I am poured out like water: and all My bones are scattered. My heart is become like wax, melted in the midst of My bowels. My strength is dried up like a potsherd, and My tongue hath cleaved to My jaws: and Thou hast brought Me down into the dust of death. For many dogs have encompassed Me. The council of the malignant hath besieged Me. They have dug My hands and feet. They have numbered all My bones. And they have looked and stared upon Me. They parted My garments amongst them, and upon My vesture they cast lots."[62]

20. The canticles of the servant of God. However, by far the most striking prediction concerning the Passion of the Messiah is to be found in the canticles of the servant of God, found in the book of Isaiah. There are four of these canticles, each depicting with surprising wealth of detail some observable aspect of the ministry and death of Jesus. These by themselves as well as with the other predictions which

---

61 Ps. 68:5, 8–9, 20–22.
62 Ps. 21:2, 7–9, 12–19.

are manifestly verified in Jesus of Nazareth, constitute an intellectual miracle of the first order, and thus a motive of credibility accessible to the intelligence of all men, even to the spirit of our own age.

The first of these canticles depicts the dignity and beneficence which will characterize the work of the Messiah. "Behold My Servant, I will uphold Him: My Elect, My soul delighteth in Him. I have given My Spirit upon Him. He shall bring forth judgment to the gentiles. He shall not cry, nor have respect to person. Neither shall His voice be heard abroad. The bruised reed He shall not break and smoking flax He shall not quench. He shall bring forth judgment in truth. He shall not be sad nor troublesome, till He set judgment in the earth. And the islands shall wait for His law. Thus saith the Lord God that created the heavens and stretched them out: that established the earth and the things that spring out of it: that giveth bread to the people upon it, and spirit to them that tread thereon. I the Lord have called Thee in justice, and taken Thee by the hand, and preserved Thee. And I have given Thee for a covenant of the people, for a light of the gentiles. That Thou mightest open the eyes of the blind, and bring forth the prisoner out of prison, and them that sit in darkness out of the prison house."[63]

The second canticle expounds the glory of this servant. "Give ear, ye islands, and hearken ye peoples from afar. The Lord hath called Me from the womb. From the bowels of My mother He hath been mindful of My name. And He hath made My mouth like a sharp sword: in the shadow of His hand He hath protected Me, and hath made Me as a chosen arrow. In His quiver He hath hidden Me. And He said to Me: Thou art My Servant, Israel, for in Thee will I glory. And I said, I have labored in vain. I have spent My strength without cause and in vain. Therefore My judgment is with the Lord, and My work with My God. And now saith the Lord that formed Me from the womb to be His Servant, that I may bring back Jacob unto Him, and Israel will not be gathered together. And I am glorified in the eyes of the Lord, and My God is made My strength. And He said: It is a small thing that Thou shouldst be My Servant to raise up the tribes of Jacob, and to convert the dregs of Israel. Behold I have given Thee to be the light of the gentiles, that Thou mayst be My salvation, even to

---

63 Isa. 42:1–7.

The Witness of Prophecy

the farthest part of the earth. Thus saith the Lord the Redeemer of Israel His holy One, to the soul that is despised, to the nation that is abhorred, to the servant of rulers: Kings shall see, and princes shall rise up and adore for the Lord's sake, because He is faithful, and for the holy One of Israel who hath chosen Thee."[64]

The third describes the courage of this Servant. "The Lord hath given Me a learned tongue, that I should know how to uphold by word him that is weary. He wakeneth in the morning, in the morning He wakeneth My ear that I may hear Him as a Master. The Lord God hath opened My ear, and I do not resist, I have not gone back. I have given My body to the strikers, and My cheeks to them that plucked them. I have not turned away My face from them that rebuked Me and spit upon Me. The Lord is My Helper, therefore am I not, confounded. Therefore have I set My face as a most hard rock. And I know that I shall not be confounded. He is near that justifieth Me. Who will contend with Me? Let us stand together. Who is My adversary? Let him come near to Me. Behold the Lord God is My Helper. Who is He that shall condemn Me? So they shall all be destroyed as a garment, the moth shall eat them up."[65]

However, the fourth canticle gives the most circumstantial picture of the suffering Redeemer. "Behold My Servant shall understand. He shall be exalted and extolled, and shall be exceeding high. As many have been astonished at Thee, so shall His visage be inglorious among men, and His form among the sons of men. He shall sprinkle many nations, kings shall shut their mouth at Him. For they to whom it was not told of Him have seen; and they that have not heard have beheld. Who hath believed our report? And to whom is the arm of the Lord revealed? And He shall grow up as a tender plant before Him, and as a root out of a thirsty ground. There is no beauty in Him, nor comeliness. And we have seen Him, and there was no sightliness, that we should be desirous of Him: Despised and most abject of men, a man of sorrows and acquainted with infirmity: and His look was, as it were, hidden and despised, wherefore we esteemed Him not. Surely He hath borne our infirmities and carried our sorrows. And we have thought Him as it were a leper, and as one struck by God

---

64 Isa. 49:1–7.
65 Isa. 50:4–9.

and afflicted. But He was wounded for our iniquities. He was bruised for our sins. The chastisement of our peace was upon Him, and by His bruises we are healed. All we like sheep have gone astray. Every one hath turned aside into his own way. And the Lord hath laid on Him the iniquity of us all. He was offered because it was His own will, and He opened not His mouth. He shall be led as a sheep to the slaughter, and shall be dumb as a lamb before His shearer. And He shall not open His mouth. He was taken away from distress and from judgment. Who shall declare His generation? Because He is cut off out of the land of the living. For the wickedness of My people have I struck Him. And He shall give the ungodly for His burial, and the rich for His death: because He hath done no iniquity, neither was there deceit in His mouth. And the Lord was pleased to bruise Him in infirmity. If He shall lay down His life for sin, He shall see a long-lived seed, and the will of the Lord shall be prosperous in His hand. Because His soul hath labored, He shall see and be filled. By His knowledge shall this, My just Servant, justify many, and He shall bear their iniquities. Therefore will I distribute to Him very many, and He shall divide the spoils of the strong, because He hath delivered His soul unto death, and was reputed with the wicked, and He hath borne the sins of many, and hath prayed for the transgressors."[66]

21. Jesus as the Servant described in Isaiah. Line for line, these canticles describe with considerable detail and perfect accuracy the Passion of Jesus and the events which led up to it. The forty-second chapter of Isaiah describes the Servant of God as working unostentatiously. We have already seen how, time after time, Jesus of Nazareth forbade His disciples, the beneficiaries of His miracles, and above all the evil spirits to publish the news of His wonders and of His supernatural wisdom. The Jews themselves were forced to acknowledge that He was not a respecter of persons and that He taught truth.[67] Alone among the prophets of Israel, Jesus presented a message which was intended for the gentiles as well as for those of his own nation. The forty-ninth chapter describes the Servant of God as one whose mission it was to bring salvation to the ends of

---

66 Isa. 52:13–15; 53:1–12. For a modern scientific investigation of these prophecies see R. P. F. Ceuppens, O.P., *De Prophetiis Messianicis in Antiquo Testamento* (Rome, 1935).
67 Matt. 22:16; Mark 12:14; Luke 20:21.

the earth. This corresponds exactly to the injunction which Jesus, alone among the teachers in Israel, gave to His disciples.[68] The fiftieth chapter describes One who receives a teaching from God. Many times, as we have already seen, Jesus asserted that His doctrine had been given Him by the Father. Only Jesus suffered the revolting indignities described in the sixth verse of this chapter. The historical accounts of His captivity in the house of Caiphas and what we know of the fate of condemned prisoners in Oriental countries combine to show the graphic accuracy of the description in Isaiah. Furthermore, this same chapter describes the courage of the Servant. History tells us with absolute certainty that Jesus of Nazareth was never overcome by fear during the dark hours of His agony.

However, the fourth canticle contains the greatest wealth of detail. The abject appearance of the Servant in the prophecy constitutes a vivid and accurate description of a man who was scourged and crucified. The book of Isaiah tells of a willing Victim, and both the express words of Jesus and the verifiable historical records of His arrest show that He could have avoided capture and death. Jesus had said, "Therefore doth the Father love Me: because I lay down My life, that I may take it up again. No man taketh it away from Me, but I lay it down of Myself. And I have power to lay it down and I have power to take it up again. This commandment have I received of My Father."[69] The freedom which Jesus claimed, and which the Resurrection proved Him to possess, was that described in Isaiah. Naturally the truth is far more perfect and striking than the description of it in the prophetical book. Nevertheless, the prophetic description is accurate and manifestly beyond the natural competence of any creature, actual or possible. Furthermore, this fifty-third chapter of Isaiah insists that the Servant is to die and to be counted among the wicked and reprobate.

The psalter of David describes details of the suffering which this Servant of God was destined to undergo. That suffering embraced thirst, the piercing of the hands and feet of the victim, nudity, abandonment, and absolute rejection by His own people. All of these circumstances are verified fully and solely in the agony of Jesus.

---

68 Cf. Matt. 28:19; Mark 16:15.
69 John 10:17–18.

22. The death on the cross. There is one point in these prophecies which deserves special mention. The Jews at the time of St. Justin the Martyr and in our own day alleged as a reason for rejecting the messianic claims of Jesus the fact that He died hanging on the cross. They cite the text of the pentateuch. "When a man hath committed a crime for which he is to be punished with death, and being condemned to die is hanged on a gibbet: his body shall not remain upon the tree, but shall be buried the same day, for he is accursed of God that hangeth on a tree: and thou shalt not defile thy land which the Lord thy God shall give thee in possession."[70] As a matter of fact the Man of Sorrows spoken of in the prophecy of Isaiah is recognized as taking upon Himself freely the guilt of others and suffering for sins He did not commit. St. Paul gave an explanation alone consonant with the doctrine of the prophecy and with the history of Jesus, "Christ hath redeemed us from the curse of the law, being made a curse for us: for it is written: Cursed is every one that hangeth on a tree."[71]

Even the title "Servant of God" fits the character and the claims of Jesus perfectly. There was no other who could say "I do always the things that please Him."[72] The composite picture is such that any reasonable man can recognize it as a prophecy. It would be manifestly far above the natural competence of any man to predict with certainty the series of details which as a matter of fact appeared in the messianic prophecies. When Jesus of Nazareth appeared and when everything which had been foretold about the sufferings and death of the Messiah actually happened to Him, the prediction was clearly manifest as a true prophecy and thus an effective motive of credibility.

23. Apostolic preaching about the prophecies. We must not forget that the Apostles appealed to prophecies about the Resurrection in the Old Testament. Jesus Himself had asserted that His rising from the dead, as well as the other events in His life, had been foretold in the ancient writings.[73] The Pentecost sermon of St.

---

70 Deut. 21:22–23.
71 Gal. 3:13.
72 John 8:29.
73 Luke 8:31–33; 24:26–27.

Peter pointed out the place of that prophecy and St. Paul recalled it many times during the course of his own preaching.[74] The prediction was contained in one of the psalms of David. "The Lord is the portion of My inheritance and of My cup: It is Thou that wilt restore My inheritance to Me. The lives are fallen unto Me in goodly places: for My inheritance is goodly to Me. I will bless the Lord, who hath given Me understanding. Moreover My reins also have corrected Me even till night. I set the Lord always in My sight: for He is at My right hand, that I be not moved. Therefore My heart hath been glad, and My tongue hath rejoiced. More over My flesh also shall rest in hope. Because Thou wilt not leave My soul in hell: nor wilt Thou give Thy holy one to see corruption. Thou hast made known to Me the ways of life. Thou shalt fill Me with joy with Thy countenance. At Thy right hand are delights even to the end."[75]

St. Peter explained that the prophecy could not have been applied to David himself, since the royal psalmist had died and since the tomb in which his body was enclosed was visible even while he was preaching on that first Christian Pentecost. Manifestly the only Teacher of the divine Word who died but whose body never saw corruption was Jesus of Nazareth. To this day that explanation retains its validity. A teaching which men accepted as divinely revealed and consequently as sovereignly true could never have been understood other than in a way compatible with that truth. Since David had died, like all the kings and prophets after him, the Jewish people could not have imagined that the promise of incorruption applied to any of them. Only Jesus of Nazareth rose from the dead. In Him alone the prophecy was verified.

24. Prophecy about the birthplace and homeland of Christ. Two more messianic prophecies of high apologetical importance are cited by the evangelists. The first referred to the birthplace of the promised Redeemer. St. Matthew explains how this prediction, with its messianic implications, was known to the Jewish leaders at the time Jesus was born. "When Jesus therefore was born in Bethlehem of Judah in the days of king Herod, behold there came wise men from the east to Jerusalem, saying: Where is He that is born King

---

74 Acts 2:24–33; 12:23; 17:2; 26:22.
75 Ps. 15:5–11.

of the Jews? For we have seen His star in the east, and are come to adore Him. And king Herod hearing this was troubled, and all Jerusalem with him. And assembling together all the chief priests and the scribes of the people, he inquired of them where Christ should be born. But they said to him: In Bethlehem of Judah. For so it is written by the prophet: And thou Bethlehem, the land of Judah, art not the least among the princes of Judah: for out of thee shall come forth the captain that shall rule My people Israel."[76] Later the Jews in Jerusalem, ignorant of the fact that Jesus had really been born in Bethlehem, urged that He could not be the true Messiah, since the promised Redeemer was to be born in this town. "Of the multitude therefore, when they had heard these words of His, some said: This is the prophet indeed. Others said: This is the Christ: But some said: Doth the Christ come out of Galilee? Doth not the Scripture say that Christ cometh of the seed of David, and from Bethlehem, the town where David was?"[77]

In both of these cases the Jewish leaders obviously referred to a statement found in the book of Micah. "And thou Bethlehem Ephrata, art a little one among the thousands of Judah: out of thee shall He come forth unto Me that is to be the Ruler in Israel. And His going forth is from the beginning, from the days of eternity."[78] It is obvious, of course, that the Pharisees and the other Jews, conserving jealously the meaning contained in the divine message at least substantially, recognized this as a true prophecy about the Messiah. The fact that Jesus, who fulfilled in such marvelous accuracy of detail, all the other predictions about the Messiah was also born in Bethlehem, vindicates this prophecy, and shows it as a valid and effective motive of credibility in favor of His own doctrine.

Again there was a distinct reference in an ancient prophecy to the region where the Messiah would begin His ministry. "At the first time the land of Zabulon, and the land of Nephthali was lightly touched: and at the last the way of the sea beyond the Jordan, of the Galilee of the Gentiles was heavily loaded. The people that walked in darkness have seen a great light. To them that dwelt in the region of

---

76 Matt. 2:1–6.
77 John 7:40–42.
78 Mich. 5:2.

the shadow of death, light is risen."[79] St. Matthew, when he mentions that Jesus left Nazareth to carry out His ministry in Capharnaum and in the other sea-coast cities, states that this town was on the border of Zabulon and Nephthali and sees in the initial preaching of Jesus a fulfillment of this old prophecy.[80]

25. Jesus and the prophecies about John the Baptist. Jesus also appealed to the prophecies of John the Baptist as confirming the intellectual miracles of the Old Testament predictions. "You sent to John: and he gave testimony to the truth. But I receive not testimony from man: but I say these things that you may be saved. He was a burning and a shining light. And you were willing for a time to rejoice in his light. But I have a greater testimony than that of John. For the works which My Father hath given Me to perfect: the works themselves which I do, give testimony of Me that the Father hath sent Me. And the Father Himself who hath sent Me hath given testimony of Me. Neither have you heard His voice at any time nor seen His shape. And you have not His word abiding in you. For whom He hath sent, Him you believe not. Search the Scriptures, for you think in them to have life everlasting, and the same are they that give testimony of Me . . . Think not that I will accuse you to the Father. There is one that accuseth you. Moses, in whom you trust. For if you did believe Moses, you would perhaps believe Me also, for he wrote of Me. But if you do not believe his writings, how will you believe My words?"[81]

That was the appeal of Jesus. As far as the teaching of John was concerned, many Jews freely acknowledged that he had prophesied concerning Jesus. "And He went again beyond the Jordan into that place where John was baptizing first: and there He abode. And many resorted to Him, and they said: John indeed did no sign. But all things whatsoever John said of this man were true. And many believed in Him."[82] The Church from the time of the Apostles and the first apologists has never ceased to allege the prophecies of the Old Testament as intellectual miracles, guaranteeing the divine origin of that doctrine which Jesus of Nazareth proposed to men.

---

79 Isa. 9:1–2.
80 Matt. 4:12–16.
81 John 5:33–39; 44–47.
82 John 10:40–42.

26. The prophecies as criteria of revelation. The messianic prophecies to which we have made explicit reference are those of primacy and unquestioned apologetical value. Even the most cursory reading will assure the student that the Old Testament abounds in figures and in predictions which are fulfilled in the new dispensation under Jesus Christ. As a matter of fact the theologians have always maintained that the truths of the Old Testament are made manifest in the new, while the verities of the new dispensation or covenant are foreshadowed in the old. However, not all of the doctrine about Jesus and about the Church of which He is the Founder and the Head can be said to have full demonstrative force in the science of apologetics. Only those events which were clearly foretold, and which were publicly verified in the conduct and teaching of Jesus can obtain full and perfect historical recognition as intellectual miracles. In the science of apologetics as we know it, the most effective criteria of divine revelation in the line of intellectual miracles are those prophecies which have been so clearly fulfilled that we can compare the accomplishment, known as a plain historical fact, with the prediction and the literal meaning with which it was endowed among the chosen people. Where the prophecy itself must serve as a reason for the acceptance of the fact, it is manifest that this condition is not verified.

27. Prophecies about the birth of Jesus. Thus, for example, the virgin birth of Jesus was foretold long before He came into the world by Isaiah the prophet. "And the Lord spoke again to Achaz, saying: Ask thee a sign of the Lord thy God, either unto the depth of hell or unto the heighth above. And Achaz said: I will not ask, and I will not tempt the Lord. And He said: Hear ye therefore O house of David: Is it a small thing for you to be grievous to man, that you are grievous to my God also? Therefore the Lord Himself shall give you a sign. Behold a virgin shall conceive and bear a Son, and His name shall be called Emmanuel."[83] The prophecy evidently has reference to the birth of the Messiah, for only the promised Redeemer was ever acknowledged among men as possessing the name and the dignity of the living God. Furthermore, the reference is obviously to a virgin birth in the strict and miraculous sense of the term. A tremendous

---

83 Isa. 7:10–14.

and awful sign, given by God to a fearful but unrepentant king, and, as it were forced upon him despite his refusal to petition God would manifestly be in the miraculous order. It would have been the height of naïveté to suppose that, under the circumstances, Achaz or anyone else for that matter would have been able to find anything extraordinary in the prediction that a young woman who had been a virgin had conceived and borne a child in the natural manner. The extraordinary portent must obviously be the conception and birth of a child by and from a woman who remained a virgin. There is no room for serious doubt on this point.

Moreover it is a fact that Jesus of Nazareth was born in the way described in this prophecy. The first gospel says explicitly "And Joseph rising up from sleep, did as the angel of the Lord had commanded him, and took unto him his wife. And he knew her not till she brought forth her first born Son: and he called His name Jesus."[84] The evangelist moreover cites the conception and birth of Jesus precisely as the fulfillment of this prophecy. "Now the generation of Christ was in this wise. When His mother Mary was espoused to Joseph, before they came together, she was found with Child of the Holy Ghost. Whereupon Joseph her husband, being a just man and not willing publicly to expose her, was minded to put her away privately. But while he thought on these things, behold the Angel of the Lord appeared to him in his sleep saying: Joseph, son of David, fear not to take unto thee Mary thy wife: for that which is conceived in her is of the Holy Ghost. And she shall bring forth a Son: and thou shalt call His name Jesus: for He shall save His people from their sins. Now all this was done that it might be fulfilled which the Lord spoke by the prophet saying: Behold a virgin shall be with child and bring forth a Son. And they shall call His name Emmanuel, which being interpreted is, God with us."[85]

In the third gospel we learn of the actual message which God sent to Mary. "And the angel said to her: Fear not Mary, for thou hast found grace with God. Behold thou shalt conceive in thy womb, and shalt bring forth a Son, and thou shalt call His name Jesus. He shall be great, and shall be called the Son of the Most High. And the Lord

---

84 Matt. 1:24–25.
85 Matt. 1:18–23.

God shall give unto Him the throne of David His father. And He shall reign in the house of Jacob forever. And of His kingdom there shall be no end. And Mary said to the angel: How shall this be done, because I know not man? And the angel answering said to her: The Holy Ghost shall come upon thee, and the power of the Most High shall overshadow thee. And therefore also the Holy which shall be born of thee shall be called the Son of God."[86]

Now the virgin birth was obviously not the sort of event which would ordinarily fall within the competence of historians. As a matter of fact it is a fact, and moreover a fact which we believe. When we offer a theological explanation of this Catholic belief, it is only reasonable that we should follow the example of St. Matthew and cite the prophecy which foretold this very occurrence. The person who examines the prophecy of Isaiah scientifically and impartially is bound to see that it predicts a virgin birth. If that person accepts the content of the Old Testament as true on the authority of God revealing, he would naturally be certain that the Messiah would appear in the world of men in this manner. If He examined the claims of Jesus to the messianic honor and dignity, he would be bound to see that, as St. Justin Martyr said to Trypho the Jew, "Now it is evident to all that in the race of Abraham according to the flesh, no one has been born of a virgin or is said to have been born of a virgin save this our Christ."[87] This would constitute a serious, though not an apodictic proof for the credibility of Christ's doctrine as the statement stands in Justin.

The person who sincerely accepted the prophecy as the Word of God would have no scruples about believing that the virgin birth was possible to God. He would, if he came to accept the credibility of the Christian message because of the innumerable other signs which attest its divine origin, be ready to accept as strictly true the account of the virgin birth. Thus the prophecy of Isaiah is of tremendous importance for scholastic theology properly so called and for what is called the apology of dogma as well. However we would harm our cause by placing this fact, absolutely true as it is, on a level with the Resurrection and the prophecies which were verified in public and manifest events as motives of credibility. It has not the first or most

---

86 Luke 1:30–35.
87 St. Justin Martyr, Dialogue With Trypho, Ch. 60.

important place in the scheme of apologetics, even though, in this very science, it retains a certain power.

28. Prophecies not yet fulfilled. These are some prophecies which have not yet been fulfilled. These Old Testament predictions refer to the second coming of Christ. As such they constitute objects of belief rather than motives of credibility. The prophecy that is clear, and that is manifestly fulfilled, is the manifest intellectual miracle which attests to any man ready to examine the evidence the divine origin of the doctrine with which it is connected. A man does not have to accept the content of that prophecy with an act of divine faith to see its demonstrative force as a motive of credibility. He merely ascertains that at a certain time this definite event—A— is predicted. He knows that no created mind would or could be in a position to foretell that event with certainty. He examines his evidence and finds that this—A—has really taken place, in the manner in which it was prophesied. The obvious and necessary implication is that the prediction was an act of the divine knowledge. If a man has uttered it, he has manifestly received from God information which is valid and effective as a motive of credibility. The man who possesses an accurate natural knowledge about God is quite well aware that the Creator, all wise and just as He is, will never be party to a lie, and will never prostitute His seal to the cause of deception. Since the verified and apologetically effective prophecies of the Old Testament speak of the Messiah as a Bearer of a message from God, the seal of the divine approval is manifestly attached to the Person in whom these prophecies are fulfilled. Manifestly His teaching, proposed as a divine message, is rationally credible for what it claims to be.

29. The prophecies of Jesus. No less important but far less difficult to study are the prophecies uttered by Jesus of Nazareth and verified in the sight of all men. It is to our distinct advantage to list a number of these intellectual miracles, remembering that a knowledge of hidden truth in the past or present is fully as much an evidence of the divine mind as a certain and verified prediction of future events.

In the first place Jews of Nazareth manifested a knowledge of men's thoughts and hidden past life beyond that of which any creature would be naturally competent. The Apostles as a group acknowledged this: "Now we know that Thou knowest all things, and Thou needest not that any man should ask Thee. By this we believe that Thou comest forth from God."[88] An exercise of this power had influenced Nathanael to believe.[89] The Samaritan woman acknowledged Jesus as the Messiah when she saw an example of such an intellectual wonder.[90]

Jesus foretold with certitude and absolute accuracy events which were about to take place but which could never have been foreseen by any creature whatsoever. He foretold the finding of the ass and its colt, upon which He made His triumphal entry into Jerusalem.[91]

In the same way He gave the Apostles directions for entering into Jerusalem and finding the man with the water vessel, who was to lead them to the house where they would eat the last supper.[92]

We have already seen, in the previous chapter, how Jesus clearly predicted His own Passion, death, and Resurrection. He foretold the treason of Judas, at first in such a way that the faithful Apostles could not know the identity of the traitor, then finally at the last supper clearly, at the instance of John who had been moved to question the Master by Peter.[93] He predicted the denial of St. Peter at the very moment when this ardent and impetuous Apostle was protesting his own undying faith and loyalty.[94] He foretold the fate of St. Peter and of St. John,[95] the former of whom was destined to be crucified, and the latter to die a natural death.

Very clearly He predicted the bloody persecutions which would be raised against the Apostles and their successors.[96] He announced that the Jews would accept impostors who would claim the dignity and the office of Messiah. "I am come in the name of My Father, and you receive Me not. If another shall come in his own name, him you will receive."[97] This prophecy was abundantly fulfilled when a great

---

88 John 16:30.
89 John 1:49.
90 John 4:19.
91 Matt. 21:1–8; Mark 11:1–8; Luke 19:19–36.
92 Matt. 36:17–19; Mark 14:12–16; Luke 22:7–13.
93 Matt. 26:70–71; Mark 14:18–21; Luke 22:21–23; John 6:70–71; 13:21–30.
94 Matt. 26:33–35; Mark 14:29–31; Luke 22:33–34; John 13:36–38.
95 John 31:17–23.
96 Cf. John 16:2; Matt. 10:17–18; Mark 13:9–10; Luke 21:12–19.
97 John 5:43.

number of the Jewish people accepted adventurers like the nameless Egyptian and later Bar Chochebas.

Finally He predicted the utter ruin of Jerusalem within the lifetime of those who listened to His voice. According to Jesus the temple and the city would be utterly destroyed at the hands of a victorious army after a military siege conducted in the orthodox tactical manner. In the accounts of this prophecy, given in the three synoptic gospels, the teaching on the destruction of Jerusalem is interspersed with instruction relative to the end of the world and the second coming of Christ. However, St. Matthew notes[98] that the reply answered two distinct questions put by the Apostles to Jesus. One question was, "When shall these things be?" These things were the events which would transpire during the destruction of the holy city. The other was, "What will be the sign of Thy coming and of the consummation of the world?" According to the express declaration of Jesus "these things" were to happen during the lifetime of His own generation.[99] The end of the world would take place at a time which God had not revealed to any creature and which the Son of God was not commissioned to insert into that doctrine which He offered to the world as divine public revelation.[100]

History tells us very clearly that the followers of Christ in Jerusalem left the city before it was besieged by the Romans. "The whole body however of the Church at Jerusalem, having been commanded by a divine revelation, given to men of approved piety there before the war, removed from the city, and dwelt at a certain town beyond the Jordan, called Pella.[101] Eusebius mentions a divine revelation or prophecy but does not identify this with the words of Jesus. However the fact stands. Those who were the recipients of that instruction which the Master had given were prepared for this fall. Books which manifestly were written before that event describe it in detail, and ascribe the prophecy to Jesus.

30. The demonstrative power of these prophecies. However the scientific apologist must be prepared to encounter a somewhat bizarre

---

98 Matt. 24:3.
99 Malt. 24:34; Mark 12:30; Luke 21:32.
100 Matt. 24:36; Mark 12:32.
101 Eusebius, *The Ecclesiastical History*, Book III, Ch. 5.

attitude with regard to prophecy even on the part of men whose learning and competence enable them to work more intelligently. A couple of citations from an eminent modern work will illustrate this attitude better than any words could describe it. "Little that is certain can be said as to the date at which the three oldest gospels arose. The passage on the End of the World and the parousia of Jesus give a hint in Luke's case, for instead of Mark's enigmatic wording 'When ye see the abomination of desolation standing where he ought not,'[102] Luke says 'When ye see Jerusalem compassed with armies.'[103] Whoever wrote like that had been through the siege and destruction of Jerusalem. Hence Luke's Gospel and Acts were written after AD 70." ... If then the story of the empty grave was first published by Mark, the assumption is not remote that this took place at a time when the location could no longer be pointed out—otherwise there would probably have been a search. Hence even our oldest Gospel arose only after the destruction of Jerusalem, i.e., after AD 70.[104]

Now all of this is quite interesting. The learned professor, however, has set out to propose an hypothesis to explain the origin of New Testament literature. The hypothesis is ingenious. A very considerable amount of erudition is expended in explaining it. However, as the professor propounds it, the explanation remains a mere hypothesis. The conclusions which he states so decisively happen to be drawn, not from the certain and evident content of the New Testament books nor from ancient testimony about them and about their origin, but from the very hypothesis he started out to demonstrate and to elucidate. That hypothesis supposes the impossibility of motives and prophecies. It supposes the radical inaccuracy of the New Testament literature. It is clever, but unfortunately it happens to be at variance with naturally ascertainable facts. Professor Dibelius may believe that no one knew about the empty grave of Jesus until well after AD 70. The important fact, however, is that the Christians and their enemies among the Jewish leaders labored under no such delusion. He may be persuaded that St. Luke and the other synoptic authors could not

---

102 Mark 13:14.
103 Luke 11:20.
104 Martin Dibelius; *A Fresh Approach to the New Testament and Early Christian Literature*, English Translation (New York, 1936), pp. 64–66.

have written their accounts of the prophecies uttered by Jesus until after the destruction of Jerusalem. Frankly all the scientific evidence, both from internal and from external sources, is against him. The accumulation of erudition he displays (and that erudition is vast and exceedingly helpful) can never make up for a lack of science in the Aristotelian sense of the term. His conclusions are certainly not self-evident. No one can say that they are validly and rigidly inferred from proper evidence and principles. Science, in the strict and Aristotelian sense, shows very clearly that true prophecies, manifestly fulfilled and manifestly attached to the message of Jesus, marked that message as rationally credible and acceptable on divine faith. We will be recreant to our duty as apologists if we fail to exploit, for the glory of God and the benefit of mankind, this available and strictly scientific resource.

Chapter 18

THE CHURCH AS A MOTIVE OF CREDIBILITY

1. Jesus and miracles of the social order. Effects which are manifestly beyond the natural competence of any creature and which serve as authentic and effective signs of divine revelation can exist in many orders. In the first place they can take place in the world of bodily activity, and these motives of credibility are miracles in the strict sense of the term. A prophecy is a miracle in the intellectual order, the manifestation of some knowledge which evidently could belong naturally to God alone. When, in the life of an individual man we find moral and mental excellence of unlimited perfection and consequently beyond the natural sphere of man's capacity, we rightly designate these qualities as moral or sapiential miracles. The only other sort of objective or external motive of credibility available to man and useful as a guarantee of the divine origin of some doctrine must be sought in the social order. God could produce and sustain in the world some society which is visibly beyond the natural power of man either to originate or to continue. The Catholic Church proposes herself as such a sign of divine revelation.

Jesus of Nazareth Himself appealed to signs in the social order which were to be indicative of His divine mission. "That they all may be one, as Thou, Father in Me, and I in Thee, that they also may be one in Us: that the world may believe that Thou hast sent Me, and the glory which Thou hast given Me, I have given to them; that they may be one, as we also are One. I in them, and Thou in Me: that they may be made perfect in One, and the world may know that Thou hast sent Me, and hast loved them, as Thou hast also loved Me."[1] He intended that the unity of His disciples should stand as a firm indication that

---

[1] John 17:21–23.

His message was actually the teaching of God. As the doctrine on the kingdom of God has shown us, He intended that union among His disciples to be social and supernatural. They were to be one with Him and with each other insofar as they sincerely loved one another as fellow members of an organization of which He was at once the Founder and the Head. That love, the principle of ecclesiastical unity, was meant to be the affection for God or charity which is the source of all holiness, and the principle of all full perfection in the life of man. Thus, when Jesus of Nazareth insisted that the disciples, insofar as they were to be one, would constitute a true motive of credibility, He pointed out that all of those characteristics dependent upon that unity might denominate the Church as a true social miracle.

2. The natural competence of man in the social order. It is perfectly obvious, of course, that man is naturally competent to found and to continue societies. However, it is equally manifest that none of these social organizations will surpass the limits imposed upon the power of those who brought them into being or who compose them. The natural force of man is finite. He produces a limited effect. He can found a society, but the organization thus brought into being will, insofar as it is *proportioned* to the natural strength of man, be effective in one time or among people of one racial or social group. To imagine for a moment that the opposite could possibly be true would be to indulge in the idle fancy that an effect could be greater than its principal cause.

A society which is manifestly unlimited by any of those factors which encompass works proportioned to the natural force of any creature is manifestly an effect which is proportioned to the infinite power of God. As such it is a true motive of credibility, attesting the divine approbation for claims made in favor of that doctrine with which it is connected. Now the Catholic Church is such a society. It is the business of the apologist to point out those aspects of the Church and of her activity which most effectually and convincingly manifest and exhibit its character as a miracle in the social order.

3. The characteristics by which the Church is recognizable as a criterion of revelation. The fathers of the Vatican Council pointed out five of these characteristics.[2] According to their teaching,

---

[2] The Vatican Council, The Constitution, *Dei Filius*, Ch. 3.

the Catholic Church is a true and perpetual motive of credibility and an unwavering indication of her own divine commission because of

1. Her admirable propagation
2. Her exalted holiness
3. Her marvelous and unlimited fruitfulness in all good things
4. Her catholic unity
5. Her unconquered stability.

We must realize that we do not use these manifest qualities of the Catholic Church in the same way that the four notes are used in Ecclesiology. The historical sources at our disposition show us very clearly that Jesus of Nazareth actually instituted a Church which was one, holy, catholic, and apostolic. Thus, when the student of Ecclesiology finds evidence that the Roman Catholic Church alone is endowed with these characteristics, he can rightfully infer that this organization has the sole right to propose herself as the true Church of Jesus Christ. All that is required for this purpose is to ascertain that the Church manifestly possesses those qualities with which Jesus of Nazareth endowed the society He founded.

The task of the apologist who uses the Church as a true motive of credibility is something quite distinct. The apologist considers the qualities with which he is concerned, not insofar as they were described by Jesus of Nazareth, but precisely insofar as they could not have been brought about by the natural power of any creature in any society. Our work will not have been accomplished successfully unless we can bring forth evidence that no created agency could have produced and maintained an institution which was propagated and which endured like the Catholic Church, and which still maintained in holiness, beneficence, and unity.

4. The marvelous propagation of the Church—the political background. The founding of the Catholic Church is historically a miraculous phenomenon because the natural created causes which were brought into play were in no way proportionate to the effect achieved. There are two ways in which we can ascertain the manifestly miraculous character of this foundation. In the first place, it is obvious that the agencies which have been used to propagate the Church were in themselves incapable of bringing about a powerful and international organization. In the second place it is historically evident that there were forces thrown against the nascent Christian Church which would most certainly have destroyed any organization which depended upon the natural power of creatures for its subsistence. In order to have a scientific understanding of these facts, we must take many circumstances into consideration.

We must not forget that the Church was first propagated by a group of Jews, devoid of any special education and certainly without political influence. We know very well that the Romans and the Greeks during the first century and the second looked upon the Jewish race with particular disfavor. At first they were despised as superstitious and antisocial, as enemies of the human race. Later they were attacked and hated as fierce but unsuccessful rebels against the power and the authority of Rome. The Christians insisted that all men must worship as God this Jesus of Nazareth, a Jew who had been condemned to the humiliating and terrifying death of the cross.

At a time when religion and the state were inseparably joined together and when the adoration of the national gods was considered as a part of the recognition due to the state itself, the Christians not only proposed their crucified Lord as an object of worship, but steadfastly refused to recognize the civic deities at all. At a time when certain types of vice were permissible or even fashionable, they insisted upon the full observance of the moral law. Humanly speaking the twelve Apostles could perhaps have worked for the institution and maintenance of those little sects that flourished for a time among the Jews. Their natural powers were totally insufficient for the foundation and support of a worldwide and forceful society.

Moreover, from the first, the infant Church was faced with the hatred of the governments and the peoples to whom the gospel of Jesus was preached. The healing of the lame man in the Beautiful Gate of the temple was followed by a discourse of Peter. As a result of this sermon Peter and John his companion were arrested by the Jews. From that time on the opposition to Christianity among the Israelites was bitter and unrelenting. The Apostles were imprisoned,[3] they were scourged and threatened by the Sanhedrin itself.[4] The heroic deacon Stephen was stoned according to the judicial mode of

---

3 Acts 5:18.
4 Acts 5:40.

execution among the Jews.[5] Paul was maltreated continually.[6] James was put to death by Herod, who saw that his persecution pleased the people.[7]

At first the Romans held themselves aloof from what they considered an internal quarrel of a despised and ignorant people. However the infamous Nero made the Christians, who were manifestly in great disrepute among the pagans, the scapegoats for himself when he was accused, rightly or wrongly, of setting the fire which destroyed a good portion of the imperial city during his reign. From that time until the edict of Milan in 313,[8] the followers of Christ lived under the official ban of the Roman empire. During a good portion of that time they enjoyed a certain *de facto* toleration. However, very frequently the government of what the old Celts used to call the King of the World employed every device of craft and force to induce its subjects to abandon Jesus. Only the most naïve student could imagine for a moment that a society thus hated and proscribed by Jews and Romans alike and directed by men of no social or political prominence could have been propagated by forces natural to any creature.

We must remember that the Church did not advance with members inseparably bound to one another by ties of race or by the hope of material booty. The Christian leaders enjoined cheerful obedience to political masters and insisted, as had Jesus Himself, that the kingdom they sought was not of this world. The Christians themselves embraced their faith freely and intelligently. They suffered and lived, not as barbarian fanatics, but as reasonable men, ready and willing to give an account of the hope that was in them. With all of these factors which humanly would have condemned the Catholic Church to relative impotence and restricted it to a small membership, the Church as a visible society very soon overflowed throughout the known world. As the frontiers of geographic knowledge have advanced, the cross has gone ahead with them. Today there is no

---

5 Acts 5:57–59.
6 2 Cor. 11:23–33.
7 Acts 12:1–3.
8 Cf. Lactantius, *De Mortibus Persecutorum*, Ch. 48; Kidd, *Documents Illustrative of the History of the Church*, Vol. 1, No. 182.

considerable portion of the earth upon which the Catholic Church does not exist and carry on its salvific work.

The change of dynasties and of cultures has never prevented this propagation. The missions of the Church are active during the present war as they were during the lifetime of the Apostles themselves. It goes without saying that no other religious organization can boast of such a record. There were powerful and important religious societies in existence when the Catholic Church embarked upon her missionary career. They have changed or perished. All of them have found that *limitation* which inexorably characterizes all things merely human.

We must not lose sight of the fact that we are dealing with the Catholic Church as a motive of credibility even when we consider this aspect of her marvelous propagation. The Church claims to be and is a perfect society. She must be judged according to the norms applied to societies and compared with other organizations. Thus it is more than a religious movement and more again than a dogmatic system. The thing whose marvelous propagation we can easily recognize is a society with a definite monarchical and hierarchical form of government. The men who embraced the teachings of Jesus Christ became incorporated into this society. They acknowledged and obeyed its leadership. At times that *society* found itself opposed and even proscribed by the state. It propagated itself as a society. It claimed and exercised the right of expelling disobedient and unworthy members. It never allowed a mere nominal membership in its adherents, but imposed upon them the works of faith and penance and charity. The Catholic Church, humanly speaking, is an institution which would spread itself throughout the world with considerable difficulty. Its propagation is manifestly a work beyond the competence of any created nature.

Sometimes there has been a tendency to ascribe the missionary success of the Catholic Church to the political or diplomatic astuteness of her leaders. A glance at the ascertainable facts will show any student that this strategic skill, when it existed at all, could not be the adequate cause of any such propagation as we find in the Catholic Church. We will find in the history of this society that it has frequently been directed by men of consummate genius. Some of the first minds that God has given to the children of men have been proud to consecrate themselves to the work of spreading the Catholic Church and thus serving the cause of Jesus. Nevertheless, even a brief study will show us that the missionary effort of the Church has not always been carried on along lines suggested by human genius. Moreover the definite failings of her own children have frequently hampered or prevented her progress. The Catholic Church insists upon the fact that some of her members do not follow and have not followed the moral teachings of Christ. A society whose membership or whose missionary corps consisted entirely of men like St. Paul or St. Francis Xavier would naturally have made tremendous strides in the line of growth and new foundations. However, the Church has very frequently found that incompetence or carelessness which would have ruined any merely human organization within her own ranks. Neither this nor any other factor could limit or prevent a work which is manifestly supernatural.

5. Miracles in the primitive Church. The first propagation of the Church was accompanied and aided by manifest miracles. The history of the primitive Church mentions a good many of them specifically. The throng at Pentecost heard the announcement of Christ, each man in his own language although the members of that crowd were from every section of the diaspora. "And they were all filled with the Holy Ghost, and they began to speak with divers tongues according as the Holy Ghost gave them to speak. Now there were dwelling at Jerusalem Jews, devout men out of every nation under heaven. And when this was noised abroad, the multitude came together, and were confounded in mind because that every man heard them speak in his own tongue. And they were all amazed and wondered saying: Behold are not all these that speak Galileans? And how have we heard every man our own tongue wherein we were born? Parthians and Medes and Elamites and inhabitants of Mesopotamia, Judea, and Cappadocia, Pontus and Asia; Phrygia and Pamphilia, Egypt and the parts of Lybia about Cyrene, and strangers of Rome; Jews also and proselytes, Cretes and Arabians: We have heard them speak in our own tongues the wonderful works of God."[9]

The miraculous cure of the lame man in the Beautiful Gate of the temple was an outstanding event in the life of the early Church and

---

9 Acts 2:4–11.

one which resulted in the accession of many converts. "Now Peter and John went up into the temple at the ninth hour of prayer. And a certain man who was lame from his mother's womb was carried: whom they laid every day at the gate of the temple which is called Beautiful, that he might ask alms of them that went into the temple. He, when he had seen Peter and John about to go into the temple, asked to receive alms. But Peter with John, fastening his eyes upon him said: Look upon us. But he looked earnestly upon them, hoping that he should receive something from them. But Peter said: Silver and gold I have none: but what I have I give thee: In the name of Jesus Christ of Nazareth, arise and walk. And taking him by the right hand, he lifted him up, and forthwith his feet and soles received strength. And he leaping up stood and walked: and went in with them into the temple, walking and leaping and praising God. And all the people saw him walking and praising God. And they knew him that it was he who sat begging alms at the Beautiful Gate of the temple: and they were filled with wonder and amazement at that which had happened to him."[10] The Sanhedrin, apprised of this event attempted to prevent the Apostles from preaching about Jesus, but they were in no way able to deny the reality of the miracle. "But they threatening sent them away: not finding how they might punish them, because of the people: for all men glorified what had been done, in that which had come to pass, for the man was above forty years old in whom that miraculous cure had been wrought."[11] When Ananias and Saphira his wife lied to Peter, they were immediately struck dead by the divine power.[12]

The text of the Acts recounts that many unnamed miracles were wrought by the Apostles, so that even those not glorying in the Christian name hastened to take advantage of the healing power manifest in the witnesses of Jesus. "And there came great fear upon the whole church, and upon all that heard these things. And by the hands of the Apostles were many signs and wonders wrought among the people. And they were all with one accord in Solomon's porch. But of the rest no man durst join himself unto them: but the people

---

10 Acts 3:1–10.
11 Acts 4:21–22.
12 Acts 5:1–10.

magnified them. And the multitude of men and women who believed in the Lord was more increased, insomuch that they brought forth the sick into the streets, and laid them on beds and couches, that when Peter came, his shadow at the least might overshadow any of them, and they might be delivered from their infirmities. And there came also together to Jerusalem a multitude out of the neighboring cities, bringing sick persons and such as were troubled with unclean spirits; who were all healed."[13]

The Apostles as a group were liberated from prison by the ministry of an angel,[14] as was St. Peter alone at a later date.[15] St. Stephen, one of the first deacons, is mentioned as having performed miraculous works, which drew upon him the hatred of his countrymen.[16] St. Philip, one of his companions, did likewise.[17] The conversion of St. Paul was certainly a moral miracle of the first order.[18] The intellectual miracle of prophecy was found among the Christians. "And in these days there came prophets from Jerusalem to Antioch. And one of them named Agabus, rising up, signified by the Spirit that there should be a great famine over the whole world, which came to pass under Claudius."[19] St. Paul cast out an evil spirit from a girl in Philippi,[20] and obtained a reputation as a miracle worker in Ephesus. So great was his fame that the Jewish exorcists attempted to expel devils from possessed persons by the use of his name. "And God wrought by the hand of Paul more than common miracles: so that even there were brought from his body to the sick handkerchiefs and aprons. And the diseases departed from them and the wicked spirits went out of them. Now some also of the Jewish exorcists who went about attempted to invoke over them that had evil spirits the name of the Lord Jesus, saying: I conjure you by Jesus whom Paul preacheth. And there were certain men, seven sons of Sceva, a chief priest, that did this. But the wicked spirit answering said to them: Jesus I know, and

---

13 Acts 5:11–16.
14 Acts 5:18–20.
15 Acts 12:5–11.
16 Acts 6:8.
17 Acts 8:6–8.
18 Acts 9:1–19.
19 Acts 11:27–28.
20 Acts 16:16–18.

Paul I know: but who are you? And the man in whom the wicked spirit was, leaping upon them and mastering them both, prevailed against them, so that they fled out of that house naked and wounded. And this became known to all the Jews and the gentiles that dwelt at Ephesus: and fear fell on them all, and the name of the Lord Jesus was magnified."[21] On two occasions the Apostles restored life to persons who had died. St. Peter raised up Dorcas at Joppe and St. Paul a young Christian Troas.[22]

As a matter of fact the place of miracles in the early church was so well recognized that St. Paul was compelled to remind his disciples that the power of performing them was only one of the many gifts which God had vouchsafed to His followers, and that it was by no means the most excellent of these gifts. "Now there are diversities of graces, but the same Spirit, and there are diversities of ministries, but the same Lord. And there are diversities of operations, but the same God who worketh all in all. And the manifestation of the Spirit is given to every man unto profit. To one indeed, by the Spirit, is given the word of wisdom: and to another, the word of knowledge according to the same Spirit: to another faith, in the same Spirit: to another the grace of healing in one Spirit: to another the working of miracles, to another prophecy, to another the discerning of Spirits, to another diverse kinds of tongues, to another interpretation of speeches."[23]

The Church which possessed and exercised this power spread abroad and flourished in spite of official and popular resentment against it. It manifested no political ambition. As a matter of fact the pagans declaimed against it precisely because it had a tendency to turn men away from offices of civic preferment. It offered no inducement of earthly pride and luxury. Yet, a bare three centuries after its Founder had died on Calvary, the Roman emperor Constantine was proud to act as the patron and protector of this organization. In itself this would constitute a manifest social miracle, but the marvelous propagation of the Catholic Church can be seen in its proper background only when we consider it with reference to the holiness and other qualities mentioned by the Council.

---

21 Acts 19:11–17.
22 Acts 9:36–42; 20:9–12.
23 1 Cor. 12:4–10.

6. The exalted holiness of the Church. This characteristic is perhaps the easiest to recognize of all those qualities by which the Church can be distinguished as a social miracle. Holiness consists in a firm and perfect adherence to good, coupled with an absolute aversion from evil in the moral order. As an organization, the Catholic Church manifests this holiness to an unlimited extent. Thus it appears certainly as a society beyond the natural competence of any creature to organize or to maintain.

The Church, according to the promise of her divine Founder, and also in the light of history and experience, is and has been an organization which includes within its membership both good and evil men. As a result it is worse than idle to attempt an appreciation of that sanctity which characterizes the Catholic society from the point of view of some constant and universal holiness in all of her children. The Church is an organization, and as such she must be described and judged. Now this society manifests an exalted holiness precisely insofar as any organization can show it.

Primarily the way in which this organization manifests its holiness is by devoting itself corporately to the worship of God. The Catholic Church, as a society, has its central and essential function in the sacrifice of the Mass. The person who takes the trouble to examine this activity can see immediately that, in the ineffable profundity and complexity of its nature, it is an operation of outstanding holiness. Jesus of Nazareth commanded His Church to repeat, in memory of Him, the solemn sacrificial act which He instituted in the upper room the night before He died. "Do this for a commemoration of Me."[24] The act consisted in the double consecration. Jesus took bread and said to His Apostles, "This is My Body," and then took wine and said "This is the chalice of My Blood."[25] The Church has interpreted this sacrificial act into a prayer of ineffable beauty and holiness, a prayer which is, in the last analysis, a kind of paraphrase of that petition which Jesus Himself had commended to the Apostles and which we know as the Lord's Prayer. The action, as sacrificial, is pre-eminently social in its nature. It is meant to express and to vivify the corporate petition of that society which wills that which Jesus Himself intended

---

24 Luke 22:19.
25 Matt. 26:26–28; Mark 14:22–24; Luke 22:19–20.

and which He still intends. The object of the petition which is set forth in this sacrifice is the glory of God through the eternal salvation of men. In order that men may enjoy this unending happiness, Jesus and the Church He founded will that they may enjoy peace and prosperity in this world.

For the Church, as for Jesus Himself, a sincere and benevolent love of God is inseparable from a true philanthropy. When God is glorified, the benefit accrues not to Him, but to those intellectual creatures who honor and reverence Him. As a result the Church seeks unfailingly to bring men to an eternity of eternal happiness. Conscious of the fact that Jesus Himself laid down baptism, which is the sign of entrance into her communion, as a necessary condition for salvation, she does all in her power to bring all men to recognize the validity of her claims to believe the teaching which Jesus has given her with the assent of divine faith, and finally to enter and persevere in her communion.

Centering around the Eucharistic sacrifice, the Church exhibits to the world six other sacraments, all of them calculated to bring man closer to God and to remove him from that condition of sin which alone could prevent him from enjoying eternal happiness. Around these sacraments she has constructed a liturgy of outstanding perfection and purity. All of her effort has been expended in bringing about the fulfillment of that intention which animates her central sacrifice.

The teaching of the Catholic Church unmistakably expresses this same high holiness. In her official instruction she has labored incessantly to preserve pure and inviolate the complete message which Jesus of Nazareth entrusted to her care. Every pronouncement in all of her dogmatic history has been made either to repel some fatal misinterpretation of that communication or to bring its meaning home even more effectively to her children. The Church instructs its members about God, about human nature, and about the world, showing the divine sanctity of which all human holiness is meant to be a sharing and an imitation. At the same time it holds up to its members the divine command that they should be holy as their heavenly Father is holy.[26]

---

26 Cf. Matt. 5:48.

This fact has a great deal to do with the manifest and miraculous holiness of the Catholic Church. Naturally there is nothing remarkable about an organization which intends to raise its members up in the standard of human virtue. Nearly every society, religious or civic, intends some moral excellence on the part of its own members. However, it is one thing to enjoin the practice of some moral virtues and quite another to insist upon a complete and ever increasingly perfect observation of the divine law. This latter intention is visibly the characteristic of our Church. This organization sternly forbids the practice of any vice and at the same time refuses to allow any individual within its ranks to be satisfied with the degree of moral excellency already attained. In this way she manifests herself as a society of outstanding or extraordinary holiness, a social miracle in the strictest sense of the term.

The basic commandments upon which the Catholic Church insists are distinctly positive in character, the active benevolent and sincere love of God and of our neighbors. Thus a man who follows the instruction of this Church realizes that he does not possess the perfection which God expects of him merely by omitting certain operations or flying from some temptations. The motive which underlies all his obedience to the divine law is a real and active affection for that God who has designed to call him to the dignity of an adoptive sonship. The Church does not allow him to lose sight of the fact that God is so good that any affection we may conceive for Him is unworthy of Him, and that therefore he should strive unceasingly to love God ever more effectively and intensely.

At the same time the Church obviously conforms and has conformed to the negative exigencies of real sanctity. She has been in existence for nearly two millennia, and during all that time she has consistently and conspicuously refrained from any official complacency in or toleration of moral evil. During these two millennia naturally enough a good many moral vices have become fashionable or popular at one time or another. The Church could obviously have kept the loyalty and the affection of England and consequently of the British Empire as a whole, had she been willing to condone the divorce of Henry VIII. She refused to tolerate this act, just as she has condemned the pernicious practices of birth control and mutilation in our own day.

We are perfectly aware that in these similar events not all the men who have been influential in determining the policy of the Catholic Church need necessarily have been motivated by a pure love of holiness. All that entered into the individual conduct of such ecclesiastical personages is, in the last analysis at least, quite impertinent to the question of corporate sanctity. The manifest fact of the matter is that in every case the Catholic Church as a society has refused to countenance sin in any form whatsoever. The fact that an organization could act in this way while at the same time it counts within its membership men and women not remarkable for sanctity itself constitutes a manifest and striking social miracle.

7. The saints. We would not sufficiently appreciate the exalted holiness of the Catholic Church unless we realized that this holiness of doctrine and intention produced practical effects within the membership of this organization. From the very beginning of its existence until the present time there have been persons of eminent and manifest sanctity who have lived according to the tenets of the Church and whose sanctity was the vital expression of that teaching which they received from this society. Many of these individuals are inscribed among the saints, venerated by the Church itself. It is a striking tribute to the effective holiness of the Church as a teacher in modern times that no less than one hundred and fifty members of the Catholic Church who lived during the nineteenth century have been seriously proposed for canonization. Many of these have been recognized as authentic saints, worthy of the veneration of their fellows by reason of the eminent and heroic sanctity which characterized their earthly lives.

Naturally individual holiness is a quality quite difficult to ascertain. As a result the Catholic Church insists that every individual raised to its altars should have his holiness attested by well-authenticated miracles, performed through the intercession of the candidate for canonization. The men who are acquainted with the processes which govern the administration of the Church are well aware of the intense scrutiny to which these miracles are unfailingly subjected. These miracles are accepted only when they are manifestly and unquestionably motives of credibility, signs of the divine approval for the claim that this definite person has lived a life of eminent holiness and is now enjoying his eternal reward. The miracles are facts, and the realist must accept them as such or deny the actual.

8. The martyrs. In every age, and most especially in the past two centuries, the Church has been manifest as a motive of credibility through the heroism of innumerable martyrs who have sacrificed their lives rather than betray the message and the love of Jesus. In the nineteenth century there were mass executions of Catholics in Japan, Korea, China, Uganda, and Paris. Our own century has seen bloody persecution in Russia, Mexico, and particularly in Spain under the bolshevist reign of terror. History informs us that there have been martyrs in the Catholic Church since the days of St. Stephen. The Church which can evoke that type of adherence from men and women of every age and social class is obviously a reality which could not have been produced and maintained by any merely created agency.

Naturally enough we do not hold that the Catholic Church is manifestly a society of which God is the principal Cause merely because some persons have died for her sake. History shows us very clearly that there is hardly a cause, however worthless or evil it might have been, which has not claimed the lives of some of its adherents. There have always been fanatics delighted to have the opportunity of accepting death for one reason or another. However, it is perfectly manifest to any man who takes the trouble to investigate the matter that the Catholic martyrs can be explained by no merely natural cause or reason. Their fortitude and perseverance bespeaks much more.

In the first place these martyrs could never, as a group at least, be classified as fanatics. Among their number we find such eminent literary figures as SS. Justin and Cyprian. We have at our disposal the intensely human letters of SS. Isaac Jogue and John de Brebreuf. The students who crowded the old Angelico classroom of Father Joseph Garcia-Diaz knew him as a gentle and brilliant professor. Yet, only a few short years ago he laid down his life in Barcelona in glorious martyrdom. The martyrs suffered freely. They accepted a death which was in itself most horrible because they would not abandon the living doctrine of Jesus. Thus they were pre-eminently *witnesses* to the truth of that doctrine. Only an absolutely universal and unlimited Cause could have produced this effect.

9. The fruitfulness of the Church in beneficial works. The Church again is visible as a social miracle precisely because of the good effects in her ministry. Any person who is at all acquainted with the activity of this organization knows very well that there is hardly a branch of philanthropic work in which she is not prominent. The property of any diocese or religious community is invariably devoted to the welfare of the people as a whole. Those who have given their lives to the service of the Church are engaged in activity which is uniformly beneficial. This unique characteristic of the Church marks it as an organization beyond the natural power of man to organize and maintain.

The reason for this beneficial activity must be sought in the basic intention of the Church. Intending the supernatural and eternal happiness of all men, she works sincerely to bring about the conditions of peace and prosperity in which men can most effectively work out their final destiny. Naturally the greatest service she renders to mankind is to be found in her central activity, the conduct of the Eucharistic sacrifice, the attendant administration of the sacraments, and the preaching of the divinely revealed message. However we cannot consider this work as a valid evidence of credibility, since it is good only in the supposition that the teaching offered by the Church actually is what it claims to be, a message communicated in a supernatural way by God to man. Still there are visibly philanthropic works so common in the life of Catholicism that they can serve easily as evidence of the sublime origin of the Church itself.

First there is the work of instruction. Prescinding for a moment from the teaching of the mysteries, the Church obviously proposes to all men an accurate certain and universally attainable natural knowledge about God. To this end she works with an educational system far greater in extent and in perfection than any other school system in the history of the world. Any thoughtful man can easily see that such a notion of God is by far the greatest natural intellectual benefit attainable to the human race. With this accurate natural knowledge about his Creator, man can recognize an objective moral order, both in the individual and in the social sphere. Without it he is hopelessly involved in mental darkness. No institution has done as much as the Catholic Church to bring this accurate natural notion of God to men.

Moreover the Church has always devoted a great part of her energy to alleviating bodily suffering among men. History tells of the many occasions when the leaders of this society were willing and able to relieve want in the districts confided to their care even to the extent of selling the possessions of the Church to procure necessary food and clothing for the afflicted. The charities of the Church are enormous. Her hospitals and dispensaries are scattered throughout the world ready and able to give assistance to those who are in need of it.

On the other hand, there is no activity foreign to the best interests of man upon which the Church has ever embarked. This is a strong statement, but one which can be verified easily enough from the available datum of history. It is perfectly true that there have been and that there actually are Catholics quite unworthy of their high calling. At the same time, however, the organization as such, in her laws and in her corporate activity, has confined her activity to works manifestly beneficial to the human race.

Naturally enough this aspect shows the Church as a social miracle when it is taken in conjunction with the other four enumerated by the Council of the Vatican. The Church which was propagated in a marvelous way, which is eminently and manifestly holy, which rejoices in a Catholic unity and which has endured in the face of difficulties which most certainly would have destroyed any merely human organization, is even more evidently a social miracle when we consider its *unlimited* fruitfulness in all good things for mankind. The Church is not a social miracle merely because it is a philanthropic organization, nor for that matter merely because its activities are purely beneficial. It is outstanding, a source of wonder in the created universe because its activity for good is totally unrestricted. It was beneficial to the Romans and the Persians. It is beneficial today in America and in China. Wherever it exists it manifestly adapts itself to the temper, to the requirements, and to the capacities of the peoples who rejoice in its presence.

A society within the natural compass of human achievement can obviously be of benefit to some peoples at some times. Only the Catholic Church, among the visible organizations laboring in the world in which we live, has proven an unmixed blessing to the men of all lands and of all ages. We do not speak, of course, of the beneficial capacity of the Church. We are concerned only with the visible benefits actually conferred upon the human race throughout the world in the past and now being produced across the face of the earth.

As we have seen, a created power, by the very fact that it is created, necessarily finds a limited object. Thus when we learn of an institution which produces good effects with no sign of circumscription at all, an organization which is fully as much at home among and beneficial to the men of the first century, the twelfth, and the twentieth, we have every reason to say that this society could never have been produced and maintained by any natural power. We have a right scientifically to assert that it is an effect freely produced by the living God above and independently of the natural forces active in the world. It is manifest as a work which has God alone as a principal Cause. Attached as it is to a doctrine which is presented as a divinely revealed message, the Catholic Church is an obvious and powerful motive of credibility, an evidence that the teaching it presents has really come from God.

10. The Catholic unity of the Church. Unity and Catholicity are notes of the true Church which Jesus of Nazareth founded in the world. In other words, it is manifest, from the reliable historical documents which tell us of His activity, that He meant to establish a religious organization which should subsist throughout the entire world and which should be undivided as a social entity. Thus it is obvious that only some society actually endowed with these qualities can have the right to claim that it is the organization which Jesus constituted and which He wished men to enter. On the contrary, any religious movement which does not possess these marks is manifestly a society quite foreign to the true Church of Christ.

When we say, however, that the Church is a manifest social miracle by reason of its catholic unity, we affirm that an organization so constituted is manifestly beyond the natural competence of creatures to form and to continue. Man has always found it quite impossible to set up any sort of a strictly universal kingdom which functioned successfully. Time and again the world has been plagued with would-be conquerors who were avid to bring the entire earth under their sway. And, each time such an individual has appeared, the world has very soon enjoyed the pleasure of seeing his efforts overthrown.

This tentative universality is all the more difficult in the religious field. One after another the great religious bodies which have achieved some sort of international power have seen that the men of one nation were quite unwilling to accept definite direction from the citizens of another region. Alone among all the religious organizations in history, and manifest as a miraculous organization, the Catholic Church has penetrated every quarter of the globe and has peacefully received the rule of that man, who as the successor of St. Peter, the prince of the apostolic college, speaks to men with the voice of Christ. Thus the Church constitutes a supernatural and highly unique phenomenon among the societies of the world.

We find the centrifugal tendencies of religious organizations sufficiently manifest on even a national scheme. Of the two hundred fifty-seven religious societies mentioned in the Selected Statistics for the United States by Denominations and Geographic Divisions,[27] we find that no less than seventy-seven have changed their names or broken off from other groups since the religious census of 1906. Only a few of the two hundred fifty-seven can honestly be said to be "at home" in this country. Certainly no society other than the Roman Catholic Church is organized and at home in every section of the earth.

Yet with all of its universality, the Church retains its inflexible social unity. Manifestly it has one visible head or ruler whose commands are obeyed by Catholics throughout the world. It has one body of dogma, manifest and explicit, which all its members hold with the certain assent of divine faith. It has one sacrifice and one sacramental system. It has one episcopate and one priesthood.

Moreover, the dogma of the Church does not consist in a series of pronouncements like the thirty-nine articles of the Protestant Episcopal Church, which every member is practically free to interpret and to accept in whatever sense he chooses. The doctrinal unity of the Catholic Church is a plainly realistic affair. The Church claims and exercises the right of declaring the meaning of Holy Scripture and of the dogmatic formulae she has hitherto pronounced. She claims

---

27 Washington, The Department of Commerce, Bureau of the Census, 1941.

and exercises the faculty of deciding, once and for all, whether such a meaning is actually contained in a book and intended by a given author. Enthusiastically and with absolute certitude the members of the Church accept this direction. We need not inquire what would happen to the organization of any other religious body which attempted a like function.

11. The unconquered stability of the Church. One of the attributes or qualities of the true Church, founded and maintained by Jesus of Nazareth, is its indefectibility. It is characteristic of this society that it will endure, substantially unchanged until the end of time. Naturally enough we hold that the Church is indefectible by an act of divine faith, for we have no means of acquiring evidence about future times. However, we can see very well that the Church has endured and still continues in the face of obstacles which would manifestly have destroyed any organization within the natural competence of man. Hence we can realize that the Church, living in spite of these forces which have been brought into play against her, constitutes a true social miracle and as such a true and evident motive of credibility.

When we speak of the Church's unconquered stability, we take cognizance of the definite and naturally overwhelming attempts which have been made to destroy her. In the first place, there have been open and formidable persecutions in which secular authorities have exerted every effort to destroy this society by trying to force its members to disclaim their affiliation and to prevent others from joining it. It is plainly evident that these attempts would have been plentifully sufficient to dissolve any organization within the natural competence of man. Furthermore, we can easily see that the Church does not possess the *natural* means which other societies have exploited in order to survive persecutions. We must bear in mind that the attack upon Christianity has been universal. The history of the Church shows us that, in general, faithful adherence to this society has been surrounded with difficulties during the greater part of the time since Jesus of Nazareth brought it into existence. In only a relatively small number of cases has membership in this organization been anything other than a political and social handicap.

To limit ourselves to the official persecutions suffered by Christians, we must still contemplate a corporate or composite force infinitely greater than that brought into play against any other society in the history of the world. The Church did not, and by its very nature could not, adopt the tactic of ambitious and organized counterforce which might possibly have overcome some of the efforts made against it. She did not seek or did she acquire financial or military control which would have protected her against her enemies. Furthermore, it would be a lamentable inexactitude to state that the prudence, the zeal, or the natural courage of her members or her directors could be considered a sufficient and principal cause of her survival.

From the year 70 until 313 the Catholic Church was under the official ban of the pagan Roman empire. Nero, the inaugurator of the persecution, put a great many Christians to death, as did Domitian. Under Trajan and Aelius Adrian the Christians suffered both from official persecution and from rioting among the people. The coldly philosophical Marcus Aurelius Antoninus showed his contempt for the Church by putting a considerable number of its members to death. Septimius Severus, Gallus, and Valerian were still more vicious. The persecutions under Decius, Diocletian, and other emperors associated with this latter were by all means the most sanguinary that the Church was called upon to endure under the pagan states. During the earliest period of its existence the Church suffered sanguinary opposition from the Jewish Sanhedrin, from the ruler Herod Agrippa, and from the impostor Bar Cochebas.

During the fourth and fifth centuries the Great Kings of Persia resolved to extirpate the Catholics from their dominions. We have records of sixteen thousand individual Christians who suffered death under one of them, Sapor II (340–399). At the same time the faithful Catholics in northern Africa were tormented by the lawless Donatists, whose fanatical zeal spread death and destruction throughout the province.

The Arians within the Roman empire, particularly under Constantius II, by far the most brilliant and successful opponent the Catholic Church has ever faced, brought about conditions under which it seemed humanly impossible that this society could endure. Outside the empire the Vandals, imbued with this heresy carried out a relentless persecution of the Church until well into the sixth century.

The Protestant revolution made the lives of Catholics exceedingly difficult and even placed them in serious danger in what had been the best provinces of the Church. The reformers themselves made no pretense of dealing fairly with members of the ancient Church. Luther, Calvin, and Melanchthon all made themselves obnoxious by seeking the violent destruction of Catholic leaders and the dissolution of the Church as a society. Beza considered liberty of conscience as a diabolical teaching. In France, Belgium, and Holland the greatest cruelty was practiced upon Catholics, while martyrdom was visited upon the faithful by the Calvinists in Switzerland and Hungary.

The English who remained as members of the Church were persecuted and often put to death from the time of Henry VIII until that of Queen Anne. However, the most atrocious treatment was accorded the clergy and the people of Ireland. Every device of cruelty and corruption was brought into play in order to induce the people of that glorious land to abandon their allegiance to the successor of St. Peter.

The Mohammedan nations habitually treated their Christian and particularly their Catholic subjects with brutal severity. The Greco-Russian schismatics never lost the opportunity of arousing and intensifying a hatred of Catholicism among their peoples. In the field of foreign missions, throughout Africa, Asia, and Oceania the members of the Catholic Church have been subjected to barbarous persecutions. However, the cruelty of "liberals" during the French Revolution, and in the infamous Commune of Paris, in Russia, in Mexico, and in Spain has gone far beyond the savagery of pagan tribes.

At this moment the Catholic Church is the object of hatred to governments which control a very considerable number of the world's inhabitants. In other places Catholics have been and still are considered as "citizens of the second order" and deprived practically of the positions and influence which they are naturally entitled to possess. The forms of literature, of popular education, and of finance have been thrown into the fray against the Church. Despite all of these forces the society flourishes and endures.

An infinitesimal fraction of the power which has been exercised against this organization would manifestly have sufficed to destroy any merely human society. Only a Church equipped with absolutely unlimited force, or, to put the thing in other words, a Church assisted and maintained by the living God could have survived and prospered. This the Church has done.

She has lived precisely as an institution that claims to possess and to propound a divine revelation. If God has accomplished and continues to bring about this visible social miracle, it is evident that He wishes to affirm and to seal the verity of those claims advanced by and for this institution. The message which Jesus of Nazareth preached as a divine communication, and which the Catholic Church offers to mankind in His name is thus attested as rationally credible by every type of objective motive of credibility.

12. Catholicism and the internal motives of Credibility. Our own reactions to the Christian message constitute the internal motives of credibility. In so far as the Catholic dogma actually satisfies man to an extent utterly beyond the capacity or any other religious teaching, it gives evidence of having been formed by that same divine Agent who has created the world and who is the Master of human activity. The satisfaction or joy which men have derived from the acceptance of Catholic dogma has been and is plainly manifest. From it we know at least that this system of religious teaching does not run counter to the legitimate and basic tendencies of human nature. Thus the response of the individual man to the Catholic faith constitutes a real and valuable *negative* motive of credibility. From this point of view, as from every other, there is no valid objection against the authenticity of those claims advanced in favor of that doctrine which Jesus of Nazareth preached to men.

In so far as it represents an individual reaction, the marvelous satisfaction experienced in the act of Catholic faith has efficacy as a *positive* sign of revelation also. However, in this case it does not offer a full and objective certitude. After all, the claims put forth in favor of Catholic teaching are too far reaching to be judged merely in the light of an individual's response to that doctrine. Catholic dogma presents itself as a message revealed to man in a supernatural manner and containing truths and mysteries of a definitely and intrinsically supernatural character. When we assent to this doctrine with the certain act of divine faith, we feel that this teaching has actually come from the living God who has created us. This experience affords us a high degree of probability that the message is what it claims to be. In ordinary cases at least it offers nothing more. The satisfaction we find in Catholic faith tells us only that this is the sort of message we might expect from the infinitely perfect God.

In their proper place, then, the internal motives of credibility perform a humble yet valuable service in the central demonstration of apologetics. However, certain teachers and writers have managed to slip into dangerous errors on the subject of Christian faith precisely by misusing these motives. As a group the Modernists, condemned by Pope Pius X for their utter misinterpretation of Catholic dogma, ascribed to these internal motives the sole efficacy in supporting the contentions of dogma. They refused to accept the external motives at all as effective means for demonstrating the divine origin and consequently the rational credibility of that message which Jesus Christ had taught. In attempting to elevate the internal motives out of their proper sphere, they destroyed their effectiveness and utterly misconstrued the very doctrine they had ostensibly set out to defend.

The errors of modernist apologetics, like practically all of the mistakes which have been made in the field of this science, spring from a false notion of God and an utter misconception of the basic doctrines contained in the Christian message. The contention of the modernists would have been true if there were no one true God, infinitely perfect and absolutely distinct from the created universe, whose existence can be proved and demonstrated by a strict and certain scientific process. The motives of credibility are acceptable to men precisely because they manifest the free and intelligent activity of a Being of whose existence and of whose attributes we are naturally aware. When that naturally ascertainable and correct teaching about God has been ignored or distorted man can never understand the true significance of revelation itself or of its discernibility.

The modernists, in refusing scientific and demonstrative value to external or objective motives of credibility, tried to make man himself the measure of divine revelation. They considered this revelation as "nothing else than man's acquired consciousness of his own relation with God."[28] With such confused notions, it is hardly remarkable that they preferred internal motives of credibility to all others.

---

28 Pius X, *The Decree "Lamentabili,"* July 3, 1907 (Denzinger, 2020).

We can and should consider the internal motives of credibility in their universal as well as in their individual manifestations. The satisfaction which men of all ages and of all nations have found in the acceptance of Catholic dogma manifestly constitutes a psychological miracle. As such it is an evident divine work, clearly performed in support of the contention that God Himself is the Author of that message which is set forth in His name. The internal motives of credibility seen in their universal aspect correspond to the miraculous holiness and wisdom seen in the Catholic dogma itself.

13. The summary of St. Thomas. In all the history of Catholic apologetics there is no more effective and conclusive statement of the motives and their adequacy than that contained in the *Summa Contra Gentiles*. "Those who give faith to such truth to which human reason does not attain do not believe without reason 'following learned fables' as it is said in the second epistle of St. Peter.

"For the divine Wisdom Itself, which knows all things most perfectly has deigned to reveal these secrets of the divine wisdom to men. It has shown Its own presence and the truth of Its doctrine and inspiration by most fitting demonstrations when, to confirm those truths which surpass natural knowledge, It has shown visibly works which surpass the competence of all nature. It does this in the marvelous cure of ailments, in the raising of the dead, in the marvelous movement of heavenly bodies and in what is still more wonderful, the inspiration of human minds so that unlearned and simple men, filled with the gift of the Holy Ghost, attain in an instant the highest wisdom and eloquence.

"Moreover, through the power of this above-mentioned proof, not by the violence of arms nor by the promise of sensual delights and, what is most remarkable, amid the tyranny of persecutors an innumerable throng, not only of untutored men but also of those most perfectly versed in wisdom has gathered to the Christian faith, in which truths surpassing all human understanding are preached, in which the pleasures of the flesh are restrained and in which they are taught to despise all earthly things. It is the greatest miracle to have the minds of mortal men assent to such doctrines and it is a manifest work of divine inspiration that men should condemn visible things and desire only that which they do not see. This, however, has taken place neither without warning nor by chance, but, by a divine disposition it was made manifest that this would occur. Long ago God foretold by many pronouncements of the prophets that He would bring about these things. The books of these prophets are venerated among us as giving testimony in favor of our faith.

"This mode of confirmation is meant in the statement 'which (that is human salvation) having begun to be declared by the Lord was confirmed unto us by them that heard Him. God also bearing them witness by signs and wonders and divers miracles, and distributions of the Holy Ghost according to His own will.'[29] This so wonderful conversion of the world to the Christian faith is a most certain index of the past miracles, so that there is no longer any need to repeat these ancient signs, since they appear manifestly in their effects. For it would have been more wonderful than all the miracles if the world had been led by men devoid of learning and nobility, without miraculous signs to believe doctrines so hard to accept, to accomplish works so difficult to perform and to hope for such lofty benefits. As a matter of fact, however, God does not cease, even in our own times, performing miracles by the instrumentality of His saints for the confirmation of our faith.

"But those who have introduced the sects of error have acted in quite another way. This is evident in Mohammed, who enticed the people by promises of sensual delights to the desire of which their carnal appetite spurred them on. He also gave commandments consistent with those promises. He relaxed the reins of fleshly pleasure precepts which carnal men are prepared to obey. He offered no documents of truth other than those which any man of ordinary culture could know very readily. Then he mingled the truths he taught the people with fables and with the most erroneous doctrines. He set forth no supernaturally performed miracles, by which alone a fitting testimony for divine inspiration is advanced, since the visible operation which cannot be other than divine points out the teacher of truth who is invisibly inspired. He said, however, that he was sent in the power of arms, which sign even robbers and tyrants possess.

"Moreover, neither men well versed in the doctrine about God, nor those experienced in divine and human sciences believed in him from

---

29 Heb. 2:3–4.

the beginning. His followers were savages dwelling in the deserts, ignorant of all teaching about God. By the force of the arms of this multitude he compelled others to accept his law.

"No divine pronouncements of the ancient prophets bear witness to him. Rather he adulterated almost all the documents of the Old and the New Testaments with mythical stories. Hence astutely he forbade his followers to read the books of the Old and the New Testaments lest he himself should be convicted of falsity through them. Thus it is manifest that those who accept his faith believe imprudently."[30]

---

[30] St. Thomas, *Summa Contra Gentiles,* Book 1, Ch. 6.

Chapter 19

THE CONCLUSION OF APOLOGETICS

1. The Fact of Credibility. The evidence of the signs of revelation is amply sufficient to show that Catholic dogma is really credible for what it claims to be, a message from God to man, supernatural both in the manner in which man has received it and in its central and essential content. Since the subject matter of divine faith is something which can be scientifically demonstrated as credible, then it follows that the act of faith itself is eminently a reasonable and prudent human operation. Beyond this conclusion the science of apologetics, properly so called, does not advance.

The positive proof supposes, as does every other section of fundamental dogmatic theology, the transcendent and all-important fact that a personal God really exists. There is, as the Catholic Church officially proclaims "one true and living God, the Creator and Lord of heaven and of earth. He is omnipotent, eternal, unlimited, incomprehensible, and infinite in understanding, in will and in all perfection. Since He is one singular, entirely simple and immutable spiritual substance, He must be considered as really and essentially distinct from the world, most blessed in Himself and of Himself, and ineffably exalted above all things which are or can be conceived apart from Him.

"This only true God, by His own goodness and His omnipotent power, neither to increase nor to acquire His own beatitude, but to manifest His own perfection through the good things which He vouchsafes to creatures, has most freely, 'together from the beginning of time made from nothing both types of creatures, namely the spiritual and the corporeal, that is, the angelic and the mundane, and finally the human as something common to both as being constituted of both spirit and body."[1]

"God guards and governs by His providence all the things He has established, 'reaching from end to end strongly and disposing all things sweetly.'[2] For 'all things are bare and open to His eyes'[3] even those things which are going to come about by the free action of His creatures."[4]

This God can be known with certitude and can even be demonstrated in the natural light of reason by the things that are made; that is by the visible works of creation as a cause is known and demonstrated through its effects.[5] This is the great and all-important fact upon which the proof of credibility is based.

Since God is infinitely perfect in understanding and in will, He knows all the circumstances which surround the performance of one of His miracles. He could not possibly perform a miracle which is attached to a doctrine that He knows to be untrue. The true motive of credibility is a seal of the divine approval. When it is performed in support of a doctrine that claims to be divinely revealed, it constitutes the best possible indication that God Himself has actually given this teaching to men.

The existence of a God who is infinitely wise and just can be and is demonstrated with absolute certitude by an examination of naturally ascertainable evidence. We have the most perfect historical evidence to the effect that Jesus of Nazareth preached a definite and distinct doctrine, claimed that this teaching was divinely revealed, and then adduced motives of credibility plentifully sufficient to demonstrate the validity of His claim. We have naturally attainable scientific historical certitude that the Apostles and their successors proposed the very doctrine that Jesus had given and then offered ample evidence of its divine origin with manifest signs of revelation. Finally the existing Catholic Church, as it is, constitutes a great and spectacular miracle

---

[1] The Vatican Council uses the words of the Fourth Lateran (Denzinger, 428).
[2] Citation from Wisd. 8:1.
[3] Citation from Heb. 14:13.
[4] The Vatican Council, The Constitution, *Dei Filius* (Denzinger, 1782–1784).
[5] Cf. The Anti-Modernist Oath (Denzinger, 2145), and the Vatican Council (Denzinger, 1785).

in the social order. An infinitely wise and just God could not have allowed these things to happen in support of an erroneous assertion.

2. The obligation of faith. However, once we have ascertained the naturally evident credibility of Catholic dogma, we must investigate its implications in the line of human conduct. We have already seen that the very doctrine which gives naturally demonstrable evidence of credibility offers itself as a benefit, doubly necessary to mankind. It is proposed as something apart from which man cannot obtain the eternal and supernatural happiness God wishes him to enjoy. Furthermore, man stands in moral need of this revealed truth in order that there may be an accurate and certain natural knowledge about God, readily available to all men. Consequently once man has realized the validity of those claims that Catholic dogma actually is divinely revealed, he can see that it is to his best interest to accept this teaching with the certain assent of divine faith.

We must realize, of course, that the act of faith is by no means forced by the evidence of credibility. As a matter of fact the judgment of credibility itself is essentially in the natural order. It is based upon evidence available to any man who is willing to examine it and to accept the truth. However, the act of faith itself is definitely and essentially in the *supernatural* realm. It belongs to the order of mysteries, having to do with the intimate life of God Himself. Furthermore, the act of faith is inherently *free*. When a man says, "I believe," he accepts with absolute and unwavering certitude statements for which he has no direct evidence whatsoever. All the naturally attainable objective evidence points to the fact that God attests the validity of the claim that the doctrine of the Blessed Trinity, for example, has been divinely revealed. It is not evidence that in the ineffable unity of the divine nature there coexist three distinct, equal, and consubstantial Persons. This latter statement is one which man can accept with absolute certitude only on the authority or on the Word of God Himself. In spite of naturally ascertainable evidence to the effect that God attests the divine origin of this statement, and the perfectly sure naturally attainable truth that God is and must be infinitely veracious and omniscient, men can refuse to believe Him.

There are two ways in which a man is free in affairs of this kind. In the first place, there is what is called the freedom of exercise. A man need not apply his mind to the consideration of any given problem. Naturally if he does not consider the problem, he will not be in a position to make any statement whatsoever.

However, in certain cases, when a man has considered the matter itself, he still retains a freedom of specification, even in the intellectual realm. Evidence as such, if it is clear enough, forces itself upon the mind. Thus I am not free to deny that two plus two equals four. But objective evidence is the only factor competent to act upon the mind so as to remove its freedom of specification. Where there is no such evidence, the mind can make a certain assent only insofar as it is moved by the will. In other words, a man can make a fully certain assertion where there is no immediate evidence for it only because he wills to do so. This is the case in the act of faith.

Precisely because it is free and distinct from the evident judgment of credibility, the act of faith can possess a firmness and certitude far surpassing those which characterize this judgment. After all the conclusion that Catholic dogma is rationally credible as divine revelation is only as strong as human science can make it even though it is sufficiently firm to set aside all possibility and danger of error. The act of faith, however, partakes of the power inherent in the divine mind itself. The believer accepts this truth not as evident to natural reason but as seen in the knowledge of God Himself.

There is a definite naturally ascertainable moral obligation to accept Catholic dogma with an act of divine faith. This obligation, like the doctrine on the existence of a personal God, is no less naturally attainable because it has been set down with scientific nicety by the Catholic Church itself. "Since man depends utterly upon God as upon his Creator and his Lord, and since created reason is entirely subject to uncreated truth, we are bound to offer God in faith the full service of understanding and of will."[6] Once again our grasp to this truth is entirely dependent upon our appreciation of the fact that there is an infinitely perfect God who has created us and who watches over us, from whom we derive every fiber and aspect of goodness which we possess and enjoy. We know His existence through the examination of naturally and ascertainable evidence. All

---

6 The Vatican Council, The Constitution, *Dei Filius*, Ch. 3 (Denzinger, 1789). Cf. also Denzinger, 1810.

of the reasoning requisite for demonstrating His existence and His primary attributes is perfectly within the natural competence of man.

3. The obligation of religion. Once we are realistic enough to take cognizance of this transcendently important fact, the obligation of religion is apparent. Objectively religion is the service of recognition which we *owe* to God precisely because of His infinite excellence. Subjectively considered it is the virtue by which a man is prepared to render God this honor or cult which is due to Him. Religion is a virtue because it belongs to a good man. One who refuses to give God the tribute of service which is due to Him has failed signally in his human life. He has withheld something which a good man is ready and eager to render. Lacking this moral virtue, a human being lives as an evil man.

Now the service of religion obviously includes the act of faith, whenever and wherever there appears a doctrine which gives certain evidence that it has come from God. The man who refuses to accept such a teaching is by that very fact unwilling to acknowledge fully God's infinite excellence in the line of veracity and omniscience. In itself then the message which possesses credibility as divine revelation enjoys *credentity* by reason of the firm demands religion makes upon us. The man who refuses to accept this doctrine has failed in that worship he owes the living God.

4. Two concepts of religion. We are, of course, perfectly aware of the fact that the world abounds in definitions of religion quite distinct from our own. Monsignor Fulton Sheen, among others, has done excellent work in the scientific field by pointing out the existence and the futility of "religion without God." The somewhat popular and colorful account which Lewis Browne gives of the origin of religion may serve to show the general trend of these doctrines. This eminent writer offers a vivid description of the thought-processes in primitive man that "poor gibbering half-ape nursing his wound in some draughty cave." The first emotion that arose in "his poor dull pate" was fear, a terror based upon the unfortunate fellow's conviction that all the objects in the world were intentionally hurting him. From this condition he finally evolved faith and religion. "Instinctively he too wanted to thrash whatever seemed to bring him evil. Only he was afraid. From experience he knew that fighting was useless, that the enemy objects, falling boulders that maimed him, and the flooding streams that wrecked his hut, were in some uncanny way proof against his spears and arrows. That was why he was finally forced to resort to more subtle methods of attack. Since blows could not subdue the hostile rocks or streams, our ancestors tried to subdue them with magic. He thought words might avail: strange syllables uttered in groans, or meaningless shouts accompanied by beating tom-toms. Or he tried wild dances. Or luck charms. If these spells failed, then he invented others; if those in turn failed, then he invented still others. Of one thing he seemed most stubbornly convinced: that *some* spell would work. Somehow the hostile things around him *could* be appeased or controlled, he believed; somehow death *could* be averted. Why he should have been so certain, no one can tell. It must have been his instinctive adjustment to the conditions of a world that was too much for him. Self-preservation must have forced him to that certainty, for without it self-preservation would have been impossible. Man had to have faith in himself, or die—and he would not die.

"So he had faith—and developed religion."[7]

The author is quite explicit in describing his notions of religion and of faith. "Religion, is not all of faith, but only a part of it. By the word faith we mean that indispensable—and therefore imperishable—illusion in the heart of man that, though he may seem a mere worm on earth, he nevertheless can make himself the lord of the universe. By the word religion, however, we mean one specialized technique by which man seeks to realize that illusion."[8]

We would only deceive ourselves were we to imagine that, using the definition employed by Mr. Browne and approved by a great many modern leaders, we could arrive at any satisfactory conclusion in the science of apologetics. Apologetics, after all, is a realistic discipline, and it demands a realistic outlook on life and on the world. God does exist, and a realist must take cognizance of this fact. We do owe God a tribute of service and love. Taking these transcendent facts into consideration, only the objective and traditional notions of faith and of religion are valid.

---

7 *This Believing World*, p. 29.
8 *Ibid.*, pp. 29–30.

Naturally enough the nonrealistic writers are as consistent in their line of thought as the realists are in the science of apologetics. If religion is the illusion Mr. Browne says it is, he is perfectly correct in considering one technique as pretty much the same as another. But, if we wish to take cognizance of the evident facts which lie before us, we must realize that obedience to God is accomplished only in that form of worship which He has designated. The unique testimony which He offers in favor of one body of religious teaching is ample indication that He wishes to be served and honored according to the precepts contained therein.

However, we have both the right and the duty, as apologetics, to inquire into the reason which justifies the two diverse definitions of religion, offered by the non-realists and by the traditional teachers. It is perfectly obvious that they do not refer to the same thing. The service which is seen as due to an evidently existing and infinitely perfect God has absolutely nothing in common with the specialized technique by which man seeks to realize the illusion that he can make himself the lord of the universe. Taken literally this second type of "religion" would be merely the procedure of a megalomaniac.

Now the first type is readily understood. Religion, in this sense, is the thing which Moses and Plato and St. Paul and Mohammed all professed, at any rate, to describe. The world knows what it is. It has been the motive force in the lives of the saints. It has been the essential business of the Church and the synagogue during the passage of two millennia. The term religion applies to this reality and to the technique for realizing an illusion in much the same way that the word "bank" designates a financial institution and the side of a stream or that the term "pitcher" denominates a vessel from which liquids are meant to be poured and a member of a baseball team. To speak of "Christianity" in connection with religions of this second type is as ridiculous and absurd a procedure as to include a life of Lefty Grove in a treatise on early American pottery.

5. The necessity for teaching Catholic dogma. The obligation of real religion obliges men to accept the message of Jesus Christ with the firm and unwavering assent of divine faith. This message comes to them today, as it has in the past since the time of our Lord Himself, in the form of Catholic dogma. As Catholic dogma it is verified not only by those motives of credibility which surrounded the life of Jesus but also by the various miracles which have taken place within the Church since the apostolic age, and particularly by that outstanding and spectacular social miracle which is the Catholic Church itself. This doctrine is not left idly in the world as a prize which pious men are expected to seek out and find entirely by their own devices. As a matter of fact it is carried to men through all the strife and operations of the world. Jesus of Nazareth preached that message openly. The Apostles whom He sent and their successors in the sacred ministry have brought this teaching to every quarter of the globe. St. Paul commanded Timothy his disciple "I charge thee before God and Jesus Christ, who shall judge the living and the dead, by His coming and His kingdom: *preach the word*, be instant in season, out of season: reprove, entreat, rebuke in all patience and doctrine."⁹ The teaching Church has throughout its history obeyed that precept to the letter. The men who have been entrusted with the task of presenting the divine message of Jesus Christ to the world have exploited every resource of human ingenuity in bringing this teaching to those who are meant to profit by it. The Catholic dogma, manifest as credible through ample signs of divine revelation, is presented to men, one might even say forced upon their attention, as an exclusive and ultimate body of doctrine.

We must not lose sight of the fact that our Lord Himself had specifically stated that His message, and His alone, was to be preached until the end of time. "And Jesus coming spoke to them, saying: All power is given to Me in heaven and in earth. Going therefore teach ye all nations: baptizing them in the name of the Father, and of the Son, and of the Holy Ghost: *Teaching them to observe all things whatsoever I have, commanded you,* and behold I am with you all days, even to the consummation of the world."¹⁰ The only message, then, which the Apostles were commanded and commissioned to teach was the actual doctrine of Jesus.

6. Liberalism and Christianity. St. Paul made that teaching quite explicit. "I wonder that you are so soon removed from Him that called you unto the grace of Christ, unto another gospel: Which is

---

9 2 Tim. 4:1–2.
10 Matt. 28:18–20.

not another, only there are some that trouble you, and would pervert the gospel of Christ. But though we, or an angel from heaven, preach a gospel to you besides that which we have preached to you, let him be anathema. As we said before, so now I say again: If any one preach to you a gospel, besides that which you have received, let him be anathema."[11] In her doctrinal pronouncements the Church has reaffirmed this same position. "If any one should say that the position of the faithful is like to that of those who have not arrived at that faith which alone is true, so that Catholics can have a just cause for calling into doubt, with suspended judgment, the faith which they have already received under the magisterium of the Church until they have completed a scientific demonstration of the credibility and the truth of their faith, let him be anathema."[12] Likewise Pius IX stigmatized the following statements under the heading of indifferentism and latitudinarianism in the Syllabus of December 8, 1864.

15. Each man is free to embrace and to profess that religion which, led by the light of reason, he might consider true.

16. Men can find the way of eternal salvation and can achieve eternal salvation in the cult of any religion whatsoever.[13]

7. Claims for non-Catholic doctrine. The message of Christ presented to us in the form of Catholic dogma is manifestly credible. The claim of exclusive and ultimate effectiveness in presenting divine public revelation constitutes manifestly an integral part of the Christian message. As a result the realistic approach to the conclusion offered by and in the science of apologetics demands an acceptance of this fact. When the message of Christ has presented its credentials, the virtue of religion will not allow a man to proceed to further inquiries. The direction of duty is clear. Only by an immediate and complete acceptance of Catholic dogma in the act of divine faith by the man who is aware of its credentials can the obligations of true religion be satisfied.

However, we have no fear that any other religious teaching can or will rival Catholic dogma in either its claims or its credentials. In this respect the most valuable practical manual is to be found in the

---

11 Gal. 1:6–7.
12 The Vatican Council, Canon 6, *De Fide* (Denzinger, 1815). Cf. also Denzinger, 1794.
13 Denzinger, 1715–1716.

results of the religious census, taken every ten years by the bureau of the census in the Department of Commerce. The results of this census of religious bodies give, among other valuable information, the history, doctrine, and works of all the religious societies existent within the United States of America.[14] With calm impartiality the book in which these results are set forth advances the claims and the guarantees cited by the various organizations.

There are several religious groups professing doctrines entirely or in a great measure independent of the Christian message. Buddhism, Brahmanism, professed by the Vedanta Society, Spiritualism, Christian Science, Mormonism, and Judaism are examples of such doctrines. Here we are faced, not with teachings which have been accepted in the past, but with the attitudes and doctrines influential in the world today. Thus, for example, the Jewish congregation claim that they have no distinct and obligatory articles of faith at all. "The Jewish religion is a way of life and has no formulated creed, or articles of faith, the acceptance of which brings redemption or salvation to the believer, or divergence from which involves separation from the Jewish congregation. On the other hand it has certain teachings, sometimes called doctrines or dogmas, which have been at all times considered obligatory on the adherents of the Jewish religion."[15] The "dogmas or doctrines" enumerated in this volume are for the most part beautiful and true. But in no case is there any inference that God wills all men to accept this doctrinal content of the Jewish religion as it is presented today. This teaching does not present itself with those claims which are made for Catholic dogma. Certainly there is no evidence of any divine seal by which such claims might be attested. The other distinctively non-Christian religious teachings sometimes, as in the case of Mormonism, propose themselves as divinely revealed. They give no appreciable evidence, by either internal or external motives of credibility, of any divine origin.

The Christian groups naturally claim to present the teaching of Jesus. Yet, without exception, every non-Catholic religious teaching glories in some origin subsequent to and distinct from Christ Himself. Their ever shifting multitude, taken concretely and corporately, is a

---

14 Vol. II, parts 1 and 2, Washington, 1941.
15 *The Census of Religious Bodies,* 1936, Vol. *2,* p. 763.

clear indication that men can never successfully change the content of Christian teaching. As a matter of fact only the Catholic Church claims to have been instituted by Christ. Historically her assertions are unquestionable. Her identity with the Church of the Apostles is just as manifest as is the identity of the great nation in which we live with the United States of which George Washington was president. Only her teaching is set forth as the message of Christ, presented to the world unchanged unto this day.

8. The beneficial and credible message. Finally the science of apologetics should bring us to see that the message of Jesus constitutes the great blessing for mankind. Here again we depend upon the realistic and accurate natural knowledge about God which the science of apologetics demands and gives. The God whose existence and perfection we know through natural reason is not like some tyrant who forces his will upon his subjects. God, infinitely holy and just, reveals His message to man in order that man may derive from it blessings incalculable, blessings in this world and in the next. The doctrine which He manifests as credible is pre-eminently a *beneficial* teaching. The obligation to believe, imposed by the virtue of religion, binds man to what is his own supreme good, now and forever. God does not drag us down to defeat. He lifts us up for an eternal victory. The divine Prophet, with whom the apologist is privileged to stand has made that clear. "These things I have spoken to you, that in Me you may have peace. In the world you shall have distress: but have confidence, I have overcome the world."[16] "This is the victory which overcometh the world, our faith."[17]

---

16 John 16:33.
17 1 John 5:4.

Chapter 20

THE STORY OF APOLOGETICS

1. Background of the study. A treatise of this sort would be hopelessly incomplete without some indication of the stages through which the science of apologetics has passed in attaining its present condition of methodological perfection. It is very definitely a science with a history. Each thesis set forward within that science has, at one time or another during the life of the Catholic Church, been asserted against serious opposition. The claims and the verification of the claims asserted in scientific apologetics were both put forward by Jesus of Nazareth. Since the time He ascended into heaven, the men of the Church have been faced with the necessity of presenting both the claims and the proofs of Jesus to men who have denied His teaching and tried to discountenance His organization.

It is axiomatic that each of these men who has been privileged to stand with Christ and to defend Him against the assaults of His enemies has contributed something to the science of apologetics. Each has grasped, in some particular way, according to the intellectual force with which God has endowed him, some aspect of apologetics in which the credibility and inherent beneficence of the gospel message has been more effectively presented. However, in a volume of this type, we have no room for any extensive or detailed treatment of the history of apologetics.[1] It is merely our intention to point out some of the most illustrious among these champions for Christ and

---

[1] As a matter of fact the twentieth century has been remarkably remiss in this field. Dr. Karl Werner's *Geschichte der Apologetischen und Polemischen Literatur der Christlichen Theologie* (Schaffhausen, 1861), 5 vols., is still the most complete text. Acceptable outlines have been written by Maisonneuve, Seitz, and Charles F. Aiken for the *Dictionnaire de Théologie Catholique, Lexikon fur Theologie und Kirche,* and the *Catholic Encyclopedia* respectively. Acceptable summaries appear in the manuals of Dieckmann and Michelitsch.

to see the most general stages through which scientific apologetics has progressed.

2. The apostolic fathers. Among the writings of the apostolic fathers, the so-called Epistle of Barnabas, probably written at some time during the first third of the second century, contains the elements of apologetical demonstration. The author, obviously writing to those who knew the Old Testament Scriptures and who were inclined to follow them, seeks to prove that the sacrifices and rites therein described are no longer pleasing to God. He refers to the Resurrection of Christ and to the messianic prophecies. About the same time lived Ariston of Pella, to whom the seventh-century writer, St. Maximus the Confessor, attributes the first apologetical work against the Jews. This was a book entitled *The Debate Between Jason and Papiscus on the Subject of Christ*. It is possible that the long list of similar works, including the famous *Dialogue With the Jew Trypho*, by St. Justin the Martyr, contain doctrine actually set forth in this volume.

3. The early Greek apologists. We have seen the lone citation of Quadratus the apologist which has come down to us. In this apology to Aelius Adrian, most probably written about the year 124, he made special reference to the reality of those miraculous cures which had been wrought by Christ. The long lost but recently discovered apology of Aristides, the Athenian Philosopher, written about the same time and likewise dedicated to Adrian, distinguishes the religious teaching of the Christians from that of the Greeks, the Barbarians, and the Jews. After showing the manifest errors of idolatry and pagan mythology, and after claiming that the religious practice of the Jews honored angels rather than God (an assertion occasionally repeated by ancient Christian writers), he proceeds to show that the Christians alone possess the truth. He appeals to the Resurrection of Jesus and to His miracles and mentions the written account of our Lord's life which Adrian is at liberty to consult if he chooses to do so. However, his chief argument for the acceptability of Christian teaching is to be found in the miraculous holiness of the Church as visible in its precepts and in the lives of the faithful, together with the outstanding and manifest wisdom of the message itself.

The author of the letter to Diognetus, written during the second third of the second century, has left us a masterpiece of early apologetical reasoning. Like Aristides he considers Christians as the "soul of the world." He appeals chiefly to the miracle of the Church itself as evidence for the acceptability of its doctrine. Marcus Aurelius mentions a Diognetus who was his own teacher. The pagan to whom this letter was sent may possibly have been this individual.

By far the most powerful and important of these early apologists was St. Justin the Martyr, who suffered death because of his faith about the year 165. From him we have three works of paramount importance, the two apologies addressed to Antoninus Pius, while he shared the throne of empire with Marcus Aurelius and with Lucius Verus. The two apologies were written in an attempt to induce the authorities to abandon the cruel persecution then raging against the Christians. In these works Justin appeals to prophecies uttered by Jesus to the miraculous holiness of Christian doctrine in itself and in its effects upon believers, but most of all to prophecies about Christ. He spoke of miracles as signs attesting the divine origin of messages which claimed to be prophecies, but made no special appeal to the miracles of our Lord. In the *Dialogue with Trypho* he developed the argument from the messianic prophecies magnificently, demonstrating that Jesus was really the redeemer expected by the Jews.

Justin contended that the pagan philosophers had derived their best doctrines from the revealed monotheistic system set forth by Moses. As a result he was willing to concede a great value in their works, even while he asserted that they were utterly inferior to the Christian writings. He looked incessantly for parallels between Catholic teaching and the religious philosophical tenets of the pagans, holding that the emperors had no business to persecute the Christians when even the pagans themselves accepted teachings somewhat similar to theirs. He blamed the persecution of the Church on the demons who misrepresented the teaching of Christ to men.

Tatian, the bitter and brilliant disciple of St. Justin, died during the last third of the second century after having fallen into the heresy of the Encratites. His one apological work is the *Discourse to the Greeks* in which he manifests a much more pessimistic attitude about pagan culture than had his master. Athenagoras, writing to Marcus Aurelius and to his son Commodus, refutes the charges of immorality made against the Christians and insists upon the visible and marvelous truth of their teaching about God and about human morality. He also wrote a treatise on the Resurrection showing that this article of Christian belief was in conformity with reason. St. Theophilus of Antioch wrote, shortly after the year 180, three books of a *Discourse to Autolycus*. Like his predecessors, Theophilus insists upon the silliness of idolatry and polytheism and points to the innocence of Christians. He insists upon the attributes of the living God and makes specific appeal to prophecy as a motive of credibility. He is most concerned with the temporal and sapiential superiority of the Old Testament books over the pagan narratives.

St. Melito of Sardis, who died about the year 195, has left fragments of an apology addressed to Marcus Aurelius. The *Oration* falsely attributed to him is a Syriac treatise on the one God, probably composed shortly after his death. His contemporaries, Miltiades and Apollinaris, both wrote treatises against the Greeks and against the Jews but these early works of apologetics have not come down to us.

4. Early Latin apologists. During the second half of the second century there appeared the first of the Latin apologists, Marcus Minucius Felix, author of the famed *Octavius*. In this book, written with a literary brilliance far surpassing that of the contemporary apologists, Caecilius, a pagan, is represented as setting forth all of the stock arguments against Christianity. Octavius, a Christian, responds to these charges, triumphantly demonstrating the superiority of the Christian doctrine and exposing the shameful weakness of polytheism. In this book, as in most of the Greek apologetic works we have considered, the author is mainly concerned with showing the acceptability of Christian teaching about the one God. In the *Octavius* we meet for the first time the pagan contention that it would be unwise to embrace Christianity since Rome has prospered under the cult of the pagan Gods. Both Arnobius and St. Augustine faced that same objection generations afterward. The men who wrote in Latin were obviously more concerned with the fate of the empire than were their Greek confreres.

The *Apologeticus* of Quintus Septimius Florens Tertullianus resembles the *Octavius* of Minucius Felix so closely that it would seem that either one was based upon the other or both upon some common source. The resemblance is limited to sections of the text, since the works differ greatly in literary style and in spirit. Tertullian does not plead for cessation of persecution against the Christians. He demands it. In the five books which he wrote on the field of apologetics this turbulent genius excoriated the errors and evils of the pagans, pointed out the moral miracle of Christian martyrdom and showed its effects in the spread of Christianity, taunted the pagans with the failure of their efforts to destroy the faith in Jesus, and then showed that the messianic prophecies demonstrated clearly the divine legateship of Jesus. The death outside the Church sometime after 222 of this dauntless champion is one of the great tragedies of Catholic history. The rigorism which eventually drove him to embrace the cause of Montanism, if not permanently to affiliate himself with their organization, is all too evident in his apologetical works, as well as in the other books he devoted to the cause of Christ. St. Cyprian, the Bishop of Carthage who suffered a glorious martyrdom in 258, followed the lead of Tertullian, whom he called his master, with three books of *Testimonies* against the Jews. These books are collections of prophecies contained in the Old Testament and manifestly fulfilled in the life of Jesus and His Church. By far the most important doctrinal work of St. Cyprian was done in the field of ecclesiology.

5. St. Irenaeus. Although St. Irenaeus, who died a martyr in 202 or 203, is not as well known in the field of apologetics as he is in that of controversy, he wrote an apologetical treatise, the *Demonstration of the Apostolic Preaching*. His masterpiece, the five books *Against the Heresies*, contains material of great service to the science of apologetics, particularly insofar as it shows the unwavering and enlightened tradition in the early Christian Church.

6. The Great Alexandrians. Titus Flavius Clemens, whom we know as Clement of Alexandria, died between the years 211 and 216. One of his works is a book, the *Exhortation to the Heathen*, in which he begs the pagans to accept the Christian faith. The motives alleged are the manifest errors in pagan teachings and the obviously supernal wisdom in the doctrine of Jesus. However, by far the most illustrious and important treatise in apologetics during the third century came from his successor as master in the Didiscalium of Alexandria. This is the volume, in eight books, *Against Celsus*, written by the great Origen. Celsus, an Epicurean philosopher had written a treatise in four books and called it *The True Discourse*. In this work he set out to demolish the pretensions of both Christianity and of Judaism. However, his hatred of our Lord would seem to have surpassed the dislike he felt for His fellow countrymen, so he began his work with a resume of the various objections raised against Christianity within the Jewish world of that time. The remainder of the work was taken up with carefully thought out attacks on what he regarded as the common ground of the two religious systems he detested. This was the work which Origen set out to answer.

His response was certainly one of the most brilliant treatises in all the long and rich history of Christian letters. After a sublime prologue and a worthy opening, Origen answered the charges of Celsus point by point. As a matter of fact, *The True Discourse* itself has long since vanished from the face of the earth, and the only text we possess is incorporated in the books of his triumphant and outstandingly brilliant adversary. There is hardly an objection which modern opponents of Christianity have raised which Celsus did not press and which Origen did not demolish. Celsus came forward as an enlightened philosopher, a scientist, and a literateur. Origen met him on his own ground. Carefully and with a meticulous impartiality he analyzed each objection. He took cognizance of the points which Celsus held and those which he denied. Under the skillful and scientific searching of Origen the very enemies of Christianity are seen as testifying to the truth of her contentions.

We would be greatly mistaken were we to imagine that the *Contra Celsum* is merely a piece of negative apologetic. Supremely competent as he was, and certainly gifted with scientific acumen far beyond that of his contemporaries, Origen contrived to bring out an adequate apologetic in the process of refuting Celsus. He followed the order of the old Epicurean. He cited his words, even those in which the pharisaical insults against the Person of our Lord are conveyed. But in and through his examination he managed to demonstrate, with faultless accuracy, that the message preached by Jesus of Nazareth and proposed by the Catholic Church was guaranteed by unquestionable motives of credibility as authentic divine revelation. Origen died at Tyre about the year 254. It is safe to say that among those who have been privileged to stand with Christ and defend Him during the ages, none has accomplished his work more perfectly than the great Alexandrian.

7. Later Latin apologists. Among the Latin apologists of this time, Commodianus, who lived during the latter half of the third century, is more remarkable for the fact that he wrote in verse than for any particular excellence of doctrine. In his work *Adversus Gentes,* Arnobius, who died in 327, made better use of miracles as motives of credibility than had any of his predecessors with the possible exception of the great Origen himself. Furthermore, he applied himself to show that the spread of Christianity was in no way responsible for the evils the Roman empire endured in his own times. His pupil and successor Lactantius, who seems to have survived him a short time, was the first Latin apologist to write after the peace which came to the Church through the edict of Milan. Even so, his masterpiece, the *Divine Institutions,* constitute a contrast of Christian doctrine with the now fading pagan teaching, rather than an apologetic in the strict sense of the term.

8. The last antipagan writers. After the great Council of Nicea, the attention of the great patristic writers was focused on the *homoousian* controversy rather than on apologetics as such. Nevertheless, several of these men contributed to the literature of apologetics, and one at least instituted a new method. Eusebius of Caesarea, halfhearted proponent of Arius though he was, labored valiantly toward perfecting the literature of apologetics. In his *Ecclesiastical History* he conserved sections of ancient writings which otherwise would have been entirely lost. However he did yeoman service in discounting once and for all the legend of Apollonius of Tyona. This Neo-Pythagorean philosopher had flourished during the first century of our era and had been known as a magician. The empress Julia Domna, wife of Septimius Severus (211), had prevailed upon the savant Philostratus to write his life. The book may have been animated by that hostility for Christianity which characterized its author's patroness. At any rate it represented Apollonius as a wonder-worker whom contemporaries of Eusebius (and for that matter our own) suddenly patronized as a rival to Christ. The suave and erudite Bishop of Caesarea examined a work written by Hierocles, governor of Bithynia under Galerius, in which the author compared Apollonius and our Lord. The result of his painstaking research (for Eusebius was a man of tremendous ability and learning) seems to have embittered the eminent historian. Eusebius unhesitatingly declared Apollonius as a rival to Jesus was "like a jackass covered with the skin of a lion." The book *Against Hierocles* regrets that no more formidable figure could have been selected by a dying paganism as its champion. Eusebius also wrote a book called *The Evangelical Preparation,* in which he shows the superiority of Judaism and Christianity over the decadent heathen doctrines, and another entitled *The Evangelical Demonstration,* which demonstrates the messianic dignity of Jesus from acknowledged prophecies in the Old Testament.

St. Athanasius (373), the outstanding ecclesiastical figure of the fourth century, has left us a *Discourse Against the Greeks* in which pagan errors are noted and refuted. Julian the Apostate wrote three books *Against the Gospels and Against the Christians.* St. Cyril of Alexandria (444) found little difficulty in refuting the imperial assailant of Christianity in his *Contra Julianum Imperatorem.* Theodoret of Cyr (458) closes the list of great Eastern apologists with his *Curing of Pagan Ills,* a work in which he showed that the teachings of the great philosophers would and could lead a man toward Christianity.

It was given, however, to St. Augustine (430) to make the most outstanding contribution to the science of apologetics in the later patristic period. In his treatise *De Vera Religione* he laid the groundwork for later books on apologetical methodology, showing how God leads men to truth by authority and reason. In the monumental *City of God* he carried out the work which had been begun by Minucius and Arnobius. He makes a definitive examination of pagan doctrine and then elaborates an apologetical philosophy of history by pointing out the contrast between the two cities, of God and of the world.

9. Anti-Mohammedan controversy. With the death of St. Augustine, St. Cyril of Alexandria, and Theodoret, the conflict of the Church with the pagans ceased. Almost immediately, however, a new enemy of Christianity appeared, an enemy to challenge the attentions of the apologist rather than of the controversialist. The heretics, Arian, Nestorian, and the like, had required the services of an apologist of dogma to confute their errors. The Mohammedans, like the Jews themselves, were foemen from the outside. They opposed Christianity as such. St. John Damascene (749) was the first of the important ecclesiastical writers to take the field against them. His *Dialogue Between a Christian and a Saracen* was the model for many subsequent works. The same writer, in his *Philosophical Chapters,* contributed toward the establishment of fundamental dogmatic theology by establishing standard definitions which could be of service in the sacred discipline.

After the time of St. John Damascene, because of the regrettable schism in the orient, Greek writers had for all practical purposes no influence whatsoever in the development of the science of apologetics as we know it. The western or Latin writers who continued the tradition of apologetics did so chiefly by means of treatises directed against the arguments of the Jews. Such writers were St. Isidore of Seville (636) and Rabanus Maurus (c. 856). Agobard (876), bishop of Lyons, wrote to refute the talmudic diatribes against our Lord as did St. Peter Damian (1072) and Peter the Venerable (1156). Raymond Martin (1278), in his *Pugio Fidei adversus Mauros et Judaeos,* relied mostly on the messianic prophecies in demonstrating the excellence and the divinity of Catholicism.

10. St. Thomas and his successors. The thirteenth century, however, saw the production of one book which has had a tremendous individual influence on the development of scientific apologetics. It was the *Summa Contra Gentiles,* written by St. Thomas Aquinas (1274). The university circles of his day were troubled by a group whose admiration for Mohammedan philosophical scholarship had turned them away from Catholic dogma. They received the appellation of Averroists, after the brilliant Saracen commentator on Aristotle whom they idolized.

St. Thomas distinguished those statements of Catholic dogma which had been revealed supernaturally but which still remained within the field of man's natural intellectual competence from the mysteries of the faith themselves, those truths which were intrinsically and essentially supernatural. He set out to demonstrate the first order of doctrines apodictically, utilizing every device at the disposal of a medieval philosopher. Then he showed clearly that the mysteries themselves were manifestly and rationally credible because of the motives of credibility which pointed out their divine origin. Finally he pointed out, for each mystery of faith taken individually, that there could be no true variance between revealed doctrine and naturally ascertainable truth.

The following centuries saw still more books written to help in converting Jews and Mohammedans. Some of these volumes were eminently successful in their own times, but they contributed very little toward the advancement of scientific apologetics. Among the more prominent authors who produced such books we must number Ricoldus a Monte Crucis, Hieronymus a Sancta Fide, Paul of Burgos, Abdallah, and the Franciscan Alphonsus de Spina. Pedro de la Cavalleria wrote, in 1487, a layman's book of apologetics in which he stressed the internal motives of credibility. The English Carmelite, Thomas Netter Waldensis (1430), wrote against the Wycliffites a treatise which was to have important influence in the development of fundamental dogmatic theology. Savonarola (1448), the platonist Marsilius Ficinus (1499), and Cardinal Nicholas of Cusa (1464) defended Catholic dogma during the first years of the Renaissance, although only the great Dominican managed this work along lines of scientific excellence.

11. Controversialists during the Reformation. With the advent of the Reformation a new and glorious chapter in the history of Catholic apologetics appears. Attacks upon Catholic doctrine by Protestants were soon followed by the works of deists, rationalists, and naturalists. In the face of this opposition the men who were privileged to guard and propose the doctrine of Christ renewed their examination of its motives of credibility. Melchior Cano, a Dominican bishop (1560), is rightly listed as the founder of fundamental dogmatic theology by reason of his *De Locis Theologicis*, although he made wide use of earlier writers, among others of Thomas Netter Waldensis and John Turrecremata (1468). The great Catholic controversialists, men like John Eck (1543), Bishop Frederich Nausea (1552), John Cochlaeus (1552), Ruard Tapper (1559), John Driedo (1553), Bishop Ambrose Catharinus (1553), Albert Pighius (1542), and James Latomus (1546) perfected that portion of apologetics which deals with the Church as such. Outstanding contributions in this line were made by St. Robert Bellarmine (1621), Thomas Stapleton (1589), and Cardinal William Allen (1594).

12. The Post-Tridentine theologians. The great scholastics and commentators made what might be termed the immediate preparation for modern and scientific apologetics, particularly when they dealt with the treatise on faith. Particularly valuable work in this regard was done by Francis Suarez, S.J. (1617), Gabriel Vasquez, S.J. (1604), and William Estus (1613). Francis Sylvius (1649) and the Dominican John of Saint Thomas (1644) considered the problems of apologetics quite directly. The great seventeenth-century polemic theologians, the brothers Van Walenburch, Adrian (1669), and Peter (1675) already considered the problems of credibility.

During the seventeenth century the brilliant Blaise Pascal (1662) began his project of apologetics. He wrote a series of notes, left uncompleted at his death, and later gathered together and edited many times as the *Thoughts*. He was in vital contact with the scientific world of his own time and he possessed the genius and foresight to expound the acceptability of the Catholic religion as such, in the face of opposition which denied the need and the validity of any systematic or supernatural religious doctrine whatsoever. He used internal motives of credibility freely, but at the same time he used the external signs, miracles, and prophecies much more scientifically and effectively than did some of his scholastic contemporaries. The bishops Jacques Benigne Bossuet (1704) and Daniel Huet (1721) used history to show the divinity of Christianity. The latter, however, utilized some rather eccentric scientific methods which did little to augment the value or utility of his writing.

13. Apologists of the eighteenth century. During the eighteenth century what has been called the traditional form of scientific scholastic apologetics began to appear. In 1747 Antonine Valsecchi published at Venice his work, *De Fundamentis Religionis,* in which he traced the path of apologetics through proofs of the existence of an all-just and omniscient God and of the immortality of the human soul to the final conclusion that the Catholic Christian message has been divinely revealed. Vitus Pichler, S.J. (1736), had covered much the same method very successfully. Cardinal Vincent Gotti (1742), Martin Gerbert (1793), Claude Regnier, S.S. (1790), and Peter Maria Gazzaniga, O.P. (1799), are intimately connected with this rise of the scholastic method. Daniel Concina, O.P., had given in his treatise on faith in the *Theologia Christiana* a magnificent explanation of the various motives of credibility.

From that time on we can easily recognize twin currents of scientific and literary apologetics. During the early part of the nineteenth century a great many defenders of the faith seriously compromised their own position and weakened their arguments by a somewhat credulous confidence in the edicts of Emmanuel Kant. Drey, Kuhn, Schell, and Klee lost much of their effectiveness in this way. The literary apologists, Vicomte Francois-Rene de Chateaubriand (1848), Count Joseph de Maistre, and Frederick Ozanam (1853) set the fashion for a militant Catholic interest in the credentials of the Catholic message.

14. Apologetics in the nineteenth century. The scholastic apologists of the nineteenth century are too well known to need any special explanation. They continued, with some variations, the order that had been followed by Pichler and Valsecchi during the previous century. Naturally some of them were more effective and scientific than others. Certain proponents of popular and ofttimes quite eccentric systems have unjustly blamed the group for faults which are found in only a few scattered individuals. It is a fact that some among the traditional scholastic apologists in the past century (and a few in our own time for that matter) have been rather cavalier in their attitude toward demonstration, doubtless imagining that any process of proof is acceptable if it is used for the truth. So it has happened that the carelessness of some writers has brought objections against the effectiveness of scholastic demonstration when, as a matter of fact, these men were ineffective precisely because they failed to conform their works to the exigencies of such proofs.

Among the most eminent of these traditional apologists of the nineteenth century we must list Bishop Bouvier (1854), Louis Brugere, S.S. (1888), Jeremias Dalponte, J. V. DeGroot, O.P., Bishop Francis Egger (1917), Cardinal John Baptist Franzelin, S.J. (1885), Hugo Hurter, S.J., Bernard Jungmann (1895), Archbishop Francis Patrick Kenrick (1863), Joseph Kleutgen, S.J. (1893), Albert Knoll a Bulsano, O.M.Cap., Gustavus Lahousse, S.J., Bishop Henry Lambrecht, Bruno Francis Liebermann (1844), John Lottini, Cardinal Camillus Mazella, S.J. (1900), Joseph Mendive, S.J. (1896), Parthenius Minges,

O.F.M., Patrick Murray (1882), Norbertus a Tux, O.M.Cap., Ignatius Ottiger, S.J. (1891), Dominic Palmieri, S.J. (1909), Carlo Passaglia (1887), Joseph Perrone, S.J. (1876), Francis Henry Reinerding, George Reinhold, Louis de San, S.J. (1904), Constantine Schaezler (1880), Santo Schiffini, S.J., Francis X. Schouppe, S.J. (1904), Clemens Schrader, S.J. (1875), John Schivetz, Archbishop Joseph Stadler (1917), Ferdinand Stentrup, S.J. (1898), Angelus Stummer, O.M.Cap., Ad. Tanquerey, S.S., Bernard Tepe, S.J. (1894), William Wilmers, S.J., and Cardinal Thomas Maria Zigliara, O.P. (1893).

These men wrote in Latin. Father Devivier, S.J., and the German apologists, Frances Hettinger (1890) and Paul Schanz, also wrote traditional treatises which have been translated into English and have exercised a powerful influence upon American Catholic thought.

Catholic writers during the nineteenth century did not by any means confine themselves to what was soon termed the traditional method in asserting the acceptability of their dogma. Theodore Paul De Broglie (1895) preferred to use a properly historical method and to manifest the contrast between the effects produced by the Christian faith and those brought about by other religious doctrines. Cardinal Victor Augustus Deschamps (1883) developed the use of the Church herself as a motive of credibility. Bishop Emil Bougaud (1888) preferred what he called the "intimate" method and strove to show particularly how the Catholic dogma corresponded with the most profound exigencies of the human heart. At the same time, however, he acknowledged the value of the external motives of credibility and actually made use of them in his apologetical demonstrations. The same attitude, if not the same method, was manifest in the works of the great Cardinal John Henry Newman (1892) in England.

15. The Vatican Council and apologetics. The Vatican Council in 1870 was pre-eminently concerned with fundamental dogmatic theology. It stated clearly that "in order that the service of our faith should be conformed to reason, God has willed to join with the internal aids of the Holy Ghost external proofs of His divine revelation, that is to say, divine works and first of all miracles and prophecies which, since they manifestly indicate the omnipotence and the infinite knowledge of God, are most certain signs of divine revelation and accommodated to the understanding of all. Hence both Moses and the prophets, and especially Christ the Lord Himself gave out many and most evident miracles and prophecies, and we read of the Apostles 'But they going forth preached everywhere, the Lord working withal, and confirming the word with signs that followed'[2] and 'we have the more firm prophetical word: whereunto you do well to attend, as to a light that shineth in a dark place.'"[3] The corresponding canon is still more explicit. "If anyone should say that no miracles can take place and that consequently all the accounts of them, even those contained in Holy Scripture, are to be classified as fables or myths; or that miracles can never be known with certainty and that the divine origin of the Christian religion cannot properly be demonstrated by them, let him be anathema."[4]

At the same time the Council, in expressing the dogmatic teaching of the Church, took full cognizance of the fact that the Church herself is a great and ever present living motive of credibility, as Cardinal Deschamps had pointed out in his writings. The Fathers of the Council acknowledged the traditional correctness of the Cardinal's stand when they stated "To the Catholic Church alone belong all those things, so many and so wonderful which are divinely disposed to the evident credibility of the Christian faith. Moreover, the Church by herself, by reason of her admirable propagation, her exalted sanctity, and her unexhausted fruitfulness in all good, by reason of her Catholic unity and her unconquered stability is a certain great and perpetual motive of credibility and an unwavering testimony to her own divine mission."[5] But even in making these decisions and in insisting upon the necessity of external motives, the Church acknowledged the existence and the limited efficacy of purely internal reasons. "If any one should say that divine revelation cannot be rendered credible through external signs, and that consequently men should be moved to faith by the internal experience of each one alone or by private inspiration, let him be anathema."[6]

---

2 The citation is from Mark 16:20.
3 The citation is from 2 Pet. 1:19. The words of the Vatican Council, the Constitution, *Dei Filius,* are to be found in Denzinger, 1790.
4 The Vatican Council, Canon 4, *De Fide* (Denzinger, 1 and 13).
5 The Vatican Council, the Constitution, *Dei Filius,* Ch. 3 (Denzinger, 1794).
6 The Vatican Council, Canon 3, *De Fide* (Denzinger, 1812).

16. The Modernists. The matter was clearly enough defined. Yet there remained certain Catholics of literary ability who had lost confidence in the actual effectiveness of these external motives. In 1893 the then young Maurice Blondel published his dissertation *L'Action*. It was his contention that "Greek Thought" or Aristotelian philosophy had been overthrown in that ideological movement of which the writings of Henri Bergson constituted the most powerful expression. As a result he had little place in the scheme of things for that system of apologetics, which was taught in the traditional manuals of the school. He felt that he could show that the full and perfect activity of man would be impossible without the force we know as Catholic dogma or the Christian religion. Some of his disciples, notably La Berthonniere and Le Roy, carried his ideas further than he did himself, and thus drew upon their books the condemnation of the Church. The movement was one of those which entered into the teeming complexity and confusion of modernism. With the condemnation of that movement during the first decade of our century there came a renewed impetus to scientific apologetics.

17. Contemporary apologetics. In general, the manuals of apologetics which have appeared in our own time are appreciably better than those of the past century. The twentieth-century apologist has superior material at his disposal, although we must not forget that through the efforts of nineteenth-century savants, and particularly through the work of Jacques-Paul Migne (1875), they were very well equipped for their tasks. The careless simplicity of the nineteenth-century unbeliever who imagined that a little scientific archeology, history of dogma, or biblical criticism would overthrow the Church's claims has vanished entirely. The naïve sentimentalism of Schliermacher and Renan, the pretentious skepticism of Kant and Boyle, the crude fancies of Strauss, Reimarus, and Baur are out of place in a century that loves and needs realism.

New objections are ever present, but the corps of Catholic apologists is and has demonstrated itself to be adequately master of the situation. As a group the apologists of the twentieth century have shown themselves much more perfectly in contact with the world about them than did some at least of their predecessors. The twentieth-century apologist knows full well that he is privileged to cooperate toward the extension of Christ's kingdom in the world. He has no merely defensive attitude. In order to spread the Word of God through the world, he knows full well that he must know both the attitudes of those whom he means to benefit and the content and credentials of the message with which he is entrusted.

Of prime service to the twentieth-century apologist was the methodological gem, *La Credibilite et l'Apologetique*, by Father Gardeil, O.P. Excellent manuals have been written by Reginald Garrigou-Lagrange, O.P., Christian Pesch, S.J., Herman Dieckmann, S.J., Aemilius Dorsch, S.J., Bishop Hilarinus Felder, O.M. Cap., Archbishop Valentine Zubizarreta, O.C.D., John MacGuiness, C.M., and J. V. Bainvel, all in the Latin tongue. In the various languages of Europe the vernacular works of Mariano Cordovanni, O.P., Nicolas Marin Negueruela, Joseph Mausbach, and Gerhard Esser, John Brunsmann, S.V.D., Eugene Duplessy, and Canon Boulenger are readily available. A system somewhat resembling that of Blondel has appeared in France in the writings of Henri Morice. Eugene Masure has written well on the theory of apologetics.

Besides the source collections, numerous dictionaries and encyclopedias have combined to make the work of the modern apologist more effective and scientific. Among others we must note the American *Catholic Encyclopedia*, the German *Lexicon fur Theologie und Kirche*, the French *Dictionnaire de Theologie Catholique*, the *Dictionnaire Apologetique de la Foi Catholique*, and the various symposia which issued from the publishing house of Bloud et Gay.

18. Apologetics in the English language. In the English language and particularly in the United States of America the science of apologetics flourishes. The Catholicism in English-speaking countries has always abounded in good polemic writers. That tradition began with the valiant exiles of Douay and Louvain, with Cardinal Allen, Thomas Stapleton, Richard Smith, Matthew Kellison, Edmund Campion, S.J., and Gregory Martin. It was preserved in the scholarship and courage of Bishop John Milner (1826). Here in America it grew with the writings of England and Kenrick and Spalding, worthy episcopal contemporaries of the great English cardinals, Wiseman and Newman and Manning. Orestes Brownson brought all the resources of his literary power to the service of American apologetics.[7]

We have books of popular apologetics beyond number. In the line of Latin scholastic works America has as its own the texts of Archbishop Francis Patrick Kenrick, and of two brilliant modern Jesuits, John Langan and Anthony Cotter. Aiding in the preservation of that accurate notion of God which is requisite for all work in this science have been John Moran, S.J., William Brosnan, S.J., and Father John T. Driscoll. *The Theory of Revelation,* by Joseph Baierl, is acknowledged as one of the best works extant on this section of apologetics. Brilliant monographs by Monsignor Fulton Sheen have done a great deal for this science in our own country.

English-speaking Catholics have always been well supplied with translations of foreign works in apologetics. Nevertheless, they have at their disposal manuals of lasting excellence written in their own language. Prominent among these are the two books by T. J. Walshe, and volumes written by Paul Glenn and Archbishop Sheehan.

Perhaps the greatest asset the American apologist possesses is his conviction that no work of his can measure up to the excellence of that Master he is honored to serve. The ideal apologist was Jesus Christ our Lord. It is the task of the modern apologist to strain every resource at his disposition in order that men may see effectively the goodness and the credentials of the divine message He preached. The ideal apologetic *is* Jesus Christ. That is why the apologist today must point to Him and to what He has said and done. The man who is privileged to stand with Jesus would only spoil the effect if he allowed some error, some personal bias, to stand in the way and distract men's attention from the Master. Because men must know and love Him, the apologist will polish and perfect his demonstrations, and will search out every possibility by which men may see the signature of God in His message.

---

[7] Information on early American apologists can be found *Catholic Apologetical Literature in the United States (1784–1858),* by Robert Gorman. This book, a doctoral dissertation, was written under the brilliant direction of Msgr. Peter Guilday.

Index

Abdallah, 486
Acts of the Apostles, 121
Adler, Mortimer, 311
Agnosticism, 13, 42 f., 49
Agobard, 485
Agrapha, 118
Allen, Cardinal William, 486, 492
Alphonsus de Spina, 486
Analogy, in theological process, 30
Apocalypse, 122, 261
Apologetics, analogy in, 17 f.; and apology of dogma, 3; and canonical sources, 120 ff.; and controversy, 3; and ecclesiology, 9 (note); and messianic prophecy, 389 f.; and polemics, 3; and proofs for God's existence, 12; and prophecy, 388f.; and signature of God, 5 f.; and the Vatican Council, 468 f.; arrangement of matter in, 102; basic theory of, 2 ff.; certitude in, 8 f.; conclusion of, 465-475; definition of nominal, 1 (note); divinity of Christ, 202 f.; historical evidence in, 109; procedure in, 104 ff.; story of, 477-493; work of, 1-9.
Apology, term applied to second century works, 1 (note)
Apology of dogma, and apologetics, 3
Apostles, and messianic prophecies, 425; as witnesses for Christ, 263 ff.; their attitude toward the divinity of Christ, 207 f.
Apollonius of Tyona, 483
Arendzen, J. P., 120 (note)

Aristides the apologist, 478
Aristotle, 240, 283, 306, 308 ff.; on religion and morality, 63 f.
Arnobius, 84 (note), 343, 397, 480 f.
Ascension of Christ, gospel accounts of, 363
Athanasius, St., 1, 484
Atheism, 49
Athenagoras, 1, 479
Augustine, St., 1, 62, 116, 309, 480, 484
Averroists, 485

Baierl, Joseph J., 35 (note), 45 (note), 54 (note), 87 (note), 89 (note) 493
Bainvel, Joseph, S.J., 492
Bar Chochebas, 390, 410, 433
Barnabas, the so-called Epistle of, 478
Bauer, Bruno, 136
Baur, Christian, 136, 265, 491
Beatific vision, 28 f.
Beatitudes in the teaching of Jesus, 200
Bergson, 491
Binet-Sanglé, 275 ff.
Blondel, 491 ff.
Bossuet, James, 487
Bougaud, Emil, 489
Boulenger, Canon, 103 (note), 492
Bouvier, 488
Brillant and Nédoncelle, 120 (note)
Brosnan, William, S.J., 479
Browne, Lewis, 232 (note), 379 f., 469 ff.
Brownson, Orestes, 492

Brugere, Louis, O.P., 474
Brunsmann, John, S.V.D., 34 (note), 478

Campion, Edmund, S.J., 492
Cano, Melchior, 486
Canonical sources, use of, in apologetics, 123 ff.
Catharinus, Ambrose, 486
Cayré P., A.A., 128 (note)
Celsus, vii, 1, 116 (note), 131, 282, 311 f., 328, 377 f., 481 f.
Certitude, and judgment of credibility, 91 ff.
Chateaubriand, 488
Chrestus, substituted for the word Christus, 109
Christ, and divine law, 216; and forgiveness of sin, 217 f.; and His Mother, 279 f.; and love of God, 285 ff.; and messianic prophecies, 416 ff.; apocryphal Christian sources for life of, 119 f.; apostles as witnesses for, 263 ff.; as a divine messenger, 141 f.; ascension of, 3563 attributes of God claimed by, 213 ff.; authority of, 183; beneficence in life of, 288 ff.; beneficent character of teaching, 171 f.; betrayal of, as predicted, 413 ff.; canonical sources on life of, 120 ff.; Chrestus for Christus, 110; Christian sources about life of, 117 f.; claims of, 139-172; consubstantial with God the Father, 224 f.; creative sanctity in the life of, 293 ff.; denounces pharisaic tradition, 184 f.; discernibility of holiness in, 291 ff.; divine honors claimed by, 169 f.; divinity of, 202 ff.; divinity of, and Caiphas, 212; divinity of, and commission of the apostles, 213; divinity of, and glorification of the Father, 207 f.; divinity of, and voice of the Father, 209; divinity of, apostles attitude toward, 207 ff.; divinity of, asserted in gospel stories about His infancy, 205 f.; divinity of, fourth gospel on, 220 ff.; divinity of, synoptic gospels on, 203 ff.; doctrinal content of message, 173-258; ecschatology of, 189 ff.; freedom from sin in, 290 f.; gospels on life of, 120 ff.; holiness of, 273, 295, 297; intrinsically supernatural character of teaching, 169 f.; Jewish legends about, 282 f.; Jewish sources on life of, 113 f.; messianic claims of, 147 f.; miracles of, 218 f., 315 ff., 328 ff.; miracles of, and the divine attributes, 337 f.; miracles of, as a motive of credibility, 339 ff.; miracles of, their cumulative force, 336 f.; moral teaching of, 148; mosaic dispensation in teaching of, 177 f.; pagan sources on life of, 109 ff.; papyri on life of, 118 (note); prayer of, 146 f.; prophecies of, see prophecy; redemptive death of, 234 f.; relations of, 140 f.; resurrection of, see resurrection of Christ; role at the Last Judgment,

216 f.; Roman sources on life of, 109 ff.; salvific mission of, 232 f.; servant of God, 420 ff.; social acceptability of, 278 f.; teaching of, credible, 144 f.; teaching of, moral, 192; teaching on beatitudes, 200 f.; teaching on charity, 194 ff.; teaching on created spirits, 187 ff.; teaching on end of world, 211 f.; teaching on eternal reward for men, 191 f.; teaching on faith, 192 f.; teaching on God the creator, 185 f.; teaching on the Holy Ghost, 226 ff.; teaching on hope, 193 f.; teaching on judgment, 189 ff.; teaching on prayer, 197 ff.; temperance in life of, 283 f.; title of Christ claimed by, 159 ff.; uncompromising opposition to sin in the teaching of, 297; unlimited holiness in the teaching of, 295 f.; wisdom of, 273-314; wisdom of, as a motive of credibility, 312 f.

Church, as a motive of credibility, 104 f., 437-464; fruitfulness of, in good works, 452 ff.; holiness in, 447 ff.; persecution of, 456 ff.; saints in, 450 f.; stability of, 456 ff.; unity in, 454 ff.; unity of, in Catholic epistles, 260 ff.; visible, 256 f.

Claudius, and troubles among Jews occasioned by Chrestus, 110 f.

Clement of Alexandria, 118 (note), 126, 265 (note), 368, 481

Cochlaeus, John, 486
Commodianus, 483
Concina, Daniel, O.P., 487
Constitution, Dei Filius, see Vatican Council
Controversy, and apologetics, 3
Cotter, Anthony C, S.J., 45 (note), 54 (note), 493
Council of Trent, 270 (note)
Counsels, the evangelical, 183 f.
Credibility, and Catholic dogma, 4 ff.; and prophecy, 87 f.; and revelation, 4; certitude in judgment of, 92 f.; Christ's holiness as negative motive of, 273; Christ's holiness as a positive motive of, 286, 298 ff.; Christ's wisdom as negative motive of, 273; Christ's wisdom as positive motive of, 304 ff.; Church as motive of, 104 f., 437-464; fact of, 459 ff.; general conditions of, 69 f.; internal motives of, 91, 459 ff.; judgment of, 8 ff.; judgment of and certitude, 92 ff.; meaning and demonstration of, 4; miracles as motives of, 77 f.; motive of, and transsubstantiation, 78 (note); motives of, 69-100 negative motives of, 71, 73
Cyril of Alexandria, St., 484

Dalponte, 488
De Broglie, 489
De Grandmaison, Leonce, S.J., 2 (note), 114 (note), 120 (note), 147 (note)
De Groot, J. V., 488
De Maistre, Joseph, 488

Index 495

De San, Louis, S.J., 489
Decree Lamentabili, 9 (note), 23, 92, 461
Deschamps, 489
Devivier, W., S.J., 103 (note), 489
Diatesseron of Tatian, 128
Dibelius, Martin, 435
Didiscalion of Alexandria, 126
Dieckmann, Hermannus, S.J., 26, 54 (note), 70 (note), 75 (note), 86 (note), 107 (note), 477, 492
Diognetus, the letter to, 478
Divinity of Christ, see Christ
Dodd, C. H., 174 f.
Dogma, and credibility,. 3 ff.; and the New Testament, 176 f.; an intrinsically supernatural revelation, 25 f.; as mediate revelation, 34; defense of, 2 ff.; definition of, 2; immutability of, 2; necessity for teaching of, 471 f.; necessity of, 471 f.; origin of, 11; rational acceptability of, 2 f.; supernatural obtainal of, 19 ff.
Donovan, John, S.J., 121 (note)
Dorsch, Aemilius, S.J., 26, 54 (note), 107 (note), 492
Drey, 488
Driedo, John, 486
Driscoll, John T., 87 (note), 493
Duplessy, Canon Eugene, 103 (note), 492

Ecclesiology, and apologetics, 9 (note)
Eck, John, 486
Egger, Franz, 488
Ehrle, Cardinal, S.J., 240 (note)
Ephraem, St., 128

Epictetus, 287, 306 ff.
Esser, Gerhard, 492
Estus, William, 487
Eusebius, 1, 84 (note), 113 (note), 114, 125 ff., 251 (note), 368, 412 f., 434 (note), 483 f.

Faith, and reason, 30 ff.; certitude in judgment of, 94 f.; intrinsically supernatural, 29 f.; motive of, 95 ff.; nature of, 467, obligation of, 467 ff.; relation to natural reason, 30 ff.; ultimate resolution of, 97 ff.
Felder, Hilarinus, O.M.Cap., 54 (note), 103 (note), 107 (note), 120 (note), 147 (note), 275, 492
Fenton, J.C., 4 (note), 27 (note), 28 (note), 120 (note), 123 (note), 197 (note)
Ficinus, Marsilius, 486
Fideism, 13
Franzelin, Cardinal, S.J., 488
Frazer, 226 (note)

Gardeil, Rev., O.P., 9 (note), 103, 106, 492
Garrigou-Lagrange, Reginald, 2 f. (note), 27 (note), 32 (note), 39 (note), 42 (note), 45 (note), 54 (note), 75, 87 (note), 96, 103, 107 (note), 177 (note), 311, 492
Garvie, Alfred E., 86 (note)
Gazzaniga, Peter, O.P., 487
Gerbert, Martin, 487
Glenn, Paul, 493
God, accurate natural concept of, based on proofs of exis-

tence, 13; center of the intrinsically supernatural order, 27 f.; fatherhood of, in Jewish teaching, 206 f.; known in the natural light of human reason, 13 ff.; natural knowledge about, 13 ff.; proofs for the existence of, 14 ff.
Gorman, Robert, 493 (note)
Gospels, antilogies of, 133; eschatological explanation of, 137; genuineness of, 125 ff.; patristic testimony on, 125 ff.; veracity of, 130 ff.
Gotti, Cardinal Vincent, 487
Grace, requisite for faith, 6f.
Guilday, Msgr. Peter, 493 (note)

Hadrian, letter to Caius Minucius Fundamus, 112 f.
Hegesippus, 411 f.
Hettinger, 489
Hierocles, 483
Hieronymus, Sancta Fide, 486
Holy Ghost, in teaching of Christ, 226 ff.
Hort, 129 (note)
Hort and Westcott, 134 (note)
Huby, J., S.J., 120 (note)
Huet, Daniel, 487
Hugueny, C, O.P., 177 (note)
Hurter, Hugo, S.J., 488

Ianssens-Morandi, 121 ff.
Ignatius of Antioch, St., 294 f.
Irenaeus, St., 1, 84 (note), 125 f., 368, 481
Isidore of Seville, St., 485

James, Montague Rhodes, 119 (note)
James, St., letter of, 122
Jesus Christ, see Christ
John, St., gospel of, 122 f., letters of, 122
John Damascene, St., 197, 485
John of St. Thomas, O.P., 487
Josephus, Flavius, 113 ff.
Judas of Galilee, 390
Jude, St., letter of, 122, 261
Julian the Apostate, 484
Jungmann, Bernard, 488
Justin Martyr, St., 1, 59 (note), 110 (note), 113 f., 127, 373 (note), 378, 424, 430 f., 451, 478 f.

Kant, Emmanuel, 488
Kellison, Matthew, 492
Kenrick, F. P., 488, 492
Kenyon, Sir Frederick, 118 (note), 128 (note), 133 f. (note)
Kidd, B.J., 110 (note), 111 ff., 441 (note)
Kingdom of God, consummation of, consummation of, 250 ff.; membership in, 244, rejection of, 246 ff.; reward of, 249 f.; rulers in, 254 ff.; value of, 244; watchfulness in, 251 ff.
Klee, 488
Kleutgen, Joseph, S.J., 488
Knoll, Albertus a Bulsano, O.M.Cap., 35 (note), 54 (note), 107 (note), 488
Kuhn, 488
La Berthonniere, 491
Lactantius, 441 (note), 483
Lagrange, M.J., O.P., 316
Lahousse, Gustavus, S.J., 488

Index

Lambrecht, Henry, 488
Langan, John T., S.J., 35 (note), 45 (note), 493
Latomus, James, 486
Lavergne, C., O.P., 177 (note), 316 (note)
Lebreton, Jules, S.J., 206, 212
Le Roy, 491
Liberalism and Christianity, 472 f.
Liebermann, Bruno F., 488
Lietzmann, Hans, 151 (note)
Life of Christ, see Christ
Logia, 118
Lomer, Georg, 275 f.
Longinque Oceani, 65 (note0
Lottini, John, 488
Luke, St., gospel of, 121
Lumen gloriae, 28

MacGuiness, John, C.M., 492
McCown, Chester C., 174, 204 (note), 275
McNabb, Vincent, O.P., 64 (note)
Maisonneuve, 103 (note), 477 (note)
Man, supernatural end of, 57
Manning, Cardinal, 492
Marcus Aurelius, 286, 306, 475, 479
Marin, Negueruela, Nicolas, 54 (note), 492
Mark, St., gospel of, 120
Martin, Gregory, 492
Martin, Raymond, 485
Martyrs, testimony of, 450 f.
Masure, Eugene, 492
Materialism, 50 f.
Matthew, St., gospel of, 120 f.
Matthews, W.R., 174 (note)
Maurus, Sylvester, S.J., 240 (note)

Mausbach, Joseph, 492
Mazella, Cardinal Camillus, 488
Melito of Sardis, 480
Mendive, Joseph, S.J., 488
Messianic character, Christ recognized by the Apostles from the outset, 159
Messianic dignity, claim of made at the beginning of Christ's public life, 157 f.
Messianic Kingdom, 224 ff.; growth of, 243
Messianic prophcies, cited by Christ, 157 f.
Messiah, and the times and peoples, 402 f.; as a divine messenger, 148 f.; betrayal of, predicted, 403 ff.; crucifixion of, as prophesied, 424 f.; erroneous teachings about, combated by Christ, 155 f.; eschatological concept of, 153 ff.; precursor of, predicted, 427 f.; predicted as a triumphant King, 403 f.; predicted as descendant of Abraham, Isaac, and Jacob, 408 ff.; predicted as Son of David, 406 ff.; prediction of precursor for, 395; prophetical office of, 148 f.; prophetical office of, claimed by Jesus, 165 f.; rabbinical concept of, 150 f.; rabbinical concept of, repudiated by Christ, 151 ff.; rejection of, 405 f.; royal office of, 149; royalty of, claimed by Jesus, 159 f.; sacerdotal office of, 149 f.
Micklem, Nathaniel, 173
Migne, J.P., 491

Milner, John, 492
Minges, Parthentus, O.F.M., 488
Minucius, Felix, 480, 484
Miracles, and order in the universe, 81 f.; as divine marks, 80 f.; as motives of credibility, 71 f.; demonstrative, force of individual, 335 f.; discernibility of, 77 f.; in the primitive Church, 443 ff.; of the moral and social order, 90 f.; of the social order, 437 f.; on the Sabbath, 322 f.; possibility of, 82 f.; purpose of, 85 f.; testimony of, 315-354; true and counterfeit, 83 f.; types of, 77 ff.; witnesses of, 323 ff.
Miracles of Jesus, see Christ, Miracles of
Modernism, 13, 92 (note)
Modernists, 491
Moore, George F., 175, 181 (note), 232 (note)
Moran, John, S.J., 493
Morice, Henri, 492
Morrison, Charles C, 174
Mosaic dispensation, and the teaching of Christ, 177 f.
Mosaic ritual, 178 f.
Muratorian fragment, 127
Murray, Patrick, 489
Mysteries, kinds of, 32 f.
Mysteries of faith, intrinsically supernatural, 28 f.

Nausea, 486
Necessity, hypothetical and absolute, 53
Nédoncelle and Brillant, 120 (note)

Nero, and first Roman persecution of the Christians, 110 f.
New Testament, and Catholic dogma, 176 f.; and lectionaries, 134 (note); authenticity of texts, 133 f.; manuscripts of, 133 (note); veracity of writers, 131 ff.; see also Gospels
Newman, Cardinal John, 489, 492
Nicholas of Cusa, 486
Nock, A. D., 389 f.
Non-Catholic doctrine, claims for, 473 f.
Norbertus a Tux, O.M.Cap., 489

Oath against modernism, 3 (note), 13, 72 f.
Old Testament, moral teaching of, in new law, 179 ff.
Orange, Second Council of, 94 f.
Origen, vii, 1, 84 (note), 114, 116 (note), 126, 128 f., 265 (note), 282, 311, 328, 368 f., 377, 383 (note), 481 f.
Ottiger, Ignatius, S.J., 489
Oxyrhynchus papyri, 118 (note)
Ozanam, Frederick, 488

Palmieri, Dominic, S.J., 489
Pantaenus, 125 f.
Pantheism, 39 f., 49 f.
Papias, 125 f., 265 (note), 368
Papyrus, Rylands, 134 (note)
Parable of the Evil Husbandmen, 141, 152, 210 f., 246 f., 414
Parable of the sower, 242
Parables, nature of, 240 f.; reason for use of, by Jesus, 241 f.; use

of, by Christ, 400 ff.
Pascal, Blaise, 487 f.
Passaglia, Carlo, 489
Paul, St., letters of, 122; on the teaching of Christ, 266 ff.; witness of the resurrection, 326 f.
Paul of Burgos, 486
Paulus, Gottlieb, 135
Pedro de la Cavalleria, 486
Perrone, Joseph, S.J., 489
Pesch, Christian, S.J., 492
Petavius, Dionysius, S.J., 310
Peter, St., divinity of Christ, 207 f.; letters of, 122
Peter Damian, St., 485
Peter the Lombard, 311
Peter the Venerable, 485
Pichler, Vitus, S.J., 487 f.
Pighius, Albert, 486
Pirot, L., 122 (note), 123 (note)
Plato, 240, 306, 308 ff., 471; on religion and morality, 63 f.
Pliny the Younger, 111 f.
Polemics, and apologetics, 3
Polycarp, 126, 128 f.
Porphyry, 306
Pothinus, St., 128
Preternatural, meaning of, 26
Progressive method, 106
Prophecies, appealed to by Christ, 391 f.; as a motive of credibility, 85 ff.; as to birthplace of Christ, 426 f.; by Jesus, 432 ff.; concerning Christ, 416 ff.; concerning servant of God, 420 ff.; demonstrative power of Christ's, 434 ff.; messianic and apotolic preaching, 425; messianic and the second coming, 431 f.; messianic, existence of, 389 ff.; messianic in primitive Christian teaching, 417 ff.; messianic in the message of Christ, 387-436, 416 f.; messianic relative to the second coming, 431 f.; messianic use of, in Catholic apologetics, 388 f.; place of, in Catholic apologetics, 387 f.; true and counterfeit, 88 ff.

Quadratus, 84 (note), 210 f., 246 f., 414

Rabanus Maurus, 485
Ramussen, Emil, 275 ff.
Reason, and dogma, 30 ff.; and faith, 29 ff.
Recognitiones Clementis, 58
Reformation, Catholic controversialists during, 486
Regnier, Claude, S.S., 487
Regressive method, 106 f.
Reimarus, 135, 491
Reinach, 226 (note)
Reinerding, 489
Reinhold, 489
Religion, concepts of, 469 ff.; obligation of, 469 f.
Renan, Ernest, 136, 491
Resurrection of Christ, a motive of credibility, 345; appearances of Christ, 358 ff.; deception theory to account for, 376 f.; gospel accounts of, 347-357; in apostolic preaching, 365 ff., in the apocryphal "Gospel of Peter," 370 f.; in the catechesis of St. Paul, 369 f.; properties of risen Christ, 381 f.; proph-

esied, 382 ff.; swoon theory to account for, 380 f.; testimony of His enemies to, 372 ff.; vision theory to account for, 377 ff.
Revelation, 139; and civic honesty, 66 f.; and credibility, 4; and cultures, 60 f.; and democracy, 64 f.; and patriotism, 66 f.; as teaching, 23; beneficial character of, 55 f., 61; characteristics of, 26-36; concept of, 11-24; considered as an act, 11; considered objectively, 12; criteria of, 69-100; discernibility of, 69-100; freely granted by God, 50 f.; immediate, 35 f.; intrinsically supernatural, 25 ff.; mediate, 34; mediate, possibility of, 45 f.; moral necessity of, 59; necessity of, for man, 53-68; nominal definition of, 12; possibility of, 37-52; private, 34; proof for possibility of, 38 f.; public, 36 f.; public, possibility of, 45; purpose of, 47 f.
Ricoldus a Monte Crucis, 486
Ritschl, Albrecht, 136
Robert and Tricot, 120 (note)
Robert Bellarmine, St., 486
Rufinus, 113 (note)
Rylands Papyrus, 134 (note)

Sanhedrin, recognized the reality of Jesus' miracles, 325 f.
Savonarola, 486
Schaezler, Constantine, 489
Schanz, 489
Schell, 488
Schiffini, Santo, S.J., 489
Schouppe, Francis, S.J., 489
Schrader, Clemens, S.J., 489
Schivetz, John, 489
Scrivener, Frederick, 134 (note)
Second coming, and messianic prophecies, 431 f.
Sheehan, Archbishop, 103 (note), 493
Sheen, Msgr. Fulton, 469, 493
Smith, Richard, 492
"Son of David," 168 f., 406
"Son of Man," 162 ff.
Spalding, Archbishop, 492
Spinoza, 311
Spiritual, distinct from supernatural, 33 f.
Stadler, Joseph, 489
Stapleton, Thomas, 486, 492
Steinmueller, John E., 123 (note), 127 (note)
Stentrup, Ferdinand, S.J., 489
Strauss, David, 136, 491
Stummer, Angelus, O.M.Cap., 489
Suarez, Francis, S.J., 312, 487
Suetonius, 109 (note), 110
Supernatural mysteries, and Catholic dogma, 4, 6; and human reason, 29 ff.; distinct from spiritual, 33 f.; possibility of, 45
"Syllabus of Errors," 473 f.
Sylvius, Francis, 310, 312, 487
Synoptics, 123

Tacitus, 110 f.
Talmud, 115 f., 282
Tanquerey, Adolphe, S.S., 103 (note), 489
Tapper, Ruard, 486

Tatian, 128, 479
Tepe, Bernardus, S.J., 45 (note)
Tertullian, 110 (note), 118 (note), 130, 481 f.
Theodoret, 470
Theologia Wirceburgensis, 107 (note)
Theology, process of, 29 ff.
Theophilus of Antioch, 480
Theudas, 390
Thomas Aquinas, St., 8 (note), 29 (note), 35 (note), 38 (note), 40 (note), 54, 56, 60, 78, 87, 96, 387, 485
Thomas Netter Waldensis, 486f.
Toledot Ieschu, 115,1 17
Tradition, and the teaching of Christ, 262 f.
Traditionalism, false, 12
Tricot, 120 (note), 134 (note)
Trajan, 112, 412. 457
Turrecremata, John, 486

Vacant, 3 (note), 49 (note), 52 (note)
Valsecchi, 487
Van Noort, G., 123 (note)
Van Walenburch, Adrian and Peter, 487
Varro, on the three theologies, 62
Vasquez, Gabriel, S.J., 487
Vatican Council, and apologetics, 490 f.; on faith, 91; on God, 47 f.; on revelation, 47 f.
Vatican Council, Constitution Dei Filius, 4, 11 ff., 25 f., 30 ff., 31, 48, 54, 72 ff., 90, 101, 104 f., 202, 305, 438 f., 466 ff., 490 f.; definition of Catholic dogma, 2

Vincent of Lerins, 106 (note)
Vitoria, Francis, O.P., 312
Vogels, 207 (note)
Voste, 242

Walshe, T. J., 28 (note), 32 (note), 39 (note), 42 (note), 45 (note), 54 (note), 75, 87 (note), 311, 493
Werner, Karl, 477
Westcott and Hort, 134 (note)
Wilmers, William, S.J., 489
Wiseman, Cardinal, 492

Zigliara, Cardinal Thomas, O.P., 489
Zubizarreta, Val., O.C.D., 492

www.ingramcontent.com/pod-product-compliance
Lightning Source LLC
Chambersburg PA
CBHW051047230426
43666CB00012B/2593